Kitchener

The Man not the Myth

Anne Samson

Helion & Company

Helion & Company Limited
Unit 8 Amherst Business Centre
Budbrooke Road
Warwick
CV34 5WE
England
Tel. 01926 499 619
Email: info@helion.co.uk
Website: www.helion.co.uk
Twitter: @helionbooks
Blog: https://helionbooks.wordpress.com/

Published by Helion & Company 2020. Reprinted in paperback 2023
Designed and typeset by Mach 3 Solutions Ltd (www.mach3solutions.co.uk)
Cover designed by Paul Hewitt, Battlefield Design (www.battlefield-design.co.uk)

Text © Anne Samson 2019
Images © as individually credited

ISBN 978-1-804513-84-2

British Library Cataloguing-in-Publication Data.
A catalogue record for this book is available from the British Library.

For details of other military history titles published by Helion & Company Limited contact
the above address, or visit our website: http://www.helion.co.uk.

We always welcome receiving book proposals from prospective authors.

KITCHENER
The Man not the Myth

*Field Marshal the Rt Hon HH Earl Kitchener of Khartoum, KG,
KP, GCB, OM, GCSI, CGMC, Col Commandant Royal Engineers,
Col Irish Guards, Secretary of State for War*[1]

Wot sets the Colonel cravin' for a just so rank and file?
Wot sets the Sergeant's swearin' so particularly vile?
It ain't his blamed anxiety to keep the Rooshian out;
It's a 'horrid sort o' feelin' of a K somew'ere about.
It's K – yus; K.
An' there's none to say 'im nay.
There's a flutter in the dovecotes w'en like Nemysis 'e stalks.
'E's a corker, and an 'cro, as a bogey man, they say.
For 'e's always hup an' doin' while the others sits and talks.[2]

---

1   Title as per Reginald H Brade's (Permanent Under Secretary of
    State for the War Office) instruction for period of mourning.
2   In Warwick James Price, 'K', in *The Sewanee Review*, vol 24, no 4
    (Oct 1916) pp.486-9.

Contents

List of Illustrations

Plates

Maps

Timeline of Kitchener's life[1]

Date [Age]	Country/place	Activity
1850 Jun 24	Ireland: County Kerry	Birth, years at Ballylongford
1863/4	Switzerland: Villeneuve	Schooling: Grand Clos on Lake Geneva
1867 [17]	England: Cambridge, London	Cramming for Woolwich
1868 Jan – 1870 Dec	England: Woolwich	Royal Military Academy, Woolwich
1870 – 1871 [20]	France	Franco-Prussian War
1871 Jan 6	England: Chatham	Lieutenant Royal Engineers
1873 April	Austria: Hanover	Attends manoeuvres Improve German; study German engineering and von Moltke's military reforms of the German Army
1874 [24] Summer Nov	England: Aldershot Hanover Palestine	Mounted troops of Royal Engineers Leave Palestine Exploration Fund
1875 Mar 15 Jun 10 Sep 11-28 Oct 1 Dec	Palestine England France: Dinan	Returns to work after fever in Jerusalem Wounded Safed riots Trial at Acre re Safed riots Recovering With father
1876	England	Palestine Exploration Fund Royal Albert Hall with Conder Publication of *Photographs of Biblical sites*
1877 [27] Feb 6 Feb 11 Feb 24 Apr 11 Jun 24 Jul 10 Jul 21	Palestine Palestine – Galilee Lebanon	Replaces Conder to lead survey of Palestine Arrives Beirut Damascus Haiffa Safed Phonecia Completed survey of Galilee/Northern Palestine Four weeks leave

1   Depicting main travel and detail for some periods to show gruelling schedule.

Date [Age]	Country/place	Activity
Aug 23	Palestine	Back to work in Beersheba
Sep 2		Arrives Jerusalem via Sidon, Tyre, Acre, Nazareth,
Sep 28		Jenin, Nablur
Nov 22		Survey of Western Palestine complete
Nov 26		Sends staff home
Dec 12	Turkey	Sails for Constantinople
Dec 25		Adrianople, Sofia, Kamerleh
		Left Constantinople
1878 Jan –	England: London	In flat with father
Aug 16	Ireland	Dublin
Sep 3		Appointed to survey Cyprus
Sep 10		Hands over maps and memoirs for Palestine
Sep 19	Cyprus	Leaves for Cyprus; Mapping under Wolseley
1879 Feb	Anatolia, Kastamanu	Military Vice Consul (8 months)
1880 Mar 15	Cyprus	High Commissioner Major-General Robert Biddulph, Director of Survey for Cyprus
1881 Jul	England	Annual leave
Oct 7		Arrives at Larnca, Cyprus from Alexandria
1882 Jun 15 [32]	Cyprus	Honorary Secretary to Cyprus Museum
Jul 2	Egypt	In Alexandria on leave of absence
Dec 28		Egyptian Army under Sir Evelyn Wood
1883 Jan 1	Egypt	Leaves Limassol for Egypt
Jan 4		Captain British Army; Major Egyptian Army; Intelligence Officer
Mar 18		Appointed new Egyptian Army, Second in Command cavalry regiment
		Initiated La Concordia Lodge No 1226, Cairo (Lodge erased 1890)[2]
Nov 10		Leaves Suez to survey Sinai Peninsula and south of Dead Sea
1884 Jan 6	Egypt	Arrives Ismalia after 200 mile desert ride; Sudan for survey work; Intelligence officer to desert column
1885 Jan 17		Battle Abu Klea (Intelligence, Desert Column)
Jun 15		Brevet Lieutenant Colonel
Jul 3 [35]	England	Break after Gordon's death
Jul 15		Queen at Osborne House
		Stays with Pandeli Ralli for first time in London; father at The Manor House, Cossington,
Nov 29 –	Zanzibar	Leicestershire
		Boundary Commission; letter of appointment 17 Oct 1885
1886 Jan 25	Zanzibar	Founder Drury Lane Lodge No 2127, London
Sep 7	Sudan	Governor General Eastern Sudan and Red Sea Littoral (Suakin)

2   Freemason chronology

Date [Age]	Country/place	Activity
1888 Jan 17	Sudan	Battle of Handub, Kitchener wounded
Feb	Egypt	Recovery in Cairo
Mar 15	Suakin	
May 26		Leaves for England
Jun 11	England	Annual leave (stays at Hatfield with Lord Salisbury)
Jul 13		Gazetted as Colonel; promoted 11 April Pasha in Egypt
Sep 13	Egypt	Egypt
Dec		Aide de Camp to Queen Victoria
		Adjutant General Egyptian Army under Francis Grenfell
		Command 1st Brigade Soudanese, Returns to Cairo
1889 Aug 17	Egypt	Battle of Toski
Summer	India	Visits brother Walter
		CB (Companion of the Bath) for Battle of Toski
Nov 2	Egypt	Joined Bulwer Lodge No 1068, Cairo
1890 [40]	Egypt	Temporary Inspector General Egyptian Police
Feb 12		Exalted at Bulwar Chapter, Cairo
Mar 8		Joined Grecia Lodge No 1105
1892 Apr 13	Egypt	Appointed Sirdar, Egyptian Army with rank of Major-General
Nov 15		Joined Star of the East Chapter No 1355
1893	Egypt	Cecil Rhodes and Kitchener meet
1894 Feb		CMG – Companion of the Order of St Michael and St George
Jul 21	London	KCMG – awarded for work in Egypt
		War Office meeting
1895	Egypt	Founder and Honorary WM of the Fatish Lodge (National GL of Egypt)
Apr 5		Past Senior Grand Warden of Egypt
Jul		Dinner at Savoy
1896 Jan 8	Egypt	Honorary WM of El Lataif Lodge (National GL of Egypt)
		Appointed Grand Third Principal of Grand Chapter of Egypt
Jun 7	London	Appointed Past Third Grand Principal of Grand Chapter of Egypt
Nov 9		KCB & Major General following Battle of Hafir
		Battle of Firket
		Sees PM/Chancellor for funds; lunch with Queen
		Commander-in-Charge River War
1897 Jan	Sudan	Starts railway from Wadi Halfa to Abu Hamed;
	England	occupies Berber
		Appointed Junior Grand Warden (Past Rank)
		United GL of England (special Queen Victoria Jubilee Celebration Meeting)
		Appointed Grand Scribe Nehemiah (Past Rank)
		Supreme Grand Chapter of England
1898	Sudan & Egypt	Governor Sudan
Apr 8		Battle of Atbara
		Leave in Cairo

Date [Age]	Country/place	Activity
Sep 2		Nile to Omdurman
Sep 10		Omdurman to Fashoda/Kodok
Sep 19		Fashoda
Oct 6		Cairo
Oct 27 –	Calais – Dover	Stays at Hatfield, Balmoral and Windsor
	England	Lunch with Queen Victoria
Oct 31		Baron Kitchener of Khartoum
Nov 3		Gaity Theatre
Nov 4		Freedom of London, Guildhall; Mansion House
Nov 8		dinner
Nov 24		Dinner at Chatham with Royal Engineers
Nov 28		Cambridge Honorary Degree; freedom of city
Nov 29	Scotland	Sandringham with Prince of Wales
		Edinburgh honorary degree, guest of Lord
Dec 2	Wales	Rosebury; launch Gordon college fund; freedom
Dec 7		of city
Dec 28	Khartoum	Cardiff honorary degree
		Leaves England on steamer *Dover* from Folkstone
		With Cromer
1899 Jan 4	Khartoum	Foundation stone for Gordon Memorial College
		District GM Egypt and the Sudan
Jun –	England, Ireland	Visits Lord Roberts re India and South Africa
Jun 17-19		With Count and Countess of Jersey
Jun 21	Osterley	Honorary Degree with Cecil John Rhodes et Oxford
Jul 18	Oxford	Fishmongers' Company dinner
Dec 10	London	Leaves for Egypt
Dec 21	Egypt	Arrives Cairo from Khartoum, train having
Dec 24	Malta	derailed at Luxor
Dec 26	Gibraltar	Meets up with Lord Roberts en route to South
		Africa on *Dunnottar Castle*
1900 Jan 10	South Africa	Arrives Cape Town
Feb 6		With Roberts leaves for Front
Apr 23		Bloemfontein. Attends English Constitution
		Rising Star Lodge No 1022 (Roberts also present)
Nov 29 [50]		Command of South African forces
1902 Jun 20		Leaves South Africa
Jul 12	England	Arrives Southampton
		Stays with King and PM
Sep 22		Viscount; award of £50,000
		Ipswich; Honorary membership British Union
		Lodge No 114 Province of Suffolk
Oct 17	England – France	Leaves Dover for Paris
Oct 22	Italy	Rome
Oct 27	Egypt	Alexandria
Nov 1		Aswan Reservoir works
Nov 4		Khartoum
Nov 7		Joined Khartoum Lodge No 2877
Nov 8		Opens Gordon College
Nov 17		Cairo
Nov 27		Appointed District Grand Master Punjab
Nov 28		Bombay, Command of Indian Army
Dec 2		Delhi
Dec 12		Leaves Delhi

Date [Age]	Country/place	Activity
1903 Apr 13	India	Joins Himalayan Brotherhood Lodge No 459 Simla Founder Kitchener Lodge No 2998 Simla
1906		Fitzgerald replaces Maxwell (the Brat) as aide de camp
1907 Feb 2	India	HM Habibullah Khan, Amir of Afghanistan initiated to Lodge Concordia, No 3102, Calcutta
1909 Jul 9	India	Deakin invites to Australia
Aug 7		Announced High Commissioner Mediterranean
Aug 20		Farewell speech United Service Club
Aug 31		Masonic Banquet
Sep 6		Leaves Simla
Sep 9		Lays down Indian Command
Sep 10	Poona	
Sep 12	Tuticorin for Ceylon	
Sept 13	Columbia	
Sept 20	Singapore	
Sep 24	Saigon	
Sep 27	Hongkong	
Sep 29	Canton	
Sep 30	Hongkong to Shanghai	
Oct 3	Sharkha	
Oct 5		Curio shops in 'Native City'
Oct 6	Nanking	
Oct 12	Peking	
Oct 16	Winter Palace	
Oct 17	Summer Palace	
Oct 18	China	Received by Chinese Regent
Oct 20		Inspects Chinese Imperial Guard
Oct 21		Personal tour of Russo Japanese war with Japanese
Oct 23	Port Arthur	officer
Oct 23		Leaves Port Arthur
Oct 24	Liaoyang	Battlefield
Oct 25	Mukden	Telegram of sympathy on assassination of Prince
Oct 27	Seoul to Japan	Ito
Oct 29	Tokyo	
Nov 2		Stays at Shiba Palace
Nov 5		Leaves for Japanese manoeuvres
Nov 10	Tokyo	Reviews north and south armies with Mikado
Nov 11		
Nov 12		Lunch Admiral Baron Saito (Minister of the
Nov 13	Tokyo – Kyoto	Navy); dinner at British embassy
Nov 16	Osaka	Inspects Chrysanthemums at Akasaka Palace
Nov 18	Kobe for Shanghai	
Nov 19	Hongkong	
Nov 26	Singapore for Java	
Dec 2	Batavia	
Dec 6	Sourabaya – Australia	
Dec 11	Darwin	Tours Jaich
Dec 16		
Dec 21	HMS *Encounter*	Boat *Van Outhoorn* grounds near island of Wetter,
Dec 25	Queensland	refloated undamaged
Dec 30		Joins after visiting Koepang, Eimor and Dilli Thursday Island

Date [Age]	Country/place	Activity
1910 Jan 1	Australia: Melbourne	Start of six-week tour
Feb 17	New Zealand South Island United States of America	Continuation of tour
Apr –	England	San Francisco
Apr 7		London: applies for Viceroy of India position; stays
Apr 26 [60]		Balmoral, Wellbeck, Powis, Hatfield
May 6		Edward VII dies; Unemployed
Sep 29		Ireland
Nov 5	Tour: Europe,	Asquith offers Kitchener unpaid seat on CID
Nov 27	Turkey	Rome, Venice, Vienna
Dec		Constantinople
1911	Egypt & Sudan	
Mar 7	British East Africa	Safari Lake Victoria to Mombasa; Buys coffee farm
		Appointed command troops at Coronation of
Mar 22		George V
	Venice	Leaves Mombasa
Apr 2	England	Meets Kaiser at Lady Layard's House
Apr 6		
Apr 26		Buys Broome House
Jun 15		Introduction to House of Lords
Jun 22		Meets Louis Botha in London
Jul 12		Oversees Coronation of George V
Jul	Ireland	Meeting with Edward Grey re Egypt
Jul 16	England	Investiture Knight of St Patrick
Sep 28	Egypt: Alexandria	British Agent Egypt following Gorst's death
		Arrives as British Agent
1912 May 29	Malta	Kitchener meets Churchill and Asquith
1913 Jul 11 –	England	Arrives
Sep 3-8		Balmoral
Sep 29	Italy	Leaves Venice for Egypt
Oct 2	Egypt	Arrives Cairo
Dec 29		Flight with airman Olivier
Dec 31		Leaves for Sudan
1914 Jun 14	Sudan	Arrives Khartoum
Jun 18		Leaves Egypt, travels via Trieste
Jun 19		Annual leave
Jun 23 –	Marseilles	Stays with Desboroughs
Jun 29	England	
Jul 21		Lunch German Ambassador, London; meets
		Churchill and Asquith
Aug 5		Recalled to War Office: *remains in England except for the following dates*
Aug 25	England – Dover	First speech House of Lords
Aug 29	France	Rumoured at Le Havre
Sep 3	France (Dunkirk) Returns same day	Assisting Joffre
Nov 1	France	Meeting Poincare, Cambon, Joffre, Foch
Dec 2	Belgium: Hazebrouck	Meeting Poincare, Joffre, King Albert, Lord French and Mayor of Hazebrouck

Date [Age]	Country/place	Activity
1915 Jul 2		Department of Munitions formed
Jul 5 [65]	France: Calais	Conference of Allied Ministers
Aug 15-18	France	Meeting with Joffre and Millerand
Nov 5	Ship	Leaves for Near East; Dardanelles
Nov 12-30	St Helles, Athens, Rome,	
Dec 4-11	Paris	
	France: Calais	
1916 Feb 15	France	Returns England
Mar 23 – Apr 3	France: Paris	Paris War Council
Jun 2	England	Meets with Parliament
Jun 3-4		Broome House
Jun 5 [19 days short		To Scotland
of 66]	Scotland: Scapa Flow	5.00pm embarks HMS *Hampshire*
		7.45pm HMS *Hampshire* en route to Russia sinks[3]

3   For the list of men on HMS *Hampshire* when it sunk see hmshampshire.org [accessed 24/6/2019].

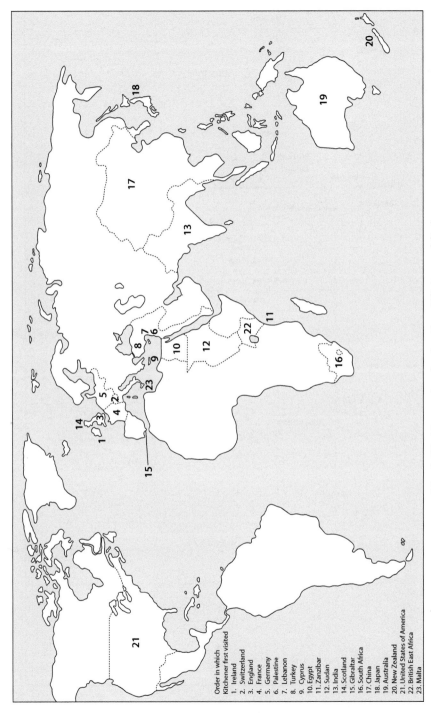

Map 1 World map, showing locations Kitchener visited.

Order in which
Kitchener first visited
1. Ireland
2. Switzerland
3. England
4. France
5. Germany
6. Palestine
7. Lebanon
8. Turkey
9. Cyprus
10. Egypt
11. Zanzibar
12. Sudan
13. India
14. Scotland
15. Gibraltar
16. South Africa
17. China
18. Japan
19. Australia
20. New Zealand
21. United States of America
22. British East Africa
23. Malta

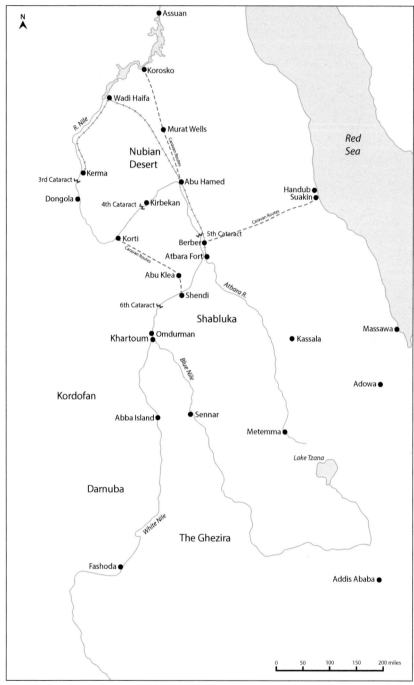

Map 2 The Sudan.

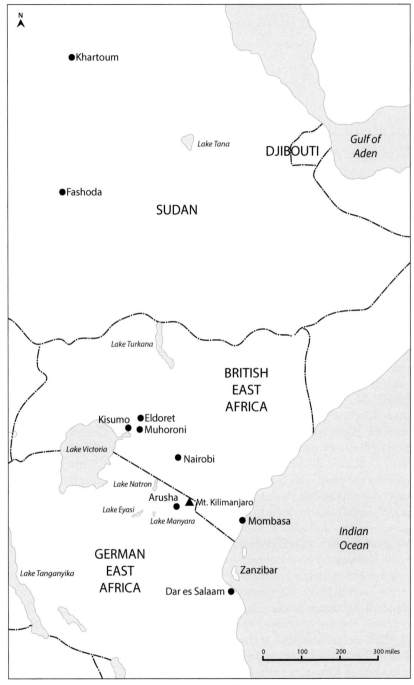

Map 3 East Africa.

Foreword

Given the number of casualties, understandably the focus of the centenary years of the Great War was the man in the trench; the fighting soldier, who endured inconceivable privations and the constant risk of death or injury on our behalf. Those who led them, 'the Generals', were ignored by the media or if addressed written off as out of touch and cold blooded incompetents. A caricature, however unjustified, most effectively and damagingly captured in Alan Clark's 1961 book *The Donkeys*.

Lord Kitchener, until his death in 1916 the most senior General of the day and certainly the most well-known through the recruiting poster that featured him pointing his finger at potential recruits with the words 'Your country needs You', is often portrayed as the guiding spirit behind Great Britain's herd of donkeys. Yet in his day Kitchener was a legendary indeed almost heroic figure who dominated headlines for his courage, leadership, strategic brilliance, and patriotism. Now few know of him and if scrutinised at all he seems best known for perceived military blunders and imperial atrocities.

In this biography, Anne Samson astutely unpacks the enigma that is Kitchener. She breaks the mould by focusing on rarely discussed aspects of the man universally known as 'Kitchener' or more simply 'K' or 'K of K'. Tracing how and why his reputation evolved, Anne challenges the current perception of 'the Generals' by exploring Kitchener's desire for peace and concern for the well-being of his men as well as the emphasis he placed, almost uniquely in C19th British military culture, on education. She explores the power play between politician and soldier as well as the complex relationship between the British metropole and one of its colonial children, who despite a paucity of helpful connections rose to the top of the military tree. Not being a specialist in military strategy and tactics, Anne draws attention to a variety of less conventional factors which impact on decisions in the field. She shows that most Generals, and especially Kitchener, are very human beneath their often rather austere demeanours.

Anne Samson modestly assumes her reader will have read at least one of the other fifty-three biographies on the man, or will be tempted to do so to find out more about the 'standard' Kitchener. In my judgement there is no need to do so. In this beautifully written book, the author brings a complex, demanding, but very human man to life. Amid all the virtues and flaws of the era in which he lived, *Kitchener: The Man not the Myth*, describes through fresh and sympathetic eyes an exceptional soldier who helped shape the British Empire at and to its height.

General The Lord Richards of Herstmonceux GCB CBE DSO
June 2019

Introduction

> Earl Kitchener was not England's foremost soldier, – if only on the ground once taken by Moltke, that he had never been called upon to endure the supreme test of conducting a retreat. That he was the greatest military administrator of this country is generally granted, however; even, perhaps, the greatest of the world to-day.[1]

In the United Kingdom, 2019, the name Kitchener elicits looks of confusion and questions of 'who is he?' Mention the poster 'Your country needs you' and you generally get the response 'that man with the moustache?' or 'the man pointing his finger?'[2] In contrast, mention Lord Kitchener in South Africa and you will receive a barrage of 'he was responsible for the concentration camps' and other unfavourable comments. This, however, is from a limited section of the population. Ask someone from the Caribbean and the response is likely to be, 'The Calypso musician?'[3]

It is almost inconceivable to think that between the 1890s and 1920s, the name Kitchener dominated headlines and news and would have been on everyone's tongue, at least in the British Empire. He was one of the celebrities of the day, but who was he, and why publish a biography of him in 2019 (or even 2013 when the idea was conceived) when there are already more than fifty?

Most of his biographers treat him as British, which technically he was, having been born to British parents before 1926 and within the British Empire.[4] However, his upbringing and early adult years were informed by experiences outside Britain. These helped create and form the man to whom everyone in Britain looked to see them through the conflict which became known as the Great War, the First World War or

---

1   In Warwick James Price, 'K', in *The Sewanee Review*, vol 24, no 4 (Oct 1916) pp.486-9.
2   The poster, by Alfred Leete, first appeared on the cover of *London Opinion* on 15 September 1914; Trevor Royle, *The Kitchener Enigma* (M Joseph, 1985) p.2; James Taylor, *'Your Country Needs You': The Secret History of the Propaganda Poster* (Glasgow: Saraband, 2013).
3   Lord Kitchener, the Calypso singer, born Trinidad, 18 April 1922, died 11 February 2000.
4   The most recent biography, Brad Faught, *Kitchener: Hero and Anti-Hero* (London: IB Tauris, 2016), follows the style of previous biographies, although some aspects are reconsidered in light of today's values.

World War One. As Kitchener himself told Lord Riddell in April 1915, 'When the war is over I shall shake the dust of this country off my feet and go to the East! The people here do not understand me and I do not understand them!'[5]

Despite the unanimous vote of confidence in Kitchener at the outbreak of the 1914 war, by mid-1915 he was being criticised and side-lined by colleagues and, when he died unexpectedly on 5 June 1916, became the scapegoat for many of the ills in Britain's management of the war – purely as he could not defend himself. This was political. For the general man on the street and the soldier in the trench of working-class stock, the demise of Kitchener was a huge shock evinced in the outpouring of biographies which flooded the market – ten in 1916 and 1917, in three languages.

For all his faults, and he had a few, Kitchener, aged 64, was regarded as the best military man available to steer the British Empire through the troubled times which began in August 1914. The Earl of Birkenhead, Frederick Edwin Smith, believed that 'every contemporary military figure in the Empire will shrink into insignificance' when compared with Kitchener.[6]

Is there place for another biography on Kitchener?[7] Most definitely. AM Gollin recalled that when he started his research into Alfred Milner, he was asked 'why I wanted to become concerned with "that vile brute", while another told me that "I should discover what a great and good man Lord Milner was."'[8] Similar sentiments have been expressed about Kitchener. A biography in the centenary years of the Great War provides an opportunity to '[humanise] history as it reflects life – its heroism, nobility, endurance, folly, ignorance, weakness and brutality,' and not just of Kitchener, but of all involved.[9] As RG Collingwood noted, 'In History, as in all serious matters, no achievement is final [and] every new generation must rewrite history in its own way.'[10] Each generation, and individual historian, looks at the past through a different lens, building on what has come before with the added benefit of the discovery of 'new', previously unused, sources of information, experience and insight.

5   Lord Riddell, *War Diary 1914-18* (London: Ivor Nicolson & Watson, 1933) p.20.
6   The Earl of Birkenhead, FE Smith, Correcting Lord Esher's critique of Kitchener in 1922. *Points of View*, p.2. Frederick Edwin Smith, born 12 July 1872, died 30 September 1930, Lord Esher (1852-1930), Reginald Elliot Brett, 2nd Viscount Esher, historian and liberal politician. Head of British Intelligence in France 1914-18 and author of the Esher Committee Report on War Office Reorganisation.
7   See Bibliography for the complete list.
8   Alfred M Gollin, *Proconsul in Politics: A Study of Lord Milner in Opposition and Power, with an Introductory Section, 1854-1905* (Anthony Blond, 1964) p.x.
9   FA Mouton, '"The good, the bad and the ugly": Professional historians and political biography of South African parliamentary politics, 1910-1990', in *Journal of Contemporary History*, vol 36, no 1 (June 2011) p.74.
10   Andrew Porter, 'The South African war and imperial Britain: a question of significance?', in Gregory Cuthbertson, Albert Grundlingh & Mary-Lynn Suttie, *Writing a Wider War: Rethinking Gender, Race and Identity in the South African War, 1899-1902* (Cape Town: David Phillips, 2002) p.287.

Having grown up in South Africa with the myths surrounding Kitchener and then exposed to others in Britain, I found a completely different picture emerge through my study of the First World War in East Africa.[11] I wanted to find out about this soldier who was so totally against war in that theatre that he had to be removed from his post at the War Office for action to be sanctioned. Professor Tony Stockwell, one of my thesis supervisors, rightly challenged my challenging the myths – and in doing so ensured my conclusions were well established in fact. I hope the rigour instilled over fifteen years ago concerning my investigations into the man Kitchener has remained and that this reappraisal does justice to both.

A few books have come close to doing what I have attempted in these pages. AJ Smithers's *The fighting nation*, Trevor Royle's *The Kitchener Enigma* and John Pollock's mammoth *Kitchener*.[12] All are relatively recent publications (1994, 1985 and 1988/2001 respectively) and attempt to shed light on specific aspects of Kitchener's life. As usual when working with biography, one needs to exercise caution, particularly when authors are gushing in praise or are overly critical. Concerning Kitchener, George Arthur's three volume biography is overly favourable.[13] Arthur, a Kitchener acolyte from 1914, could say nothing against his leader. However, his work should not be ignored. Rather, it is a 'must' read for demonstrating the fervour which Kitchener engendered in his 'team'. The biographies which came to light in 1916 and 1917 deserve the same cautious approach that Arthur's merits. They are an outpouring of grief and shock at a time when the country was in great need of heroes. The loss of a hero such as Kitchener could only elicit popular and positive texts. The texts which appeared in French acknowledged the support and friendship Kitchener gave France, whilst the German biography was an occasion to explain that Germany had not intentionally targeted the *Hampshire*. Its sinking was purely accidental due to mines which had been laid.[14]

It is in the report of the Dardanelles Commission and texts that appeared in the post-war years, once Britain had emerged victorious, that erstwhile colleagues pointed the finger at Kitchener and blamed him for the ills of the nation during the early days of the First World War. Lords French and Northcliffe and Colonel Repington lead the way. These in turn, resonate with feelings and perceptions of Kitchener formed in South Africa after the 1899-1902 (Second Anglo-Boer) war and so have been little

---

11   Anne Samson, *Britain, South Africa and the East Africa Campaign, 1914-18: The Union Comes of Age* (London: IB Tauris, 2005); Anne Samson, *World War 1 in Africa: The Forgotten Conflict of the European Powers* (London: IB Tauris, 2013).

12   AJ Smithers, *The fighting nation* (London: Leo Cooper, 1994); Trevor Royle, *The Kitchener Enigma* (London: Michael Joseph, 1985); John Pollock, *Kitchener Comprising The Road to Omdurman and Saviour of the Nation* (London: Constable, 2001).

13   George Arthur, *Life of Lord Kitchener*, 3 volumes (London: Macmillan, 1920).

14   Henry D Davray, *Lord Kitchener: his work and prestige, With a Prefatory Letter by S.E. Monsieur Paul Cambon* (London: T Fisher Unwin, 1917). There are numerous books dealing with the sinking of the *Hampshire* and conspiracies around Kitchener's death. They do not form part of this study.

challenged to date. David Lloyd George's memoirs are difficult to place: they reflect his vacillating emotions and reactions, which together with recorded conversations in Lord Riddell's *War Diary*, provide a fairly balanced view of Kitchener. Few would have expected Lloyd George at the time of the munitions' crisis, January 1915, to record Kitchener lamenting: 'They want me to send soldiers there – but I don't mean to. It would be murder. I never mind ordering a soldier to face danger in the ordinary way, but I will not have soldiers murdered ... All war is an outrage.'[15]

The starting point for this study was to work through all the available biographies on Kitchener, and as many related texts as possible with archival sources utilised to support and enhance the narrative. Quotes, which tend to be repeated in biographies, have been checked to ascertain validity and the argument presented. The advent of the Internet has without doubt been of great value in identifying many memoirs, while space constraints have played their part in limiting what has been included. Emphasis has been given to previously unpublished or scarce accounts, rather than rehash the oft repeated, but the incidents and events have not been ignored. They are integral to understanding the man, Kitchener.

A word of caution: this biography does not dwell on the military as the author is not qualified to pass judgement on such issues. The purpose of this book is to shed light on the political and interpersonal relationships against which the military activities and decisions took place, showing how Kitchener learned along the way. Neither is the author an expert on the European War of 1914-18. This may well have its drawbacks, but being able to step back and see the forces at work behind the scenes without an intimate knowledge of what actually took place can only support a more balanced view of the man. The same arguments apply to the author's knowledge of the other major events in Kitchener's life – the Sudan, India and Egypt, and even South Africa. Despite being taught the 'Boer War' every year at school and university, the detail failed to take hold – in fact the 'Boer War' had such an impact that at one stage the author never wanted to look at South African history again! Kitchener, however, has forced her to engage with that much-studied aspect of South Africa's past. Readers expecting a judgement to be passed on Paardeberg and other military actions will remain unsatisfied. What does this then leave to discuss in a study of a soldier? A phenomenal amount – covering social and political reform, technological advancement and innovation, a strategic overview of military matters few others had, and a decisive mind which could be as cruel as it was loyal, and a sense of humour and sensitivity not usually associated with a man of war. A study of Kitchener's time in the War Office highlights in one the achievements and frailties of the man and provides an opportunity to explore some of the dominant beliefs of the day.

It seems fitting that a new biography of Kitchener be released in the centenary years of the peace treaty discussions. One can only imagine how Kitchener would have reacted to the Versailles talks, especially as he believed Germany should retain

15   Riddell, *War Diary*, p.50.

its colonies to ensure future peace. Considering 'what ifs' is beyond the scope of this study, but what it does is provide a prompt to consider how a man of war came to be a diplomat seeking reconciliation whilst the diplomats became aggressors seeking revenge.

Tracing Kitchener's life allows themes and trends to be identified and provides a context for some analysis of the man before the final chapters consider his time at the War Office and death. Most revealing has been the extent of Kitchener's relationships with men and women, his sensitivity and strict adherence to principles he held dear and the total disregard of others. He was an astute student but not in the traditional sense, although he valued the latter for others. He was generous, exacting, intolerant of those who did not stand up to him, and shy – his awareness of his shortcomings masked by a cloak of aloofness and severity. His life was duty to his monarch and the empire that was British.

A study of this kind would not have been possible without input by others, especially given the gaps in the author's knowledge. Professor Tony Stockwell whose robust challenging in effect spawned this book. Professor Stephen Badsey provided invaluable help, insights and information on Kitchener as an Engineer and Cavalry officer as well as offering suggestions of other texts to read on Kitchener's relations with Lord French.[16] Attendees at the various papers I presented on Kitchener in South Africa, at Val on railways and at the South African Military History Society in 2012 and 2015 and those who subsequently entered into correspondence about the subject. Sandy Buchanan has been a phenomenal help in understanding railways and trying to trace various connections Kitchener had. Colleagues at conferences in Maynooth, Ireland 2014 and UNISA 2015 asked probing and pertinent questions regarding Kitchener's identity which have helped frame the text. Professor Ian van der Waag provided a generous sounding board, as did Dr Suryakanthie Chetty. Nicholas Southey needs to be singled out for the challenge he set on Kitchener's identity. Colleagues in the History and Archive Section of Countess Mountbatten's Own Legion of Frontiersmen inspired questions and access to obscure material, and it is hoped this study will go some way to resolving a few of the many unanswered questions concerning the Legion's involvement in the First World War. Professor Rod McCarthy generously shared information and diary snippets on Sam Steele.

Many archives kindly provided access and permission for material to be used, while texts quoted are either out of copyright or fall into the fair usage category. The (British) National Archives (TNA) for access to the Kitchener papers and relevant Crown Copyright correspondence. Lucy McCann at the Bodleian Library has, as always, been more than generous with pointing me in the right direction of material and information, Anna Petre, Assistant Keeper of the Oxford University Archives for information on the granting of Honorary Doctorates to Kitchener and Rhodes,

16   John Denton Pinkstone French, 1st Earl of Ypres, born 28 September 1852, died 22 May 1925.

Parliamentary Archives, Templar Study Centre at the National Army Museum, the Manuscripts Department, Asian & African Studies at The British Library. The staff in Rare Books helped track down missing items and knew just when and how to pacify a frustrated researcher. The staff at Hertfordshire County Archives & Local Studies Centre and Hatfield House in Hertford and at Brenthurst Library in South Africa made me feel at home. Thomas Kiely at the British Museum for his patience and enthusiasm in email correspondence.

A special thanks to Dr Christopher Brice who having spotted the potential of this biography, diligently edited it, providing valuable advice along the way, and Duncan Rogers at Helion for agreeing there was something in it. It has been a refreshing and, I hope, worthwhile journey. The support of family and friends is hugely appreciated – this book would not have been completed had it not been for your patience, under-standing and reminders about work-life balance.

To military colleagues in the Great War in Africa Association, Legion of Frontiersmen, King's African Rifles & East African Forces Association and General The Lord Richards of Herstmonceux, thank you for your patience, encouragement and acceptance of the views of this non-military-trained historian treading on your toes. This book is dedicated to you all, especially those born, working in 'alien' lands and not always understood.

1

The formative years: Ireland and Europe, 1850-1874

The man we 'know' as Kitchener did not just happen. Like all human beings he went through stages of development where experiences and encounters moulded him into the person who took control of the War Office in August 1914. He made mistakes along the way, but learned from them and, in certain respects, mellowed with age, while becoming more dogmatic in others. Those he reported to and those he worked closely with provide astute observations on his personality, behaviours he learned to manage publicly but which came to the fore at times of extreme pressure.

Horatio Herbert Kitchener was born in Ballygunner (Gunsborough House) near Listowell, County Kerry, Ireland, on 24 June 1850, the third of five children and named after his father's hero, Lord Horatio Nelson, victor of Trafalgar. His childhood years were spent in Ireland and Switzerland where he was initially home-schooled. The move to Villeneuve in Switzerland in 1863 was the result of his mother's ill-health. It failed in its objective, and she died a year later when Kitchener was only fourteen years old. Soon after, 10 January 1867, his father remarried at the British Legation in Berne, Switzerland and moved to New Zealand, leaving Kitchener, his two brothers and sister at school in Switzerland. His fifth sibling was a half-sister born in New Zealand.[1]

As with all children, these early years were to influence Kitchener later. He was used to the 'quirky' – his father did not believe in comfortable living and used only newspapers to keep warm at night during winter. Self-regulation was encouraged with the children meting out punishment on each other for perceived and real injustices. There is a story of Kitchener's sister pinning him down spread-eagled, tied to croquet rings, for a day because he had teased her.[2] Much time was spent outdoors, horse riding and swimming. Another account tells of him aged twelve, swimming out

1   Frederick Arthur Crisp (ed.), *Visitation of England and Wales*, vol 19 (private print, 1919) p.295.
2   Philip Magnus, *Kitchener: Portrait of an Imperialist* (London: Penguin, 1958) pp.20-1.

to sea and getting caught in seaweed. Turning on his back, he waited for the tide to turn, disentangled the seaweed and swam back to shore. He was an expert swimmer.[3]

On arrival at boarding school, the young Kitcheners discovered that for all their home-schooling, they were not well-versed in the requirements of the formal education system and curriculum and had quite a bit of catching up to do. Perseverance and determination aided by some fatherly threats enabled them to do so: the family motto was 'thorough' which Kitchener took to heart.

Having completed his schooling, Kitchener determined to follow in his father's footsteps and join the army – two brothers did likewise[4] – but he was not an outstanding student, coming 28/56 in the examination for entry to Woolwich Academy.[5] Here, he trained as an engineer; mathematics being one of his strong subjects. On conclusion of his studies, and whilst waiting for his first appointment, Kitchener visited his father who was then in Dinan, France. His visit coinciding with the Franco-Prussian War of 1870, the young soldier could not resist the opportunity of seeing action for himself.

Lessons in preparation and planning: France, 1870-1871, England 1871-1874

Kitchener, and friend Henry Dawson, enlisted in the French Army, joining General Chanzy at Loire where he served as an ambulance-man, but there is no evidence that he met Henry Brackenbury who had taught him at Woolwich and later played a role in his time in Sudan.[6] While in France, 4 January to 15 March 1871, Jean Jules Jusserand, one-time ambassador to England and friend, recalled:

3   Cora Rowell, *Leaders of the Great War* (New York: Macmillan, 1919) pp.85-6.
4   *Henry Elliot Chevalier Kitchener*, 2nd Earl Kitchener, born 5 October 1846, joined the army 1866, commissioned 46th (South Devonshire) Regiment of Foot and Duke of Cornwall's Light Infantry in 1881. Served in Franco-Prussian War alongside his brother (*The Gleaner*, p.1, 5 July 1916), Instructor at Curragh Camp 1876-1878, Instructor military topography at Royal Military College 1879-1886, Burma 1891, Deputy Adjutant General; West Indies depot Jamaica Dec 1898, retired Colonel 1903. Remained in Jamaica until he went to East Africa in 1915, died Kenya 27 March 1937, aged 90. His son HFC Kitchener was on HMS *Ajax* in 1914. *Frances Emily Jane (Millie) Kitchener*, born 1848, died 10 February 1925, married 24 June 1869. *Arthur Buck Kitchener*, FGS, born 1852, died from pneumonia in Lucerne, March 1907. Studied minerology and mining engineering. Nottingham *Evening Post*, 6 March 1907, p.5. *Frederick Walter Kitchener*, born 26 May 1858, joined the army 1876, served Egypt, Afghanistan, Transvaal, India, Governor Bermuda, died 6 March 1912. Half-sister, *Henrietta Letitia Emma Kawara Kitchener*, born 1867, died 7 October 1926.
5   *The Times*, 24 January 1868 in JB Rye & Horace G Groser, *Kitchener in His Own Words* (London: T Fisher Unwin, 1917) p.28; Magnus, p.23.
6   Christopher Brice, *The Thinking Man's Soldier: The Life and Career of General Sir Henry Brackenbury 1837-1914* (Solihull: Helion & Co Ltd, 2012) chapter 9; Henry Brackenbury, *Some Memories of My Spare Time* (London: William Blackwood & Sons, 1909) p.224.

[Kitchener was told he was] 'the only officer of engineers among us, you must blow up the bridge.' He was greatly embarrassed; theoretically he knew from books how to blow up bridges, but he had never tried his hand at it; what if he failed? But he reflected that, if other things were wanting, there was no lack of powder, and moreover no one was wise enough to object to anything he might do; he therefore had sufficient powder laid to blow up 'a city'; the bridge was scattered into the air and he was warmly complimented.[7]

In France, having gone up in an air balloon, Kitchener contracted pneumonia,[8] and on his return to the United Kingdom, was severely chastised by the Commander-in-Chief, the Duke of Cambridge, for almost causing an international incident. His dressing down over, the Duke informed the young Kitchener that he would have done exactly the same had the opportunity arisen. Kitchener thus learnt early on that he could get away with taking risks and breaking protocol, but it was also a salutary lesson for the young officer. Later in his life, Kitchener would maintain his austere and harsh reputation yet treat subordinates with consideration and humanity; the circumstances dictating his level of understanding and tolerance.

The lesson [Kitchener] seems to have learnt [in France] was that to go into battle ill-prepared has unpleasant results; certainly all his own battles in the future would occur at the end of long, careful preparations. Kitchener was to belong to the school of generals who believe that battle should only be offered if it is thought to have been won already.[9]

Eventually, in 1913, he received his campaign medal for France.[10] As a military engineer, he was well placed and trained in the latest technological developments. His post training experiences would ensure he remained aware of developments and, by all accounts, he was to experience a number of firsts as a British soldier. The situations in which he found himself, together with his training, meant he was not afraid to experiment, or take risks, to achieve a goal. His hot air balloon excursion exposed him to the potentials of the balloon for military service twenty years before the British Army got its first balloon in 1890,[11] and his poor experience of medical treatment led to him taking a particular interest in this area as far as finances would allow. It was a fine line to tread and not one he always got right.

On his return to England, 16 March 1871 to 20 April 1873, Kitchener spent time with the Sappers at the School of Military Engineering at Chatham, studying

7   JJ Jusserand, *What Me Befell* (London: Constable, 1933) p.115; TNA: WO 25/3914/304 (part 7, p.77) service record.
8   Royle, p.24.
9   Philip Warner, *The Man Behind the Legend* (New York: Atheneum, 1986) p.16.
10   Magnus, p.25.
11   Warner, p.62.

photography, ballooning, surveying, submarine mining and fortifications.[12] He is then listed as being at Aldershot from 21 April to 30 June 1873. This coincides with the period Pollock claims Kitchener was aide-de-camp (ADC) to George Richard Greaves attending manoeuvres in Austria as part of the silver-jubilee celebrations for Frans Joseph. When Greaves fell ill, Kitchener stepped in to attend dinners with the Arch-Duke in Vienna.[13] He also used the opportunity to find out about river cross-ings, and went to Hanover to improve his German, develop his knowledge of German engineering, and to study von Moltke's military reform of the German Army.[14] On return he was posted to Royal Engineering Training from 1 July 1873 to 20 December 1874, where he was, according to Groser, responsible for training troops in field teleg-raphy and further developed his survey skills.[15]

12   Rye, p.28; Magnus, pp.25, 27; TNA: WO 25/3914/304 (part 7, p.77).
13   Pollock, p.27. George Richard Greaves (1831-1922) served India, Gold Coast and Cyprus; Kitchener is not mentioned in Greaves' autobiography, or that he missed dinner with the Kaiser due to illness. (*Memoirs of General Sir George Richards Greaves*, written by himself, London: John Murray, 1924).
14   Magnus, p.27; Smithers, p.22-3.
15   Rye, p.28.

2

Personal development: The Middle East, 1874-1892

The next twelve years saw Kitchener, 24 to 36 years of age, in a variety of roles. He was ambitious, out to prove himself and to climb the career ladder. That he had not been schooled in England other than the years of his initial military training meant he was an unknown entity to his fellow officers and colleagues. In habit, he was unpolished, the result of his childhood freedoms reinforced by his years in the Middle East and Sudan, but was able, outwardly, to carry himself as a gentleman should, no doubt having learnt to do so whilst at Aldershot and Woolwich.

Finding his feet: Palestine, 1874-1878

Military action remained scarce, so Kitchener accepted a posting to map Palestine with the Palestine Exploration Fund in November 1874.[1] Claude Reignier Conder[2] had recommended Kitchener be approached to replace CF Tyrwhitt Drake who had died and, on 15 July 1875, Kitchener succeeded Conder himself when the latter suffered poor health. Kitchener and Conder had known each other at Woolwich, and at the house of Reverend George Frost in Kensington Square where they studied Hebrew together.[3] Four years later, 10 September 1878, a week after being appointed to survey Cyprus, Kitchener handed in his report on Palestine.[4]

---

1 Others in the party were Conder, Corporals Armstrong, Brophy and Junor as well as a Syrian scribe, Palestine Exploration Fund, *Quarterly Statement* January 1875, pp.3, 109. More can be found at The Palestine Exploration Fund, online: https://www.pef.org.uk/history/ [accessed 7 Sep 2019].
2 Claude Reignier Conder, born 29 December 1848, died 16 February 1910.
3 John James Moscrop, The Palestine Exploration Fund: 1865-1914 (PhD, University of Leicester, 1996) p.108. Arthur, p.7.
4 For a comprehensive overview of Kitchener's time in Palestine, see Samuel Daiches, *Lord Kitchener and His Work in Palestine* (London: Luzac, 1915).

In completing the Palestine survey, he covered 1,000 square miles in eight months at a cost of £1,000.[5] He rescued Conder from drowning on 5 April 1875, having returned less than a month earlier from sick leave. Suffering from 'Jericho fever' in January 1875 he had been left at Jerusalem to recover, returning on 15 March.[6] Not long after, at Safed, on 13 July, 'Kitchener was seriously injured on the thigh with a huge stone …' Despite his injury, he again saved Conder, receiving a blow to the head and a wounded arm, and he narrowly missed being shot.[7] The outcome was the suspension of mapping exercises to allow order to be restored and also for a cholera outbreak to be brought under control. On 11 April, they 'made a most successful entry into Safed.' Having been met by the leaders of the town, 'we rode […] in quite a triumphal procession. […] Today I had the Governor, the British Consul, and our old enemy, Ali Agha Alan, the cause of the row; the latter expressed deep sorrow for what he had done, as well he may, as I hear he and the Mogrebbins are all but ruined.'[8] As a result, the perpetrators' fine was reduced at Kitchener's instigation.

In addition to mapping the land, Kitchener took over fifty photographs of significant places and artefacts, some of which were published in a Guinea Book, *Photographs of Biblical sites*, in 1876.[9] By all accounts it had been his photography which led to the appointment.[10] Reading through Kitchener's reports to the Palestine Exploration Fund, it becomes apparent that he was well read, an interest which developed whilst there.[11] In describing the land around the Sea of Galilee in April 1877, he wrote:

> The best views of the lake are from a distance on the many heights from which it is visible, as thus seen in the evening it is particularly lovely. Deep blue shadows seem to increase the size of the hills, and there is always a rosy flush in the sky and over snow-clad Hermon.
>
> The road at the southern end of the lake passes through Kerak, which appears to have been a fortified place of considerable strength. Two castles, one on either side of the road, with a wall joining them, seem to have guarded this entrance to the shores of the lake … It also must have required a large garrison owing to the great size of the plateau.
>
> Josephus describes Vespasian as advancing to the attack of Iberias from Seythopolis or Veisan: 'He then came with three legions and pitched his camp thirty furlongs off Tiberias, at a certain station easily seen [by the innovators]; it is named Sennabris.'

5   *Church and State*, 14 September 1878, p.10.
6   Conder in Rye, p.31.
7   Conder in Rye, p.32.
8   Daiches, *Kitchener in Palestine*, p.37.
9   Palestine Exploration Fund reports, July 1876, p.111.
10   Harold Begbie, *Kitchener: Organizer of Victory* (Boston: Riverside Press Cambridge, 1915) chapter 5.
11   Begbie, Chapter 5; Moscrop, *The Palestine Exploration Fund*.

> Measuring 30 furlongs north from Kerak it brings us well within the ruins
> of the ancient town of Tiberias, though not up to the walls of the present city.[12]

Kitchener continues that the 'large artificially levelled plateau' could have been the remains of the Roman camp described, and that it was the Sennabris road. The earliest reference for the text quoted by Kitchener is by Flavius Joseph, circa AD77, whose work was translated from Greek into English and republished in numerous editions, one in 1873 four years before Kitchener wrote his report.[13]

In the same report, he observed:

> The site of Capernaum is the most interesting of all the places around the lake.
> I cannot help thinking, with Dr Robinson, that it was at Khurbet Minyeh. The
> guard-house, where the Centurion resided, was probably on the great Damascus
> road at Khurbet el 'Aureimeh, which seems to be the ruin of such a station.[14]

What is noticeable in all Kitchener's reports of this time is the clarity of his logic and thinking in explaining why, or why not, a specific location is identified as such. Where an inaccuracy is found, he details the extent to which they went before making the final decision. 'Thorough' comes to mind.

On 28 March 1877, Kitchener received a telegram informing him that war had been declared between Turkey and Russia. 'I hope this sad news will not interfere with the successful completion of the survey of Galilee,' concluded his March 1877 report to the funders.[15] He must have been anxious to take the opportunity of being so close to seeing how the war was developing, yet stayed to complete the work he had been commissioned to do. Having completed his survey of northern Palestine on 10 July 1877 in the course of which he collected 2,773 names and visited and described 476 ruins, Kitchener started the paperwork and prepared for starting a survey of the south in September. The committee, on receipt of this report took the opportunity to note:

> ... their high sense of Lieutenant Kitchener's ability and zeal. He has conducted
> the work for six months without any accidents during a period of suspicion and

12   Palestine Exploration Fund report, 30 April 1877 from Meiron, pp.120-1.
13   Flavius Josephus & William Whiston, *The Works of Flavius Josephus, the Learned and Authentic Jewish Historian and Celebrated Warrior*, with three dissertations, concerning Jesus Christ, John the Baptist, James the Just, God's command to Abraham etc (T Nelson, 1860) p.670; Flavius Joseph (Рипол Классик) *The works of Josephus* (1873); William Whiston first published in *The Genuine Works of Flavius Josephus, the Jewish Historian* (trans. William Whiston, 1737) online: https://lexundria.com/j_bj/0/wst [accessed 16 Feb 2019].
14   Palestine Exploration Fund report, 30 April 1877 from Meiron, p.123.
15   Palestine Exploration Fund report, 30 April 1877 from Meiron, p.125.

excitement. His reports, which are in the hands of the General Committee, are careful and intelligent, and his monthly accounts show due regard to economy. He has hitherto managed to conduct the Survey for a monthly sum less than that which the Committee gave him as a maximum.[16]

The work Conder and Kitchener undertook would 'give the world such a geography of Palestine as will make the topography of the Bible for the first time completely intelligible.' The map consisting of twenty-six sheets, would be accompanied by its own memoir containing '... some thousands of names, very many of them of Biblical places heretofore not identified, together with many of those found in Talmudic, early Christian and Crusading histories.'[17]

On leave from 11 July, Kitchener went to the Lebanon, returning to work on 23 August 1877. From Aleih, he wrote:

> We arrived here safely on the 21st [August], after a hot march from Haifa. I have now started office work in a room close to our camp, and I think we shall have a month or more hard work; everything has to be made in duplicate, and all observations, descriptions, etc, have to be copied out.[18]

Kitchener's return had been delayed, '... as I could not have moved one of my horses ...' He left on 24 August for Jerusalem from where he wrote on 7 September that he had 'presented the gun to Abdallah Agha' and reported that, 'The Arabs show no great patriotism for their co-religionists at war; they hate the Turk, and do not care which way the war goes.'[19]

The survey of the final 200 square miles of the south was completed in October, but not the repair of Jacob's well as the territory had become too dangerous, according to Kitchener attributed 'to the elation felt by Mohammedans at having been able to best so large a Christian power as Russia.'[20] On 3 November Kitchener had stones thrown at him in Nablus which did not interfere with completing the outstanding work on 22 November.[21] This included drawing 29 plans and taking 19 photographs. On 26 November Kitchener left for Constantinople, having been granted a month's leave.[22]

16   Palestine Exploration Fund Meeting of the General Committee 17 July 1877, p.193.
17   Palestine Exploration Fund report, W Hepworth Dixon, Chairman of the Executive Committee, January 1878, Quarterly Statement, p.6.
18   Daiches, *Kitchener in Palestine*, p.44.
19   Daiches, *Kitchener in Palestine*, pp.4-7.
20   Palestine Exploration Fund report, 1 November 1877 from Nablus, p.15.
21   Rye, p.40.
22   Palestine Exploration Fund report, 23 November 1877 from Jerusalem, p.67.

During this period of leave, Kitchener went to observe the Russo-Turkish war, 1877-1878, with someone identified only as T.[23] In November 1877 he was at Kamerleh (Karmarli) in Bulgaria, paying special attention to the Turks. Magnus reports Kitchener as being 'mildly startled' at seeing Bulgarian corpses hanging from lampposts at Tatar Bazardjik,[24] however, in his own account, he found:

> The town was in a state of siege, and no one was allowed out in the streets after dark. At almost every corner, three pieces of wood projected into the street, forming, as I thought, a point to suspend a lamp; these were gallows, and were in full use about three weeks before our visit. Even now there was considerable fear of a Bulgarian rising in the town against the Turks.[25]

Failing to obtain transport to the front, disguised as a wounded Turk he travelled with Dr Smith of the Red Crescent Ambulance who was overseeing a convoy heading in the same direction. Kitchener's Arabic stood him in good stead too. Struggling through snow after leaving Vakerall, '… it was very distressing to meet a long convoy of bullock-carts full of wounded soldiers slowly creeping along the road we had come, only covered by a few blankets given out by the Compassionate Fund. These poor men would have to be jolted along all night in such weather.'[26]

On 20 December Kitchener and his companion rode out to Tashkessen, about an hour from Kamerleh. Again, Kitchener noted the contrasts, this time between the Arab and Bosnian soldiers giving him insight into how men from warm climes would cope with freezing weather: 'There was a marked difference between the Arab and Bosnian battalions. The former appeared shrivelled up and scarcely capable of moving, whilst the latter were lively, and working to make their huts more comfortable.'[27]

Here, on 21 December, he met Valentine Baker Pasha (former Commander of the 10th Hussars) serving with the Turkish Army. With Baker, he climbed a 6,200-foot mountain. Jastrzembski claims Kitchener recognised that:

> Baker Pasha is the only general who has looked after the interior economy and sanitary arrangements of his men, and his division's camps are in striking contrast to those of the rest of the army. The men are very fond of the Inglese Pasha as they call him, and have a thorough confidence in him.[28]

---

23   HHK, 'A visit to Sophia and the heights of Kamerleh – Christmas 1877', in *Blackwood's Magazine* (Feb 1878) p.194.
24   Magnus, pp.38-9.
25   HHK, *Visit to Sophia*, p.195.
26   HHK, *Visit to Sophia*, p.196.
27   HHK, *Visit to Sophia*, p.198.
28   Frank Jastrzembski, *Valentine Baker's Heroic Stand at Tashkessen 1877: A Tarnished British Soldier's Glorious Victory* (Barnsley: Pen & Sword, 2017) p.185, quoting HHK, *Visit to Sophia*, p.198.

Despite not being able to speak Turkish, Valentine was idolised. This would have reinforced Kitchener's view that being with your men was more valuable than commanding or leading from a distance. Kitchener had to leave on Christmas day to return to Constantinople and then London but T remained behind, 'Poor Fellow! He was caught by the Russians two days later, when they at last advanced on Tashkessen.'[29]

Kitchener arrived back in London in January 1878 and stayed for nine months. He completed his maps and memoirs on Palestine and, on a visit to Dublin in August, gave a talk to the Geographical section of the British Association of Archaeologists explaining how he went about the work. It was no small task triangulating places, the task taking eight days, building on what they had done in 1875. Their camp, well situated at Hattin, '… consisted of five Egyptian tents, seven little Arab horses, seven mules, four Europeans, ten natives, and two bashi-bazouks with their horses, attached to us by the Government.'[30] Kitchener had requested the support of the bashi-bazouks after the previous troubles at Safed. Understanding local conditions and beliefs was important in completing the work:

> During our triangulation we found some little difficulty from the natives, who thought we were magicians, with power to find hidden treasure under the ground and that our cairns were marks to remember the places by. It was an unfortunate idea, […] in the night time our cairns often disappeared, and the natives groped through any earth to the rock below, hoping to forestall us. After making the offenders rebuild the cairns on one or two occasions these annoyances ceased.[31]

On accuracy of spelling and names, he explained:

> Each surveyor had a guide with him, who gave the names of the different places. The surveyor wrote them down as near as he could to the sound, and on returning to camp he repeated them in front of the guide and the scribe. The guide then pronounced the names correctly, and the scribe wrote it down from him. I afterwards transliterated the Arabic in accordance with Robinson's method,[32] and the

29   HHK, *Visit to Sophia*, p.200.
30   HH Kitchener, Survey of Galilee, A paper read before the Geographical Section of the British Association, [in Dublin] August 1878, p.161.
31   Kitchener, Survey of Galilee, p.163.
32   Edward Robinson was a Biblical scholar who travelled Palestine in the 1830s accompanied by a previous student and missionary fluent in Arabic. Philip J King provides a useful oversight of Robinson and his approach in 'Edward Robinson: Biblical scholar', in *The American Schools of Oriental Research*, vol 46, no 4 (Dec 1983) pp.230-2 online: http://holyland.oucreate.com/wp-content/uploads/2016/01/Philip-King-Edward-Robinson.pdf [accessed 16 Feb 2019]; for an understanding of the complexities of Arabic translation see Adolph August Brux, 'Arabic-English Transliteration for Library Purposes', in *The American Journal of Semitic Languages and Literatures*, vol 47, no 1, part 2 (Oct, 1930) pp.1-30.

proper spelling was thus obtained and written on the map. Every possible check on the veracity of the natives was employed by asking numbers of people independently the names. Dishonest guides were dismissed, and as these people are peculiarly susceptible of sarcasm, the offenders were not happy when they were laughed out of camp for not knowing it.[33]

Kitchener also gave some insight into Christian-Muslim relations at the time. On his arrival at Dibl, the Christians were looking to move out, but decided to stay with the arrival of the survey group which they believed could protect them.

A Christian village can be known from a distance by the greenness of its vineyards and fields, in striking contrast to the barren desolation surrounding most Muslim villages. The terrible fatalism of their religion destroys the country. 'If God wills that fruit trees or vineyards should grow they will grow,' says the Moslem, as he sits and smokes.

[... The Christians] were very anxious to buy arms and defend themselves, but that course might have led to what they most dreaded. I am glad to say that our influence in the country at this crisis caused these poor Christians to remain in their villages, which if they had deserted would have been seized by the Moslems, and would undoubtedly have led to a grave disturbance.

I must also bear testimony to the stringent orders sent from Constantinople to the Turkish governors and officials to protect these Christians, and to put down any attempt to drive them out of the country. There was more cause to fear this, as the ignorance of the people led them to believe the war was one of religion – Moslem against Christian, instead of Turk against Russian.[34]

Not long after, Kitchener entertained eighty Bedouin Arabs with their wives and families travelling to Joshua's tomb so their chief's son could get healed. Having organised a goat to be killed and 'rewarded them with lumps of sugar' for their dancing and entertainment in the evening, the following morning, they had gone. Two days later, the chief returned to thank Kitchener for the medicine.[35]

His work for the Palestine Exploration Fund near completion, on 3 September 1878, Kitchener accepted a role with the Foreign Office to map Cyprus. Failing to reconcile his father and step-mother, he left London and 'did not spend another winter in England until 1914.'[36] This appointment had been organised by Thomas Cobbold,[37] a distant cousin, who had been in the Diplomatic Service and was Conservative MP

33   Kitchener, Survey of Galilee, p.164.
34   Kitchener, Survey of Galilee, p.169.
35   Kitchener, Survey of Galilee, p.170.
36   Magnus, pp.40-1.
37   Thomas Cobbold, 22 July 1833 to 21 November 1883.

for Ipswich. For this posting Kitchener would report into Lord Salisbury[38] at the Foreign Office, the War Office unable to decide which department was responsible for the task.[39]

Encounters with authority: Cyprus, Kastamanu & Egypt, 1878-1882

Cyprus had become a British protectorate in 1878 following a secret agreement between the Ottoman Sultan and Lord Beaconsfield (Benjamin Disraeli) on 8 July. Intended to be a temporary defensive base from which to protect the Ottoman Empire and Eastern Mediterranean from Russian encroachment, Garnet Wolseley was appointed the first High Commissioner on 22 July 1878.[40] Kitchener arrived on 15 September and five months later met the explorer Samuel Baker whom he piloted '… to the celebrated springs about three miles above the village [Kythrea].' Baker recalled that, 'With this excellent guide, who could explain every inch of the surrounding country, we started upon a most interesting ride.'[41]

Kitchener's knowledge of the land and peoples was set out in an unattributed article he submitted to *Blackwood's Magazine* in 1879. In addition to commenting on the Island's Greeks and Turks, the influence of religion on social and cultural norms and the countryside, his ever-present military eye led to suggestions, which if they had been adopted, could have presented a different scenario when the 1914-18 war broke out. Kitchener explained:

> The army of those who are to be our future allies should also be attended to. We know what splendid fighting material there is in the Turkish soldier. We also know their wants – good officers, discipline and commissariat. By raising and maintaining a Turkish regiment in Cyprus, we could find out by experience the reforms necessary. It would become the training school for officers, who would be capable of carrying out the same reforms in Asia Minor; and in case of war, we should have men able to raise troops amongst the many warlike tribes of Syria and Asia Minor who would follow an English leader to the death.

---

38   Robert Arthur Gascoyne-Cecil, 3rd Marquess of Salisbury born 3 February 1830, died 22 August 1903, Secretary of State for Foreign Affairs 2 April 1879–28 April 1880; 24 June 1885–February 1886; 14 January 1887–11 August 1892; 2 June 1895–12 November 1900; Prime Minister 23 June 1885–28 January 1886; 25 July 1886–11 August 1892; 25 June 1895–11 July 1902.

39   Magnus, p.40.

40   Gail Dallas Hook, *Protectorate Cyprus: British Imperial Power Before World War I* (London: IB Tauris, 2015) pp.16, 33; Cyprus was annexed by Britain in 1914 and became a Crown Colony in 1925. Hook, p.24. Sir Garnet Joseph Wolseley (1833-1913) served in Burma, Crimea, Gold Coast, Cyprus, War Office.

41   Rye, pp.48-9.

By thus employing Cyprus we should make its possession politically of the vastest importance, and we should really possess the key of the East.[42]

Kitchener's view on the Turkish Army, and on having Turkey as an ally, was no doubt influenced by his observations of the Russo-Turkish war a few years before. One of his reasons for preferring Turkey over Russia was that despite religious differences and his preference for Christianity, the 'Muscovite yoke [was] twice as heavy as the Ottoman'; it would be difficult to challenge and change.[43] Other themes starting to run through Kitchener's writing are those of Britain taking the lead in educating and influencing how people lived, as well as looking to Britain's security. In his reports on Palestine, Kitchener had already expressed his belief in British imperialism, and this continued during his time in Cyprus; his view bringing him into conflict with Wolseley.

Kitchener, a perfectionist, had fallen out with Wolseley when he wanted to do a far more detailed job than Wolseley thought necessary, or financially possible. Wanting to raise a Turkish regiment in case of a general war did not help matters either.[44] On 14 June 1879, the War Office received the following from the Foreign Office:

> We are sending you an official letter of approval of the services of Lieutenants Kitchener and Hippesly [Richard Hippisley, Kitchener's assistant] in Cyprus. Their work was brought to a sudden conclusion in consequence of objections raised by the Cyprus Government to the expense of carrying out the survey and it is feared that they may have been exposed to some hardship and inconvenience by the unexpected termination of their employment. Lord Salisbury proposes to provide for Lieutenant Kitchener by offering him an appointment under Major Wilson in Asia Minor and a letter asking for his services in that capacity has been sent to the War Office.[45]

Two weeks later, Kitchener was appointed to Kastamanu in Northern Anatolia from 2 August 1879, where he spent eight months as Vice-Consul to Charles Wilson.[46] Wilson knew Kitchener through the Palestine Exploration Fund, himself having been involved in the feasibility study for the mapping of Western Palestine which Kitchener completed. Both were Royal Engineers and members of the British Association of Archaeologists. It was also at this time that Kitchener's name became known to

---

42   Camp Levkouiko, 'Cyprus, Notes from Cyprus', in *Blackwood's Magazine* (Aug 1879) pp.150-7.
43   Levkouiko, p.157.
44   Magnus, pp.41-2; Warner, p.25.
45   Arthur Hodges, *Lord Kitchener* (London: Thornton Butterworth, 1936) p.44.
46   TNA: PRO 30/57/1/2, 26 June 1879; Magnus, pp.46-7; Charles William Wilson, born 14 March 1836, died 25 October 1905.

Lord Salisbury, Secretary of State for Foreign Affairs, responsible for Britain's role in ensuring the terms of the treaties between Russia and Turkey were adhered to.[47]

While in Anatolia, Kitchener wrote various letters about the Circassians who were troubling the Christians and Muslims. He thought the Turkish government was doing little to alleviate the plight of the Circassians and until this was done, or a stand made, the suppression of the inhabitants would continue. Bribery and maladministration were rife and needed addressing so that order and stability could be introduced.[48] Kitchener's experiences of the poor being suppressed and the link to lawlessness and unrest, seen here and in Palestine, no doubt influenced the later reforms he was to introduce in Egypt: if people had nothing, the law meant nothing, survival became everything. On reading Kitchener's report of the situation, Lord Salisbury wrote: 'I request that Your Excellency [Austen Henry Layard] will have the goodness to convey to Mr Kitchener my thanks for the information contained in this document (the Report), which I have read with much interest.'[49]

Kitchener returned to Cyprus on 15 March 1880 at the request of the new High Commissioner, Robert Biddulph following Wolseley's appointment to South Africa.[50] He wrote to Walter Besant, secretary of the Palestine Exploration Fund:[51]

> Here I am back at my old work of surveying [March 1880]. I think I was wrong giving up the diplomatic line, but I could not let another pull my points about, so when the General [Biddulph] offered it to me I could not well refuse as he put in increased pay and better position ... I enjoyed Anatolia immensely, such lovely country. I met Wilson at Marsovan looking awfully well. He moves about in great state and is well received everywhere. He showed me some copies of the Memoir. How about the map [of Palestine]? I should much like to have a run up to Constantinople to present it to the old Sultan in my best Turkish (no small accomplishment now) to tell him what it is, why it was done, who did it, and how glad he ought to be to get it, with some hints of a *firman* for increased powers of excavation in Jerusalem or the survey of Haman. A flourish afterward by the Times correspondent whom I know and a letter from Lawrence Oliphant will start the whole thing gain in grand style.[52]

47   Charles Moore Watson, *The Life of Major-General Charles William Wilson, Royal Engineers* (London: John Murray, 1909) pp.108-9.
48   Rye, pp.54-64.
49   Rye, p.64; Austen Henry Layard, born 5 March 1817, died 5 July 1894, was an archaeologist and from 1877 to 1880 was British Ambassador to Istanbul.
50   Magnus, p.47; Robert Biddulph (1835-1918) replaced George Robert Greaves as High Commissioner, the latter serving after Wolseley from May to July 1879. Biddulph remained in Cyprus until 1886. Hook, pp.88, 91.
51   Walter Besant, born 1836, died 1901, author, historian, philanthropist, Freemason, Acting Secretary of the Palestine Exploration Fund 1868-1885. Annie Bessant was his sister-in-law.
52   Hodges, p.45.

Kitchener must have felt rather constrained by Cyprus. Not long after taking up his post in 1880, Biddulph refused to allow him to accept an offer by the British Museum to lead an archaeological expedition to Assyria and Babylon, places which would have greater appeal to his religious nature than Cyprus. This offer was made whilst he was on leave in Britain in July and August 1881.[53] Instead he 'excavated in Cyprus for the South Kensington Museum and for several years administered the Land Registry Office, earning the respect of Greek, Turkish and French residents for his "zeal and intelligence" in administration and in his protection of Cyprus sites.' In recognition of his work, Kitchener was appointed curator and honorary secretary of the new Cyprus Museum by Biddulph in June 1882. When he eventually left the island, Kitchener received letters from the Archbishop, the Bishop of Kyrenia, the Abbot of Kikko amongst others, and a letter from Turkish inhabitants regretting his departure and thanking him for 'the preservation of the antiquities of this island.'[54] Apart from safeguarding items for the museum in Cyprus, Kitchener had added to his private collection started whilst in Palestine.[55]

The lure of action, though, was too strong and when an opportunity arose in July 1882, Kitchener took leave to travel to Egypt where he conducted intelligence work dressed as an Egyptian Arab, even allowing himself to be taken prisoner to obtain information and emotionlessly watched a fellow spy be tortured to death. During one of his forays, he travelled 200 kilometres across the desert developing a slight squint by refusing to wear dark glasses.[56]

Kitchener's visit to Egypt was against regulations. The accounts of how he got to Egypt are rather confusing when held up to scrutiny. However, it is worth considering Kitchener's version as set out to FGE Warren,[57] Chief Secretary to the Cyprus Government in 1884.

I dare say you know I have a very bad mark placed against me in the War Office, owing to my having left Cyprus for the bombardment. I may be wrong, but I think I was hardly treated – you were not in the island at the time. The facts were these. [Chief Justice of Cyprus, Sir Elliot] Bovill was staying with me when news was brought that the fleet, in which was one of my relations [not identified], had arrived at Alexandria. I discussed the matter with him and thought I would try to run over and see them. The post-boat was leaving Larnaca next day, so I telegraphed to the General, who was in Troodos for a week's leave – no war had been declared, and as you know, it was a very outside chance that the bombardment would take place [officers were not allowed to travel to war zones during their leave]. I have got the General's telegram granting me a week's leave,

53   Magnus, p.50.
54   Rye, pp.76-7.
55   Pollock, p.47.
56   Lord Kitchener, *New Zealand Herald*, 28 February 1910, p.12.
57   Falkland George Edgeworth Warren, born 18 June 1834, died 19 March 1908.

and I started in the post-boat next day, arriving on the 4th July. At Alexandria, Major [AB] Tulloch made use of me, and telegraphed for an extension of my leave. I also wrote to the General, little dreaming he was very angry with me. Major Tulloch did not tell me the General had refused my extension until after the post-boat had gone. He had made an appointment with me that morning to go on a reconnaissance to Kep Zaya. The post-boat left for Port Said earlier than usual, and when I met Major Tulloch it was gone. I returned to Cyprus by the very first opportunity in a gun-boat leaving for Port Said and was six days over my leave. [...][58]

By all accounts, Kitchener was aware there was to be a bombardment of Alexandria. It was at dinner in Cyprus with his assistant, SCN Grant, and ER Kenyon, attached to the department of Public Works in Cyprus, in June 1882 that he became aware that the British fleet was to attack Alexandria. Despite recovering from fever, his response was, 'I'm going to Alexandria.' The other guests at dinner, Mr Williamson and Mr Rees, both businessmen in Cyprus had let it be known they had obtained a contract to supply the fleet, which was leaving that night, with provisions. 'Kenyon laughed' at Kitchener's response, saying, 'The only way you can get there is by going with Rees tonight. The mailboat sails from Limassol tomorrow morning and Biddulph has ordered that no one shall apply for leave by telegraph unless absolutely necessary, and that full particulars must be given. Of course if you say you want leave to go to Alexandria you won't get it.' Retreating into gloomy silence, Kitchener announced, 'I'm going.'[59] He sent a telegram to the Chief Secretary asking for ten days' leave and packed, 'taking the precaution to prepare his paper of particulars to be sent in later.' At midnight, he received permission to go, sending in 'the particulars in the usual way.' He left with Rees the next morning.[60] There is a further account that Dr Heidenstam, the Health Officer at Limassol, '... saw Kitchener putting off from the flag-ship in a small boat.' Biddulph received the news of Kitchener's departure at dinner with Williamson, possibly the following night, and considering Kitchener's move one of insubordination ordered him to return immediately.[61]

Meanwhile, in Egypt, Tulloch recalled, 'One morning when I was engaged writing on board the *Invincible*, a tall, thin subaltern of Engineers, named Kitchener, came to see me; he had got a few days' leave from his General at Cyprus, and as he could speak Arabic, had come to see if he could be of any use to me.' He continued: '[...]

---

58   Peter's Finger, 'Lord Kitchener and the bombardment of Alexandria', in *Journal of the Society for Army Historical Research*, vol 18, no 72 (1939) pp.230-1. Peter's Finger is clearly a pseudonym but given the standing of the Journal, the author would have been known to the editor(s) and the article accepted as credible. An attempt was made to obtain the identity of the author.

59   Hodges, p.49.

60   Hodges, p.50.

61   Hodges, p.51-3.

K's General at Cyprus telegraphed more than once for me to send him back. I replied that I could not spare him, but on the 9th or 10th, as soon as I saw the screw of the passenger steamer, which should have taken him back, begin to turn, I wired, "Finished with K. He has been very useful but can now return".' He ends, 'Had we been aware what a genius was with us, not all the Generals in the Mediterranean would have prevented our keeping him.'[62]

The officer commanding was Wolseley, Kitchener's nemesis, who wanted to know whether it was possible to follow Napoleon's route from Cairo to Alexandria via the Nile as it had been dry when Napoleon did it; his aim being to bring Egypt under British control to protect the Suez route to the East. Tulloch and Kitchener, dressed as Levantine officials, left on the Suez train. Having determined the route was not feasible, Tulloch feigned illness and he and Kitchener left the train. A week later, a Syrian was found with his throat cut on the platform at Kafr ez Zaiyat, the station where Kitchener and Tulloch had alighted. The Syrian had a similar look to Tulloch suggesting the Egyptian-Syrian intelligence was working effectively. Eventually, on 11 June 1882, the bombardment of Alexandria began, but Kitchener had to watch from on board as he was not on active service. He then returned to Cyprus where he faced Biddulph.

No black marks had, in fact, been placed against Kitchener's name by either Biddulph or Wolseley. Peter's Finger points out that, 'The brevet promotions to Major in 1884 and Lieutenant-Colonel in January, 1885, quite dispel any such illusion.'[63] But, Biddulph's secretary Charles King-Harmon in the 1890s noted that if conscience came into conflict with self-interest, self-interest would win where Kitchener was concerned.[64] He clearly had experience of Kitchener manipulating circumstances to his own advantage. Kitchener continued to believe that his involvement in Egypt was acceptable '... because he was free to roam at will from end to end of Cyprus in the course of his survey work and an application for "leave of absence" could only mean permission to quit the island.'[65] This seems a long stretch even for Kitchener. Francis Grenfell[66] clearly had the measure of Kitchener: 'an exceptionally gifted officer but of the type which obeys the orders he likes but fails to understand the others.'[67]

Towards the end of his Cyprus contract, Kitchener suggested he be appointed British Consul to Mosul where he could survey the area and be consul. However,

62   AB Tulloch, 'Recollections of Forty Years' Service' in Peter's Finger, 'Lord Kitchener and the bombardment of Alexandria', p.229, Alexander Bruce Tulloch, born 2 September 1838, died 26 May 1920.
63   See fn 57 above; Peter's Finger, p.232.
64   Pollock, p.50.
65   EWC Sandes, *The Royal Engineers in Egypt and the Sudan: The Reconquest Reappraised* (Chatham: The Institution of Royal Engineers, 1937) p.54.
66   Francis Wallace Grenfell, 1st Baron Grenfell, GCB, GCMG, PC, born 29 April 1841, died 27 January 1925, no relation to Willy Grenfell, Lord Desborough, but was uncle to Frank Maxwell.
67   Warner, p.70.

'It did not, [...] seem as ideal to his commander-in-chief [Biddulph] who, although generally sympathetic to his ideas, had formed the opinion that Kitchener was beginning to chase too many hares for a young officer in the British Army.' Biddulph further noted that Kitchener was '... rather impulsive and does not always foresee results.' Kitchener's preference though was to go to Egypt where there would be more action. He desperately wanted to see active service, especially having earlier been turned down in 1879 by Wolseley for a post in South Africa, when the latter replaced Chelmsford[68] who had been defeated by the Zulu at Isandlwana, and became General Officer Commanding and Governor of Natal and Transvaal.[69]

Not his way: The Egyptian Army and death of Gordon, 1883-1885

Eight days after disbanding the Egyptian Army, following its defeat by Wolseley, Evelyn Wood telegrammed to Kitchener inviting him to join him in Egypt. When Kitchener declined, his tenure in Cyprus having another year to go, Wood told him, '... write your plans as we wanted you for second in command cavalry regiment.'[70] The offer followed when it became known that Kitchener spoke both Arabic and Turkish. Kitchener reluctantly accepted the post, the only one on offer. The new force was intended to maintain internal order, consisting initially of six thousand men led by 25 British officers, who were described as '... either poor men attracted by the high rates of pay, or ambitions allured by the increased authority.'[71] Kitchener returned to Cairo in February 1883 with the rank of Captain and second-in-command to Billy Taylor of the 19th Hussars commanding an Egyptian cavalry regiment.[72] On 17 March 1883 he took up his new position and, 'Whatever his deficiencies as a horseman, [...] was equal to any, and superior to most, in endurance, subtlety and courage. [...] possessed seemingly of an inborn understanding of Arab mentality, he was soon to be in his element among the mounted tribes of the desert.'[73]

'Deficiencies in horsemanship' contrast with his success on the race course. In Cyprus, at Nicosia, Kitchener won cups for racing on the flat and over sticks riding his own horses, *Selim* and *Kathleen*, and served as a whip to the local hunt.[74] The 'deficiencies' highlight that Kitchener was not trained as a cavalryman: he was an outsider, a 'professional soldier' rather than a 'gentleman'.[75] The fact that he had not attended

68   Frederic Augustus Thesiger, 2nd Baron Chelmsford, born 31 May 1827, died 9 April 1905.
69   TNA: PRO 30/57/1, 2 August 1882; Warner, pp.32, 34, 40.
70   TNA: PRO 30/57/1, 28 and 30 December 1882.
71   Churchill, *River War*, pp.187-90; Peter's Finger, p.232; Sandes, p.54.
72   Hodges, p.56.
73   Sandes, p.53.
74   Magnus, p.50; Hodges, p.54; Rye, p.65.
75   Christopher Brice, The military career of General Sir Henry Brackenbury 1856-1904 (De Montford University, PhD, 2009) p.14.

public school in the United Kingdom and did not understand, or pay regard to, the class proprieties, meant '… to his contemporaries, [Kitchener] was almost unknown, a mere name in the Army List, [with] no opportunity to distinguish himself in any of the colonial campaigns of the period […]. Against that he had some unusual credentials. He had seen a little of great European armies at war, he was a considerable linguist, was accustomed to working on his own and to living amongst people of other races. He was strong and tough, had had his courage tested and was expert with both horse and camel.'[76]

On 7 October 1883, Kitchener turned down an opportunity to study the Jordan valley and the Dead Sea. He wrote to Bessant, 'No doubt the trip will be delightful and I should like nothing better than to go on it, but not alone.' He had previously told Wilson he would require one or two assistants and further explained, 'I have not been home now for over five years and by taking my two months' leave for this trip I cut off all chances of getting home for some time to come.' This was followed with, 'If I could have had Sergeant Armstrong [one of his NCOs in Palestine], I should be satisfied, but no steps seem to have been taken, although he is quite willing to come and entitled to leave.' This appears to have had some effect as on 8 November, Kitchener met with Professor Edward Hull, his medical doctor son Gordon, Mr Hart, Mr Lawrence and Sergeant Armstrong and three weeks later they were at Akaba heading towards the Dead Sea, 125 miles distant.[77] Their trip, however, was interrupted by the news from Evelyn Baring that William Hicks[78] and his force had been massacred by the Mahdi in the latter's struggle for liberation. Despite the urge to return, Kitchener saw the expedition safely to Gaza before returning to Ismailia, going straight through the desert:

I considered the road by Al Arish to Egypt was already well-known, so by myself with four camels and four Arabs, I made my way across to Ismailia, about two hundred miles. One of the Arabs had been part of the road fifteen years before, none of the others knew anything of it, but they were good men from the Egyptian Huweitât under a relation of the Sheikh Ibn Shedid. We passed a good many Arabs of the Tarabin and Ma'azi tribes and I was received amongst them as Abdullah Bey, an Egyptian official, thus reviving a name well known and much revered amongst them … I was well received and heard many expressions of disgust the Arabs have for [Professor Edward Henry] Palmer's murderers [along with Hicks] … My route, for there was no path or road, was a good deal on rolling sand dunes with no water supply. At one time we held a council of war whether we should go back for water or push on to Ismailia, but as we had

76 Smithers, pp.4-5, 77.
77 Hodges, p.57; Edward Hull, *Mount Seir, Sinai and Western Palestine: Being a Narrative of a Scientific Expedition* (London: Richard Bentley, 1885).
78 William Hicks, British Indian army officer, born 1830, died commanding the Egyptian Army at El Obeid 5 November 1883 during the battle of Shaykan.

brought as much as we could carry from the last supply I insisted on pushing on, and we reached Ismailia without loss but at our last gasp for water. A trip I have no wish to make again.[79]

It had taken Kitchener five weeks to reach Ismailia: he arrived on 6 January 1884 and later that month, on 24 January, Charles Gordon[80] landed. By the time Gordon arrived in Khartoum in March, Kitchener was at Korosko, from where Gordon had started crossing the desert to Khartoum. Kitchener's instructions were amongst others:

1.   [to] proceed as quickly as possible to Berber.
2.   [...] render all possible assistance to Huessin Pasha Khalifa. [...] use every endeavour to open the Berber Suakin road. [...] if possible communicate with Gordon Pasha at Khartoum or elsewhere. [...] spare no expense to effect this object. On opening communications with Gordon Pasha [...] carry out any instruction he will receive from him.[81]

Berber being too dangerous to access, Kitchener volunteered to scout to the south to ascertain the attitude of the local inhabitants; the Egyptian officer initially tasked with the job having demanded a reward of £10,000 to do so.[82] Set up at Korosko, 'living in a mud hut on the banks of the Nile', on 2 August 1884, dressed as a Bedouin leader, Kitchener together with twenty camel riders, arrived at Dongola, a six-day cross desert journey, to ascertain local intentions. He wanted to keep an eye on the leader, Mustafa Yawar, which meant setting up a base at Debbah, with 100 Arabs, which was also six days closer to Khartoum. Whilst Wolseley and Wood were discussing Kitchener's promotion, Kitchener assumed the higher rank of Bimbashi (Brevet Major) as 'an inferior [rank] would not have carried sufficient prestige in the eyes of the natives.' Formal notification of the promotion came through in due course.

Kitchener did his best with what native labour he could commandeer, to make it habitable and put it into defensible shape. The garrison made it difficult for him, committing various atrocities, robbing and maltreating the tribes in the vicinity, but, although he was alone and surrounded by outlaws and fanatics, he managed to maintain an authority over them. Besides, he was getting messengers through to Gordon, and with three friendly sheiks had gone to within three days' march of the beleaguered city.[83]

79   Hodges, pp.58-60.
80   Charles George Gordon, born 28 January 1833, died 26 January 1885 defending Khartoum, known as Chinese Gordon, Gordon Pasha and Gordon of Khartoum. Saw service in Crimea, Siege of Sevastopol, China, Sudan.
81   Hodges, pp.70-1.
82   Sandes, p.94.
83   Hodges, pp.74-5.

Bennet Burleigh of the *Daily Telegraph* recorded that he 'found one Englishman within the mud walls of Debbeh [...] He gave me a hearty welcome and added to my debt of gratitude by producing two bottles of claret, his whole store, which we drank most loyally at dinner. [...] In manner he is good-natured, a listener rather than a talker, but readily pronouncing an opinion if it is called for.'[84] Sandes puts this as the location where Kitchener '... carried his life in his hands [and] was present one day at the execution of a supposed spy who was tortured so horribly that Kitchener thereafter carried a small bottle of poison about with him.'[85] A relative told a separate story which seems to have become conflated with the execution story:

> Two Arab spies had been caught and confined in a tent. They pretended to be deaf, and Kitchener could get nothing from them. Another spy was captured soon afterwards and promptly pushed into the tent. The three started to talk, freely exchanging confidences. The third spy then demanded to be taken to headquarters. He was Kitchener himself. His talent for disguise was so extraordinary, thinking that he was an Arab who had no business prowling around.[86]

In 1885, Kitchener managed to make contact with Gordon besieged in Khartoum. Kitchener urged, '... one good fight close to Khartoum will see the matter through', but Baring was prevented from acting by Prime Minister Gladstone.[87] Eventually, Secretary of State for War Hartington[88] threatened to resign if nothing was done and a relief party was put together under Wolseley. Kitchener was assigned as intelligence officer to Charles Wilson who replaced Herbert Stewart on 18 January 1885 at Abu Kru, when the latter was fatally wounded in the follow up to the battle of Abu Klea the day before.[89] On 12 January, Wilson spent the day with Kitchener at Gadkul where he instructed the latter to return to Korti, which he reluctantly did two days later accompanying Stanley Clarke's convoy.[90] Willoughby Verner, another intelligence officer with Wilson, claimed Kitchener was sent back to 'look after the

84   Sandes, p.94 from Edwin Sharpe Grew, *Field Marshal Lord Kitchener: His Life and Work for the Empire* (Gresham, 1916) vol 1, p.116.
85   Sandes, p.94.
86   Sandes, p.94.
87   TNA: PRO 30/57/4 D22.6, 18 August 1885, William Ewart Gladstone, born 29 December 1809, died 19 May 1898.
88   Spencer Cavendish, Lord Hartington, born 23 July 1833, died 24 March 1908, Eighth Duke of Devonshire.
89   Kitchener served in Anatolia under Charles Wilson. In 1885 Wilson commanded the Nile Flotillas near Khartoum. BL: MAP DMO/ADD/12 Kitchener's Notes on the fall of Khartoum, p.4. Herbert Stewart, born 30 June 1843, died 16 February 1885.
90   Charles Wilson, *From Korti to Khartoum* (Edinburgh: William Blackwood, 1886) pp.13-6.

Emir of Dongola, who was our doubtful ally.'[91] Wilson eventually reached Khartoum on 28 January, having travelled some part of the way on a naval vessel, two days after Gordon was killed. Kitchener returned with Redvers Buller on 11 February and was bitter. He had been refused permission to send an escort to protect Stewart, Gordon's second-in-command, when he left Khartoum with the result that Stewart and his men were trapped by a local sheik and killed. It was 'murder by Red Tape', and Kitchener made his views publicly known through Samuel Baker and his father.[92] This exposure in the press would go some way to instilling his name in the public mind, particularly after Gordon was killed, and was to lay the ground for his later actions to avenge Gordon's death.

Kitchener's experiences at this time would influence his later management of campaigns and would lead to one of his biggest challenges in the 1914-18 war: efficacy of equipment. During the battle of Abu Klea, the column suffered from inadequate equipment: a Gardner gun kept jamming as it had done in the battle of Tamai a year earlier, ammunition stuck in the Henry Martin rifles and bayonets bent during contact and were not sharp.[93] Kitchener was horrified at the loss of life which could have been avoided had the military equipment been up to standard. Another outcome of the battle was his friendship with Pandeli Ralli.[94] On hearing of Stewart's death, Ralli wrote to Kitchener requesting details which began a correspondence.[95]

In March 1885, Kitchener wrote to Bessant, 'I daresay I shall be home before long as everything here is looking dark and gloomy for us in the Egyptian Army and I for one do not care to draw pay if I do not do the work.' He was annoyed and frustrated at not being allowed to go to Gordon's relief.[96] His frustrations grew when the government ordered the withdrawal from Dongola, handing the Sudan back to the Mahdi.[97] His report on the situation was not accepted and on 3 July 1885, he resigned his commission in the Egyptian Army and returned to England. He was introduced to the Queen at Osborne House on 14 July, and over the summer started studying Ottoman law.[98]

Kitchener's time in Egypt had been affected by his run-in with Wolseley in Cyprus.[99] A year before Kitchener's resignation, his father had reported:

91   Willoughby Verner, 'With Kitchener in the Gordon relief expedition', in *The Nineteenth Century* (August 1916) pp.284-5, William Willoughby Cole Verner, born 22 October 1852, died 25 January 1922.
92   Royle, pp.60-63.
93   Churchill, *River War*, p.170; Mike Snook MBE, Wolseley, Wilson and the failure of the Khartoum campaign: An exercise in scapegoating and abrogation of command responsibility (Cranfield University: PhD, 2014) p.319.
94   Pandeli Toumazis Ralli, born 22 May 1845, died 22 August 1928, Liberal politician.
95   Hodges, p.80; TNA: PRO 30/57/5 E25, Kitchener's letter to Ralli dated 12 January 1885.
96   Hodges, p.84.
97   Royle, p.71.
98   Arthur, p.143.
99   Hodges, p.85.

... Wolseley and Herbert having come to loggerheads as to how the Cyprus maps should be brought out and as I know W doesn't forgive or forget, he having refused Herbert the medal although he was under command on board the Flagship at Alexandria, and since in two cases I have seen he has not forgotten their disagreement, I think it is not unlikely when the time comes Herbert may not get all he deserves, and as Wolseley is fond of and fears the Press I cannot but think that if at the right time something suitable came out in the papers it might be of benefit to him.[100]

In October 1885, Kitchener was ordered to join the Royal Engineers in Dublin. Hodges suggests this order might have been Wolseley's doing but the timing may well have been influenced by French journalist Henri Rochefort's attempt to implicate Kitchener in the death of Olivier Pain. Pain was a journalist with links to the Mahdi and believed to spy for him. It is said a bounty of £50 had been put on his head by Kitchener who watched him be '... shot at Abondou, on April the 18th.'[101] Pain had in fact been buried in the desert after fainting, his colleagues thinking he was dead.[102] However, before Kitchener left for Dublin, Salisbury sent notice that the War Office had loaned him to represent Britain on the Zanzibar Commission. As Kitchener and Salisbury had not met at this stage, 1888 appears to be their first encounter, it is probable that Kitchener was appointed because of his fluency in Arabic and diplomatic and survey skills of which Salisbury was aware, and to remove him from proximity to the press which had been running accounts of the Pain saga from mid-August to mid-September 1885.[103]

On 18 October 1885, Kitchener wrote to Biddulph in Cyprus:

I have today received the Egyptian Medal for the Nile Expedition, and it therefore cannot be considered medal-hunting for me to ask your good offices with Lord Wolseley to obtain for me the Alexandria clasp, without which I shall not wear the medal unless ordered to do so. [...] I would have waited to see you in

100 Hodges, pp.86-7; Lady Fanny Blunt records the appointment of Kitchener by Wolseley to investigate some situation. Her cousin Sir Edward Zorhab, 'Under Secretary of War for Wolseley' had suggested Kitchener. By all accounts her version is an amalgamation of various incidents in Kitchener's life in Egypt. Its value lies in reinforcing the dislike between Kitchener and Wolseley. Lady Fanny Blunt, *My Reminiscences* (London: John Murray, 1918) pp.223-5.

101 Cablegram from our correspondent, 'Death of M Oliver Pain', in *The Morning News*, Belfast, 17 August 1885, p.7; Lord Newton, *Lord Lyons: A record in British diplomacy*, vol 2 (London: Edward Arnold, 1913) pp.358-9, Victor Henri Rochefort, Marquis de Rochefort-Luçay, born 30 January 1831, died 30 June 1913, Olivier Pain, born April 1845, died 15 November 1884.

102 Edward Vizetelly (Bertie Clere) *Cyprus to Zanzibar by the Egyptian Delta* (London: C Arthur, Pearson, 1901) pp.271-3.

103 Hodges, p.87; *Evening Standard*, August-September 1885.

London on the subject, were it not that I am leaving at once for Zanzibar, where I have been appointed by Lord Salisbury to delimitate the Sultan's territories – one advantage of my writing you is that you will be able to see Sir E Bovill should you care to do so. I do not expect an answer, and as you will be at the War Office so soon I only hope that you may see fit to mention the matter then.[104]

Kitchener had again pleaded his innocence over leaving Cyprus to participate in the bombardment of Alexandria. Biddulph in his reply explained how '… medals are refused always to officers on leave' and that being on leave, '… officers are not allowed […] to go to the seat of war.' On the matter of Kitchener not wearing the '… medal which you earned in '84 unless you can get a clasp for a previous campaign[,] It is not so much of a compliment to the soldiers who went through the Nile Campaign, to reckon it as inferior to one day's bombardment for the forts at Alexandria.'[105] According to Peter's Finger,

> Kitchener's resentment over the whole affair lasted for many years and showed itself as late as 1898-99, in incidents which occurred during that period, known to the writer, but which need not be recounted. There is no doubt that in Kitchener's youthful character were to be found those traits, peculiarly Irish, of suspicion, nursing a grievance real or imaginary, and considering oneself to be treated unfairly.[106]

The reference to Kitchener having 'peculiarly Irish' traits is intriguing especially in light of Kitchener's later involvement in Irish recruitment and the Irish Rebellion of 1916.

Diplomat in training: Zanzibar, November 1885

The Zanzibar Commission's task was to determine where the Sultan's territory ended and how the mainland (today's Kenya and Tanzania) should be divided between Britain and Germany. Of five commissioners,[107] Kitchener was the only soldier. When he said, 'a strip of the mainland some forty miles deep was part of the Sultanate of Zanzibar,' he annoyed the Germans who felt he was favouring the French. Officially Kitchener was rebuked for appearing to support the French, however, Secretary of

---

104 Peter's Finger, p.233.
105 Peter's Finger, p.234.
106 Peter's Finger, p.234.
107 Assa Okoth, *A History of Africa: African Societies and the Establishment of Colonial Rule 1800-1915* (Nairobi: East Africa Pub, 2006) pp.143, 146-51.

State for Foreign Affairs Rosebery,[108] offered his private support as Kitchener told his sister:

> I must say Ld Rosebery has done me very well. He sticks up to the Germans like fun. I admire him. I gave him a hint of a dirty trick the Germans were playing [insider trading] & he positively almost frightened me by the persistence which he rubbed it in at Berlin.[109]

As with all such investigations, the final decision was made over the heads of the delegation by the politicians in Europe. The Sultan got Zanzibar, Pemba and Mafia as well as a 600 mile stretch of coast land ten miles wide. Britain got Kenya or British East Africa whilst Germany received Tanganyika or German East Africa, including Mount Kilimanjaro. France was given the Cemaro Islands near Madagascar to pacify its desires on the East African coast.[110]

Within ten years, Britain had acquired Zanzibar as a protectorate. With support from Salisbury and John Kirk, British Consul at Zanzibar, pressure was put on the Admiralty to develop the port of Mombasa,[111] which Kitchener had seen as both strategically and economically important.[112] Developing Mombasa as a naval base would counteract the Germans at Dar es Salaam and the French at Madagascar. Kitchener further recommended a railway line parallel to the Suez Canal, occupation of Socotra, a lighthouse on Cape Gardafui and 'guns on Perim' to 'cork the southern end of the Red Sea.'[113] The outcome of Kitchener's reports and advice from Zanzibar was the transfer of Heligoland and the Anglo-German treaty of 1 July 1890.[114]

Whilst in East Africa, Kitchener spent his free time in the Arab quarter of Mombasa getting to know the locals, his Arabic enabling him to make friends; men he met again in 1911.[115] Having experienced the territory, he advised Salisbury in 1888 to get rid of William Mackinnon from the Imperial British East Africa Company if British East Africa was to develop.[116] In July, on route to England, he learned he was destined for the Eastern Sudan and Red Sea Littoral.

---

108 Archibald Philip Primrose, Fifth Earl of Rosebery, born 7 May 1847, died 21 May 1929.
109 Royle, p.77; Arthur, p.149.
110 Royle, p.77.
111 Hodges, pp.91-2. See Arne Peters, *Carl Peters and German Imperialism 1856-1918: A Political Biography* (Wotton-under-Edge: Clarendon, 2004) pp.106-12 for a different interpretation.
112 Warner, p.62; HH Kitchener, 'Notes on British Lines of Communications with the Indian Ocean' (1886).
113 Smithers, p.8; Royle, p.77.
114 Okoth, p.130.
115 Okoth, p.133; Hodges, p.191.
116 Okoth, p.133, William Mackinnon, 1st Baronet, born 13 March 1823, died 22 June 1893.

Lessons in civil administration and battle: Red Sea Littoral and Suakin, 1888-1889

Kitchener returned to north Africa as Governor-General of the Red Sea Littoral and Commandant of Suakin (Eastern Sudan) where his task was to regulate trade through the Red Sea. It was his first independent posting and, not surprisingly, he made mistakes.

The appointment had been rather sudden. Charles Watson the incumbent Governor-General received no warning of the change in governor and felt it only right to resign on hearing of Kitchener's appointment. Kitchener appeared just as surprised, thinking Watson had already resigned. He offered to withdraw his acceptance until he was told that if he did not accept the offer it would be given to someone else, not Watson.[117] Although ambitious, Kitchener's sense of honour would not see him usurp another. In August 1886 he assumed his post.

Five months before arriving in Suakin, the dervishes had been defeated by Gerald Graham,[118] the British troops withdrawn, and the town left under the control of the native garrison. Osman Digna, leader of the local dervishes, had been defeated but not broken and in 1887 started to advance on Suakin once again. In response, and to restrict the influx of weapons to the dervishes, Kitchener curtailed trade through the ports. In addition, he organised excursions to gather intelligence, an action Winston Churchill claims led to the surrounding tribes being 'harried and raided.'[119] Eventually Suakin was besieged by Osman Digna who threatened to cut the water supply.

Refused British support to ease the situation, Grenfell allowed Kitchener to use the resources he had to hand. This led to a series of building projects as Kitchener worked to balance the budget and prepare to bring the dervishes to heal; the success of which was recognised by James Charlemagne Dormer,[120] chief of staff, who wrote to the War Office in Cairo: 'With regard to the military works and defences of the town [Suakin], I was much struck with the great improvement that has been effected by Colonel Kitchener since my last visit to Suakin in the autumn of 1884.'[121]

In addition, Kitchener sanctioned a force of irregulars, police, and friendly tribesmen, supplemented with some of his Somali-trained cavalry in disguise, and on 17 January 1888 attacked Osman Digna at Handub.[122] Kitchener, though, misjudged

117 Sandes, pp.82-3.
118 Gerald Graham, VC, GCB, GCMG, born 27 June 1831, died 17 December 1899.
119 Churchill, *River War*, p.190.
120 James Charlemagne Dormer, born 26 January 1834, died 3 May 1893.
121 Churchill, *River War*, p.191.
122 Osman Digna (1841-1926) was of the Diqnab tribe, Anatolian in origin. Studied Islamic Law, theology and astronomy, opposed Turkish occupation. Mahdi appointed him *amir* over Eastern Sudan. Died aged 85 having spent many years a prisoner in Wadi Halfa. Ismat Hasan Zulfo (trns Adam Clark) *Karari: The Sudanese Account of the Battle of Omdurman* (London: Frederick Warne, 1980) pp.81-4.

his foe nearly costing his men their lives. Arriving to support the local force and finding them defeated, Kitchener organised an action to cover their retreat.[123] Despite this rash action, the operation gave a boost to the Egyptian Army showing how much it had developed. The final result was 200 of Osman Digna's men dead compared to only nineteen of Kitchener's. A further twenty-eight were wounded including Kitchener himself who had been shot in the face. 'Dr Galbraith,[124] who happened to be near, tried in vain to persuade Kitchener to dismount. Reeling in his saddle from loss of blood, Kitchener merely stopped to bandage up his wound with a policeman's cummerbund and continued to direct the operations.'[125] He eventually handed over to Thomas Edgecumbe Hickman[126] who withdrew the remaining force to Suakin.

Sent to Cairo, Kitchener managed to swallow the bullet which had lodged in his throat, saving himself from suffocation.[127] Warner suggests Kitchener's rash action was spurred by the death of his fiancée Hermione, Valentine Baker's daughter, aged 18 from typhoid on 21 January 1885.[128] More likely Kitchener's misreading of the situation was a combination of factors, including Stewart and Gordon's deaths, the death of Hermione's father Valentine on 17 November 1887 as well as the public censure he had over Pain and Zanzibar. He needed a break.

Kitchener's perseverance and what is known as military *good luck* had seen him through, and as with others before and after, his victory, despite being barely gained, had the effect of wiping out all his errors – at least for the British. In March 1888, Kitchener returned to Suakin and not being completely recovered, resigned his governorship and left for England.[129] On 11 June 1888, aged 38, Kitchener was gazetted a Colonel, and won a great supporter when he was appointed aide-de-camp to Queen Victoria.[130] Not one to waste time, he continued reading up on Turkish Law and how he could legally break money-lender power in Egypt.[131] On 13 September 1888, Charles Holled-Smith,[132] replaced him as Governor-General of the Red Sea Littoral.

Later that same month, Kitchener joined Grenfell in Cairo as Adjutant-General where he was given command of the 1st Brigade Soudanese. In December 1888 under Grenfell's command, Kitchener participated in the battle of Gemmaiza (Mataris)

123 Churchill, *River War*, p.191.
124 Francis Reginald Wingate, *Mahdiism and the Egyptian Sudan: Being an Account of the Rise and Progress of Mahdiism, and of Subsequent Events in the Sudan to the Present Time* (London: Macmillan, 1891) p.353 he is described as Surgeon Major Galbraith, unable to trace more detail.
125 H.C. Jackson, *Osman Digna* (London: Methuen, 1926) pp.134-5.
126 Thomas Edgecumbe Hickman, DSO, born 25 July 1859, died 23 October 1930.
127 Jackson, *Osman Digna*, pp.134-5.
128 Warner, p.63; Jastrzembski, *Baker's Heroic Stand*, p.159.
129 Warner, pp.60, 63-70; Royle, pp.80-4.
130 Rye, p.96.
131 Warner, p.60.
132 Charles Holled-Smith, born 12 September 1846, died 18 March 1925.

against Osman Digna, after whose defeat he remained in Suakin with a garrison of 2,000 Sudanese maintaining 'a purely defensive attitude.'[133]

In June 1889, the Mahdi's successor Wal-el-Nejumi began to advance on the Egyptian forces. On 2 July he attacked Colonel Wodehouse at Purguin near Wadi Halfa and on 17 August after a seven-hour battle at Toski, Wadi-el-Nejumi and half his force had been killed,[134] ending the Khalifa's ambitions in Egypt. During this operation, Kitchener had charge of the cavalry acting as decoy for Grenfell. Reminiscent of his action at Handub, Kitchener's mixed mounted force, one squadron 20th Hussars and his personally trained Egyptian Cavalry, '... by skilful manoeuvring [...], lured the Dervishes to destruction.'[135] This outcome was peace until 1893 and for his actions, Kitchener was made Companion of the Order of the Bath (CB).[136]

The succeeding period of inaction was too much for Kitchener who liked to be kept busy and on the move. Between 1890 and 1891, in command of the Egyptian Police, he took every opportunity to visit and inspect outlying garrisons, earning the nickname, 'he who must be obeyed.'[137] Baring had appointed Kitchener to Inspector-General of the Egyptian Police in 1890, a role Kitchener accepted after being reassured it would not negatively impact his replacing Grenfell as Sirdar when the latter retired.[138] His task was to reform the police, end the torture of prisoners and witnesses and introduce promotion on merit. To do this, he '... converted the ghafirs from unpaid watchmen reporting to the village umda into a part of the national police force.' He introduced a new tax to pay the force and the ghafirs underwent military and weapons training in order to be proactive. Failure to report crimes resulted in being fined or imprisoned.[139]

It was not enough, though, to keep Kitchener from slipping into one of his depression states, as he saw little chance of becoming Sirdar. Valentine Chirol, a friend (and journalist) visiting at the time, convinced him to stay, predicting that within two years he would be Sirdar.

133 Sandes, p.84.
134 Magnus, p.100; Royle, p.87; Joscelyn Heneage Wodehouse, born 17 July 1852, died 16 January 1930.
135 Colin R Ballard, *Kitchener* (London: Newnes, nd) p.59.
136 Magnus, p.100.
137 Ballard, pp.54-8.
138 Ballard, p.60; for more on the Egyptian Police and greater context, see Harold H Tollefson, Jr. 'The 1894 British takeover of the Egyptian Ministry of Interior', in *Middle Eastern Studies*, vol 2, no 4 (1990) pp.547-60.
139 Nathan Brown, 'Brigands and state building: The invention of banditry in modern Egypt', in *Comparative Studies in Society and History*, vol 32, no 2 (Apr 1990) p.278.

3

Hero: Egypt as Sirdar, 1892-1899

Chirol was not too far out with his prediction. When Grenfell resigned as Sirdar, Evelyn Baring (Lord Cromer) appointed Kitchener Sirdar over the more popular and experienced JH Wodehouse. His appointment, effective 13 April 1892, was generally unpopular amongst British officers, but Cromer felt Kitchener's desire to recover the lost Sudanese territory for Britain was strong, as was his desire to avenge Gordon's death.[1] Simply, Kitchener was more ambitious, and goal focused. As Sirdar, his main achievement would be the defeat of the Dervishes in 1898,[2] an act celebrated in a board game based on snakes and ladders called *Gordon-Kitchener*, and included in game packs Queen Alexandra sent out to the troops in South Africa.[3]

In July 1894, Kitchener on leave in England received his KCMB, and contemplated resigning over the 'Abbas Affair' where the young khedive insulted the Egyptian Army, in effect insulting Kitchener, the army's commander. On 21 July, a chiromancer named Cheiro interviewed him at the War Office and obtained an impression of Kitchener's hand. Cheiro confirmed that, 'One of his greatest qualities, at once useful and charming, is his accessibility. Anybody who has anything to say to him can approach him; anybody who has anything to teach him will find a ready and grateful learner.'[4] Within a month, his father had died with Kitchener at his bedside.[5]

Kitchener returned to Egypt to bide his time, although Charles Vere Townsend suggests he visited England in July 1895 as he attended a dinner with Curzon and

1   Rye, pp.105-6.
2   See later for discussion on whether Kitchener was out to avenge Gordon's death or whether this was a front for political and media purposes.
3   Paul Fox, *Severed Heads: The Spoils of War in the Egyptian Sudan* (Making War, Mapping Europe, 2015) p.22; Lady Briggs, *The Staff Work of the Anglo-Boer War, 1899-1901* (London: Grant Richards, 1901) p.416.
4   Cheiro, *Palmistry for All: Containing New Information on the Study of the Hand Never Published Before* (London: Herbert Jenkins, nd) p.v.
5   Pollock, p.88.

the actor Arthur Roberts at the Savoy.[6] Eventually, on 12 March 1896 Kitchener was authorised to launch an expedition into Dongola province and occupy Akasha. Six days later, Archibald Hunter led a small column to create an advance base. The sudden decision by the British government to undertake the Dongola expedition was political; to assist the Italians at Kassala.[7] A year earlier, the focus was on building the Aswan Dam, but politics has a habit of changing military priorities. Salisbury, now Prime Minister and Foreign Secretary, explained: 'we desired to kill two birds with one stone, and to use the same military effort to plant the foot of Egypt rather farther up the Nile. For this reason we preferred it to any movement from Suakin or in the direction of Kassala, because there would be no ulterior profit in these movements.'[8] The Egyptian Army was tasked with the work to give extra credence to Britain's position. However, London was concerned about leaving proceedings to the man on the ground: he was perceived to be too young and therefore impatient and reckless. What London had not taken into account was the pressure notifying the press of a proposed attack on Dongola had put on the Sirdar and his forces in Egypt.

When Kitchener then bought 5,000 camels, there was 'some disquietude' in London: 'the camels will operate on the Sirdar's mind as a powerful temptation to go on to Berber – and possibly to Khartoum.' In fact, Kitchener had only bought 2,000 camels and was not likely to act rashly. Cromer knew that, but London did not.[9] Salisbury's concern was exacerbated when he learned that the Indian contingent to occupy Suakin was asked to ensure its camel regiment was included. Cromer had to do much reassuring with the result that the War Office took no part in the campaign; it was instead a 'Foreign Office War'. Salisbury's concern translated into a request for personal weekly reports which were written by his son, Edward Cecil, Kitchener's ADC.[10] Kitchener had asked Cecil to send his father weekly reports, reprimanding him for his 'cold' style, whereas the 'model [...] he had dictated would have made the most hardened ink-slinger of the *Daily Mail* blush.'[11] By this time, Kitchener was a regular visitor at Hatfield House, suggesting Salisbury's concern was in response to hearsay. Getting regular first-hand updates would also reduce any untoward surprises.

That summer, Kitchener left Khartoum suddenly not telling his officers where he was going. He had gone to London to discuss funding with the Treasury.[12] On 27 November 1896, Salisbury wrote to Cromer that Kitchener's:

6   Erroll Sherson, *Townsend of Chitral and Kut* (London: William Heinemann, 1928) p.119; Charles Vere Townsend, born 21 February 1861, died 18 May 1924.

7   TNA: FO 78/4892.

8   Marquess of Zetland, *Lord Cromer* (London: Hodder & Stoughton, 1932) p.223; Evelyn Wood, born 26 February 1841, died 29 January 1917, 1st Earl of Cromer.

9   *Cromer*, pp.225-6.

10   Magnus, p.121; Viscountess Milner, *My Picture Gallery 1886-1901* (London: John Murray, 1951) p.90.

11   Edward Cecil, *The Leisure of an Egyptian Official* (London: Hodder & Stoughton, 1921) p.191.

12   *Townsend*, p.142.

... campaign against the Chancellor of the Exchequer was not the least brilliant, and certainly the most unexpected of all his triumphs. But all his strategy is of a piece – the position was carried by a forced march and a surprise. In fact, I had to give my approval at the end of a moment's notice, when the train by which Kitchener was to go away was already overdue. I need not say I was very glad to do so; and the Cabinet, to whom the whole matter was stated on Wednesday, entirely approved.

Kitchener had secured a loan of £800,000 which freed Cromer from European complications had he had to use the £500,000 made available by the jointly French and British managed *Caisse*.[13]

The first steps taken, it made sense politically, militarily, and financially to complete the dream: the conquest of Sudan. A speech by the Chancellor to the House of Commons on 5 February 1897, authorised Kitchener to proceed from Wadi Halfa. British assistance would be required for this final attack, but significantly the local Egyptian commander, Kitchener, would retain control. On 8 January 1897, Cromer had advised Salisbury that he would '... hear some military mutterings due to jealousy of Kitchener ...' but he had '... not a shadow of a doubt that the decision to keep Kitchener in command [was] wise.' Similarly, keeping Cromer in overall command was just as important to prevent 'great confusion' if control was taken over by the War Office in London which did not fully understand the situation on the ground.[14] It paid to have a direct link to the Prime Minister.

Kitchener had wasted no time planning his advance from the Red Sea. Exploring his options, he had George Frederick Gorringe[15] build a causeway from Trinkitat across the swamps to the mainland so supplies could be transported to Tokar. According to Sandes, the intention was to construct a railway from Suakin to Kassala passing Trinkitat and Khor Baraka, whilst another was contemplated for a line past Sheikh Barghut to Sinkat and Berber.[16] Gorringe recorded:

Much of the work which I was ordered to carry out between January 1893 and November 1895 though nominally to improve the accommodation for the troops, was really, in Kitchener's mind, preparation for an advance from Suakin. For example, I was ordered to build a new prison. I suggested a site, away from the water's edge. The Sirdar did not approve, and another site was selected where dhows would come alongside. I was told to make large, roomy buildings as he wanted the convicts to be comfortable. This I did. At his next inspection he came to see the finished work, and then remarked, 'I don't like this building for

13   *Cromer*, p.229.
14   *Cromer*, pp.231-3.
15   George Frederick Gorringe, born 10 February 1868, died 25 October 1945.
16   Sandes, p.86.

the convicts. They must build another prison on more healthy ground *outside the walls*. What you have built will make an excellent *Nuzl* (Supply and Ordnance Store).' Needless to say, that is what he intended from the first; but, having no funds, he had the building erected by convict labour for practically nothing![17]

Kitchener's economising was '... never enforced at the expense of health or efficiency. Under Kitchener's rule, the Egyptian conscript soldiers developed such smartness and confidence that they bore no resemblance to the rabble who fled at El Teb.'[18] However, on occasion men did suffer due to military exigencies and miscalculations.

In an action pre-empting that which caused the conflict with Curzon in India and criticism in the 1899-1902 war in southern Africa, Kitchener on appointment as Sirdar,

> ... reorganized the Headquarter Staff. He abolished the appointment of Quarter-Master-General [...] and became his own QMG. The Director of Military Intelligence (Major FR Wingate, RA), Chief Engineer (Capt C Godby, RE), Financial and Military Secretaries, Directors of Stores and Supplies, PMO and the DAAG 'B' (Lieut HG Lyons, RE), worked directly under him. The Adjutant-General was assisted by an AAG and a DAAG 'A'. The DAAG 'B' dealt with all QMG questions except those concerning the Intelligence, Stores, Supplies and Medical departments, most of the routing papers being taken to the AG for signature. Thus the Sirdar was able to give his instructions to the DAAG 'B' on all questions in matters in which he was personally interested, while the AG relieved him of all 'A' matters, such as discipline, recruiting, etc.[19]

Kitchener knew what he wanted in material and manpower, and leaving nothing to chance, he:

> ... interviewed every candidate for the Egyptian Army, and usually did so in a small room facing the top of the grand staircase in the Junior United Service Club in London. Selected officers joined as *Bimbashis* (Majors) on a two years' contract at £E540 per annum, though at first Kitchener allowed them only £E440 per annum (£E1 = approx. £1 0s 6d).[20]

The benefit of his approach was recorded by Henry Rawlinson[21] who further noted that Kitchener's system of not keeping records and his giving verbal instructions,

17   Sandes, p.86.
18   Sandes, p.148.
19   Sandes, fn 1-2, p.149.
20   Sandes, fn 1-2, p.149.
21   Henry Rawlinson, born 20 February 1864, died 28 March 1925, 1st Baron Rawlinson.

... was carrying things too far, and may, some day, lead to some bad misunderstanding in a crisis, but I admit that we in the British service go to the other extreme and, as a rule, write far too many orders. The system works because of K's wonderful memory and because they are all good men in the Egyptian Army. He has got the pick of the service and they understand him, and he them.[22]

Kitchener's team was good. The decision to attack Dongola had been made by a team led by Cromer; the decision being whether to take Dongola, create a feint or not undertake the expedition at all. There was full faith in the Soudanese Army on whom the task would fall; the question rather was whether they could withstand the conditions in which they found themselves.[23] On 22 March 1896, Kitchener left with Wingate and Rudolf Slatin[24] to start an operation which would end two and a half years later. He had £800,000 to complete the campaign. This meant weighing up the cost-benefit ratio of bringing in foreign forces, such as the Indians to garrison Suakin,[25] who were expensive to maintain. Additional pressure was added when the British Government announced in the press that a move was being made on Dongola. The government motivated to assist Italy, unwittingly undermined the preparations in Sudan, the Mahdi having been warned what was to come. Kitchener could not move his forces around and create diversions but rather had to ensure that towns and villages were garrisoned sufficiently to defend themselves. To cope with this and the concern British regiments had about the ability of the Egyptian Army and Fellahin, Kitchener felt it necessary to have a total of four British regiments in support.[26]

The period between 1896 and the battle of Omdurman on 2 September 1898, '... provides the best example of organisation which has ever been seen in the British Army'.[27] Ballard explains:[28] Kitchener's 'power was supreme'. His 'knowledge of the people, their language and their resources' as well as his experience of working with the local troops stood him in good stead. 'His record of service' led others above and below him to have confidence in him. He had the firm support of Baring and the backing of the British public. 'The War Office allowed [him] a free hand,' despite a very limited budget with which to work. The operations did not require a large force, only 25,000 men and the problem he was facing 'dealt only with concrete facts'. In carrying out his expedition, he followed the same planning process that von Moltke

---

22   Frederick Barton Maurice, *Life of General Lord Rawlinson of Trent from His Journals and Letters* (London: Cassell, 1928) p.34.
23   James Rennell Rodd, *Social and Diplomatic Memories, 1902-1919* (London: E Arnold, 1922) pp.89-91.
24   Rudolf Anton Carl von Slatin, born 7 June 1857, German captured by the Mahdi. Managed to escape, worked with British Intelligence until the outbreak of war in 1914 when he joined the Red Cross. Died 4 October 1932.
25   Ballard, p.66.
26   TNA: FO 78/4892, various correspondence March 1986.
27   Ballard, p.57.
28   Ballard, pp.61-3.

had used against Austria and France in 1867 and 1870 respectively. This was not surprising; in 1873 Kitchener had travelled to Hanover to improve his German and to study von Moltke's military reforms.

Living in different countries, together with his learning of languages, lead Kitchener to develop sensitivity to other cultures. His brother recalls visiting him in London on one of his rare occasions (4 June 1878), only to find him sitting 'cross-legged like an Oriental' on the floor as he had learnt in Egypt. The room had been 'fitted up entirely in Eastern fashion.'[29] Kitchener had found the company of Egyptians far more engaging than that of his fellow officers at the time, which led to him being ostracised by his colleagues. He had to tread carefully though when he became friends with Nubar Pasha, the Egyptian Prime Minister, who was mistrusted by the Resident Agent (Baring, Lord Cromer) who could influence Kitchener's future. Pasha taught Kitchener much about 'Eastern diplomacy' which enabled him to resolve a number of conflicts in years to come when he initiated reforms to improve the lot of the peasant farmer,[30] and had clearly helped in his intelligence work. On his visit to New Zealand when welcomed at Ngati Apa Kitchener insisted on having the welcome said in Maori as he could read the English later. This no doubt won him respect amongst the community.[31]

Kitchener's 'Band of Boys'[32]

The elite force of Kitchener's army whilst he was Sirdar comprised six battalions of Sudanese troops under Hector MacDonald,[33] John Maxwell and David Francis 'Taffy' Lewis who were in control of Infantry training whilst Leslie Rundle,[34] his Adjutant-General and who had been with him in 1884, was responsible for sourcing arms from Vickers and instructing the gunners. They were all overseen by Archibald Hunter. Edward Cecil, or Niggs, Salisbury's son, was Kitchener's ADC.[35] Percy Girouard, responsible for the railways in Sudan, was to play an important role in Kitchener's life.

The choice of Sudanese had been Kitchener's, their being deserters from the Khalifa's army. Training was delegated to those who had actual fighting experience and as much as he hated paperwork, Kitchener turned to administration, delegating by word of mouth. He preferred men who had honed their skills in the field rather

29   Magnus, pp.38-9.
30   Royle, p.55.
31   Address of welcome to Lord Kitchener, from the Ngati Apa, Whanganui, Rangitaane, and Muaupoko tribes 1910, Museum of New Zealand online: https://Collections.tepapa.govt. nz/object/1359276 [accessed 16 March 2019].
32   Royle, p.94.
33   Hector Archibald MacDonald, born 4 March 1953, suicide 25 March 1903 in Paris hotel.
34   Henry Macleod Leslie Rundle, born 6 January 1856, died 19 November 1934.
35   Smithers, p.14; Royle, pp.95-96.

than in 'the street or club.'[36] This was similar to Lord Roberts' view,[37] garnered from Sydney Cotton who maintained that '... parade grounds were simply useful for drill and preliminary instruction, and that as soon as the rudiments of a soldier's education had been learned the troops should leave their nursery, and try as far as possible to practise in peace what they would have to do in war.'[38]

Where possible, Kitchener handpicked his staff, knowing the skills and personalities needed for the men they would command and what he wanted them to do. If he trusted someone, they were given complete freedom[39] – men such as Archibald Hunter, William Birdwood and Ian Hamilton give testimony to this, as did William 'Wully' Robertson appointed CIGS during the First World War. Kitchener's loyalty and trust extended to his brothers, both of whom he appointed to significant roles under his command. His younger brother, Walter, was given command of a camel corps during the desert campaign as well as a commission during the 1899-1902 war, whilst his older brother, Henry, was sent to East Africa in 1914 to ascertain the extent to which volunteers could be raised. Despite his reputation for being dictatorial and brooking no argument, the men Kitchener appointed were not scared to contradict him, Percy Girouard being the most prominent example. Despite the view that Kitchener would not employ married men, Reginald Wingate was appointed intelligence officer, Archibald Hunter had recently got engaged, and in 1894 Kitchener gave an 'At home' for Arthur Montague McMurdo on his marriage in Cairo. McMurdo had been his ADC in the 1880s and saved his life near Suakin in 1888.[40] He, too, remained a friend and business partner until his death from appendicitis in April 1914.

One who knew Kitchener well but who never became a close friend was Hunter. The two men had served alongside each other in the battle of Toski following which Sirdar Kitchener put Hunter in command of the Egyptian Infantry and left him to plan the defeat of the Dervishes. The plans were 'fully accepted by Kitchener' who accompanied the river column alongside Hunter. However, in detail they differed, Kitchener pushing men across the desert whereas Hunter would have taken the river route, Hunter wanted to rush Dongola after Firket, but Kitchener preferred to sort out his transport and supply lines. Hunter, understandably angry at the loss of men and the complaints he was receiving, wrote to Kitchener in the strongest terms, yet does not seem to have been disadvantaged by his outburst. Edward Cecil talks of divided ranks in Kitchener's force; those at the front under Hunter did 'not like Kitchener' for his severity and economical ways. From the criticism levelled against Hunter by

36   Arthur, vol 2, p.80.
37   Frederick Sleigh Roberts, 1st Earl Roberts, born 30 September 1832, died 14 November 1914.
38   Earl Roberts, p.53.
39   Arthur, p.76.
40   *Auckland Star*, April 1894; p.2, George H Cassar, *Kitchener as Proconsul of Egypt, 1911-1914* (London: Palgrave Macmillan, 2016) p.199.

Cecil, it appears the two men, Kitchener and Hunter, were similar in outlook and drive, but had different early military experience. They were competitive, Hunter having been passed over as Adjutant General when Rundle was appointed. Comments Hunter passed in anger or frustration on the spur of the moment seem to have been picked up by biographers and commentators for use as the norm, especially concerning Kitchener.[41] And not dissimilar to comments passed by Kitchener.

Kitchener's shyness and reticence meant that those who were able to break through his shell and gain his trust were loyal, as he was in turn, doing what he could to protect and further their careers as well as his own. This group became known as his 'band of boys'. For those who served on the railways in Sudan, 'Ever mindful of the careers his chosen "Band of Boys", Kitchener sent to the front every young Royal Engineer who could be detached temporarily from technical work,' while his ADCs were to be remembered in his will: seventeen officers were present at Omdurman.[42] Numerous others were to see service under Kitchener's command, both in Egypt/Sudan and South Africa, who never quite understood him. Douglas Haig first saw battle at Atbara and Omdurman, as did Winston Churchill. Repington was DAAG to Grenfell at this time and remained in Cairo as liaison when Kitchener marched on Khartoum and Dongola. No doubt class issues played a part, a note in Salisbury's papers noting 'he is a commoner' at the time the Lord Mayor of London was welcoming Kitchener to the City after Omdurman.[43]

Outside the army,[44] he worked with David Beatty, Royal Navy in planning operations against Dongola and Omdurman and in designing a gunboat of the Zafir class.[45] Although Cora Rowell's narrative has to be taken somewhat cautiously, she provides insight into why Kitchener liked Beatty. Beatty was daring but not reckless: When attacking Dongola, Kitchener '... ordered Beatty to run, under fire, the passage of the river, which at this point was very narrow, and to advance as far as Dongola, thirty-six miles upstream.' At some stage Beatty and Hood managed to get their two boats up the Fourth cataract, a process which saw one man lost and two missing. After sorting his men, Beatty turned his attention to his boat. However, there was a limit to working together: A conversation between two officers suggested Kitchener did not want the boats above the Fifth cataract as that would allow Beatty to take Khartoum rather than the army.[46] The two men were of similar mind, and when Kitchener moved on Fashoda, he asked that Beatty accompany the flotilla.

41   Archie Hunter, *Kitchener's Sword-Arm: The Life and Campaigns of General Sir Archibald Hunter* (New York: Sarpedon, 1996) pp.42-56.
42   Sandes, pp.252-3.
43   Hatfield House: Salisbury papers.
44   Rye, p.22 re reading people.
45   Magnus, p.123; Smithers, p.15; Beatty was an Admiral by August 1914.
46   Rowell, *Leaders of the Great War*, pp.135-9, Horace Lambert Alexander Hood, born 2 October 1870, died 31 May 1916.

Moving an army across desert, 1896

Kitchener's success against the dervishes was due to careful planning and his ability to move his men to major bases as quickly as possible, not being reliant on waterholes to cross the desert. For this he had the latest technology available – trains. Kitchener had discovered the value of railways as a means to bypass meandering rivers when he visited Bulgaria to observe the Russo-Turkish war. Questioning the route of the railway, he discovered the rail had been laid at a fixed price per kilometre and not location to location.[47] Having witnessed the deaths of many camels and the exhaustion of men crossing the desert, as well as the time and hassle moving equipment by boat entailed, especially given the cataracts, building a railway seemed the obvious option; and it could be used later to move other goods.

The railway formed part of his plan to defeat the Mahdi. To oversee the railway construction, Kitchener employed Percy Girouard, a French-Canadian. Girouard was on route to Mauritius when he met Kitchener in London. Aged twenty-nine, at the end of March 1896,[48] Girouard arrived in Egypt. Soon he was back in London sourcing material, borrowing locomotives from Cecil Rhodes which were intended for southern Africa.[49] Kitchener, in his haste and being helpful, 'had bought a mixed assortment of rails, some from Syria, some from other light railways, which did not make the work of track-laying any easier.'[50]

Before work could begin, the rail dimensions had to be decided – Cromer wanted narrow gauge to save costs, while Kitchener wanted 3 foot 6 inch or Cape gauge (South African standard gauge) so his line could link with that of Cecil Rhodes' in the Cape.[51] Despite Cromer's charge of saving costs, Kitchener's motivation to use the 3 foot 6 inch was cost effectiveness. A line from Wadi Halfa, of standard gauge, had been approved by Ishmail Pasha in 1873, the decision to use the more expensive 3 foot 6 inch gauge being to link with the line extending north from Cape Town recommended by John Fowler.[52] By 1877 the line was 33.5 miles to Saras. However, the work had come to an end on the instruction of Gordon, eight miles short of Ambigol having cost £450,000. The railway then fell into disrepair.[53] In 1885 under orders from Wolseley, the line was refurbished in an attempt to transport material to relieve Gordon and by the end May 1885 was ten miles short of Firket. By August it had

47   Warner, p.25.
48   Roy MacLaren, *Canadians on the Nile, 1882-1898* (Vancouver: University of British Columbia, 1978) p.144.
49   Smithers, p.16.
50   RBD Blakeney in Sandes, p.179.
51   Magnus, pp.131-2; TNA: WO 32/6380.
52   John Fowler, born 15 July 1817 to 20 November 1898. Involved in developing the Forth Bridge and London Metropolitan Railway. See Thomas Mackay, *The Life of John Fowler* (London: John Murray, 1900).
53   Sandes, p.100.

reached Akasha Station. Work was again stopped on 23 August 1885, the line playing a 'valuable' role during the evacuation in 1885.[54]

In 1896, with Kitchener in command, use of the railway surfaced again. In 1893 Cecil Rhodes passed through Egypt[55] and discussed with Kitchener the route and linking Egypt with South Africa by rail and telegraph. Three years later, in 1896 the two men again met in Egypt following which Kitchener organised a cargo of Soudanese donkeys, immune to horse-sickness, for service in Rhodesia.[56] Telegrams passed between the men regarding progress.[57] Another three years later, in March 1899, having met with Kitchener and Cromer in Egypt, Rhodes met King Leopold regarding the line going through the Congo; the route through German East Africa being Rhodes' preference.[58] The same year, at the same event, Kitchener and Rhodes received honorary degrees from Oxford University, and funds were approved for Kitchener to proceed with the railway from Khartoum to Uganda. However, the outbreak of war in 1899 in southern Africa put paid to this development.[59] Ascertaining how Girouard got to know about the locomotives and with whom he negotiated to have them diverted to Egypt has not been possible to trace. By all accounts, the engines never made it south to South Africa.[60]

Before Girouard arrived in Egypt, Kitchener's forces, in a pre-emptive move, seized Akasha on 16 March and by the end of the month, with Girouard in Egypt, Kitchener joined with them in Halfa. The challenges were great. Akasha would form the starting point for the new line construction and within three months Firket had been taken too. Kitchener showed his determination when the lines were washed away by floods, getting stuck in to help repair them. This was followed by a cholera outbreak in which 19 British and 260 locals died.[61] Despite these setbacks, the line was built in record time, three hours to the mile, and within cost. Having faced accusations of cutting corners concerning medical support and using conscripted labour, James Rennell Rodd who worked with Cromer, thought the victory at Firket sweet, '… as in London

54   Sandes, p.100.
55   Magnus, pp.132, 207; Royle, p.146. According to Margot Asquith, Kitchener had no time for Rhodes, but he did like Dr Leander Starr Jameson whom he described as 'the best man I ever met'.
56   Basil Williams, *Cecil Rhodes* (New York: H Holt, 1921) pp.233, 285.
57   Not located.
58   Williams, *Rhodes*, p.310.
59   Williams, *Rhodes*, pp.312-3.
60   Email communications with Sandy Buchanan; RG Pattison, *The Cape Seventh Class Locomotives* (Kenilworth: Railway History Group of Southern Africa, 1997) pp.48-50. Kitchener makes reference to 'Western' being authorised to purchase locomotives but it is not clear if this is a person or a company, TNA: PRO 30/57/11/11, telegram 16.11.96 to Cromer.
61   Ballard, p.67.

there had been a tendency to depreciate Kitchener and to question his qualifications for conducting the campaign.'[62]

Despite the anxious moments when Kitchener thought his forces would arrive too late or be observed before they arrived, the battle of Firket on 7 June 1896 was, '... well and carefully planned, and its success in execution was complete.'[63] This gave Kitchener another fully stocked base from which to begin the next stage of railway construction. Again, during the move from Kosheh to Sadin Fanti, a distance of thirty-seven miles with no water except that brought in by camels, three hundred men were forced, by storms of rain and sand, to return to Kosheh. Eventually, sixty men out of a battalion of 700 arrived in Sadin Fanti, 1,700 having fallen out along the way. In addition to the manpower losses from the 'Death March',[64] the railway was completely destroyed by floods, but within seven days, Kitchener had the situation back under control and in functioning order. His reputation as a hard taskmaster was upheld, as was Girouard's, but Kitchener also won the support of his men as he was prepared to get his hands dirty and work with them.

For all the technology available, he could not avoid using camels. For this, he brought his younger brother Walter from India because of his experience managing camel transport.[65] Walter thought his brother at this time was 'a real autocrat – he does just as he pleases'.[66] Kitchener, though, recognised his brother's contribution:

The transport was very capably administered by Major F. W. Kitchener, Director of Transport (West Yorkshire Regiment), and the loss in camels has been exceptionally small considering the hard work, severe heat, and difficult nature of the country through which the operations were conducted; this was largely due to the camel saddle invented by Veterinary Captain Griffith and constructed by Captain Gordon, Royal Engineers.[67]

Walter had overseen:

A new solar-hat, a poke-bonnet sort of head-gear, [...] designed and tied on the pates of one thousand transport camels as an experiment to prevent sickness and sunstroke. Although the brutes have the smallest modicum of brains, they are

62   Rodd, *Memories*, p.97, born 9 November 1858, died 26 July 1941; Edward M Spiers, *Sudan: The Reconquest Reappraised* (London: Routledge, 1998) p.40.
63   Churchill, *River War*, p.215; Rye, p.112.
64   Churchill, *River War*, p.222; It is reminiscent of Jaap van Deventer's march from Kahe to Iringa in 1916. Jacob 'Jaap' van Deventer, born 18 July 1874, died 17 August 1922, South African.
65   An officer, *The Sudan Campaign 1896-1899* (London: Chapman & Hall, 1899) p.22.
66   Magnus, Letter to his wife, 9 April 1896, p.95.
67   HH Kitchener, Despatch, Dongola, 30 September 1898, online: http://www.northeastmedals.co.uk/britishguide/sudan/despatches1_dongola_hafir.htm [accessed 31 December 2018]; Gordon was Director of Stores.

very liable to attacks of illness from heat-exhaustion. That they are born in the tropics confers no immunity. Strange to say, on the march south from Assouan, of a thousand and odd only one animal succumbed to sunstroke, and that was a camel that had no sun-bonnet. If anything could have added to the naturally lugubrious expression of those lumbering freight carriers, it was the jaunty poke-bonnets with the attenuated "Oh, let us be joyful" visages grinning beneath.[68]

And in his despatch of 3 November 1896, Kitchener paid credit to his 'band', men he had pushed to complete the line not knowing when the dervishes would attack:

> The railway and telegraph services were very efficiently performed under the respective direction of Lt. Girouard, Director of Railways (Royal Engineers), and Lt. [MGE] Manifold, Staff Officer of Telegraphs (Royal Engineers). The construction of 110 miles of railway, and 250 miles of telegraph during the very trying summer, and in difficult country, involved much labour and constant supervision on the part of these officers and their assistants [...]
>
>   The rapid completion of this line, which has greatly facilitated communications, reflects much credit on Lt. Col. J.G. Maxwell, D.S.O. (Commanding Nubia District), Lt. E.P.C. Girouard, D.S.O. (Royal Engineers), and his staff and on all the officers and men employed on this undertaking, which has been successfully completed in almost record time, under great vicissitudes, and during exceptionally hot weather.[69]

The pressure was beginning to tell on Kitchener. On 6 October 1897 he wrote to Elwin Palmer, Under Secretary of Finance, when pushed to make greater savings:

> The strain on all of us and on the troops is very great. You have no idea what continual anxiety, worry and strain I have through it all. I do not think I can stand much more and I feel sometimes so completely done up that I can hardly go on and wish I were dead [...] Before next year's work in the field begins I must get some leave or I shall break down, for I have had none now for three years.[70]

Pressure continued to mount and on 18 October, Kitchener tendered his resignation: 'I do not know that the gravity of the situation is fully realised.'[71] Cromer had Kitchener to Cairo where with Grenfell's support matters were resolved and Kitchener's health restored. Sandes suggests Kitchener's resignation had been partly to test confidence in himself and to ease financial pressure to give him more freedom. Charles à Court

68   Bennet Burleigh, *Khartoum campaign, 1898: Or the Reconquest of the Soudan* (London: Chapman & Hall, 1899) pp.38-9.
69   HH Kitchener, Despatch 1898.
70   Magnus, p.111.
71   TNA: PRO 30/57/11/13, telegram Kitchener to Cromer, 18.10.1897 from Berber.

Repington, DAAG, reported on 12 November 1897 that Kitchener's '... friends, or some of them, do not think he looks well, and is showing the effects of the hard work and worry of the past campaign. I cannot say yet whether he will go home: I hope he may, as people in England do not appear to grasp the situation on the Nile.'[72] Gorringe who was with Kitchener at the time coding his messages wrote: 'I well remember the state of mind he was in [...] That evening I induced him to come out duck shooting with me, a thing he rarely did, and it took his mind off his worries.'[73] Grenfell had come out with the British troops sent to assist. Rather than outrank Kitchener in the field, Cromer insisting that the person who had planned the campaign should oversee it, Grenfell was appointed to command the army of occupation.[74] This was a significant moment for both Kitchener and the War Office; it was almost unheard of the latter relinquishing control of a force in which British troops were present.

Battles with the Mahdi, 1896-1898

Berber fell in February 1898 and in April it was Atbara; a battle described by the correspondent for the *British Medical Journal* as '... far and away the biggest battle since the Crimea if the number and severity of casualties is taken as a test.'[75] Kitchener had been undecided when to launch his attack on Atbara having received conflicting advice from his two commanders, Hunter and William Gatacre.[76] Uncharacteristically, Kitchener consulted Cromer by telegram, possibly to cover himself given the presence of the British, but before long he was back in control announcing he would attack at a time he felt was right.[77] On Good Friday, 8 April 1898, after Hunter had sent favourable information to Kitchener, the troops led by Gatacre launched their attack on Ras-el-Hudi. Kitchener gave orders personally with the result that few are recorded. However, 'Rawlinson, with his usual method, kept a record of the orders, both verbal and written, sent to the British brigade, and the final order for the night march to the *dem* or camp concludes with a noteworthy paragraph: "The Sirdar is absolutely confident that every officer and man will do his duty, he only wishes to impress upon them two words: 'Remember Gordon.' The enemy before them are Gordon's murderers".'[78] Kitchener himself 'was quite human for a quarter of an hour'[79] – whether for Gordon,

72   TNA: PRO 30/40/2, Extract from Major à Court's No 8 dated 12.11.97, f.566; Rodd, *Memories*, p.194.
73   Sandes, p.204.
74   Rodd, *Memories*, p.195.
75   Anonymous, 'The seamy side of war: A reply', in *Galliard's Medical Journal* (January 1899) vol 70, no 1, p.97.
76   William Forbes Gatacre, born 3 Dec 1843, died 18 January 1906.
77   Sandes, p.213.
78   Maurice, *Life of Rawlinson*, p.33.
79   Rye, p.126.

the achievement of his Egyptian Army or the huge and unnecessary loss of life, we will never know.

The Dervishes lost 3,000 killed and 2,000 prisoners. Mahmud was captured and paraded by Kitchener, but the main army got away. The Egyptian-British casualties were light in comparison, 500. Some authors claim field dressings were used for the first time at Atbara, however, these had been introduced into every British soldiers' kit in 1884, following an order in 1855, and were misleadingly called 'first field dressings' being designed for first application on the battlefield.[80] No doubt there had been flaws in the medical support: The battle was '... fought in a hurry; that is, rapid movements forced on us by the tactics of the enemy.' This '... perhaps did not allow of every possible independent medical arrangement being made for the British forces at this early stage in the campaign' and further '... medical organization [...] took some time to develop, as it was absolutely new to the other departments of the army with which the Principal Medical Officer of a British Army in the field is intimately tied up.' However, by the time the battle for Khartoum took place, all the deficiencies had been sorted, '... and no army ever took the field better equipped in every respect to fight the battle of Khartoum.'[81] Four thousand trained bearers had carried the wounded over forty miles from the Atbara battle front to hospital bases. Two years before, 1896, the Egyptian Army had been given its own medical team for the attack on Dongola and by all accounts during the attack on Atbara, the English and Egyptian medical teams had worked well together. Despite accusations to the contrary, the Dervishes received medical treatment, when an Egyptian doctor, Hassan Effendi Zeki, was assigned the specific task of setting up a hospital for them.[82]

In addition to the military medical support, the Red Cross Society, under the auspices of Lady Wantage who had met Kitchener earlier in the year when she and her husband visited Egypt, offered its support for the troops. Cromer and Kitchener initially declined as it would place too much pressure on the already stretched transport lines. However, when the offer was renewed, the help was 'gladly [...] accepted,' and the *May Flower* was turned into a hospital ship to transport wounded by river rather than rail between Assouan and Cairo.[83] Some, including Ballard, complained about the treatment the British received. So did Kitchener. Rawlinson recalled:

80   Thomas Longmore, *Gunshot Injuries: Their History, Characteristic Features, Complications and General Treatment* (London: Longmans, 1877) pp.507-8; Anonymous, 'The First Field Dressing', in *Journal of the Royal Army Medical Corps* (2001) vol 147, issue 3, p.371. Smithers, pp.18-9; Royle, pp.120-2.

81   The seamy side of war, pp.98-9; Spiers, *Sudan Reconquest*, pp.61-2.

82   www.kitchenerscholars.org/pages/khartoum.htm [accessed 25 Feb 2013].

83   Lady Wantage, *Memoir of Lord Wantage VC, KCB* (London: Smith, Elder & Co, 1907) pp.265-6; Burleigh, pp.268-9, Harriet Sarah Jones-Loyd, Lady Wantage, born 30 June 1837, died 9 August 1920, Robert James Loyd-Lindsay, 1st Baron Wantage, born 17 April 1832, died 10 June 1901.

K is a rum 'un, and a ripper. He is as hard as nails and as cool as a cucumber. He had a pretty anxious time from the beginning of the night march until the end of the battle, but the only thing I saw him disturbed about was the treatment of the British wounded, who, from lack of proper arrangements, suffered unnecessarily from the heat and the thirst. The medical arrangements in the British brigade were not nearly as good as those of the Egyptian Army, and K was furious.[84]

Even before the battle, Kitchener had been concerned for the British brigade who went out unprepared. Mamfold notes that on 24 March, Kitchener '... sent for Gatacre and told him to arrange for ten camels to go to Atbara and Kannur to fetch stores. Gatacre replied that he considered his troops "had everything they wanted," but Saat-el thought otherwise.'[85]

The medical correspondent explained:

When a big battle like this is going on, [Khartoum and Omdurman], spread over ten miles of country, individual responsibility and energy come a great deal into play. Any mistakes of detail should be visited on the people on the spot, and there should be no waiting for detailed orders. Red tape is responsible for much of the latter want of initiative. Throughout the whole of the Soudan campaign the Sirdar gave much direct responsibility with corresponding power, was indulgent and encouraging to slight mistakes, but visited gross mistakes with a heavy hand. This was the secret of his success, which should not be lost sight of.[86]

Changes were rapid. In May 1898 the various British military medical units were brought together in the Royal Army Medical Corps to standardise terms and conditions of service. In this capacity they served under Kitchener in the final stages of the Egyptian campaign,[87] at the end of which, Kitchener paid due recognition to the 'energy, untiring zeal, and devotion to their duty by the entire medical staff.' There were 'CBs for the two senior officers, four DSOs and six brevets [... and the] DCM [was awarded to] six NCOs and men of the RAMC.'[88]

Kitchener tried to prevent the unnecessary and innocent loss of life. He wrote to the Khalifa's son after his father's death:

84   Maurice, *Life of Rawlinson*, p.34.
85   Sandes, p.210; Sa'at el Sirdar means 'His Excellency, the Sirdar'.
86   The seamy side of war, p.100.
87   GA Kempthorne, 'Medical Staff Corps and Army Hospital Corps, 1854-1898', in *Royal Army Medical Journal* (December 1928) vol 51, issue 6, p.446.
88   Kempthorne, Medical Staff Corps, p.448.

30th August 1898, Viz., 11 Rabi Akhar, 1316 (M.E.)

From the Sirdar of the Troops, Soudan,
To Abdulla, son of Mohamed El-Taaishi, Head of the Soudan.

Bear in your mind that your evil deeds throughout the Soudan, particularly your murdering a great number of the Mohammedans without cause or excuse, besides oppression and tyranny, necessitated the advance of my troops for the destruction of your throne, in order to save the country from your devilish doings and iniquity. Inasmuch as there are many in your keeping for whose blood you are held responsible—innocent, old, and infirm, women and children and others— abhorring you and your government, who are guilty of nothing; and because we have no desire that they should suffer the least harm, we ask you to have them removed from the Dem (literally, enclosure) to a place where the shells of guns and bullets of rifles shall not reach them. If you do not do so, the shells and bullets cannot recognise them and will consequently kill them, and afterwards you will be responsible before God for their blood.

Stand firm you and your helpers only in the field of battle to meet the punishment prepared for you by the praised God. But if you and your Emirs incline to surrender to prevent blood being shed, we shall receive your envoy with due welcome, and be sure that we shall treat you with justice and peace.

(Sealed) Kitchener, Sirdar of the Troops in the Soudan.[89]

'The Khalifa's only reply had been to tear the letter up and to announce to his followers that the unbeliever would soon be delivered into his hands.'[90]

At two p.m. on 1 September, Kitchener led his forces into the city of Omdurman, having lost three British officers killed and seventeen wounded, 45 other ranks killed and 450 wounded compared to 10,000 Dervishes killed and 5,000 prisoners.[91] It had taken years of patience and planning to recapture Khartoum.[92] Many praised Kitchener's execution of the campaign, but Haig was critical of Kitchener's chaotic management.[93] Kitchener had ignored the chain of command and issued instructions directly to commanders.[94] His habit of issuing verbal instructions had developed from his time with the Egyptian Army, many, apart from officers and medical staff, being illiterate recruits from amongst the fellahin. To work in the medical services, the

89   Burleigh, pp.235-6.
90   Jackson, *Osman Digna*, p.157.
91   Ballard, p.82.
92   BL: MAP DMO/ADD/12, Major HH Kitchener, Intelligence Branch, Quarter Master General's Department Notes on the fall of Khartoum, 18 August 1885. Signed as accurate by Colonel AS Cameron.
93   Smithers, p.20.
94   Magnus, p.160; Maurice, *Life of Rawlinson*, p.33.

ability to read and write was necessary, while height and other physical enlistment requirements were foregone.[95]

Hutchinson, Frank Rhodes' biographer, summed up Kitchener's achievement:

> Fourteen years had now passed since Major Kitchener had applied for a post with the Egyptian Army: he had been with it ever since, and was at last able to test the results of those intervening years. He had been with Colonel [Frank] Rhodes at Abu Klea [17 Jan 1885], and profited from the lessons of the Baduya desert. He had seen the slow whale-boats, the thirsty troops, and the starving camels, the complete breakdown of transport, and the desperate fights against overwhelming odds – all "magnificent, but not war" [AS: a comment he was to repeat in later years in connection with trench warfare]. Now everything was changed. Civilization was due to use its own weapons in the contest with barbarism. Every detail was carefully thought out beforehand, and entrusted to tried subordinates, so that the expedition moved like some gigantic machine, unfaltering and irresistible.[96]

Following the success at Khartoum,

> A detachment from every regiment which had been engaged and nearly every officer in the force assembled at the site of the old Palace, and in the deserted garden a memorial service was held at which [Kitchener] made it a special point that the Anglican, the Roman Catholic, the Presbyterian, and the Methodist chaplains should all take part. The British and Egyptian flags were hoisted on the spot where Gordon fell, and a thunder of saluting guns proclaimed that the humiliation of fourteen years earlier was avenged.[97]

Tears were noted by his staff, Rawlinson recorded 'The Sirdar, who is, as a rule, absolutely unmoved, had great round tears on his cheeks.'[98] Rodd ascribed the 'strangely impressive ceremony' to 'a certain inarticulate sense of imagination in Kitchener.'[99]

At Berber, after the success at Atbara, Kitchener had paraded Mahmoud with his hands bound behind his back in front of the horses, a sign above his head read, 'This is Mahmoud, who said he would take Berber.' This did not go down well with the British and neither did subsequent events in Khartoum such as the destruction of the Mahdi's tomb and the suggestion that his skull had been taken for use as an inkstand or to be given to a museum.[100] Both the parading of Mahmoud and the destruc-

---

95 Kempthorne, *Medical Staff Corps*.
96 George Thomas Hutchinson, *Frank Rhodes: A memoir* (Private circulation, 1908) pp.117-8.
97 Rodd, *Memories*, pp.209-10.
98 Maurice, *Life of Rawlinson*, p.42.
99 Rodd, *Memories*, pp.209-10.
100 Magnus, p.164.

tion of the Mahdi's tomb in Khartoum had been done in accordance with local Arab and religious consultation. It was what the ignorant masses understood, ensuring the message was received loud and clear. To Cromer and Salisbury, Kitchener explained that he:

> … thought it politically advisable, considering the state of the country, that the Madhi's tomb, which was the centre of pilgrimage and fanatical feeling, should be destroyed; the tomb was also in a dangerous condition owing to the damage done to it by shell-fire, and might have caused loss of life if left as it was.[101]

The tomb was destroyed in his absence, after Kitchener had taken the advice of Mohammedan officers, '… that it would be better to have the body removed, as otherwise many of the ignorant people of Kordofan would consider that the sanctity with which they surrounded the Madhi prevented us from doing so.' He concluded that '… no Mohammedans in this country feel anything but satisfaction at the destruction of his power, together with all traces of his religion.' Cromer confirmed that '… the skull of the Mahdi was buried at Wady Halfa.'[102]

Kitchener was held accountable by the British press for the perceived inhumane slaughter at Atbara and Omdurman. There were, as usual, at least two sides to the argument: was it cold blooded murder to kill an injured Dervish, or was it acceptable to protect oneself against fanaticism knowing that if the wounded Dervish had the chance he would kill an unsuspecting soldier or medic there to help him? Kitchener denied issuing any order resulting in senseless killing. The losses were 48 dead and 434 wounded against 10-12,000 Dervishes.[103] He had also refused to attack fleeing troops as he knew they would fight to the bitter end if cornered; a far worse situation for those attacking the Dervishes.[104] After Omdurman, on 7 October 1898, he wrote to the Countess of Jersey:

> I see the [*Contemporary Review*, Ernest Bennett][105] says we kill all the wounded, but when I left Omdurman there were between six and seven thousand wounded dervishes in hospital there. The work was so hard on the Doctors that I had to call on the released Egyptian doctors from prison to help; two of them were well educated, had diplomas, and were and are very useful. We ran out of bandages and had to use our first field dressing which every man carries with him.[106]

101 Rye, p.156.
102 Rye, p.156.
103 Royle, pp.133-4.
104 Magnus, p.123.
105 Kitchener did not name the paper or Bennett, but Charles Royle does in *The Egyptian Campaigns 1882 to 1885* (London: Hurst & Blackett, 1899) fn176.
106 Margaret Elizabeth Leigh Child-Villiers, The Dowager Countess of Jersey, *Fifty-One Years of Victorian Life* (London: John Murray, 1922) pp.364-5.

A Captain of the Royal Prussian General Staff, Adolf von Tiedemann, explained:

If the Sirdar had been so bloodthirsty as the writer of the article [Bennett] in question wishes us to believe, he would have found opportunities enough at every step during his entry into Omdurman to gratify his desires, for, after the Khalifa had fled from the town, crowds of unarmed Dervishes rushed towards him, and it would have been easy enough for his escort to have cut them down. Lord Kitchener received them with kindness, and, as every one on his staff can testify, he did all in his power to put a stop to the street fighting which broke out here and there in the town. Putting aside all regard for his personal safety, he, as I saw several times, rode into narrow streets and courtyards, with uplifted hand, calling out to the inhabitants gathered there, 'Amân!' ('Peace!').

As regards the killing of the wounded on the battlefield, that was a necessary measure which was as regrettable as it was indispensable. After the first attack of the Dervishes had been repulsed, and when the Anglo-Egyptian Army was moving off by brigades to its left towards Omdurman, I myself left the staff and rode over a great part of the battlefield, but I registered a mental vow never to do so again. A wounded and apparently defenceless Dervish lying on the ground is much more dangerous than his fellow with a whole skin and arms in his hand rushing against one. One knows perfectly what to expect from the latter, while the apparent helplessness of the former makes one forget the necessary caution and also the fact that a bullet fired by a wounded man makes quite as big a hole as one fired by an unhurt person.[107]

On 19 September the battle of Hafir was fought and won with minimal loss and on 20 September, Kitchener entered the city.[108] Three days later, on 23 September, Dongola was under British control. Stanley Colville,[109] in charge of the Nile flotilla, had been replaced after an injury at Hafa by David Beatty[110] who had managed to 'impress' Kitchener, the latter arranging for Beatty being awarded the Distinguished Service Order (DSO).[111] Kitchener was made Knight Commander of the Order of the Bath (KCB) and promoted to Major-General.[112]

Rodd, based in Cairo, noted that because 'full reliance had been placed on those on the spot' rather than the war being coordinated from London, 'Kitchener's driving

107 Translated in Royle, *Egyptian Campaigns*, pp.579-80. Adolf von Tiedemann, born 24 January 1865, died 7 April 1915.
108 HH Kitchener, Despatch, Dongola 30 September 1898.
109 Stanley Cecil James Colville, GCB, GCMG, GCVO, born 21 February 1861, died 9 April 1939.
110 David Richard Beatty, GCB, OM, GCVO, DSO, PC, born 17 January 1871, died 12 March 1936, 1st Earl Beatty.
111 Rodd, *Memories*, p.105.
112 Magnus, p.128.

power and military administrative capacity [...] ensured the reconquest of the Soudan.'[113] Salisbury's gamble, breaking tradition and using a comparatively junior officer in charge of a foreign force to command British troops, had paid off and he remained Prime Minister.[114]

Mediating cultures

That the Prime Minister was prepared to risk his position over Kitchener's retaining overall command once British and Indian forces had been sent to support the Egyptian Army was quite an achievement especially for someone as unknown as the Sirdar and with his lack of 'establishment' ties. By 1898, aged 48, he had only spent seven years in England, a total of thirteen visits. Advice from Pandeli Ralli in 1885 that he make the most of the social scene if he wanted to progress his career was taken to heart and tackled with military precision. In return, association with Kitchener would help others. Ralli opened his home at 17 Belgrave Square to his friend. Within years, Kitchener had a number of aristocratic friends and supporters, many of whom had links with Egypt. One of his closest friends, William Henry Grenfell, Lord Desborough,[115] had been introduced by his brother who served with the 10th Hussars in Egypt,[116] and as with Ralli, lasted the remainder of his life. Desborough's wife, Ettie, became along with Prime Minister Salisbury's daughter-in-law, Alice Cecil,[117] one of Kitchener's closest confidents.

As Francis Grenfell's adjutant, September 1882 to April 1892, Kitchener met many people passing through Cairo, some of whom became loyal friends. Having had Kitchener stay with her at Osterley after meeting him in Cairo, on another trip Margaret Elizabeth Leigh Child-Villiers, the Countess of Jersey, described Kitchener as: '... very amusing, and when there was a difficulty about our cabins on the Nile boat he went off with us to Cook's Office and said that we *must* have two cabins instead of

---

113 Rodd, *Memories*, pp.212-3.
114 See beginning of chapter for political context.
115 No relation to Francis Grenfell whom Kitchener served under in Egypt. William Henry Grenfell, born 30 October 1855, died 9 January 1945, 1887 married Ethel (Ettie) Anne Priscilla Fane, born 27 June 1867, died 28 May 1952. Kitchener was godfather* to three of their five children: Julian* Henry Francis Grenfell, born 30 March 1888, died 26 May 1915; Gerald William* Grenfell, born 29 March 1890, died 30 July 1915; Monica Margaret Grenfell born 4 August 1893, died 17 June 1973, Ivo George Winifred Grenfell, born 5 September 1898, died 8 October 1925 and Alexandra Imogen* Clair Grenfell, born 11 February 1905, died 9 January 1969; Richard Davenport-Hines, *Ettie: The Intimate Life and Dauntless Spirit of Lady Desborough* (London: Weidenfeld & Nicholson, 2008) p.111.
116 HA: D/ERv/F132/2, Lord Desborough, *Lord Kitchener As I Knew Him.*
117 Cicely Alice Gore, born 15 July 1867, died 5 February 1955, married James Gascoyne-Cecil 17 May 1887, initially Lord and Lady Cranbourne, from 1903 4th Marquess and Marchioness of Salisbury.

two berths with which, despite our orders given in London, they tried to put us off. No one in Egypt could ever resist Kitchener's orders. He declared that we represented two aunts whom he expected. I do not mean that he told Cook this.' Kitchener and other officers had organised a similar trip for politician Joseph Chamberlain up the Nile in 1889/90. Not long after at a speech in Birmingham Chamberlain declared that 'England could not abandon the country in its present condition.'[118] Kitchener retained ties with Henry Morton Stanley after hosting Stanley at a dinner following the rescue of Emin Pasha in 1889. In 1898, one of Kitchener's first social engagements when he returned to England was to 2 Richmond Terrace, the salon run by Gertrude Tennant, Stanley's mother-in-law.[119] Kitchener looked after his friends, and in return they looked after him.

More significantly, Kitchener had become known to Foreign Secretary Salisbury when Wolseley complained to him about Kitchener's Cyprus mapping ambitions. However, on receiving Ambassador Layard's reports on Kitchener's doings in Turkey, Salisbury was sufficiently impressed that he started following Kitchener's career.[120] At some stage the two men met and became friends, most likely in 1888 as Salisbury wrote to Baring after Kitchener's action at Suakin, March 1888, that, 'Though I do not think that I have ever met him, I have been familiar with his name for many years and feel as if I know him well. He is a very gallant officer – though a head-strong subordinate.'[121] Between June and September 1888, Kitchener stayed with Prime Minister Salisbury at his country home Hatfield, the year his correspondence with Salisbury's daughter-in-law Alice started. His appointment as Sirdar in April 1892, coincided with a dinner in London where John Broderick recorded one of the guests, likely Cromer, '... observ[ing] in a carrying voice that "It's no use, Lord Salisbury, we have got to get back Khartoum. It is for me to prepare and for you to settle the right time".'[122] Cromer was absent from Egypt at the time for health reasons and to receive his title.[123]

Despite his views and background, Kitchener had made a name for himself. His complaint to his sister Millie showing how he saw things: Wolseley and his staff had,

> ... come with English ideas in everything and a scorn for native habits or knowl-
> edge of the country. The result is fatal – they work hard and do nothing absolutely

118 Countess of Jersey, p.207; Travis L Crosby, *Joseph Chamberlain: A Most Radical Imperialist* (London: IB Tauris, 2011) p.113. Joseph Chamberlain, born 8 July 1836, died 2 July 1914, was Colonial Secretary when Kitchener was serving in South Africa, 1899-1902.

119 David Waller, *The Magnificent Mrs Tennant: The Adventurous Life of Gertrude Tennant, Victorian 'Grande Dame'* (New Haven: Yale University, 2009) p.255.

120 Smithers, p.4.

121 Trevor Royle, p.82.

122 Smithers, p.13, William St John Fremantle Brodrick, 1st Earl of Midleton, born 14 December 1856, died 13 February 1942.

123 Archie Hunter, *Power and Passion in Egypt: A Life of Sir Eldon Gorst, 1861-1911* (London: IB Tauris, 2007) p.48.

except make mistakes, absurd laws etc that have to be counter-ordered. All is in fact chaos.[124]

Kitchener saw things differently. On being told by his officers that the Sudanese would not march without camp followers, Kitchener tolerated and sometimes supported them with rations. He would not reimburse them for houses that had burnt down, but had no objection to replacement huts being built so long as it was not at government expense. Allowing the women to follow helped maintain the health and morale of the troops, and reduced the chance of desertion and revolt. They played an additional role as outposts. When JRL MacDonald in Uganda refused to allow wives to accompany the force, he had to suppress a revolt by disaffected Sudanese troops.[125] Motivated by pragmatism and others' experiences Kitchener turned an eye to official policy, as he would do in South Africa when soldiers refused to burn farms.

Although more in tune with the local inhabitants he lived among, Kitchener struggled with those who had western education. Men like the young Khedive, who had been educated in Vienna,[126] developed a strong sense of nationalism and an assertive equality which countered traditional attitudes. This caused the two men regularly to clash and after Kitchener left for South Africa the Khedive's support for disaffected officers in Omdurman led to a mutiny.[127]

The complaints and criticisms of Kitchener's actions during the campaigns in Egypt appear to be by authors commenting from a British perspective, whilst more favourable views are expressed by those with a greater understanding of the cultures Kitchener was working with. Leaving the name of the commanding officer at Kassala out of his report did not help matters.[128] Who exactly Rodd is referring to is not clear, but that Kitchener, deliberately or otherwise, left off the name of a British officer 'who in the opinion of competent judges had done very well with a quite inadequate force', did not endear him to British colleagues who resented his success.[129] Had it not been for support Kitchener, effectually an outsider, garnered in high places within the British establishment, it is unlikely he would have succeeded as he did. However, had he not been good at what he did, those in high places would not have risked their careers to support him.

Being one of the first Generals ever to not use his full budget, Kitchener's financial acumen appealed to Britain's administrators.[130] For all his financial savings of

124 Pollock, p.42.
125 Ronald M Lamothe, *Slaves of Fortune: Sudanese Soldiers and the River War 1896-1898* (Woolbridge: James Currey, 2011) pp.86-8.
126 John A Wilson, *Signs and Wonders Upon Pharaoh: A History of American Egyptology* (Chicago: University of Chicago, 1964) p.68.
127 Lamothe, *Slaves of Fortune*, pp.190-1.
128 Rodd, *Memories*, p.250.
129 Rodd, *Memories*, p.250.
130 Rye, pp.140-1.

£300,000 the entire campaign cost *Egyptian* £2,354,000 (including railways of £1,100,000, gunboats of £154,000 and telegraphs of £21,000), leading Cromer to comment that if Kitchener had not been a General, he could have been one of the best Chancellors of the Exchequer.[131] A perusal of three months' accounts Kitchener kept for 1884 shows that his greatest expenditure was camels – £2,000 out of a budget of £2,679, while his personal allowance was £55.00 over two months.[132] There was no superfluous expenditure. As commander of the Egyptian police, 1890 to 1891, Kitchener only sanctioned replacement uniforms when the existing set was in rags. His force, known for its rags was looked at in disgrace, however, Kitchener knew that if his men were given new uniforms, they would be sold at the nearest market.

His '... drastic method of dealing with civil affairs [was] a never-ending source of amusement' to Cromer, his methods '... a little more masterful and peremptory' than most. When a Dervish had been captured, accused of murder, three options were offered: hanging, having his hands and right foot cut off, or giving the victim's family a bullock. Later, in response to land speculators who were using the Greeks, he suggested that every Greek who bought or sold anything without permission be expelled from the country.[133] Kitchener had spent enough time in the deserts and in the markets to know his people, although Townsend was surprised that Kitchener did not speak with the NCOs when he inspected the Egyptian troops as he, Townsend, was used to seeing happen in India.[134] Cromer acknowledged this when he supported Kitchener's appointment as Sirdar after Grenfell's resignation.[135] But, his drive for cutting costs was to backfire on occasion. Maxwell suffered a mutiny after Kitchener left Omdurman when he tried to use forced labour,[136] and Kitchener was accused of not making sufficient allowances for medical support as discussed above.

Kitchener struggled with conflicting priorities. The cause of the Omdurman mutiny dated back to his reducing the pay of the police and army whilst spending lavishly on the rebuilding of Khartoum – he put long-term gain first, and the status and power of empire above individual need. The same parallel can be seen in his decision to reduce medical support to the absolute minimum to ensure military success, although the latter was exacerbated by British misunderstanding of the environment in which they were operating.

Another trait apparent by this stage was his tendency to threaten resignation, or actually do so, when he did not get his way at crucial moments. It was a desire to break away rather than engage or confront, but it also had the advantage of strengthening his hand, giving him greater freedom which he craved. As much as Kitchener was at

---

131 Rye, p.140; Grew, p.33; TNA: PRO 30/57/10/20.
132 TNA: PRO 30/57/6, Accounts July to October 1884.
133 Zetland, *Lord Cromer*, p.247.
134 Sherson, *Townsend*, p.143.
135 George Cassar, *Kitchener's War: British Strategy From 1914-1916* (Nebraska: Potomac, 2014) p.7.
136 Magnus, pp.121, 181, 188.

a loss how to work with the establishment, so the establishment appeared uncertain how best to deal with him, and by allowing Kitchener to get his way, behaviours were reinforced which caused other difficulties and misunderstandings in later years. As Cromer noted: '... whatever may be his defects, he is unquestionably the best man I know to command the Egyptian Army for the present. However, no one is indispensable, and, if he really wishes to go, I do not want to stand in his way.'[137]

For a shy, introvert man such as Kitchener, mediating the various cultures he came into contact with placed an additional strain of which most others were unaware, not helped by the fact that he would have thought it inappropriate and difficult to discuss with others. Perhaps this accounts for his many close relationships with strong aristocratic women. They were mediating similar anomalies within their lives.

The perfect diplomat: Fashoda, 1898

Five days after Kitchener entered Omdurman, a steamer belonging to the Khalifa approached Khartoum expecting to find their kinsmen. Instead they became prisoners, the captain confirming the presence of white men at Fashoda. Three days later, on 10 September, Kitchener went to investigate, accompanied by five steamers: Beatty in charge of one, Horace Smith-Dorrien in charge of the troops and ADCs Freddie Roberts and Edward Cecil, sons of Lords Roberts and Salisbury respectively.[138]

On 19 September 1898, Kitchener dressed in Egyptian uniform, conducted his discussion with Jean-Baptiste Marchand in French. The Union Jack and other British-related links were kept well in the background, all Kitchener's officers wore the uniform of the Egyptian Army, and the flag raised was Egyptian. The talks on board the *Dal* were followed by a 'chat' over a glass of champagne and cheers given in Arabic.[139] With strict instructions for the Fashoda, soon to be renamed Kadok,[140] garrison under HW Jackson,[141] Kitchener left the real battle to be fought in the discussion chambers in Europe. Russia's refusal to back France in its African endeavours caused France to withdraw.

On 6 October 1898, Kitchener arrived in Cairo from Khartoum, a journey which had taken seventy-four hours.[142] On arrival he learned about his peerage. Ten days later, Ethel Cromer died. 'Her death was deeply felt by many, and not least by Kitchener, who at this time revealed that human side which he seldom allowed others

137 Zetland, *Lord Cromer*, p.243.
138 Ballard, p.84; Rodney Atwood, *The Life of Field Marshal Lord Roberts* (London: Bloomsbury, 2015) p.179.
139 Royle, p. 140; Burleigh, p.308; Jan Morris, *Farewell the Trumpets: An Imperial Retreat* (London: Faber & Faber, 2010) Chapter 2.
140 Royle, p.141.
141 HW Jackson, 'Fashoda, 1898', in *Sudan Notes and Records* (1920) vol 3, no 1, pp.1-11.
142 Rodd, *Memories*, p.240.

to see.'[143] Hearing that Kitchener 'burst into tears' at her memorial service, Cromer wrote, 'I liked him more for this, than anything he said or did during the lengthy relations which I had with him.'[144]

A few days later, Kitchener arrived in England, a hero. From the time he set foot on land, he was besieged by people. His two-month stay was filled with engagements and little time for rest. He negotiated a Parliamentary grant of £30,000 to accompany his peerage, recognising that on his salary he would not be able to do the title justice.[145] His biggest achievement was his scheme for Gordon College, motivated by the statement: 'Those who have conquered are called upon to civilize.'[146] Rodd recalls a rugged directness in the manner in which Kitchener demanded contributions from those he believed could afford them, and did not hesitate to indicate the amount which he considered appropriate to the donor's financial position.[147] This was attributed to Kitchener being scared of fundraising, as he explained at the Stock Exchange: 'I should not like to fail,' at which one of the company said, 'Well, Lord Kitchener, if you had doubted about your campaigns as you do about this, you would never have got to Khartoum.' Kitchener replied, 'Perhaps not, but then I depended on myself; now I have to depend on the public.'[148] Cromer laid the Gordon Memorial College foundation stone in January 1899 and the building was completed in 1902.[149]

During this stay, Kitchener met Henry Spenser Wilkinson, Sometime Chichele Professor of Military History. At lunch organised by Lord Glenesk and his son, Oliver Borthwick,

> Kitchener gave a very interesting description of the black inhabitants of the Upper Nile; they went about without any clothes and were the handsomest figures he had ever seen. With regard to the Battle of Omdurman he said: 'It's all very well for us with machine-guns to shoot down a crowd of blacks. I am wondering what will happen when the other side has machine-guns and our men are subject to their fire.' At one moment he said he would like to have a year's holiday. I asked him what he would do with it if he had it. 'I should like to go to Berlin [...] and learn the art of war.' I found him quite simple, unaffected and

---

143 Rodd, *Memories*, p.241.
144 Zetland, *Lord Cromer*, p.236.
145 Parliamentary debate granting the £30,000, HC Deb 05 June 1899 vol 72 cc327-408 online: https://api.parliament.uk/historic-hansard/Commons/1899/jun/05/supply.
146 Rye, p.144, letter to *The Times*, 30 November 1898.
147 Rodd, *Memories*, p.240.
148 Grew, p.24.
149 It was a primary school in 1902. In 1924 the Kitchener School of Medicine was opened, and with the Gordon College became the University College of Khartoum in 1951, linked with the University of London. On 24 July 1956 it became the independent University of Khartoum.

modest, yet I did not feel I should like to be under his orders. I felt that he was too peremptory for my taste.[150]

On 6 November Kitchener was best man at brother Arthur's wedding, on 1 December attended Drury Lane Lodge No 2127 to raise funds for Gordon College,[151] and 4 December accompanied the Queen to Netley Hospital to distribute Sudan medals to 180 wounded men who had fought at Atbara and Omdurman.[152] During August he had visited Ireland to observe the manoeuvres and to see Roberts about the possibility of command in South Africa if war broke out and if Roberts was given chief command. This visit had been orchestrated by Ian Hamilton and Rawlinson.[153] Hedging his bets, he also visited the India Office regarding a possible appointment as military member of the Viceroy's Council. He left both meetings satisfied.[154]

Egypt: A return, 1898-1899

On 7 December 1898 Kitchener returned to govern Sudan where he spent a year developing the territory. He started to rebuild relationships and set up government structures. Instructions were issued to

> ... provincial governors and district inspectors to acquire the confidence of the people, to develop their resources, and to raise them to a higher level. [...] Proclamations or Circulars, affect little; it is to the individual action of British officers, working independently, but with a common purpose, on the individual natives whose confidence they have gained, that we must look for the moral and industrial regeneration of the Sudan.[155]

The tribal leaders, camel and cattle-breeding nomads, were confirmed in their posts and brought within British bureaucracy, becoming local agents responsible for collecting taxes and other administrative functions. This continued a policy implemented by the Turko-Egyptian administration before 1881, the difference now that succession was not based on kinship but on a structure of hierarchy.

---

150 Henry Spenser Wilkinson, *Thirty-Five Years: 1874-1909* (London: Constable, 1933) p.229; born 1 May 1853, died 31 January 1937; related by marriage to Eyre Crowe of the Foreign Office.
151 George Turnbull in Grew, p.21.
152 *Morning Post*, 3 December 1898.
153 Atwood, *Roberts*, p.180; Royle, pp.142, 149.
154 Magnus, p.187.
155 Ahmed Ibrahim Abushouk, 'The Anglo-Egyptian Sudan: From collaboration mechanism to party politics, 1898-1956', in *Journal of Imperial and Commonwealth History*, 38:2, 207-236 (2010) p.4.

Religious leaders, though, were not permitted to continue as they had previously, '... these *Fikis*, who lived on the superstitious ignorance of the people were one of the curses of the Soudan, and were responsible in a great measure for the [Mahdi's] rebellion.'[156] They were encouraged to mix with other religious groups and leaders such as Muslim scholars and those of the Khatmiyya Sufi Order which was '... the only popular Islamic movement tolerated by the new regime.'[157] The mosque of *tariqa* was allowed to be rebuilt and Sayyid Ali was made a KCMG by Queen Victoria – all to undermine the Mahdist legacy. A similar approach was taken to Christian mission work. Llewellyn Gwynne, who had gone out shortly before to set up a Church Missionary Society base in Omdurman, was refused permission; Kitchener informed him that 'Lord Cromer and his advisers were so anxious not to give offence to the religious views of the Mohammedan (Moslem) population that any steps that might suggest efforts were being made to proselytise the people must be discouraged.' Eventually, after Kitchener left, in 1902 a mission school was opened in Khartoum.[158]

Kitchener saw the British presence as one of advising and 'civilising', that is introducing education and an ethical code independent of converting peoples of other faiths to Christianity. For many others, mission work was the means to build and support the British Empire.[159] Whilst mapping in Palestine, Kitchener had on occasion commented that areas needed a British presence, not to convert the people, but to educate and regularise trade relations which would help bring the masses out of poverty and reduce exploitation. Setting up the Gordon Memorial College was part of this process.

> What is now mainly required is to impart such a knowledge of reading, writing and arithmetic to a certain number of young men [in Khartoum] as will enable them to occupy with advantage the subordinate places in the administration of the country. The need for such a class is severely felt.[160]

The college was eventually to supply over a quarter of Sudanese civil servants in the Anglo-Egyptian administration. In his year of administering Sudan, Kitchener had set the base on which Anglo-Egyptian relations were to develop; and as Cromer pointed out, he did not always foresee or consider the consequences. It could, however, be argued that his faith in the British Empire to do right by those it ruled clouded his judgement.

156 Abushouk, The Anglo-Egyptian Sudan quoted on p.211, fn 16.
157 Abushouk, The Anglo-Egyptian Sudan quoted on p.211, fn 17.
158 James Lomote Simeon, 'Llewellyn Henry Gwynne', in *Dictionary of African Biography*. L.H. Gwynne, born 11 June 1863, died 9 December 1957.
159 John W. de Gruchy, *The Church Struggle in South Africa* (Fortress, 2005).
160 Quoted in Mark Fathi Massoud, *Law's Fragile State: Colonial, Authoritarian, and Humanitarian Legacies in Sudan* (Cambridge: Cambridge UP, 2013) p.73.

As part of his reconstruction plan, Kitchener ordered the rebuilding of Khartoum.[161] Rodd was 'unjustly critical' in his first views of the new Khartoum. It savoured *megalope-peia*, money was short and would be for some years. 'But K had imagination, and I now realise he was quite right to lay out Khartoum in the grand manner and to emphasise a contrast with the vast, mud-built, squalid metropolis of Omdurman. The new Khartoum was to have a moral significance, and results have justified the larger conception.'[162]

June and July 1899 saw Kitchener back in England when he and Cecil Rhodes were awarded honorary doctorates by the University of Oxford.

Prior to this, Cromer had been concerned, writing to Rodd:

> You know how secretive the Sirdar is. He does not tell me anything, and I am not confident he knows much about it himself. He terrorises all his people and does not encourage them to speak the truth – A Muslim army; Christian officers; the blacks capricious and almost savage; the fellaheen loathing service in the Soudan; the Khedive, to say the least, foolish; the native and the French Press doing all they can to encourage discontent; the older and more experienced English officers getting promoted; these facts are quite enough for me. – I do not think Kitchener at all appreciated the danger. Hence I insisted on giving back the field allowances. Kitchener tells me I was wrong, but I do not agree with him. It instantly put a stop to all the agitation *here*. – Kitchener must remember he has to deal with human beings and not with blocks of wood and stone.[163]

Cromer thought Kitchener 'terribly bureaucratic' and that he did '... not see with sufficient clearness the difference between forming a country and commanding a regiment,' and despite being 'cool, reliable, courageous and marvellously efficient,' there was a side of Kitchener's 'character and temperament which might cause trouble if not carefully handled.'[164] Cromer was not the only one concerned. Balfour had his doubts about the appointment having stayed with Kitchener at Hatfield and at Balmoral. He questioned 'How far he could adapt himself to wholly different and perhaps larger problems than those with which he has been dealing.'[165] Both men were justified in their concerns when, without consultation, Kitchener cut the field allowance of Egyptian officers at the time British officers in the Egyptian Army were receiving an increase so that he had money for 'other purposes'. Cromer also had Kitchener relax his leave policy for British officers, Kitchener believing time spent in Cairo was distracting and no good. Their absence from Cairo meant Cromer lost out on hearing their complaints as they did not share these with Kitchener, '... an important point, as

161 Magnus, p.183.
162 Rodd, *Memories*, p.271
163 Rodd, *Memories*, pp.249-50.
164 Zetland, *Lord Cromer*, pp.242-3; Magnus, p.186.
165 Magnus, p.175; Jane Ridley & Clayre Percy, *The Letters of Arthur Balfour and Lady Elcho, 1885-1917* (London: Hamish Hamilton, 1992) p.156.

everything depends on them, and they are all so terrified of their Chief that they do not dare to state their own grievances.'[166]

In contrast to Cromer who thought 'Kitchener had always scoffed at the idea that the Egyptian Army could ever prove dangerous' and that Kitchener's 'very stern discipline' was 'causing serious discontent,' the Egyptian Army 'grew to be a model of efficiency in war' under the command of Grenfell and Kitchener and started to attract '... every British subaltern and captain who was eager to learn soldiering or ambitious to see active service.'[167]

In the autumn, Kitchener returned to Egypt determined to bring the Khalifa to book, his whereabouts having been ascertained. Earlier in the year, Kitchener had tasked his brother Walter to lead the hunt for the Khalifa, an appointment which caused some upset as it placed Walter in command of Maxwell and MacDonald who were both his seniors and which 'was difficult to justify.'[168] Eventually in November, the Khalifa's position was betrayed and Wingate was tasked with bringing him to book. Five days later, on 24 November 1899 the Khalifa was defeated and killed at Ulm Debeikerat.[169] In the meantime on 10 October 1899 war had been declared in southern Africa.

On 18 December 1899, Kitchener left for South Africa, having received a telegram on 16 December offering him the post of second in command to Lord Roberts. He arrived in Gibraltar on 26 December having spent most of the trip suffering from sea-sickness.[170] Here, he met Roberts. Kitchener had done everything possible to ensure he was posted to South Africa: in August 1898, prompted by Rawlinson and Hamilton, he had spoken with Roberts in Ireland, and soon after his return to Egypt asked Lady Cranborne, Alice, to '... put in a word as if the Cape war comes off it will be a big thing and they might give me some billet.'[171] Both Salisbury and Queen Victoria insisted on his being appointed Roberts' Chief of Staff.[172]

On route to Gibraltar, Cromer warned Kitchener that he would not return to Sudan as Governor General. His impatience to get things done had made him autocratic and he was causing chaos with the way he manipulated the finances. His withholding of allowances and keeping areas under military control as well as introducing trade restrictions to keep weapons out of the country had not been popular.[173] Having left Egypt, other upsets came to the fore. His successor, Reginald Wingate, had more success and a positive relationship was restored with the Khedive.[174]

166 Zetland, *Lord Cromer*, pp.241-2.
167 FI Maxe, *Seymour Vandeleur: The Story of a British officer. Being a Memoir of Brevet-Lieutenant-Colonel Vandeleur, D.S.O., Scots Guards and Irish Guards, with a General Description of his Campaigns* (London, National Review, 1906) p.132.
168 Rodd, *Memories*, p.250.
169 Magnus, p.188.
170 Ballard, p.97.
171 Ian FW Beckett, *A British Profession of Arms: The Politics of Command in the Late Victorian Army* (Oklahoma: University of Oklahoma, 2018) p.225.
172 Royle, p.153; Smithers, p.25.
173 Royle, p.151.
174 Rodd, *Memories*, p.266.

4

Clay-footed hero: South Africa, 1900-1902

Kitchener and Roberts arrived in Cape Town at 1.45 p.m. on 11 January 1900.[1] Believing the Boers to be defeated following the collapse of their capitals, Roberts left in November and the War Office started to recall troops. After some discussion in London, it was agreed that Kitchener assume complete command.[2] Roberts, on his return to Britain, realising his error in judgement, pleaded with the War Office to have troops returned to South Africa.[3] However, the damage was done, and Kitchener had to constantly justify his need for additional men and supplies. By the time Roberts left, the war had already cost £80million, and saw a total of 448,435 men serve. This was more than what the East Africa campaign of 1914-18 cost (£72million),[4] and which saw the service of 89,670 troops and 646,001 carriers and labourers.[5]

The war in southern Africa was a shock and eye-opener to Kitchener. He revealed to Lady Cranborne, Alice, on 29 April 1900:

> It is quite impossible to calculate on anything in this army. I must say, I like having the whole thing cut and dried and worked out; but people here do not seem to look upon the war sufficiently seriously. It is considered too much like a game of polo with intervals for afternoon tea ... I try all I can, day and night, to get the machine to work. But a thorough organisation will have to take place before we can call ourselves a fighting nation.[6]

---

1   A Egmont-Hake (ed.) *Soldiers of the Queen: Roberts of Kandahar* (London: London Publishing, 1900) p.16. Kitchener does not have a booklet to himself in this collection, an indication that he was still relatively unknown at this time.
2   Royle, p.174, Magnus, p.210.
3   Rodney Atwood, *Roberts and Kitchener in South Africa 1900-1902* (Barnsley: Pen & Sword, 2011) pp.472-473.
4   Samson, *Britain, South Africa and East Africa*; Warner, p.123.
5   Elizabeth Riedi, Imperialist women in Edwardian Britain: The Victoria League 1899-1914 (PhD, University of St Andrew's, 1998) p.69; Great War in Africa Association, www.gweaa.com; Hew Strachan, *World War I in Africa* (Oxford: Oxford University, 2004).
6   Royle, pp.163, 198.

In Cape Town, Girouard noted:

> … chaos reigns […], chiefly because of the contradictory orders that are sent down from here […] for all departments of head-quarters wire in the name of the Chief of the Staff, usually without consulting each other, and each claims precedence for its own requirements. Kitchener, who is nominally the Chief of the Staff, is nearly always away doing odd jobs where things are going wrong, and there is no one here to pull the machinery together for the Chief.[7]

Rawlinson called for '… a staff system which shall be the same in peace as in war,'[8] agreeing with Kitchener who had insisted in Sudan that the men who trained the force had to serve with them. Later, in 1914, this was a requirement for the Kitchener Army contingents.

It did not help that at the time of his appointment, Kitchener was still relatively unknown to the other British and Indian commanders nor that he was junior to others on the Army List, including John French. Kitchener's authority came from being Roberts' mouth-piece. On arrival in South Africa he was appointed a local Lieutenant-General, a rank commensurate with his role.[9] As Chief of the Staff his role was unclear, Roberts effectively acting as his own Chief of Staff while relying on Kitchener 'on whom he could, with implicit confidence, devolve any important piece of organizing work that turned up, or whom he could [use] to "hustle" departments and subordinate members.'[10]

Yet, in Roberts Kitchener had someone of similar mind. Roberts' decision to ignore the War Office plan and to rely on railways to defeat the Boers and occupy their capital cities instantly appealed to Kitchener who firmly believed in using railway transport to support the military.[11] So, whilst Roberts set about reorganising the military and improving troop morale, Kitchener set about restructuring the transport. His attempts to centralise the transport as he had in Egypt proved unsuccessful in South Africa and a slow return was made to the old system. How much was due to the war being in progress where Kitchener responded to situations, compared to his time in Egypt where he initiated action requires closer inspection, but enough complaints were received for the War Office to issue a reprimand. This in turn led Kitchener to complain to Pandeli Ralli about '… the "old red-tape heads of departments" who quoted regulations […] "generally dated about 1870 and intended for Aldershot

---

7   Maurice, *Life of Rawlinson*, p.62.
8   Maurice, *Life of Rawlinson*, p.63.
9   Royle, pp.169-70; Atwood, *Roberts & Kitchener*, p.107, 'Kitchener was forty-first in seniority among major generals'. At least two 1899-1902 war Lieutenant Generals were more senior to Kitchener.
10 Atwood, *Roberts & Kitchener*, p.115.
11 Smithers, p.25.

manoeuvres".'[12] Despite his reputation suffering for this miscalculated move, his successful appointment of Girouard to organise and co-ordinate the Imperial military transport requirements with those of the civilian needs has gone unnoticed. Girouard was only released from his post in 1904 when military control of the railways then conflicted with economic needs which dominated.

On 17 September 1900, Redvers Buller, senior commander of the forces until Roberts arrived,[13] thought it time to return home as he '... was [not] doing any good where he was.' A month later, Roberts annexed the Transvaal and the war deteriorated into guerrilla warfare. It was, therefore, suggested that Roberts return to Britain and Buller resume command. When Kitchener heard, he did 'not want to leave' despite Rawlinson telling 'him he will probably be ordered home to ride in the triumph through London.' So, it was with some relief when Lansdowne '... replied that the Government had not sufficient confidence in Buller to leave him to finish up the war, and proposed that Kitchener should remain in command.' Roberts approved providing 'K [...] be given the rank of a full general.' He further noted that Kitchener 'was disinclined to take up an appointment at the War Office,' and that 'in the future K would best serve the state as Commander-in-Chief in India.'[14] Roberts recognised that conforming to bureaucracy and routine desk work were not for Kitchener; his skills lay elsewhere in reforming military structures. Due to sail on 29 October, Roberts' own, and family, illness delayed his departure until 29 November when he went on leave to visit his son's grave in Natal before leaving the country.

Despite misgivings, Rawlinson left for England with Roberts. On 11 December 1900, Kitchener wired to Rawlinson: 'Good-bye to you all, and the best of wishes. Don't forget those you leave behind.' Three weeks after arriving in England a telegram from Kitchener asked him to return to South Africa.[15] He arrived in March 1901 and joined Kitchener's staff. 'Living with K at the Residency', he noted Kitchener was 'in very good form now, but was evidently a bit down in January.'[16] Rawlinson was trusted with various operations in the field and when Kitchener returned to Britain, he asked Rawlinson to accompany him on board the *Orotava* which left on 23 June 1902.

The 1899-1902 conflict in the southern hemisphere raised many questions over Britain's military capabilities and with Kitchener, an outsider, in a prominent position and then in command of the campaign, his reputation suffered. His reluctance to put the record straight or accuse others of mismanagement, and that he never wrote his memoirs, have meant the reasons for his actions and extent of involvement in decision making have been conjectured by those who knew him well but also by others who

12   Magnus, p.196.
13   Redvers Buller, born 7 December 1939, died 2 June 1908, served China, Ashanti, South Africa 1878-1881, Egypt 1882-1884, South Africa 1899-1900.
14   Maurice, *Life of Rawlinson*, p.65, Henry Charles Keith Petty-Fitzmaurice, 5th Marquess of Lansdowne, born 14 January 1845, died 3 June 1927.
15   Maurice, *Life of Rawlinson*, p.66.
16   Maurice, *Life of Rawlinson*, p.67.

had a grudge. The result is that Kitchener's reputation in South Africa in 2019 is still at an all-time low amongst some of the population who believe he should be tried for war crimes during this period.[17] A book such as this, is not going to exonerate him, but it does aim to consider his actions in the broader context, and of others involved; at least showing that it takes more than one man to create and implement a policy, even in war.

This war was the first occasion where Kitchener had to deal entirely with the British Army and War Office. Before arriving in South Africa, the last time he had been in a pure British military environment was when a student at Woolwich and trainer at Aldershot. Within a month of leaving Sudan, where a few years before he had overseen the last square attack, he was thrown into a conflict four months old where technology, weapons, and tactics differed to what he was used to. And so did the enemy; a people more culturally aligned with the British and of the same religious background than the Sudanese, Egyptians, Arabs and Turks he had previously encountered. Mistakes were made, but not all his making. He perceived situations and solutions differently which caused him to clash with fellow officers and political masters. Kitchener's way of conducting war was from the front, with his men, sometimes leading the charge. During the 1914-18 war a large number of Indian and African officers were lost as they went forward with their men rather than directing from behind as was common with the white British forces, and was one of the reasons he was severely criticised for his actions at Paardeberg.

Another Kitchener personality trait which caused difficulties with colleagues at the time, and impacted on his subsequent reputation was his apparent harshness. In the same way that Jan Smuts made the wrong moral call when authorising the execution of Jopie Fourie in 1914, so Kitchener did with sanctioning those of Breaker Morant (Henry Harboard Murant) and Peter Handcock for murdering a wounded prisoner of war and eight civilians in revenge. Legally both decisions were appropriate, however they were not in keeping with popular feeling at the time and both Fourie and Morant have subsequently become national symbols. All are buried in Heroes' Acre cemetery in Pretoria, South Africa.[18] A third officer with Morant, GR Witton had his sentence commuted to life imprisonment by Kitchener. Both Field Marshals were fortunate to have friends and colleagues who were, in most cases, more people-oriented, Cromer, Broderick, Roberts for Kitchener and Louis Botha for Smuts, but it was when these mediating forces were absent that the men made unpopular decisions, technically correct but lacking sympathy. Like Smuts, when Kitchener was on a mission, little stood in his way as seen in the latter's implementation of the blockhouse system. Having issued an order that all captured loot from the Boers be handed in and

17   View of contributor at talk in Johannesburg on 27 November 2012; Bok van Blerk's song *De la Rey*.

18   DRW, *Shot at Dawn* (3 June 2017) online http://allatsea.co.za/musings/shot-at-dawn/ [accessed 9 March 2019]; Senator McGauran, Notice Paper of The Parliament of the Commonwealth of Australia, No 117, 2002-3, Wednesday 23 November 2003, pp.8-9.

auctioned, the proceeds going to the Field Force Canteen, Aubrey Woolls Sampson asked Ian Hamilton if he could keep his pony. Kitchener, happening to come by at the time, adamantly refused saying Woolls Sampson had to hand it in and repurchase it. Woolls Sampson never forgave Hamilton for ostensibly setting him up: 'They both acted according to type, and I should almost have been disappointed if either of them had climbed down.'[19] By the outbreak of the First World War though, both Kitchener and Smuts had become more media aware.

Whose failure?

In contrast to his campaign in Sudan, Kitchener's command of southern Africa started with a disadvantage. He was the third consecutive commanding officer, having been Roberts' 'sort of understudy' for the previous nine months where he had been sent 'off on independent stunts.'[20] War had been looming since 1896 after the Jameson Raid, eventually breaking out on 10 October 1899.[21] Where Kitchener had meticulously planned for Sudan, this had not been the case in southern Africa evident with the shock of Black Week in December 1899. From what Kitchener had seen in his travels around the country, he had little faith in the forces he took command of on 30 November 1900.[22] On 4 March 1900, he wrote Lady Cranborne: 'The army requires really months of hard work to get fit for the work it has to do. I never thought it was quite as bad as I have found it!' and two days later, 'I have been having rather a bad time lately ... I hope the authorities will keep their hair on; and if they want a victim to sacrifice, I am always at their disposal. War means risks; and you cannot play the game and always win; and the sooner those in authority realise this the better.'[23] Similarly, many Kitchener commanded had little faith in him.

Kitchener's actions at Paardeberg, his first fight against white soldiers, remain a matter for debate.[24] Leo Amery, military correspondent for *The Times* and the German military specialists commenting on the war believed Kitchener's actions had broken Boer morale and that Roberts was wrong not to push through with Kitchener's plan when he, Roberts, arrived back the following day. Regardless of who was right, Kitchener had lost the confidence of his generals, if he ever had it given Kelly-Kenny's response to Roberts' telegram informing him that Kitchener was in command: 'With regard to my position and Lord Kitchener's, your description of it I fully understand.

19   Ian Hamilton, *Anti-Commando* (London: Faber & Faber, 1931) pp.127-31.
20   Atwood, *Roberts*, p.204.
21   DM Leeson, 'Playing at war: The British military manoeuvres of 1898', in *War in History*, vol 15, no 4 (2008) pp.432-461 provides an interesting insight into Buller's command of the 1899-1902 war.
22   TNA: PRO 30/57/19, various letters and telegrams to Roberts.
23   Magnus, p.207.
24   Magnus, p.202.

This is not a time to enter into personal matters. Till this phase of the operations is completed, I will submit to even humiliation rather than raise any matter connected with my command.'[25]

Roberts being ill, and Piet Cronje looking like he would escape at Modder River and join up with other Boer commanders unless something urgent was done, Kitchener assumed overall command despite Kelly-Kenny being more senior. Kitchener took command on 18 February in the way he knew best: hands on.

> The Chief of the Staff wished to command in person all the units down to and including battalions, and he issued his orders direct to the latter, ignoring the regulation channels of communication and the divisional commanders. The consequence was that a strong feeling of resentment took possession of the generals [...] Their leadership was destitute of all agreeable responsibility and initiative; and this was particularly noticeable in the attitude of the commander of the cavalry division, who was otherwise so alert.[26]

Smithers concluded, 'If some of Kitchener's decisions were bad, they were a great deal better than no decisions at all.' The result was 24 officers and 279 men dead with 59 officers wounded alongside 847 men and 61 missing. 'These were formidable casualties by Victorian standards and Kitchener was greatly blamed.'[27]

There is much in common between Kitchener's actions at Paardeberg and earlier at Atbara, but in contrast to Dongola and Omdurman where careful planning and consideration of every possibility was evident. Kitchener was not good at dealing with battlefield emergencies as he failed to consider the bigger picture, dealing with what he saw in front of him. Roberts returned to the field on 19 February and felt the position could not be stormed without '... further loss of life which did not appear ... to be warranted' by the 'military emergency of the situation'.[28] Instead, he set about besieging Cronje which led, on 27 February, to Cronje's surrender. Although Kitchener remained unrepentant, the German Official History repeated his telling the US Military Attaché, Captain Slocum that, 'If I had known yesterday morning what I know today I would not have attacked the Boers in the river valley; it is impossible against the modern rifle.'[29] It was Kitchener's moment of realisation that the Boers were better equipped than the Dervishes had been. Roberts' decision to tactfully send Kitchener to Girouard at Colesburg to repair the railways and bridges there, played into the hands of the anti-war group back in London led by David Lloyd-George who felt the war was being fought to better the position of the 'gold-bugs'. Kitchener

25   Magnus, p.201, Thomas Kelly-Kenny, born 27 February 1840, died 26 December 1914.
26   Harold FB Wheeler, *The Story of Lord Kitchener* (London: George G Harrap, 1916)
       pp.185-7 quoting *German Official History*, vol 1, p.191.
27   Smithers, p.29.
28   Magnus, pp.207-8.
29   Smithers, p.29; Warner, p.117.

became the scapegoat.[30] However, it did not dent Roberts' faith in Kitchener to command on his departure. On 9 February 1900, he wrote:

> Kitchener is the only man able to manage this business and I trust he will be appointed [to the chief command when I give it up]. I cannot recommend any of those senior to him ... it is unfortunate that there are no men of military genius amongst our senior officers but I believe this has always been the case. Napoleon experienced this, and Wellington always said that he had not a single General he could trust to act alone. The only possible conclusion is that very few are fit to be Commanders of Armies and the stake is far too serious for any untried man to be appointed when a tried man is available.[31]

This was confirmed by Esher who noted that Roberts had '... no words to express his high commendation.' 'Kitchener's self-possession, his eagerness to undertake all the hardest and most difficult work, his scorn of notoriety, and his loyalty, were beyond all praise. He was the only officer who shrank from no responsibility, and no task, however arduous.'[32]

Despite having miscalculated the ability of the enemy on the occasion of Paardeberg, Kitchener quickly realised that so long as their land was under threat the Boers would fight, while Roberts felt they would surrender when the British occupied their capital cities. Having ensured British control of the main Boer economic centres, Roberts handed over command to Kitchener who was left to cope with the change to mobile or guerrilla warfare[33] which extended in turn to include the two British colonies of Natal and the Cape, all at a time the War Office was calling for troops to return to Britain and the war to be concluded. The size of the country and the nature of the landscape meant the cost of continuing the war would be astronomical. Other means therefore had to be found.[34] The result was Kitchener's adoption of policies Roberts had sanctioned, but with the methodical execution which he had become known for in Sudan.

Roberts had sanctioned the burning of farms as early as March 1900,[35] but it was Kitchener who implemented the policy and therefore blamed for the consequences. When the scorched earth or clearance policy was implemented in January 1901, safe accommodation was needed for the women, children and farm workers, both black and white, to prevent them starving. Kitchener's responsibility lies in the systematic implementation of the policies, but he cannot be held solely accountable for the

30   Royle, p.172, Magnus, p.208.
31   Smithers, p.30.
32   Lord Esher, *Journal II*, p.273 in H de Watteville, *Lord Kitchener* (London: Blackie & Son, 1939) p.177.
33   CR de Wet challenges the term as only sections of the Boer territories were under British control, not the whole. *Three Years' War* (New York: Charles Scribner) p.277.
34   Warner, p.123.
35   Atwood, *Roberts and Kitchener*, p.457; Hamilton, *Anti-Commando*, p.24.

consequences, especially as few, if any, were foreseen. According to Major Burnham, a scout:

> The order was issued because of a lack of synthetic imagination. This would have shown the two ex-Eastern potentates, Bobs of Kandahar and K of Khartoum, that the Boers were very like Englishmen and not in the least like Afghans or Dervishes. Both Bobs and K, through long service in the East, had lost something of their powers of gauging accurately the feelings of a white man of fighting race who has had his house picked out and burnt deliberately to the ground with all its little family records, in order to encourage others.[36]

Kitchener understood Boer attachment to the land, but he was constrained by a poorly planned system which he had to expand rapidly with little time for proper organisation. The speed with which the camps grew resulted in overcrowding, despite pleas by those managing the camps for forewarning of new-comers. The camps were 'hastily improvised tent camps' set alongside railway lines for 'military monitoring and supply purposes', often where there were existing camps. They were 'expected to be [a] short-lived, temporary measure' in line with Roberts' view that the war was in effect over. The inmates were regarded as British citizens and it was accepted that after the war, they would resume their place in society and vote. Where possible, the inhabitants were paid for their services including teachers, inspectors, nurses and other social services. A breakdown of the £2,5million to run the camps shows that wages formed the '... second highest item of expenditure – after food and camp supplies'; higher than that spent on the camp staff.[37]

Kitchener's challenge was exacerbated with the arrival of Emily Hobhouse around the time he took command. Hobhouse had been sent south to investigate matters on behalf of the South African Women and Children's Distress Fund following its discovery of the plight of the Boer women as a result of Roberts' farm burning policy which was one of retribution and intimidation. That she was also against the war aided the Liberal Party in its condemnation of the government. With the Colonial and War Offices not responding quickly enough to the developing humanitarian problem in South Africa, the parties turned to the press and Kitchener, at the top of the chain, again became the scapegoat.

He did not help himself by making ambiguous statements, although these show the complexity of the situation he was dealing with. Determining which Boers were refugees and which prisoners of war resulted in confusion of management and responsibility. Already in late December 1900 there were indications that Kitchener felt the

36   Hamilton, *Anti-Commando*, p.25.
37   Iain R Smith & Andreas Stuki, 'The colonial development of concentration camps (1868-1902)', in *The Journal of Imperial and Commonwealth History*, vol 39, no 3, Sep 2011, pp.417-37.

camps should be administered by the civil administration in contrast to Roberts who felt they should be military controlled. Kitchener was struggling to provide sufficient provisions, in early December resorting to a reduction in ration scales for women and children.[38] However, it was only on 17 January 1901 that it was suggested to Milner and 7 March 1901 that the handover was agreed. Confusion remained in that while internal management of the white camps rested with the Department of Burgher Refugees in Pretoria and Bloemfontein and the black camps with the Department of Native Refugees, who reported into Lord Milner, the High Commissioner, external security remained with the army. Supplies were subjected to the same conditions as for the troops, although of secondary importance.

The situation was further complicated by Milner, who had assumed responsibility for the Boer territories in February 1901, returning to England on leave between 24 May and 28 August 1901. His workload fell to the already fully employed Commander-in-Chief, Kitchener. Not only was Kitchener having to manage the military aspects but he was now responsible for civil administration as well – of a people and systems he little knew and understood. His priority was to bring the war to an end as quickly as possible, inviting Louis Botha, one of the senior Boer leaders to discuss the possibility of peace as early as February 1901, reflecting the two different attitudes towards the Boers. In June 1901, Kitchener as High Commissioner for the Transvaal and Orange River Colony wrote to Joseph Chamberlain in the Colonial Office suggesting confiscation of Boer farms and the permanent expulsion of Boers from South Africa.[39]

On 11 December 1899 Roberts had told Lansdowne at the War Office that the size of the country and the scale of operations in South Africa was too big for one commander.[40] Yet, in 1901, Kitchener had more. It is not surprising that he could not give everything his full attention and he left management of the camps to subordinates, trusting them to do what was necessary. Military recommendations for improvements coincided with those of Hobhouse so that by the time Millicent Garret Fawcett, of Suffragette fame, and her team arrived to investigate, greater order was evident, variable depending on the efficiency of the camp commandant. Her arrival helped ensure doctors, nurses and teachers were sent to South Africa. 'Indian geniuses,' as Milner called them, 'arrived in South Africa to bring Indian experiences to bear on the administration of the camps.'[41] These changes all occurred at the same time the epidemic had started to run its course and as winter came to an end.[42]

Used to the camp followers in Sudan who organised themselves, Kitchener mistakenly allowed the Boer women to organise their own camp administration and sanitary

---

38   Emily Hobhouse, *The Brunt of the War and Where It Fell* (London: Methuen, 1902) p.74.
39   TNA: PRO 30/57/16/10, letter 19 June 1901.
40   Roberts to Lansdowne in Keith Surridge, British civil-military relations and the South African War (1899-1902) (PhD, King's College London, 1994) p.85.
41   Smith & Stuki, pp.438-9.
42   See also Elizabeth van Heyningen, *The Concentration Camps of the Anglo-Boer War: A Social History* (Johannesburg: Jacana, 2013).

arrangements. Not used to living in such proximity to each other, the outcome was the horror we know about. The camps were further affected by the general supply problems Kitchener was having to deal with – his soldiers were suffering as much from a lack of supplies as were the camps as the railways were an ideal target for Boer raids. Hamilton contrasts the scorched earth policy with the 'concentration camps bungle':

> To my thinking (then and now) Kitchener, Roberts and Milner showed a lack of statesmanship in not gauging what the effect upon the world of European and American womanhood would be of thus harrying the homes of the wives and daughters of the Boers. On a point like this the force of feminine opinion was far, far more powerful in the days before women had their 'rights' and could mount platforms themselves to spout and be contradicted. Further, the moment chosen for introducing the edict so much hated by the troops into execution showed a complete absence of that cunning which is so much a part of statesmanship [...] Another couple of months and the Boer women would have been begging to be brought in and given shelter and rations. They must have done so on three out of four of the farms. [...] to burn a farm or a haystack is, according to my ethics, utterly heathen and damnable. [...] I'd sooner have stood a Court Martial than do so.[43]

Despite his behaviour, 'Kitchener somehow never got on the nerves of the Boers.' Botha even wrote to thank Kitchener for looking after the women and children.[44]

In November 1901, Fawcett sent out by the War Office to investigate the situation of the camps wrote to Milner with her recommendations. He was sympathetic but unable to do anything as the supply of additional transport was a military issue. Fawcett then asked to meet with Kitchener, who in turn requested that only two of the six-woman deputation see him.

> At the appointed hour, General [John] Maxwell arrived with a carriage to take us [Fawcett and Lady Knox] to Lord Kitchener's house. It was a charming and attractive building standing in a garden. We entered a large square hall, where we were asked to be seated while General Maxwell went into the room where Lord Kitchener was working. He left the door wide open, and we could not help hearing what he said. Again we smiled when we heard Lord Kitchener's voice inquire anxiously, 'How many are there of them?' In another minute we were shown into his room, and thereupon there ensued the most satisfactory and businesslike interview that I, at any rate, had ever had of an approximately similar nature.[45]

43   Hamilton, *Anti-Commando*, pp.26-7.
44   Hamilton, *Anti-Commando*, pp.26-7.
45   Millicent Garrett Fawcett, *What I Remember* (New York: GP Putnam's, 1925) p.171.

Her request for an additional rail truck to ensure more fresh vegetables were sent to the camps was approved. She

> ... liked him far better than any of the politicians I had gone to on deputations in London. I always say that Lady Knox and I, after this interview with Lord Kitchener, received the compliment of our lives, for, after sampling two of us, he invited the whole six of us to dinner! We did not all go; but I think there were four of us. Lord Kitchener took me in to dinner and I had much interesting conversation with him.[46]

Fawcett's business approach and Kitchener's egalitarianism ensured a successful outcome. Not one for small talk, Kitchener's experiences of meetings with women in Cairo and London had certainly made him wary and he was perhaps over circumspect following Valentine Baker's fall from grace based on the claims of a young woman in Turkey. According to Ponsonby, at a dinner with Queen Victoria in 1898, 'Kitchener related how he had been rather inconvenienced after the battle by having two thousand women on his hands. Princess Beatrice asked what the women were like and he replied, "Very much like all women, they talked a great deal".[47] He therefore avoided them where he could.

The Fawcett commission's account of their visits to the camps is surprisingly positive given the generally held view of how the Boer women were treated and the conditions in the camp. It is reminiscent of the German women giving the British and Belgian forces in East Africa a hard time in order to distract them from other tasks. The women also admitted to not telling the camp officials when they were ill or had other needs as this was not their way.[48]

Beneath the façade, Kitchener was sensitive, his confidence being obviously knocked on occasion. On 7 March 1902 Methuen was captured which caused Kitchener to miss five meals in a row.[49] Later that month, Kitchener hit another wobble when he was notified of the defeat of the Royal Horse Artillery Mounted Rifles and the Canadian Rifles under George Arthur Cookson[50] who were chasing down Koos de la Rey. Ian Hamilton believed Kitchener:

> ... could be reckoned on to keep cool as a cucumber and perfectly cheery and self-confident under one heavy stroke of misfortune on another. And now it was to be shown that, all the time, he had never been as cool as a cucumber but

46   Fawcett, *What I Remember*, p.171.
47   Frederick Ponsonby, *Recollections of Three Eeigns* (London: Eyre & Spottiswoode, 1951) p.43.
48   Fawcett's memoir and her view on the concentration camp is available online: https://www.fadedpage.com/showbook.php?pid=20170727 [accessed 10 Jan 2019]
49   Warner, p.133, Paul Sanford Methuen, 3rd Baron Methuen, born 1 September 1845, died 30 October 1932.
50   George Arthur Cookson, born 1860, died 1929.

quite another proposition, a bundle of nerves kept under control by an iron will! Either that or he was just beginning to be worked out or else, just for this once, the utter unexpectedness of a rapier thrust of fate got clean under his guard and ran him right through. [...] From the few remarks K let drop from time to time it was clear he regarded his Column Commanders in the West as babes in the wood when deprived of his guiding telegrams. The suspense was pretty bad. At last came the definite announcement that we were clean cut for an unknown time. At that K rose from his chair, went straight up to his room, and refused for the best part of two days and two nights to touch a bite. Not one single crumb. Only a rare cup of tea, and an absolute refusal to utter one word on business. We of the inner circle were aghast. Hubert Hamilton, his Military Secretary, was here, as ever, a great stand-by.[51] (Had he been by K's side in 1915 what a different war!) When I was at my wits' end what to do, and even harboured thoughts of consulting some outsider, he urged me [...] to put on a bold face to the outside world and [...] to carry on as if everything was quite normal.[52]

Kitchener's regular visitors, David Henderson[53] from Intelligence and Girouard, were 'warned off on some pretext or another.' After forty hours with lines of communication operational again, it was learned that Cookson had held back the Boers with the loss of 78 men, mostly Canadians, and 400 mules and horses. Hamilton's assessment was that '... there had been no calamity beyond an exhibition of bad generalship.'[54] When Rawlinson asked for 'someone on the spot to hold us together. Can't you send us Ian Hamilton,' followed by one from brother Walter the next day, Kitchener 'tossed' the telegrams to Hamilton saying, 'Here is that ass of a brother of mine supporting that ass Rawlinson. You had better go out to the Western Transvaal.' The result was Hamilton going, '... without any instructions at all, and not knowing whether to inspect and come back to report to K.'[55]

Hamilton had joined Kitchener at the end of 1901 when Roberts prompted Kitchener to have a Chief of Staff. Kitchener agreed, asking for someone who could provide an external perspective to help find an early end to the war. Royle, however, suggests Hamilton was sent to keep an eye on Kitchener, and having told him the purpose of his visit, Hamilton was given control of the columns working against the Boers. The result was co-ordinated and effective action, something Kitchener had been struggling to achieve.[56]

---

51 Hubert Ion Wetherall Hamilton, born 27 June 1861, died 14 October 1914.
52 Hamilton, *Anti-Commando*, pp.166-7.
53 David Henderson, born 11 August 1862, died 17 August 1921, not to be confused with George Francis Robert Henderson, born June 1854, died 5 March 1903, who had been intelligence officer for Roberts.
54 Hamilton, *Anti-Commando*, p.167.
55 Hamilton, *Anti-Commando*, p.168.
56 Royle, p.181; Arthur, vol 2, p.52.

As with all people in leadership positions Kitchener was called on to make tough decisions, such as what to prioritise: rail transport for military purposes, food for concentration camps or hospital trains. If he failed to prioritise military requirements, the war would drag on unnecessarily with financial implications as well as greater loss of life. Where he could, within what he saw as the military constraints, he tried to ease the burden on the soldier and internee. On his arrival in Cape Town with Roberts, Violet Cecil (Edward's wife) urged the two men to improve the quality of medical service for the men, as she had failed to get Milner to do so. By the spring of 1900 Roberts had doubled the number of nurses and the Cape Town hospitals had improved; it was a quick, easy solution. Recognising that the military men would have difficulty improving the hospitals immediately, she used to drag Kitchener to visit. 'He inspired awe wherever he went and I hoped that a good deal of cleaning was done from dread of these visitations.'[57] However, for greater change she ultimately turned to the press as the politicians refused to respond to her pleas. The War Office and officials seemed to be the block to improving the situation in South Africa. Violet's connections with both Salisbury and Arthur J Balfour, a cousin, were put to good use by Kitchener who used her as a conduit to complain about not getting stores and weapons: 'I imagine he did not tell me this for my *beaux yeux* so I pass it on to you.'[58] Kitchener was clearly aware that power lay with the politicians in London.[59]

The fight for peace

From the time he took command of the forces in southern Africa, Kitchener sought ways to bring about peace. His systematic clearing of the land and the blockhouse system, which had suddenly come to him one night,[60] were part of this, as were enticements to the Boers to surrender. In February 1901 he took the opportunity of sounding out Louis Botha as to the possibility of peace, using Botha's wife Annie as messenger. Annie carried a verbal message on 13 February to her husband, however, it took until 22 February for Kitchener to get the reply.[61] In anticipation of the meeting, Kitchener wrote to Broderick at the War Office that it would '… be good policy for the future of this country to treat them fairly well; and I hope I may be allowed to do away with anything humiliating to them in the surrender, if it comes off.'[62]

Six days later, Kitchener met Botha in Middleburg and discussed terms, as well as teaching him to play bridge. Importantly, trust was built which was to be repaid in

57   Riedi, *Imperialist Women*, p.13; Viscountess Milner, *Picture gallery*, p.164.
58   Riedi, *Imperialist Women*, p.16, letter to Balfour, 23 January 1900.
59   Surridge, *Civil-Military Relations*.
60   Sherson, *Townsend*, p.206.
61   Hodges, p.146.
62   TNA: CAB 37/56/27, telegram 22 February 1901 in Surridge, *Civil-Military Relations*, p.151.

the 1902 peace discussions. Kitchener reported that Botha had 'a nice unassuming manner' continuing that he '... is a quiet, capable man, and I have no doubt carries considerable weight with the burghers; he will be, I should think, a valuable assistance to the future good of the country in an official capacity.'[63]

As predicted, the talks broke off as Milner and the Colonial Office wanted unconditional surrender. Having foreseen this, Kitchener did not blame Botha,[64] despite a comment made in frustration about wanting to deport the 'savage boers'.[65] Kitchener wrote to Broderick:

> I did all in my power to urge Milner to change his views, which on this subject seem very narrow [...] there exists a small section in both Colonies who are opposed to any conciliatory measures being taken to end the war and I feel their influence is paramount; they want extermination and I suppose they will get it.
>
> [...] Milner's views may be strictly just but to my mind they are vindictive [...] We are now carrying the war on to put two or three hundred Dutchmen in prison at the end of it. It seems to be absurd and wrong.[66]

And he complained to Roberts after having been told the government would not accept amnesty for the rebels and wanted a clause accepted that black and coloured civil rights would be the same as in the Cape. 'I am much surprised the Cabinet were not more keen on getting peace as the expenditure on the war must be terrible.'[67]

The peace discussions highlighted the differences between the military and the civil in both Britain and South Africa.[68] Kitchener and Milner had a healthy respect for each other, their relationship dating to 1892 in Egypt. Despite each having habits which were annoying, the difference between a military and civilian outlook, they were similar in Imperial vision and getting the job done.[69] When Milner took three months' leave in 1901, his responsibilities fell on Kitchener, who in addition to conducting the war had to administer the British colonies of Cape and Natal.[70] He wrote to Milner reassuring him of the support his administrators were giving.[71] However, the two men clashed over what peace to conclude with the Boers. Kitchener wanted leniency whereas Milner wanted defeat and the unconditional surrender of

63   Arthur, vol 2, p.21.
64   Arthur, vol 2, p.25.
65   Smith & Stuki, p.419.
66   Hodges, p.147.
67   Kitchener to Roberts, 8 March 1901 in Surridge, *Civil-Military Relations*, p.153.
68   Surridge, *Civil-Military Relations*.
69   In 1892 when Kitchener was Sirdar and Milner Undersecretary in the Ministry of Finance, both believed it would be better for Britain to give up the charade of Egyptian control of the Sudan and to take it over completely. However, this would not work in practice. Royle, p.95.
70   Arthur, vol 2, p.28.
71   Bodleian: MS Milner Dep 175, Kitchener to Milner 31 May 1901, f.201.

the Boers.[72] Their differences brought old concerns to the fore. Milner did not trust Kitchener and saw his wanting to make a quick peace as part of his plan to further his own career.[73] Wilkinson, Chichele Professor of Military History at Oxford, believed Kitchener took the stance he did as he was tired of the war and keen to go to India which he had been promised. In addition, he believed Kitchener's compromise peace was the cause of problems in South Africa in the post-war years.[74] However, comments Kitchener made during the First World War that a lenient peace was important for the balance of power in Europe suggests his view in 1902 was not just for career enhancement. Offering the Madhi the opportunity to surrender in 1898 and a farewell speech on leaving India in 1909 further support the genuineness of the actions he took in southern Africa to bring about a conciliatory peace. When Milner failed to change Kitchener's strategy, he sought government's assistance to have Kitchener removed.[75]

With the support of Prime Minister Salisbury, the Queen whilst still alive, and, to a lesser degree, Broderick at the War Office, Kitchener remained in post. He was the only soldier at the time who stood any chance of being able to bring the war in Africa to a successful conclusion. As Hamilton identified, '... when it came to back to the wall business [Kitchener] became a king amongst his colleagues whoever they might be.'[76] By concentrating on military exigencies at the expense of politics, he was able to hold his own against Milner. He offered two options, either negotiate and have a long-lasting peace or deprive the Boers of their land completely and deport them, the latter prolonging the war indefinitely with associated expenses and the need for more troops.[77] In the short term the government hoped for the outcome of a negotiated peace through complete surrender and so prevaricated. Divisions in London led to undue pressure on Kitchener who became more obdurate, particularly when well respected officers such as George Benson were killed and others defeated. Milner having won support for his ideas whilst in London, was soon to discover Kitchener thought otherwise and on 1 November 1901, Milner wrote in exasperation:

> I do not think that my opinions, frequently expressed have any weight with the C.in.Chief ... He has probably more than the ordinary soldier's contempt for the opinions of a civilian, &, though he is always perfectly friendly & ready to listen, I find discussions of these matters with him quite unprofitable & am indisposed to continue it ... It is impossible to *guide* a military dictator of very strong views & strong character.[78]

72   Royle, p.182.
73   Royle, p.183.
74   Wilkinson, *Thirty-Five Years*, p.254.
75   Surridge, *Civil-Military Relations*, p.18.
76   Hamilton, *Anti-Commando*, p.165.
77   Surridge, *Civil-Military Relations*.
78   Milner to Chamberlain in Sturridge, pp.186-7.

Milner had also realised that trying to make two different systems work alongside each other was causing more damage than achieving a positive outcome; the camps being a case in point.

Thus, when, a year and a week later, Schalk Burger asked for permission to discuss with other Boer leaders about asking for peace, Kitchener permitted safe access and assisted them in getting together 'with unabated vigour'. However, to safeguard a return to combat, he refused to declare a general armistice but permitted local ones enabling Boer leaders to safely leave their men.[79] If the talks failed, technically fighting would pick up where it had left off. Accepting Kitchener's conditions, the Boer leaders met in Klerksdorp on 9 April 1902.[80] Later, in July 1915, Botha used a similar approach when he negotiated the conclusion of the German South West Africa campaign.[81]

Having conveyed their decisions to Kitchener, and approval from London being obtained, the Boer delegates met in Pretoria at Kitchener's Melrose House. A second meeting took place on 14 April which permitted sixty Boer delegates to confer with the people before reconvening on 13 May in Vereeniging. Following the meeting, on 17 May a commission of Boers travelled to Pretoria to negotiate with Kitchener and Milner. During these talks, the Boer leaders stayed with Hamilton, Kitchener's neighbour, a hole having been cut through the laurel hedge to enable the men to move between the two without passers-by becoming curious.[82]

Finally, on 28 May a draft proposal was handed to the Boer commissioners by Milner noting they were final, and were to be accepted as they stood or rejected within three days. The men returned to Vereeniging.[83] Independence was to be forthcoming at an undetermined date and the fate of the rebels would be determined by the Colonial governments and not as part of the peace talks. Steyn resigned as President of the Free State and eventually two days later de Wet changed his mind. According to Hodges:

> ... some of the delegates [told] Major Leggett, who was at Vereeniging at the time, [that] If we knew [...] Lord Kitchener would stay on in South Africa as Governor-General for two years, or even for a year, we are sure that the delegates would vote for peace.[84]

79   This caused some trouble for the Free State representatives as a misunderstanding of the requirements by CR de Wet and Steyn led to two days of unexpected attacks. De Wet, *Three Years' War*. Martinus Theunis Steyn, born 2 October 1857, died 28 November 1916, South African; Christiaan Rudolf de Wet, born 7 October 1854, died 3 February 1922.
80   Hodges, p.148.
81   Arthur, vol 2, p.89
82   *Rand Daily Mail*, 31 May 1961, p.4.
83   Hodges, pp.148-51.
84   Hodges, p.151.

Leggett told Kitchener who felt, 'The Government would not, nor should it, consent to the removal of Lord Milner.' After further deliberation the Boers arrived in Pretoria, an hour or so later than expected. It was not known how Milner would react; and tact was needed. Kitchener arranged for Milner to arrive an hour later, but it is not known what happened during that time. Richard Burton Haldane reflecting on the war, recalled that Milner '... was a man of most attractive qualities but was difficult to work with. I came at the end to wish that the negotiations before the war had been in the hands of a man of more diplomatic temperament and of qualities like those of Kitchener.' When de la Rey was ready to storm out of the final discussions, Kitchener restrained him with, 'Delegates cannot act so hastily. It is not civilized,' to which de la Rey conceded that Kitchener having 'been in many wars and many countries [...] knows best the manners and customs of the world.' The Treaty was approved 54 votes to six and signed on 31 May at 10.30 p.m. On signing the treaty, Kitchener shaking hands with the delegates said, 'We are good friends now.'[85]

> [T]hough the Boers had shown themselves to be good fighters, they had been badly led. Their generals, [Kitchener] explained, did not work together. Had de Wet when he entered Cape Colony been supported by other simultaneous movements, things might have been made very difficult for us. Boer farmers who were called out for a three weeks' raid obeyed the summons without hesitation, but they could not be induced to remain out for a day beyond the prescribed date, and took their departure as soon as their time was up. For Milner he had a high regard and a great personal admiration. He did not nevertheless consider that his presence at the Cape would promote reconciliation, because, quite unjustly, the Boers could not 'get it out of their wooden heads' that he had brought on the war.[86]

Haldane and Maxwell paid tribute to the diplomacy of the 'military machine': Kitchener '... strongly opposed the popular clamour for unconditional surrender, and [...] handled the British Cabinet, as well as the Boer leaders, and his principal colleague, Lord Milner, with remarkable dexterity.'[87] Objecting to the harsh terms of the 1919 Treaty of Versailles, Hamilton referred to Kitchener's role in the Peace of Vereeniging:

> How is it that the Boer War put an end to the feuds, race hatreds, bankruptcies, disorders and bloodshed which had paralysed South African progress for a generation, whilst the Great War has on the contrary inflicted race hatred, bankruptcy

85   Hodges, pp.15-4; Family tradition has it that Francis Reitz would not shake hands with Milner but did with Kitchener [Brenthurst Library: MS 272 Reitz Collection].
86   Rodd, *Memories*, chapter 1.
87   Magnus, p.230.

and murder over the best part of the old world from Ireland in the West to the Near East; including the whole of Central Europe which has been turned into a seething cauldron of hate? I'll tell you why it is; it is because our Politicians entirely ignored the ideals of those to whom we have raised this memorial by making a vindictive instead of a generous peace ... Lord Kitchener forced them to make a good peace in South Africa. For six months Lord Kitchener fought the politicians who wanted to make a vindictive peace, an 'unconditional surrender' peace as they called it; a peace which would above all things humiliate and wound the feelings of the conquered ... He beat them and made his own peace; a generous soldierly peace. He lent the Boers money; he rebuilt their farms; he rebuilt their dams; he re-stocked their farms ... within one year South Africa was smiling and so were we.[88]

Smuts, in England for Kitchener Day, 4 June 1936, spoke on the BBC. He reminded listeners that he had only met Kitchener once,

> ... during the peace negotiations at the end of the South African war. But that occasion was a very special one, where in a few days you get to know a man better than you would from years of normal intercourse. It was a testing occasion, and from it I carried away a very definite impression of Lord Kitchener. We fighters opposed to him had taken him to be a hard, ruthless, pitiless man, and in war time things are done which create that sort of impression. But our meeting revealed a different personality. [...] He revealed himself as far more human and sympathetic than I had expected. The war had taught him to entertain a high respect for his opponents, and he was anxious to avoid everything that might be wounding to them.[89]

Milner saw the Boers as defeated and needing to surrender whereas the Boer lawyers, Hertzog and Smuts, argued that the Boer Governments needed to negotiate the peace. 'This point Kitchener at once appreciated and conceded. It was a matter of form, but really of cardinal importance for the honour and self-respect of the Boer people.' Smuts then referred to the 'quiet moment' he took where Kitchener followed,

> ... and said to me that things were bound to work out better than appeared at the moment. [...] During those days of deep inner and outer conflict he made an impression on me of being a really big man with broad human sympathies and a practical knowledge of men and affairs which made him a powerful negotiator.

88   Ian Hamilton Archives 39/12/45 quoted in John Lee, 'Sir Ian Hamilton after the war: A Liberal general reflects', in Hugh Cecil & Peter H Liddle (eds), *Facing Armageddon: The First World War Experienced* (Barnsley: Pen & Sword, 2003).

89   *Rand Daily Mail*, 4 June 1936, p.7.

Lord Kitchener was not merely a great soldier, but he had real statesman-like qualities. He prevented the war from ending in a purely military surrender and did his best to create that human situation which was destined in less than a generation to work itself out to such happy results of the future peace of South Africa and the Union and its peoples. [...] When after the signing of the Vereeniging Peace, he met the Boer delegates, he addressed to them, in simple, soldiery language, words of such high praise and so soothing to their military and national self-respect that a deep and lasting impression was created and much of the sting was taken out of the sense of defeat and irreparable loss. And when 12 years afterwards he went to war again, tens of thousands of Boers fought alongside him in the same great cause.[90]

On the day South Africa became a Republic, 31 May 1961, the *Rand Daily Mail* journalist reflected on events fifty-nine years earlier: 'The warm, generous, manly Kitchener, who, in defiance of Lord Milner, had often openly expressed his detestation of the concentration camp system, rose to his feet and held out his hand to each of the Boer delegates in turn.'[91] That fifty-eight years after the Nationalists declared South Africa a republic, the one Imperialist who fought their corner is regarded with such disdain by a section of the white population shows how strong rhetoric can be, especially when a person is not able, or willing, to defend themselves.

Kitchener left for England three weeks after the peace was signed, receiving the Order of Merit for his services from King Edward VII on board the *Victoria and Albert* where the King was recuperating from an operation before the coronation. Kitchener was one of his first guests. 'Queen Alexandra burst into tears' on seeing the 'ferocious' Kitchener 'kneeling with bowed head before his master.'[92] Two months later, Kitchener attended the coronation with young Julian Grenfell as his page.

By the end of the war, Kitchener was better known to his military colleagues and politicians. Perceptions formed of him at this time were reinforced in the years to come. Hamilton captured the complexity of 'This K. of K. whom the British public with their queer flair for the Superman (however quaintly or cunningly he may disguise himself) have detected and hailed a national hero, – this inarticulate, talkative, uneducated, occasionally violent K. – and they are right.'[93]

Kitchener's duplicity was regularly used to achieve a particular goal, not necessarily personal. During the 1899-1902 war, he recommended harsh actions be taken, such as deportation, farm confiscations and stringent martial law conditions. This set the base line, however, his instructions for dealing with the reality were far more lenient. He made a clear distinction between military and civilian misdemeanours, encouraging

---

90   *Rand Daily Mail*, 4 June 1936, p.7.
91   *Rand Daily Mail*, 31 May 1961, p.4.
92   EEP Tisdall, *Unpredictable Queen: The Intimate Life of Queen Alexandra* (London: Stanley Paul, 1953) p.206.
93   Hamilton, *Anti-Commando*, p.165.

thorough consideration of incidents to ensure an accurate understanding of the underpinning motivation before passing judgment. Significantly, if a case was likely to result in the death sentence being awarded, the 'officer had to apply to Kitchener for a trial under a mixed commission, comprising a Judge of the Supreme Court and four commissioned officers.'[94] Hamilton recorded that Kitchener '... looked the other way when subordinates refused to burn, and he was all for good compensation and for rebuilding after the peace.'[95] Those close to him saw this softer, more human side, whilst others continued to see him as cold and calculating.

As a result of his achievement in South Africa, in July 1902, Kitchener was made Viscount Kitchener of Khartoum, and of the Vaal in the Colony of Transvaal, and of Aspall in the County of Suffolk.[96] A telegram to Salisbury a month before shows Kitchener's sensitivity to wider issues but also the challenges of mediating social perceptions. He wrote, '... instead of Vereeniging which is owned by Jews, I should prefer the title to be Kitchener of Khartoum and the Vaal. If there is any objection to this on account of it being a river, it is also a place.'[97] Anti-Semitism was prevalent at the time, but there is no evidence other than this statement to suggest that Kitchener may have been anti-Semitic. He spoke Hebrew, had spent years living in Palestine, had numerous Jewish friends and by all accounts was seen to be pro-Zionist in 1916.[98] In addition, the Jews who owned Vereeniging included Sammy Marks, with whom he was friendly and who gave him the statues which were supposed to surround a statue of Paul Kruger on Church Square in Pretoria.[99] This suggests Kitchener was using the jargon of the day where 'Jew' in this context referred to German or pro-German people of mainly Jewish origin who had benefited from the 1899-1902 war through their business interests in South Africa.[100]

94   CO Minutes 1900 summarised in Surridge, *Civil-Military Relations*, pp.227-8.
95   Hamilton, *Anti-Commando*, pp.27-8.
96   *London Gazette*, No 27459, 29 July 1902, p.4834.
97   Hatfield House: Salisbury papers, 11 June 1902.
98   Samuel Daiches, 'Lord Kitchener: In memoriam', in *The Zionist Review*, vol 1, no 2 (June 1917).
99   See chapter The Private Kitchener.
100   Surridge, *Civil-Military Relations*; Shira D Schnitzer, Imperial longings and promised lands: Anglo-Jewry, Palestine and the Empire, 1899-1948 (DPhil Modern History, University of Oxford, 2006) pp.28ff.

5

Lessons learnt: Reforming the War Office, 1902

Kitchener returned to England a hero – at least to the people. Politically opinions were divided as they had been before, the difference now being that some were prepared to stand up to him. Broadly speaking, the divide was to follow party political lines with Kitchener being associated as Conservative. Party politics, however, was not for Kitchener. What he did, he did for monarch, empire and Britain.

During his time in South Africa, Kitchener had been frustrated, challenged and stimulated. He relished bringing order out of chaos, but was easily frustrated and annoyed at inflexible systems and when politicians and officials refused to change and meet his demands. Some in London felt the same, no doubt spurred on by Chancellor Michael Hicks Beach's[1] concern at the cost of modernising an antiquated military system. The additional pressure of having to cope with the Boxer Rebellion in China helped to highlight further shortcomings in the British Army with the result that reform was called for. And for some, such as Haldane, Kitchener was the best placed person to oversee the reform.

Already in 1895 changes to the role of Commander-in-Chief had been made, Wolseley was unhappy at being made subordinate to a civilian, the Secretary of State for War. When Roberts was brought back from South Africa, he took over from Wolseley and after various struggles with Broderick, Under Secretary of State, was able to get greater clarification of the role. It was apparent the whole system needed upgrading.[2] Haldane on 2 October 1902, '… despaired of [the War Office] until they let loose in it somebody like Lord Kitchener,'[3] and he was not alone. Broderick had already told Kitchener in November 1900 '… that there is a very strong feeling, not only in the Cabinet, but outside, that your presence at the War Office, as soon as you can be spared from South Africa, would give much confidence.'[4] The 1899-1902 war

---

1   Michael Hicks Beach, 1st Earl St Aldwyn, born 23 October 1837, died 30 April 1916.
2   Surridge, *Civil-Military Relations*.
3   Rye, p.183.
4   Arthur, vol 2, p.118.

had brought home to the civilian establishment that pre-1900 reforms had gone too far towards reducing the efficiency of the military structure, but, as will be seen and as Kitchener feared, there was little chance of the soldiers being given too much power in any reforms.

Returning to England in mid-1902, Kitchener felt the pressure. In response to George Wyndham's suggestion that he go to the War Office, Kitchener replied:

> I would sooner sweep a crossing ... I have no intention of going to the War Office in any capacity; so if India goes to anyone else I shall have what I really want – a good long rest; and perhaps it will be the end of my military career ... Regarding the work, it is not easy to explain, but I should be a hopeless failure at the War Office, under the existing administration [...] as you say, I must not do what I wish, but what is good for the country. I am quite willing to sacrifice myself if I could do good. I sometimes wish I could get a bullet through my brain, as some of my best friends have had.[5]

Lord Minto attending a lunch hosted by the Duke of Connaught[6] was told by Kitchener that 'One could run a War Office elsewhere for a year without the War Office finding one out.' His dread of the War Office could only have been reinforced by Minto's 1902 discovery that, 'There have only been telephones at the War Office for the last few months, for fear, it is said, that some one should say something down them of which there was no record!'[7] Eventually, in October 1902 he escaped to Rome where he was '... in his element exploring the Forum and Palatinate with [Giacomo] Boni.'[8] Even there, the War Office loomed, Rodd recalling:

> As for the War Office, over which he could hardly then have foreseen he would one day be called to preside, he observed that only by digging up its foundations and beginning again from the bottom could that fossil institution ever be improved.[9]

Kitchener was in despair and anxious to get to India. Roberts, however, seemed to understand having told Lansdowne in 1900 that Kitchener was temperamentally

5   Arthur, vol 2, p.119.
6   Gilbert John Elliot-Murray-Kynynmound, 4th Lord Minto, born 9 July 1845, died 1 March 1914 was Governor of Canada from 1898 and then Viceroy of India from 1905. Duke of Connaught and Strathearn, born Arthur William Patrick Albert, 1 May 1950, died 16 January 1942, also known as Prince Arthur, was seventh son of Queen Victoria and Grand Master of the United Grand Lodge of England.
7   John Buchan, *Lord Minto: A Memoir* (London: Thomas Nelson, 1924) p.199.
8   Giacomo Boni, born 25 April 1859, died 10 July 1925, engineer, archaeologist.
9   Rodd, *Memories*.

unsuited to the position.[10] When Queen Victoria was appealed to, she tactfully remained neutral: 'Upon the very important question of Lord Kitchener's ultimate employment, here or elsewhere, the Queen thinks it not possible to decide anything yet.'[11] If Kitchener could not get India, he would '... require a rest for a while [...] having had practically no leave for a very long time.' A 'thorough change' would be welcome, possibly 'some more civil work,' and maybe 'find my way back to Egypt again.'[12]

Kitchener recognised the need for the army and support systems to change. He was a firm believer in systems being there to serve the people, not the people to serve the systems.[13] His recent experiences in South Africa had made that clear, but he was also aware what it would take having tried to implement transport changes in 1899. Before that, he had turned the Egyptian Army into a fighting machine. War brought home what reform was needed and often gave the impetus for change, but reform could only effectively happen during peace time and for Kitchener, this was the stumbling block in Britain: the country had no culture of militarisation and baulked at the idea of conscription, although this did not stop him from encouraging men to be ready and trained for time of war. As he told the men of Westpool, he hoped no campaign would last long enough to enable them to be trained in the art of war.[14]

His interest in how the War Office was being reformed remained. In 1905, an election year, Kitchener wrote to Ettie Grenfell from Simla about 'Joe's campaign'[15] and the military reforms being undertaken.

> It will be interesting to see how the war office emerges from the application of naval acquisition I can hardly believe it will be a success. Another commission, but not a soul on it that really knows what medium it would to produce and that is generally an easy consideration when a machine is being constructed. Much love to Julian and Billy what splendid boys they are I expect one of them will have to be prime minister.[16]

The following year he asked Haldane to let him have the Army Service Corps officers' course notes which had been introduced at the London School of Economics (LSE) so he could use them in India.[17] And he gave his views on what needed to change

10   Magnus, p.212.
11   Arthur, vol 2, p.118.
12   Letter in reply to Roberts dated 16 Feb 1901 in Arthur, vol 2, p.118 fn1.
13   Kellett, p.33.
14   Rye, p.183; Arthur, p.111.
15   Joseph Chamberlain who was campaigning for Tariff Reform.
16   Hertford Country Archive: DEX/789/C22.
17   Geoff Sloane, 'Haldane's Mackindergarten: A radical experiment in British Military History', in *War in History* (July 2012) vol 9, no 3, p.348.

in the British Army.[18] The army needed to be organised into standard units, peace time formations should remain intact in time of war, and the commander must know his subordinates. This latter point was more important than the necessary technical training. Specifically, he cautioned in his report after the 1899-1902 war:

> In urging the formation of a separate transport department, I would point out that there is no more important work in any branch of the Army, and none in which a thorough and careful training is more necessary, more especially at a time like the present when mechanical transport will probably be an important adjunct to the military transport system.[19]

It was a pity Jan Smuts did not take heed of this when he went into German East Africa, although knowledge and the difficulty of transport was one reason Kitchener did not want to launch an active campaign in East Africa in the 1914-18 war. Sudan had shown how transport, effectively planned, made a positive impact on the mobility of an armed force especially regards welfare, whilst the 1899-1902 war did the opposite. The role of railways became significant with Kitchener employing John Cowans[20] in 1914 to organise railway support for the British Expeditionary Force in France. In the meantime, he used what he had learned to reform the Indian Army. His experience of the East, Egypt and Turkey as well as Palestine had shown him that India was key to protecting that part of the British Empire and not having Indian experience, he '... could look at military matters from a larger standpoint than that of India alone.'[21]

18   Ballard, pp.133ff.
19   Rye, p.186.
20   John Stephen 'Jack' Cowans, born 11 March 1862, died 16 April 1921, Deputy Assistant Quartermaster General 1898, Director General Military Education for the Indian Army 1907, Quartermaster General 1912.
21   Arthur, vol 2, p.120.

6

Patriotism and Personality: India, 1902-1909

Nathanial Curzon, Viceroy of India, asked Kitchener to go to India back in 1900 and then again in 1901, however, many others, including Queen Victoria, were not keen to see him there. Once again rumour masked his true personality and they thought he would be too insensitive to the Indians. Broderick, his chief at the War Office wanted Kitchener in London to reform that office but finally gave in and told Kitchener when South Africa was over, he could go to India.[1]

In anticipation of his Indian appointment, whilst still in South Africa, Kitchener started learning Hindustani and on board ship was known to spend four hours a day working at the language.[2] Although he never publicly spoke any of the Indian languages, he could follow a conversation in Hindi and a number of dialects but preferred using an interpreter to ensure he did not cause any one group offence.[3] Kitchener was fluent in various languages, including English, French, German, Turkish and Arabic, the last he had learnt alongside Hebrew whilst in Palestine, and was one of the few British officers familiar with it.[4] His knowledge of languages extended beyond the vernacular to an understanding and appreciation of the culture; a valuable asset as he had discovered in Zanzibar (French, German and Arabic), at Fashoda (French) and being a prisoner-spy (Arabic).[5] Later in 1914, French would prove invaluable and in Egypt he would draw on his knowledge of Turkish having studied the language and Turkish law before his appointment.[6] Whilst in India, Kitchener introduced an exchange programme with Japan in which British officers proceeding to Japan were expected to learn the language; Ian Hamilton was the first

1   Royle, p.178; David Lambert and Alan Lester (eds.) *Colonial Lives Across the British Empire: Imperial Careering in the Long Nineteenth Century* (Cambridge: Cambridge University, 2006) p.302.
2   Warner, p.132.
3   Pollock, pp.201, 250.
4   Warner, pp.2-3, Churchill, *River War*, p.190.
5   Warner, p.33.
6   BL: ADD 52276B, letter 8 October 1908 Kitchener to Conk; Warner, p.60.

to go whilst Captain Otohiko Azuma was sent to India in November 1903. This followed on from a prolonged stay by General Fukushima Yasumasa who had fallen ill whilst there.[7] Feedback by Hamilton following a visit to Japan to observe the Japanese General Staff during the 1904-5 Russo-Japanese war convinced Kitchener he was doing the right thing.[8]

Within weeks of arriving in India, Kitchener observed army manoeuvres between 24 November and 22 December 1902, Rawlinson recalled Kitchener looking 'very fit' but not very impressed:

> ... the organization of the army is all higgledy-piggledy, and has no relation to what it may have to do in war. There is a rigid, narrow bureaucratic system, which he means to break down, and he groans over the number of minutes which he has to read and write. He will have a stiff job, for many of the older officers of the Indian Army will oppose him tooth and nail; but he will get support from the younger men, who are well up in their professional duties and see what he is aiming at.[9]

The Coronation Durbar took place in early January 1903. It was Curzon's moment to shine, and in the detailed record of the event, we get another glimpse into Kitchener. His camp '... quarters including an elegantly furnished dining-room tent, hung in red and white, where as many as sixty covers might be laid on a table resplendent with the gold and silver plate presented by grateful citizens.' He had stay with him, Lord and Lady Stanley, Countess of Powis, George Dashwood and Miss Dashwood, Henry Rawlinson, Richard Solomon the Advocate-General of the Transvaal who had helped draw up the terms of the Vereeniging Peace, his daughter who was to marry Percy Girouard, Mrs Adair, TY Allen, Walter Long and his wife, Pandeli Ralli, Arthur and Winifred Renshaw, Frank Rhodes and Sybil Adeline Thesiger. His brother Walter who attended the Durbar does not seem to have been part of Kitchener's camp.[10]

Intriguingly, Curzon made only one reference to Kitchener in *Leaves from a Viceroy's note-book*. This was in connection with the Coronation Durbar attended by the Duke and Duchess of Connaught and the Grand Duke Hesse. Curzon wanted to know what hymn the 'British Tommy would be most likely to sing with hearty vigour',

7   Rye, pp.241-2; Phillips O'Brien, *The Anglo-Japanese Alliance, 1902-1922* (London: Routledge, 2003); Selçuk Esenbel (ed.) *Japan on the Silk Road: Encounters and Perspectives of Politics and Culture in Eurasia* (Leiden: Brill, 2018) pp.39-40.
8   Royle, p.216.
9   Atwood, *Rawlinson*, p.81.
10 Stephen Wheeler, *History of the Delhi Coronation Durbar* (London: John Murray, 1904) p.54. Daughter of Edward Pierson Thesiger, born 16 February 1883, died 19 February 1954. In 1910 in Australia, Sybil's niece, Miss Thesiger accompanied her father Lord Chelmsford, Acting Governor General, to a banquet in Kitchener's honour [*The Sydney Morning Herald*, 11 January 1910, p.6, Richard Solomon, born 18 October 1850, died 10 November 1913.

to which Kitchener '... unhesitatingly replied, *Onward! Christian Soldiers*. [...] I was doubtful how it would be regarded by King Edward when he heard of it [it talks of end of monarchs]. So I passed my pencil through the Commander-in-Chief's choice, and selected some more innocent strophe':[11] *Fight the Good Fight with all Thy Might*, along with *O God, Our Help in Ages Past*.[12]

Contrary to general perception, Kitchener consulted. He did his homework before arriving in a way that aroused no suspicion, asking William Nicholson,[13] who had served in India from 1871 and been with him in South Africa, to explain the Indian system. On being told '... that the head of the Indian Army, corresponding to the Secretary of State for War in England, was the Military Member of Council [Kitchener] exclaimed, "Then I ought to have been Military Member of Council".'[14] Before Kitchener arrived in India, Roberts responded to Lord Glenesk[15] concerned that, 'Even if Kitchener could do the work of the Commander-in-Chief and the Military Member – which I do not admit – it is very unlikely that any future Chief would possess the ability, the energy, and the power of work that he has.' Kitchener's arrival as Commander-in-Chief ended a four-year hiatus where the Military Member had in effect been doing the Commander-in-Chief's job. Remedying matters, that is reclaiming the power the Commander-in-Chief previously had, as a minimum, would lead to friction.[16] Effectively what Kitchener did was no different to what Wolseley and Roberts himself had tried to do vis-a-vis the Commander-in-Chief role in England post 1895: ensure greater say for the military command within the constraints of the constitution.[17] But as Hamilton aptly pointed out to Marker, 'It seems such a pity that we always make such a mess of things, but it must be so where personality is stronger than patriotism.'[18]

Kitchener sought Roberts' opinion on whether Mixed or Homogenous brigades would be best in India: Mixed brigades would be good for frontier and local defence

11   Marquess Curzon of Kedleston, *Leaves From a Viceroy's Note-book* (London: Macmillan, 1926) p.20.
12   Wheeler, *Delhi Coronation Durbar*, p.145.
13   William Gustavus Nicholson, 1st Lord Ronaldshay, born 2 March 1845, retired 1912, died 13 September 1918.
14   Wilkinson, *Thirty-Five Years*, p.269.
15   Lord Glenesk, Algernon Borthwick, proprietor and editor of the *Morning Post*. Born 1830, died 1908.
16   Wilkinson, *Thirty-Five Years*, pp.269-70; George de S Barrow, *The Fire of Life* (London: Hutchinson, 1942) chapter 10. Kitchener replaced Arthur Power Palmer (born 25 June 1840, died 28 February 1904) as Commander-in-Chief.
17   Michael Roper, *The Records of the War Office and Related Departments, 1660-1964* (London: Public Record Office, 1996) p.106 summarises the situation where the Commander-in-Chief had been bypassed on military matters, resulting in a 1901 Order in Council stating that the Commander-in-Chief remained 'the principal adviser to the Secretary of State on all military questions. [...] and the general supervision of of other military departments.'
18   Peter King, *The Viceroy's Fall: How Kitchener Destroyed Curzon* (London: Sidgwick & Jackson, 1986) p.185 Hamilton to Marker.

whereas homogenous brigades were best for 'a big war, with seven or nine Divisions in the field' as supply and transport would be problematic. Kitchener therefore proposed separate Brigades which trained together and fought as Mixed Brigades locally but would be separate for other conflicts.[19] He appointed an advisory board which met weekly to consider army reforms,[20] and when ideas did not work as envisaged, changes were made and continued to be made, including after he had left, until a workable system was achieved.

Kitchener renumbered the regiments, allowed certain battalions to retain their historical titles as part of their new number,[21] and re-organised the defences. The Brigade structure was reconfigured with one British brigade for every two Indian brigades and Divisional commanders were made responsible for training. He positioned divisions across the country in a manner which allowed them to back each other up if needed.[22] Sensitive to the needs of the rank and file, he proposed a route to equality of promotion for Indians and reminded British officers of the correct etiquette when dealing with Indian officers and rank and file. He found a middle route which he hoped was acceptable.[23] People were promoted on merit, personal feelings and rites of passage aside, as noted by the appointments of Archibald Hunter, and later, in 1908 Edmund Barrow to Lieutenant General of the Inspectorate of the Southern Army.[24] He increased pay and grants for equipment and reduced the maximum age for an officer to serve from 52 to 50, determining that younger agile men who could deal with the hardship of service were required. He was reluctant to see officers in administrative or civil roles promoted,[25] the significance of which would become apparent in East Africa 1914-16 when administrators such as Wilfrid Malleson[26] took command in the field.

The war in South Africa had been complex, fought on numerous fronts compared to those fought in Egypt and provided many valuable lessons and insights, not least the need for a General Staff and men trained in the art of war, especially administration and strategy. Spurred by the prohibitive cost of travel to England, in 1905, he introduced the staff college at Quetta based on that at Sandhurst, Camberley and in

19   Arthur, vol 2, pp.166-7 quoting letter 4 Dec 1904 Kitchener to Roberts.
20   Barrow, *Fire of Life*, pp.89ff.
21   Arthur, vol 2, p.127.
22   Royle, p.216.
23   Arthur, vol 2, p.180-3.
24   Arthur, vol 2, p.140; Edmund George Barrow, born 28 June 1852, died 3 Jan 1934. Military Secretary to the India Office 1911-1917.
25   Adam John Prime, The Indian Army's British Officer Corps, 1861-1921 (PhD, University of Leicester, 2018) p.76.
26   Wilfrid Malleson, born 1886, died 1946; David Brock Katz, 'A clash of military doctrine: Brigadier-General Wilfrid Malleson and the South Africans at Salaita Hill, February 1916', in *Historia*, vol 62, no 1 (2017).

1906 Cowans was appointed Director General of Military Education in India.[27] In addition, Kitchener introduced finance responsibilities for officers. Again, his time in South Africa had shown the value of having a financial adviser available and men trained in keeping accounts.

During the 1899-1902 war, Kitchener finding the finances complex and overbearing requested assistance. Guy Fleetwood Wilson,[28] who arrived 13 March 1901, discovered many purchases 'had been made very unwisely' in Cape Town and organised an Auditing Committee. Finding appropriate officers for the task had been a challenge though as the War Office was 'literally worked to death' and the Finance branch was possibly the 'hardest-worked branch'. The chancellor was anxious 'in regard to the large expenditure of public money which was continually going on,' and had been applying pressure to reduce costs.[29] Ever cautious when it came to spending money, Kitchener had recommended local contracts be issued as it '... would admit of a great reduction in the Army Service Corps staff, that supplies could be got as well, if not cheaper, in South Africa, and that supplies would be more satisfactory.'[30] When Wilson left in July 1901, Oliver Carleton Armstrong[31] became financial adviser. However, in 1902 Kitchener's replacement Neville Gerald Lyttleton[32] did not feel one was necessary and Armstrong was instructed to resolve outstanding queries and close the accounts. Making Indian Army officers responsible for managing their own finances would go a long way to keeping costs down.

No doubt, the changes he introduced to the Indian Army ruffled some feathers, but with the support of the Viceroy and the improvement in conditions for the Indians, Kitchener could continue. However, when it came to the system of dual control and a perceived challenge to the Viceroy's authority, matters came to a head. Cromer explained: 'The Commander-in-Chief should be the servant of the Viceroy and his Council; under Lord Kitchener's system he will inevitably tend to become their master.'[33] Increased tension on the Afghan border spurred Kitchener to action: a reformed system had to be in place before war was declared;[34] and as past experience indicated, Kitchener was least effective when rushed. The outcome was that London had to make a choice – Curzon or Kitchener. Although the India and War Offices agreed with Curzon's view, supported initially by Roberts, there would be political repercussions in England if Kitchener resigned; so, as previously, they backed

27   Royle, p.216; Desmond Chapman-Huston and Owen Rutter, *General John Cowans: The Quartermaster General of the Great War*, vol 1 (London: Hutchinson, 1924) pp.125ff.
28   Guy Douglas Arthur Fleetwood Wilson, born October 1850, died December 1940.
29   *Rand Daily Mail*, 11 August 1905, p.4.
30   *Rand Daily Mail*, 11 August 1905, p.4; *The Royal Commission on War Stores in South Africa*, vol 1, Minutes of evidence (London, HMSO, 1906) pp.11-3.
31   Oliver Carleton Armstrong, born 1859, died 1932.
32   Neville Gerald Lyttleton, born 28 October 1845, died 6 July 1931.
33   Zetland, *Lord Cromer*, p.244.
34   Royle, p.209.

Kitchener.[35] Cromer, however, believed the government 'had been guilty of an unpardonable surrender' by giving in to Kitchener's threat to resign.[36]

The underlying issue concerned the separation of military and civil power.[37] In short, Kitchener looked to centralise some functions which would save costs and support the army in the field either at home or abroad in time of war, whilst decentralising other functions would allow officers to respond flexibly to any given situation they encountered. As with all systems where people are involved, and as Hamilton observed, politics and personalities got in the way and the new system was to prove just as troublesome.[38] Roberts' assessment of others in the role not being as able as Kitchener was proved right when, within three years of implementation, dual control was effectively abolished, although it continued in varied form through to 1914 when some felt the system cracked.[39] That India was able to send troops to the Western Front and Africa as rapidly and effectively as happened is credit to the changes Kitchener sought to make. His system was not perfect, and by the time war erupted in 1914, it had been tweaked on numerous occasions. While the incumbent Commander-in-Chief Beauchamp Duff,[40] worked with Kitchener until instructed otherwise, the Military Secretary to India, George Edmund Barrow, clashed with him; Kitchener having blocked Barrow's appointment as Military Supply Member in 1905 when the role of Military Member was changed.[41] In addition, when war was declared, many officers and officials were on leave in London. Blaming one man for the collapse of a system introduced a decade before seems a little unfair, particularly when many who held significant posts in the 1914-18 war had served or trained as part of that system. Men such as Haig, Birdwood, Byng and Hamilton.

On 12 August 1905, Curzon resigned. John Buchan[42] provides a view on the controversy, which, when taken with the subsequent cordial relations between the two men, warrants some consideration:

> Curzon was tired and out of health, and a difference which might easily have been settled was allowed to become a clash of adamantine principles. More serious was the other step which the Viceroy took in his last year of office. The Presidency of Bengal was proving unwieldy for a single provincial government, and Lord Curzon decided to separate the flat wet plains and jungles of

35 Royle, p.209.
36 Zetland, *Lord Cromer*, p.244.
37 King, *Viceroy's Fall*.
38 Royle, p.214.
39 Royle, p.214.
40 Beauchamp Duff, born 17 February 1955, died 20 January 1920, replaced Kitchener as Commander-in-Chief Indian Army in 1909.
41 Royle, pp.212-3; George Edmund Barrow, born 1852, died 1934; 1908 GOC Southern Army India, 1917 Member of Council of India, retired 1919.
42 John Buchan, later 1st Baron Tweedsmuir, born 26 August 1875, died 11 February 1940.

the eastern section and combine them with the province of Assam. This gave the Mohammedans a majority in the new province, and thereby inflamed the Hindus of Bengal, who saw in it a menace to their religious preponderance, and to the importance of Calcutta. The cry arose that the Bengali nation had been insulted and split in twain, and, the sensational triumph of Japan over Russia having kindled the race-consciousness of the East, in the autumn of 1905 a very pretty campaign began of boycott and agitation.[43]

Through the whole controversy Mary Curzon stood by her husband which resulted in her friendship with Kitchener coming to an end. Inadvertently, Mary might well have helped Kitchener formulate his ideas as he had come to rely on her as a sounding board and she mediated between the two men. Kitchener's '... utter dependence upon me appealed so strongly to me – more because liking me as a woman he talked to me as a man,' which gave her the confidence she needed to be a 'political wife rather than [the] wife of a politician.' During the 1905 army reorganisation Mary and Kitchener discussed the health of the Indian Army, Mary contributing new ideas she had read about concerning tropical medicine. The friendship was close. She wrote to her mother, 'Lord Kitchener has got a fourth of July [1903] dinner for me and had got American Flags made in my honour! So I shall celebrate our victory with a British Commander himself.' Curzon failed to understand his American wife's draw to celebrate aspects of her heritage. A year later, when Mary gave birth to another daughter, Kitchener seemed to deal with the situation most diplomatically, writing to her that although he knew she would have '... preferred a son, [...] the main thing is that you are well again. I was driving with the Viceroy when he got the telegram he was so thankful you had got through all right. I had a long talk with him after dinner.' Later he wrote again, 'I am so glad to hear you are pleased with the young lady who has given so much trouble and hope you are now quite well and strong again.'[44] Mary tried to keep the friendship going, but the political intrigue between those supporting Kitchener and those behind her husband proved too strong and the conflict became personal. On the day the Curzons left India, Kitchener attended for the sake of appearances, Mary recording a simple 'Goodbye' before walking on. 'Lord K never moved. He raised his white helmet and stood like a sphynx as our procession moved away.'[45] For those who knew him well, this was his way of disguising strong emotions. On 18 July 1906, Mary died aged thirty-six from a heart attack.

Milner was offered the position of Viceroy but refused as Kitchener was still Commander-in-Chief.[46] As much as the two men respected each other, Kitchener having supported the twenty-one year old Milner's initiation as a Freemason to

43   John Buchan, *Lord Minto*, pp.213-4.
44   Nicola Thomas, Negotiating the boundaries of gender and empire: Lady Curzon, Vicerine of India 1898-1905 (PhD, University of Oxford, 2001).
45   King, *Viceroy's Fall*, p.217.
46   King, *Viceroy's Fall*, p.208.

Grecia Lodge No 1105 on 2 December 1890,[47] Milner's most recent experience of working with him had shown how challenging it could be. Emotions were still raw and smarting after the South African peace discussions, and unlike Egypt where both men had senior officers to mediate, in India, as with South Africa, it would be a direct clash of styles and views. Added to the India challenge would be Milner arriving cold into the conflict whereas with South Africa, he had been in post for a number of years before Kitchener's arrival. The thirty-six year old Imperial administrator could afford to be more discerning in what he chose to do, and taking on fifty-five year old Kitchener was not one of them.

Gilbert John Elliot-Murray-Kynynmound, otherwise known as Lord Minto was prepared to work with Kitchener and was accordingly appointed Viceroy of India, arriving on 17 November 1905.[48] The issue of the Commander-in-Chief and Military Secretary had been the final straw for Curzon, but, it was to be the first issue Minto tackled. Finding Kitchener someone with '... whom he could work [...] in perfect confidence and ease, a fellow-soldier who spoke the same tongue as himself, a friend whose humour and loyalty made him an admirable colleague,' they were able to agree on a system which was implemented on 19 March 1906. The two men then worked together to articulate their concerns over Russian influence on India and Afghanistan.[49] Kitchener thought the new Viceroy 'first rate' and Secretary of State for India John 'Morley well disposed.'[50]

Not long after Minto had arrived, Kitchener threatened, or appeared to want, to resign as St Loe Stratchey wrote to Curzon that he met Morley,

> ... by chance in Edinburgh and had a long talk with him about the Indian Army question. His attitude then seemed most satisfactory but that was three weeks ago and I do not know whether there have been any recent developments. One thing I was especially pleased with was the determination wuth [sic] which Morley said that he had caused it to be intimated to Kitchener that if he threatened resignation, such resignation would be at once accepted and that no opportunity would be given for withdrawal. I do not think he has any intention of being bullied by the threat that he may be held up to the country as the man who drove the greatest soldier of the age out of the British Army. I told him that in my belief Kitchener would never resign but would stick like a limpet to his post, at all costs.[51]

---

47   MoFM: Kitchener biographical file: LF 1105.
48   King, *Viceroy's Fall*, p.208.
49   Buchan, *Minto*, pp.224-5.
50   NAM: 7807-25-39, Kitchener to Frank 2 August 1906. John Morley, born 24 December 1838, died 23 September 1923, Secretary of State for India 1905-1910.
51   PA: STR 4/17/3, St Loe Stratchey to Curzon 3 Feb 1906, pp.4-5, John St Loe Stratchey, born 9 February 1960, died 26 August 1927.

The issue with Curzon left Kitchener a wounded animal. His threatened resignation was in keeping with past actions which he had found stressful: an expression of his desire to get away and regain control of a situation. Kitchener was also keen for Lady Salisbury, Alice, and her family to visit but she could not get away.[52] By this time, he had settled into a more friendly relationship with the Viceroy, St Loe Stratchey informing Curzon that, 'Minto has so completely gone over to the Kitchener side [making] the situation particularly embarrassing for Morley.'[53] And, in September, Kitchener was refuting as 'rot' the rumours that he had the Viceroy 'under my thumb' and that 'not only have I been careful but Minto also as this is the sort of thing he was told to expect.'[54]

Minto was not under Kitchener's thumb. Rather, Kitchener valued having another soldier to discuss his ideas with and whilst the two men were in charge in India, the military reforms appeared to yield positive results. Minto however, had to work on Kitchener to accept an Indian or Native Member on the Viceroy's Council and to allow Indian rank and file to progress to officer rank. Minto threatened placing his experimental regiments under the Foreign Office if Kitchener would not accept them in the Indian Army. He informed Morley, 'Kitchener is my strongest opponent ... he looks upon the appointment as an entire subversal of the old order of things. In this I told him I entirely agree with him, but that, in my opinion, with our knowledge of what is going on around us, we cannot stay as we are [...] I am almost inclined to think he was a little shaken ...'[55]

Rank and file

Given Kitchener's drive to improve the lot of the peasant and hard-done-by in Egypt, Cyprus, and Turkey, and his support for other Indian Army reforms, his reluctance to promote Indians to positions of equal rank with whites seems out of keeping.[56] In this regard, Kitchener was a product of the times. Colour, race and religious difference were not issues where Kitchener was concerned; education and level of development were. He often commented while travelling through places that 'Britain should take control' so that trade could improve, and corruption and exploitation be minimised. Commitment and loyalty were other considerations he valued; loyalty first to the British Empire and then to him. Minto's rejection of Kitchener's reasons as not 'very sound' for refusing to accept an Indian on the Viceroy's Council and an all

---

52   NAM: 7807-25-39, Kitchener to Frank 2 August 1906.
53   PA: STR 4/17/3, St Loe Stratchey to Curzon 28 Feb 1906.
54   NAM: 7807-25-40, Kitchener to Frank 14 September 1906.
55   Mary Minto, *India, Minto and Morley: Compiled from the Correspondence Between the Viceroy and the Secretary of State* (London: Macmillan, 1934) p.104 Morley to Minto, 6 March 1907.
56   Buchan, *Minto*, pp.240-2, 253.

Indian regiment suggests it was for these reasons. He ascribed Kitchener's reluctance to consider a Native Cadet Corps and Regiment to the conflict with Curzon over who would have oversight of them and questions about their education.[57] Kitchener appeared appeased by Minto's explanation that an Indian could, if he were a member of the Indian civil service, become lieutenant-governor of a province, hold the highest position on the bench, or even Governor of Bombay or Madras, but whatever his value as a soldier he could not rise above a very inferior rank. Minto was aware that at first few Indians might be found qualified for responsible commands, but he argued: 'We want to remove the disability for promotion to such posts which now exists. We can deal with the appointments to them according to the merits of the individuals when the time comes.'[58]

For those under his command, Kitchener introduced the idea that officers put their men first. His fundamental principle was to 'treat your men as you would like to be treated' with instructions going out that officers were not to eat until their men had done so and to ensure accommodation for rank and file was sorted before they looked to their own. He took great care in writing instructions to Indian Army officers setting out exactly what he wanted them to do and how they were to avoid contracting sexually transmitted diseases. This format was again followed during the First World War when he wrote to the rank and file about the behaviour expected of a soldier. He approved the changes Julian Byng[59] made to the 10th Hussar's uniform by replacing the high collar with a standard collar and tie. Despite opposition, Kitchener fully approved and had the idea introduced for the whole army.[60]

Warner tells a story of Kitchener's bodyguard at Intombi River during the 1899-1902 war suffering from scurvy and sores because Kitchener had not shown any interest in their welfare; his attitude possibly being the little respect held for them as a fighting force given their behaviour in action.[61] This experience might well have influenced the guidance he issued to his Indian officers: he did not want a repeat performance.

Generals were particularly important in ensuring their men were ready for war. He advised them not to consistently pick fault unless they could remedy the short-comings. They should be '... trusted leaders in war, and instructors in peace, and at all times [the soldiers'] ready helpers, able and willing to promote their welfare, and to spare no effort to increase their preparedness for the stress of active service.'[62] Respect was important and this could only be achieved by a thorough knowledge and

57   Minto, *India, Minto and Morley*, pp.261-3 Morley to Minto, 14 March 1908.
58   Buchan, *Minto*, p.278.
59   Julian Byng, GCB, GCMG, MVO, born 11 September 1862, died 6 June 1935, 1st Viscount Byng of Vimy.
60   Jeffery Williams, *Byng of Vimy: General and Governor General* (Barnsley: Pen & Sword, 1992) p.52.
61   Warner, p.136.
62   Rye, p.208.

its application. Young officers – commissioned and non-commissioned – were encouraged to put their learning into practise 'in their own way', with mistakes pointed out at the end so that their impact could be discerned. And, opportunities to work with the other armed services should be found and taken to ensure that all could work together.[63]

Finance

Kitchener's austerity was well-known, on occasion causing problems when he was too frugal. He no doubt inherited this trait from his father, but other experiences demonstrated how money was wasted if contracts were not carefully negotiated. On travelling through Turkey in 1877, in answer to his question why the railway line '... twisted and turned when a straight course might have been easily kept,' he:

> ... learnt that the railway had been contracted for at so much a kilometre; and so as many kilometres were got into the level land between Adrianople and Tatar Bazardjik. Beyond this the lesser Balkans have to be crossed, so the contractor found it worth while to pay one of the pashas a good round sum and get off his contract, having made a very good thing of it.[64]

Little has been said about Kitchener's 1899-1902 financial management other than Surridge noting the continual pressure by Hicks Beach to reduce costs.[65] Did he know Kitchener's concern on this front, which is why he pushed so hard knowing that Kitchener would do what he could to work on a shoestring? Or did he not understand the demands of war? Given Lyttleton's attitude to the financial adviser, one can only conjecture at the cost of the war had Kitchener and Milner not been in charge respectively. Kitchener had little faith in non-military men making decisions about what was best for the armed forces: experience of War Office and Treasury decisions influencing his view.

Thrifty himself, Kitchener believed it important that army commanders be trained in finance and urged the post-1899-1902 commission, Royal Commission on the War in South Africa, to simplify the system of accounting to enable 'officers [...] to effectively deal with the subject.'[66] Money was not to be wasted and where it could be saved, it should be, but not at the expense of performance. Whilst Kitchener accepted the reduction imposed by the Liberal Government on army reforms, he fought to ensure the financial security of the fighting forces. In 1905, a conference

---

63   Rye, pp.209-212; Arthur, pp.169-70; Magnus, pp.169, 179, 180, 208.
64   HHK, *Visit to Sophia*, p.194.
65   Surridge, *Civil Military Relations*.
66   Rye, p.189 on evidence to the Royal Commission post Boer War, 13 April 1903.

of lieutenant-generals proposed an increase of pay for junior ranks and suggested the army rates of pay be reviewed completely. This took three years to accomplish, but did not stop Kitchener reforming where he could.[67] Uniforms were streamlined to what was necessary, grants made available and travelling allowances fixed to ensure officers were fully compensated. Pensions were revised to retain men thereby reducing recruitment costs and improving military efficiency. He also looked at the cost of travel for leave and made suitable recommendations whereby paid furlough was agreed. No aspect was ignored.[68]

Similarly, cavalry soldiers had to know how to look after their horse, crucial to preventing '... unnecessary heavy wastage in the field which it may be difficult to supply.'[69] Kitchener himself had been taken to task by his subordinates for not acclimatising the cavalry sufficiently and driving the horses too hard whilst in South Africa.[70] This was rather surprising given his horsemanship – he trained and managed his own race horses both in Cyprus and India. However, his actions could be explained by the pressures he was under to end the war.

In India, Kitchener was very aware of the cost of ammunition noting that '... a man's annual allowance would only last about two days' fighting, and we have also to allow for preliminary training.'[71] He therefore encouraged Indian factories to manufacture arms and ammunition as this would be cheaper than imports from England. Creating local employment,[72] and making India self-sufficient in terms of war material if cut off from Britain during war, would be additional benefits. He set a target of three years, from 1904, to make India self-sufficient.[73]

To make army officers responsible for finance and to reduce wastage, Kitchener introduced accountability by compiling the Indian Army Estimates 'on a Divisional basis, showing clearly all sums for the administration of which each General Officer Commanding a Division or Independent Brigade is responsible. At the same time decentralization of the Military Accounts Department [was] carried out, by means of which each Divisional General [was] provided with a Financial Adviser.'[74] To iron out inefficiencies, he introduced an element of competition between brigades.[75] Kitchener's concern about costs filtered into all aspects of his life. In organising copies of the arms of the previous Commanders in Chief to be put in India, he asked Frank

67   Ballard, p.186.
68   Arthur, vol 2, pp.194-6.
69   Rye, p.215.
70   Warner, p.138.
71   Rye, p.245.
72   Rye, p.264.
73   Arthur, vol 2, p.200.
74   Rye, pp.292-3, Financial statement of the Government of India for 1909-1910.
75   Arthur, vol 2, pp.171-2.

Maxwell to 'not go to expense. Perhaps some of your many lady friends would sketch them for me.'[76] He was always on the lookout for a good bargain.

Along with his financial dexterity, Kitchener was an organiser: but not organised. He had a clear vision of how all elements of the armed forces should work. On assuming command of the Indian Army, he wrote an order setting out the requirements for each arm and how this was to be adapted for modern warfare. He constantly reiterated the importance of training: discipline whilst allowing for 'individual and initiative' was his aim as was little disruption between peace and war formations. He wrote to Alice during his time in South Africa: 'I try all I can day and night to get the machine to work, but a thorough reorganization will have to take place before we can call ourselves a fighting nation.'[77]

Clinton Dawkins, friend of Curzon, predicted the changes Kitchener's appointment to India would bring:

> (K) is spoken of as a great organiser in the sense that he can hold 100 threads in his hands and 1,000 details in his head, but that he is a great centraliser, and has very little appreciation of the proper organisation of a great administrator. He will obliterate the distinction between Commander-in-Chief and Military Member, and insist on doing the Military Member's work himself.[78]

His 'little appreciation of the proper organisation' referred to Kitchener's avoidance of paperwork at all costs. His office was always untidy with documents strewn all over the place, and on one occasion led to Curzon calling him a liar as he claimed not to have seen a document.[79]

Wilson, Financial Adviser to Kitchener in the 1899-1902 war, believed Kitchener could be a good liar if needed and would do so to protect the empire. He had witnessed Kitchener have contracts changed through such means, and was able to call his bluff on one occasion. Kitchener had been reluctant to sign an order which he eventually did in pencil. However, Wilson sealed it with wax, to enhance the initials and ensure Kitchener could not later erase it.[80]

76   NAM: 7807-25-38, Kitchener to Frank 5 July 1906.
77   Smithers, p.30.
78   Royle, p.199; Magnus, p.121; Dawkins was Undersecretary for Finance in Egypt during Kitchener's time, born 2 November 1859, died 2 December 1905, chaired the Committee on the Reorganisation of the War Office in 1901.
79   King, *Viceroy's Fall*, pp.210-1.
80   Guy Fleetwood Wilson, *Letters to Nobody, 1908-1913* (London: John Murray, 1921) pp.15-6.

7

Celebrity with nothing to do: World tour, 1909-1910

In 1907, Morley, on behalf of the Liberal Government, offered Kitchener a two-year extension to stay in India despite their clashes. Kitchener accepted rather than go to the War Office.[1] The offer, however, was strategic as Morley admitted to Lady Minto: 'If we are accused of making radical changes in India, I want it known that anyhow we are not tampering with the Army.'[2]

India was challenging and frustrating for Kitchener. Having clashed with Curzon, he then had to deal with a Secretary of State for India, Morley, who had his own sensitivities and little time for, or understanding of, Kitchener. When Kitchener made it known that he wanted to become Viceroy after Minto in 1909, Morley refused, threatening resignation if overridden.[3] One of the reasons Morley gave for rejecting Kitchener as Viceroy was that he was a soldier, but Minto had been a soldier.[4] Morley misunderstood Kitchener writing to Minto about trouble on the Frontier in early 1908:

> I think the policy of His Majesty's Government has been amply justified in the result; and the military part of the work has evidently been done to perfection. For this I cannot but feel that we owe Lord K. a special debt. I don't suppose that he had any taste for our policy of prompt and peremptory withdrawal, and yet he manifestly (and as I learn from letters) threw himself into the execution of it with as much care, skill, and energy, as if he had thought it the best policy in the world. That's the true soldier.[5]

Minto responded: 'K. is the very essence of caution as regards the frontier. I know no one more anxious to avoid punitive expeditions, possibly no doubt because he knows that with the vastly improved armaments of the tribes a frontier war on a big scale

1   Royle, p.220.
2   Minto, *India, Minto and Morley*, p.115, Lady Minto to her husband, 4 April 1907.
3   Royle, p.225; Warner, p.161.
4   Buchan, *Minto*, p.295.
5   Buchan, *Minto*, p.271, 4 March.

would be a very serious affair.'[6] Minto did all he could to change Morley's perception of Kitchener without success. On another occasion, Minto shared: 'The more I see of him, the more I admire his ability, excellent judgement, and level-headedness [...] He is a curious personality, not attractive in manner, but has a kind heart buried away somewhere, and his inner tastes are much more artistic than military.'[7] And another confirmed Kitchener's desire for Egypt ending with praise about Kitchener's administration and being a 'big man.'[8]

A year later, on Kitchener's departure, Minto wrote:

> I shall miss K. very much, for he has supported me most loyally always, and I look upon him as a real friend. We have differed – as, of course, we must occasionally – over certain things, but I have always found him very open to conviction. He is such a different man to what the outside public suppose him to be. In my humble opinion you could not select for the *gadi* a more reliable occupant.[9]

When, eventually, in 1910 Morley got to meet Kitchener, he:

> ... was a good deal astonished, for I had expected a silent, stiff, moody fellow; behold I could hardly get a word in, and he hammered away loud and strong with manly gestures and high tones. He used the warmest language, as to which I was in no need of such emphasis, about yourself; it was very agreeable to hear, you may be certain. He has the poorest opinion possible of your Council, not as an institution, but of its present members. He talked about the Partition of Bengal in a way that rather made me open my eyes; for, although he hardly went so far as to favour reversal, he was persuaded that we must do something in bringing the people of the two severed portions into some species of unity. We got on well enough – he and I – for nothing was said about his going to India.[10]

Birdwood in his foreword to Hodge's biography twenty years after Kitchener's death wrote:

> He was impatient certainly at times, for he was by nature impetuous, but he was always possessed of the most astonishing spirit of perseverance and determination to allow no difficulties to defeat him, never failing to return to the attack until he had achieved the object on which his heart was set.[11]

---

6   Buchan, *Minto*, p.271.
7   Arthur, vol 2, p.189, 30 November 1908.
8   Arthur, vol 2, p.263.
9   Buchan, *Minto*, p.295.
10   Buchan, *Minto*, p.307.
11   Hodges, Foreword.

The Kitchener family: Henry, Millie and the future Lord Kitchener on his mother's lap, 1851. (*The Illustrated War News*)

Lord Kitchener as a cadet at Woolwich Academy, about the age of 17. (From E.S. Grew, *Field-Marshal Lord Kitchener: His Life and Work for the Empire.* London: The Gresham Publishing Company, 1916).

Kitchener's father. (*Illustrated London News*)

Kitchener as a young officer. (*Illustrated London News*)

Kitchener as a young officer.
(*Illustrated London News*)

Major Kitchener in Sudan.
(*Illustrated London News*)

Photo taken by Kitchener of a newly-discovered synagogue at Susaf, Palestine. (*Palestine Exploration Fund, Quarterly Report*, 1877)

Kitchener and his brother, Henry.
(*Illustrated London News*)

Cyprus Survey Staff, 1883. (From www.militarysurvey.org.uk)

Kitchener's Cyprus Theodolite. (From www.
militarysurvey.org.uk)

Kitchener arriving home after the Sudan,
1898. (*Illustrated London News*)

Kitchener graduation, 1898.
(*Illustrated London News*)

Crowds welcoming home Kitchener
(*Illustrated London News*)

Kitchener's design of Khartoum. (*Illustrated London News*)

The Egyptian railway. (*Illustrated London News*)

Irene Concentration Camp memorial Park. (Anne Samson)

Kitchener at the Vereeniging talks ending the 1899-1902 war. (From E.S. Grew, *Field-Marshal Lord Kitchener: His Life and Work for the Empire*. London: The Gresham Publishing Company, 1916).

Melrose House, Pretoria where peace discussions took place, 1902. (Anne Samson)

Kitchener at King Edward VII's funeral procession, May 1910. (*Illustrated London News*)

The Amir of Afghanistan.
(*Illustrated London News*)

Kitchener, Commander in Chief and Sword
Bearer, organiser of King George V's
Coronation, 1911, painting by Cyrus Cuneo
ROI. (*Illustrated London News*)

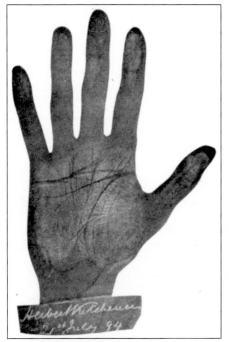

Kitchener's hand by Cheiro (From Cheiro,
Palmistry for all, New York: G.P. Putnam's,
1916)

Meeting Indian officers, 1911.
(*Illustrated London News*)

Kitchener the
traveller, 1911.
(*Illustrated London
News*)

Kitchener in Malta
1912, standing
with Leslie Rundle
on left, Fitzgerald
on right, Prime
Minister Asquith
seated. (*Illustrated
London News*)

Playing golf, 1910.
(*Illustrated London
News*)

h

With Lord
Robertson, 1916.
(*Illustrated London
News*)

Visiting Indian
wounded, 1916.
(*Illustrated London
News*)

Soldier Kitchener
in the War Office as
civilian Secretary of
State for War, 1914.
(*Illustrated London
News*)

Entertaining British wounded at Broome Park, 1916. (*Daily Sketch*)

With wounded
soldiers at
Broome, 1916.
(*Illustrated
London News*)

Visiting Indian
wounded, 1916.
(*Illustrated London
News*)

Leaving the War Office
to address the House of
Commons, June 1916.
(*Illustrated London News*)

On war business out of
uniform, 1916. (*Illustrated
London News*)

On HMS *Hampshire*, June 1916. (*Illustrated London News*)

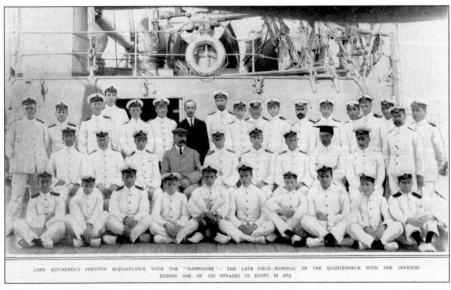

LORD KITCHENER'S PREVIOUS ACQUAINTANCE WITH THE "HAMPSHIRE": THE LATE FIELD-MARSHAL ON THE QUARTERDECK WITH THE OFFICERS DURING ONE OF HIS VOYAGES TO EGYPT, IN 1912.

The crew of HMS *Hampshire* which took him to Malta, 1912; how many drowned with him in 1916? (*Illustrated London News*)

Colleagues who drowned when HMS *Hampshire* sank, June 1916. (*Illustrated London News*)

SIR. H. F. DONALDSON,
Chief Technical Adviser to the Ministry of Munitions.

MR. L. S. ROBERTSON,
Assistant to the Director of Production at the Ministry of Munitions.

BRIG.-GENERAL WILFRID ELLERSHAW, R.A.,
On Special Service at the War Office.

MR. H. J. O'BEIRNE, C.V.O., C.B.,
Of the Foreign Office.

CAPTAIN H. J. SAVILL, R.N.,
Captain of H.M.S. "Hampshire."

Field memorial service for Kitchener, 1916. (*Illustrated London News*)

Church memorial service for Kitchener, 1916. (*Illustrated London News*)

The King and Queen
en route to say goodbye
to their friend,
Kitchener. (*Illustrated
London News*)

n

Older brother, H.E.C. Kitchener, the new Earl, 1916. (*Illustrated London News*)

Kitchener statue, Horse Guards, London. (Anne Samson)

Lord Wolseley, Horse Guards, London.
(Anne Samson)

Lord Roberts, Horse Guards, London.
(Anne Samson)

Lord Kitchener, Horse Guards, London.
(Anne Samson)

While a writer in the *Pioneer* said on Kitchener's leaving India: 'His reforms were wise, but perhaps his greatest wisdom was shown in what he left undone.' Kitchener had failed to change the way the Northern Frontier operated with bribes and different tribes playing against each other, instead he left it to the local Political Officers to manage the local situation.[12]

That Kitchener was reluctant to fight wars for the sake of fighting wars was supported by Minto: 'We both agree that we should sit tight at any rate for a little longer, although an expedition would be easy enough if we did not retire, and were permitted to occupy certain posts on our political frontier [...]'[13] In a farewell speech, Kitchener told his audience:

> It has not fallen to my lot, as it has to that of many of my distinguished predecessors, to include within my period of command the conduct of any great campaign … Perhaps you will expect me to say that I regret this – to mourn that wars, and the opportunities of distinction that wars bring to soldiers, have been so few and so fleeting during the past seven years. But, indeed, my feeling on that subject is the very reverse. It is well that the younger officers should long for war, that they should burn to show their zeal and their devotion in the fiery test of battle. But it would not be well that the Commander-in-Chief who, sitting as he does on the Viceroy's Council, takes his part in shaping the destiny of the Indian Empire, should share or allow himself to be swayed by any such consideration. He must know and feel the truth that for this, as for every nation, peace is the greatest of all blessings – so long as it is peace with honour. Such peace as that can be purchased only by readiness for war. Therefore I hold it to be the duty of every Commander-in-Chief to strive with all his might after that readiness and at the same time, while so striving, to use all his influence against the frittering away of the resources of the country in military adventures which are not demonstrably necessary or unavoidable. Those, Gentlemen, are the ideals which I have held before myself during my tenure of the command in India. I know that His Excellency the Viceroy will endorse my claim that my voice in his Council has ever been for peace: that I have striven after readiness for war will not, I think, be questioned.[14]

Controversy of some kind continued to plague Kitchener where India was concerned. It turned out that his farewell speech in Simla had been plagiarised from that of Lord Curzon's to the Byculla Club in 1905, or it was as Jerrold suggests revealing of 'an unsuspected kind of grim humour' paralleling the changes Kitchener had made for

12   Ballard, p.145.
13   Minto, *India, Minto and Morley*, pp.183ff.
14   BL: Add 52278 Marker papers.

the army as Curzon had for administration.[15] Minto, however, had to explain, especially after *The Times* ran both in parallel columns:

> At first I thought the similarity might be mere coincidence – but such a possibility vanishes when one sees the passages side by side. The best explanation I have heard – and I have good reason to think it the true one – is that K. merely told Duff that he would find some good points in Curzon's speech, but I am firmly convinced that K. never intended that he should use it as he did, and never had any idea that he had done so. But then, as I say – how is Duff's performance to be accounted for? Of course there are ill-natured explanations beneath contempt. The supposition that it was irony on K.'s part has also gone the rounds here – sheer impossible nonsense ... K. is a very bad speaker – hates having even to say a few words – always reads his speeches, and read the one in question particularly badly ... I am very sorry about it all. It is lucky for K. that he is on the high seas![16]

Thwarted in getting the posts he wanted, and having achieved what he set out to in India, Kitchener soon bored with official life after his term was extended. Instead, he immersed himself in gardening, orchids, acquiring a poodle,[17] and maintained his holiday season habit of travelling to see different parts of the country. He had acquired Wildflower Hall, close to Simla but 1,000 feet higher. American Caroline Perry Sinnickson who rented the house in 1911, was '... making great alterations that the place may be brighter and have more sun and air. Lord K paid no attention whatever to the house, never even sleeping in it more than half a dozen times – but in the garden his skill and work and care knew no bounds.'[18] Shortly before leaving India, he dined with Caroline and her husband Offley whom he met at a dinner at Viceregal Lodge: '... the great man was particularly kind and charming to me and he consented to dine with us.' Unfortunately, he could not dine with them on 4 July, '... as [he] has so many engagements he reserves Sundays to go to his Bungalow at Mashobra [Wildflower Hall].'[19]

She revealed Kitchener's caution in meeting people, no doubt Offley and Fitzgerald being friends helped on this occasion:

> One of his ADCs lunches with me on Friday to arrange the date and take my small list of guests for his Excellency to approve or change. Gen'l Sir B Duff,

15   Walter Jerrold, *Earl Kitchener of Khartoum: The Story of His Life* (London: J Johnson, 1916).
16   Buchan, *Minto*, p.296.
17   Royle, p.221.
18   Caroline Perry Shore & Alan Jones, *An Enchanted Journey: The Letters of the Philadelphian Wife of a British Officer of the Indian Cavalry* (Pentland Press, 1994) 6 March 1911 to Uncle Joe and Aunt Fanny, p.137.
19   Shore & Jones, *Enchanted Journey*, 30 May 1909, p.88.

who is good to me like a father, tells me the honour is a very personal one and we hear the Viceroy has said 'why am I not asked to dine with Mrs Offley!' Very flattering of course. We are in hopes we can tuck a letter in K's pocket to you when he goes through USA but he is a very shy man and dreads to be made much of, preferring greatly to be allowed to go quietly on his way yet always very agreeable and enjoying people.[20]

On 6 September 1909, handing over to O'Moore Creagh,[21] Kitchener left India to tour Australia at the invitation of Prime Minister Alfred Deakin and New Zealand as guest of Prime Minister Joseph Ward.[22] En route, he stopped in Japan, Korea and China to witness military manoeuvres, and the Dutch East Indies. He earned his keep, most of the trip being paid for by the British government. His visit to Japan helped reinforce the 1902 Japanese treaty which satisfied the Admiralty.[23] Despite preferring Chinese porcelain to Japanese, Kitchener '... had witnessed in China the worst maladministration he had ever seen,' and for this reason supported Japan ruling '... as far as Harbin in Manchuria.'[24] In Australia and New Zealand he advised on their defence systems. Prior to arrival, he had thoroughly researched whatever local facts and figures he could from India, including sending two officers to 'regulate his programme.'[25]

The family motto of Thorough was still a motivation for Kitchener. He realised '... the strain of passing from peace to war will absorb the energies of all engaged, even when every possible contingency has been foreseen.'[26] This had been part of his urgency for pushing through reform in India and was behind his recommendations for the two dominions he visited. During this time, Kitchener influenced the South African Defence Act 1912 when Tim Lukin and Methuen supported a '... Swiss-style military system where all adult males were members of a part-time reserve that could be mobilised quickly when required, particularly in defense of the mother country.'[27]

20   Shore & Jones, *Enchanted Journey*, 27 June 1909, p.93.
21   Arthur, vol 2, p.280, Garrett O'Moore Creagh, born 2 April 1848, died 9 August 1923.
22   Joseph George Ward, 1st Baronet of Wellington, born 26 April 1856, died 8 July 1930, New Zealand.
23   Royle, pp.228-229.
24   Ayako Hotto-Lister, *The Japan-British Exhibition of 1910: Gateway to the Island Empire of the East* (Richmond, Japan Library, 1999) p.14.
25   Arthur, vol 2, p.292.
26   Rye, pp.115-7.
27   Timothy J Stapleton, *Military History of South Africa: From the Dutch-Khoi Wars to the End of Apartheid* (Santa Barbara: Praeger ABC-Clio, 2010) p.114, Henry Timson Lukin, born 24 May 1860, died 15 December 1925.

His schedule was gruelling.[28] In Australia, Kitchener recommended coordinated development of the railway so it could be used to defend the country.[29] He also recommended establishing a military college and the formation of a Staff Corps,[30] which with a naval college were set up. On 18 February 1910, the day after he arrived in New Zealand, his report on Australian defences was published. His subsequent recommendation for New Zealand was similar, encouraging the two Dominions to work together to link their military systems for mutual defence, especially as they were completely isolated from other British territories. He then visited the United States of America taking in West Point Military Academy during a twelve day stay, which was cut short by a summons to return to England.

Kitchener built or promoted railways in Africa, India and Australia. 'One of the great needs of Australia is systematic, statesmanlike, and comprehensive railway extensions. Trunk lines opening up communication and developing the fertile districts of the interior of this vast country would undoubtedly stimulate more than anything else the growth of your population, as well as fostering trade and considerably increasing your means of defence.'[31] The same applied to the other imperial territories. In 1904, he started construction to the Frontier areas,[32] and in 1912 with Reginald Wingate, they opened the railway to El Obeid in Egypt.[33]

Kitchener, a few months shy of sixty, arrived in London on 26 April 1910 to press his claims for the Viceroyalty of India.[34] This put the government in a difficult position from which they were extricated when Edward VII died shortly before midnight on 6 May 1910, the day Kitchener had lunch with Margot Asquith, Frances Balfour, John Burns and four others. Kitchener's anxiety was noticeable, constantly checking that 'the flag was still flying at the Palace.'[35]

Between leaving India in 1909 and going to Egypt in 1911, Kitchener's star had been on the wane, partly due to the Liberal Party being in power. However, the issue was not one of politics in the traditional sense, but rather that Liberal politicians did not really know Kitchener as most of his circle of correspondents were Conservative Tories. Significant, too, was Kitchener's reputation which had been pushed into the public limelight concerning events against which the Liberals stood, for example, the 1899-1902 war and concentration camps. He was a military man, harsh and callous, who would do more harm on the diplomatic front than any good. His position was

28   An example can be found at 'Lord Kitchener, Auckland arrangements', in *New Zealand Herald*, 28 February 1910, p.7.
29   Arthur, vol 2, p.293; Peter Bastion, *Andrew Fisher: An Underestimated Man* (Sydney: University New South Wales, 2009) pp.1,198.
30   Arthur, vol 2, p.295.
31   Rye, p.314; Sydney *Herald*, 12 Jan 1910.
32   Arthur, vol 2, p.146.
33   BFI: http://www.colonialfilm.org.uk/node/1207 [accessed 9 Jan 2013].
34   Royle, p.232.
35   Mark Bonham Carter (ed.), *The Autobiography of Margot Asquith* (London: Weidenfeld & Nicolson, 1995) p.266.

not helped by his reluctance to become Governor of Malta in place of the Duke of Connaught. Despite promises of a more favourable appointment when one became available, and despite the King's telegram, Kitchener was reluctant to go to Malta. Seeing the King to receive his Field Marshal's baton, he discussed the matter. The King told Kitchener not to accept the post, 'it's a damn rotten one!' So, with the King's blessing, Kitchener declined the post learning that the King's name had been used in his role as constitutional monarch, rather than in his personal capacity.[36] Not long after the King died, Secretary of State for War Haldane took the opportunity to announce that Methuen would become Governor instead.

Hints of Kitchener's willingness to be liaison to Turkey (Ottoman Empire), where he could ensure that country's loyalty to Britain when Europe went to war, failed.[37] This was due to Edward Grey's reluctance to annoy the Unions by employing ambassadors not in the Diplomatic Service, and misunderstanding and lack of awareness of Kitchener's knowledge of Turkish culture. All Kitchener could do was watch as the Ottoman Empire/Turkey moved closer to Germany.

Kitchener was unemployed. On 22 June 1909, he wrote to Frank Maxwell about 'old Morley' not wanting him for India 'at any price' and with the Mediterranean command going elsewhere, he was 'at a loose end with nothing to do.' He '... could not stand London where I must either appear to be cap in hand to this Govt or join Ld Bobs & Charlie Beresford and criticize the military powers that be which I do not consider a sound course so I have bolted to the country of my birth and am doing some towing and trying to learn how to enjoy doing nothing.' The letter continues with news of others and ends being 'so glad' Frank was expecting another child: 'I know what it means to you and your wife.' He finishes with 'PS: I feel a bit sick at times at the result of ones work but that will pass when I can settle down to something. You are such an old friend I can tell you what no one knows – or sees. This issue went pretty deep. K.'[38] Kitchener wrote similarly to Ettie, 'Life is still worth living with such staunch friends as you have been. To you alone I will admit the issue has gone in pretty deep.'[39]

Kitchener remained unemployed but restless, writing to friends and supporters in his search for gainful employment. This endeared him little to the Liberal Party leadership having to respond to questions in parliament and the press as to why Kitchener was not employed or at least on the Committee of Imperial Defence (CID) whilst in England. When Asquith, Prime Minister and leader of the Liberal Party invited Kitchener to join the CID on 29 September 1910, Kitchener questioned why he had been rejected previously. He finally accepted on 10 October being concerned about the military arrangements Britain had with France in the event of war. His appointment

36   TNA: PRO 30/57/91/6, Birdwood to Arthur, 26 August 1916.
37   PA: STR 7/8/15.
38   NAM: 7807-25-44, 22 June 1909, Kitchener to Frank; Charles William de la Poer Beresford, 1st Baron Beresford, born 10 February 1846, died 6 September 1919.
39   HA: DEX/789/C2, 10 June 1910 from 17 Belgrave Square.

coincided with a recommendation by Louis Botha, Prime Minister of South Africa, that Kitchener's advice '... should be taken on all that pertained to the safeguarding of the Empire.'[40]

On 6 July 1910, Kitchener had embarked on HMS *Drake* at Falmouth to see the naval manoeuvres.[41] The same day he sent a telegram to Ettie 'prefer[ring] eldons [sic] place but if that is impossible, then yes very many thanks.' Lady Desborough was house-hunting so he had a place to stay when he arrived back in London.[42] A week later, 12 July, Kitchener wrote from the 5th Cruiser Squadron, HMS *Drake* at Oban, providing another insight to the man and the times:

> I have just received your letter about my coming to Taplow on the 23rd. I had, I am sorry to say, quite forgotten you had asked me and thought when I went to Ireland I was quite clear of all engagements so when Lady Lansdowne asked me to go to Bowood I replied that if I could get away from the naval manoeuvres in time I would go there on the 23rd and I wrote the other day from Falmouth that I should be able to do so – mea culpa! What am I to do – will you ever forgive me or ought I to write and make a clear breast of it to Lady Lansdowne –
>
> I should have so liked to come to Taplow and to have seen you again and thanked you for all you have done. Might I come up to London on Monday and see you there or at Taplow –
>
> I hope you will not think I am careless about engagements this is the first mistake I have made and I remember how you asked me a long time ago at Hatfield – Pray forgive me I am more than sorry for my stupidity.
>
> So many thanks for letting me see the enclosed letter which I have destroyed. I thought the transfer to St Petersburg had been finally fixed up but evidently that is not the case.
>
> You will forgive me won't you and let me see you on Monday the 25th. Yours always sincerely Kitchener.[43]

On 25 August he again wrote to Ettie, this time from 22 Ryder Street, St James' thanking her for an invitation which he would have to decline as he was due at Balmoral on 12 September for a week. He had '... been all over the country looking for a house but so far unsuccessful no one seems to want to sell a nice place. No news of any sort about my future but I do not think any is to be expected. I am sure you are having a splendid time and I only wish I was with you.'[44] From Balmoral, 13 September, he was leaving on Monday and heading immediately south 'as there is a

---

40   Arthur, vol 2, p.305.
41   HA: DEX/789/C23D.
42   HA: D/ERv/C1501/2; telegram 5 July 1910 to Lady Desborough, 19 Manchester Square, London.
43   HA: DEX/ 789/C29.
44   HA: DEX/789/C20.

lot of business to do about the new purchase.' He was '... quite pleased at having at last got a place of my own and hope there will be no hitch about titles which my lawyers are looking into.' He hoped the two Desboroughs would come and see Broome when they returned from Scotland.[45]

In keeping with his past habits and having no intention of spending a winter in Britain, Kitchener sailed for Egypt and East Africa on 5 November 1910 in the company of Fitzgerald, who had become his ADC in India when Maxwell left to get married in 1906, and McMurdo, his ADC in Egypt during the 1880s. On his travels, he had with him copies of *Country Life* and novels by Stanley Weyman.[46] In Sudan, he stopped to look at Gordon College which he had been instrumental in setting up and wrote to *The Times* appealing for funds for the cathedral in Khartoum.[47] Shooting on the Nile followed.

At the Uganda-Sudan border, they were joined by Edward Humphrey Manisty Leggett, on Kitchener's staff in South Africa, who guided them through East Africa.[48] During his visit, Kitchener negotiated with Governor Girouard the purchase of 9,000 acres forming Songhor Estates, Muhoroni near the Uganda Railway, thirty-eight miles from Victoria Nyanza and 550 miles from Mombasa;[49] the intention being to spend British winters on his farm in Africa and summers at Broome.[50] The choice of a farm was not surprising; both his father and uncle had been farmers.[51] When McMurdo died in April 1914, his shares were bought by Kitchener, Leggett and Fitzgerald from the estate, but there was never enough money injected into the property to make it a viable farming enterprise. It remained reliant on financial support from the British East Africa Corporation. Although the farm was making a loss compared to others in the area, it was developing according to the *East Africa Standard* on 15 August 1914, and repairing bridges.[52] On 7 January 1915, Khan Bahadur wrote to Governor Henry Conway Belfield enclosing coffee seeds for Kitchener's farm[53] and, later in 1915, Kitchener bought Indian Buffalo for the farm although it is not clear whether they arrived.[54] Days before he drowned, 3 and 4 June 1916, whilst at Broome Kitchener signed documents authorising a limited company to control the farm and enable finance to be raised. At this time only 200 square miles of land had been

45   HA: DEX/789/C21.
46   Magnus, p.306.
47   Arthur, p.306.
48   Edward Humphry Manisty Leggett, born 7 December 1871, died 17 May 1941.
49   Samson, p.195; Rye, p.333.
50   Magnus, p.307.
51   Rye, p.20.
52   Samson, p.195; Arthur Renshaw looked after Kitchener's personal matters when he was out of the country.
53   Samson, p.195.
54   Cory Library: Aubrey diaries.

cultivated.[55] Henry, his brother, sent to East Africa during the war, died on the farm in March 1937.

Kitchener's interest in farming was more than skin deep. He may not have had much time to spend on the farm, but he followed farming trends and technology with interest. In March 1910, he 'naturally visited the Government agricultural farm' where he came across 'Kitchener wheat' being trialled.[56] When in South Africa, some asked him for assistance to combat rust in wheat, so he had samples of Tibetan wheat sent to South Africa but heard nothing more. The result of merging these two wheats had been sent from South to East Africa and without his knowledge, the Boers had named the wheat after him;[57] so much for their dislike of the man who had 'invented' the concentration camp. Kitchener told this story during a lunch at the Suffolk Agricultural Show which he attended as High Steward of the Borough of Ipswich[58] to which he had been appointed whilst on tour. He also took the opportunity of reminding his audience that he was grandson of Dr Chevalier of Aspall who 'introduced the famous Chevalier barley.'[59] There is another Kitchener wheat which he may not have known about. One developed in Canada by Seagar Wheeler and named '... because, in his mind, it was straight and strong as Britain's soldier-hero Lord Kitchener.' This wheat originated in 1911 on his farm and was a mutant of 'sport'. Canadians did not take to it, but Colorado did. In 2018, it can be found as the base for some ales.[60]

Kitchener had an eye for farming. Reports from Palestine comment on the land, fertility, and aspects of agriculture, whilst his account in *Blackwood's Magazine* of Sophia and the Turkish front in 1877 describes '... travelling along by the side of the river Maritza, through a rich plain wonderfully well cultivated. The soil was very different to that between Constantinople and Adrianople, being much more fertile, and a good deal of irrigation runs down from the river.'[61] Later, when Agent in Egypt, he set up an experimental farm on an island which became known as Kitchener Island,[62] and sought to improve irrigation. Rodd believed Kitchener would be remembered for '... the provision of safe refuges for the roosting and breeding of the egret,' which '... had been almost exterminated by the alien plumage hunter.' The egret protected the cotton crop by eating the boll-worm. When Rodd visited Egypt in 1920, the sight of

55   Warner, p.197.
56   Jerrold, p.229.
57   Rye, p.335 quoting *The Times* 2 June 1911; Jerrold, p.299; Hoyt, p.214, Also *New Zealand Herald*, 5 June 1911, p.7.
58   His cousin Thomas Cobbold, through his mother's Chevalier lineage, had been MP for Ipswich.
59   Jerrold, p.228.
60   Jim Shalladay, *Canada's Wheat King: The Life and Times of Seager Wheeler* (University of Regina, 2007) p.103.
61   HHK, 'A visit to Sophia and the heights of Kamerleh – Christmas 1877', in *Blackwood's Magazine* (Feb 1878) p.194.
62   Pollock, p.221.

the birds in flight '... brought back a kindly thought of K. and a picture of the strong ruddy face with the light-blue eyes watching their white companies winging through the golden evening glow.'[63]

The rural life impacted his diet in that although he was partial to tinned Paysandu ox tongue, he craved fresh milk. The latter causing a cow and calf to travel with him to be on hand when needed, especially in Sudan. According to Hodges, '... on one occasion when the Sirdar's cow was following him on a Nile boat, it fell or jumped overboard and swam to the very island on which the Mahdi had been born. The flotilla came to a halt and waited whilst a company of Sudanese was landed to round it up.'[64]

Animals featured strongly in his life, perhaps because of their loyalty. Dogs were a firm favourite, their names indicative of his wit.[65] His spaniel gun-dogs in England were called Aim, Fire, Bang, Miss and Damn, which caused huge amusement when he went calling after them.[66] Two spaniels accompanied him to Egypt in 1911. The bear cub, Toby, obtained in Turkey moved to Cyprus until Toby decided to join him in his bath,[67] what happened next is unknown. In Palestine, he refused to move until a horse was better and expressed regret at the death of a baggage camel. Later, Kitchener was sad a horse died a day before its work would have been finished. The animal had died despite everything being done to help it recover.[68] Despite regret at losing a baggage camel, they were not suitable for surveying: 'I used to keep mine at a good trot for a bit until he got cross, which he showed by roaring, and then suddenly shutting up all four legs and coming with a thud on the ground, at the same moment springing up again and darting off in an opposite direction. Continued correction caused him to collapse again, and then roll, which was decidedly uncomfortable.'[69] In 1918 when Lady Northcliffe set up the Red Cross Pearl appeal, Kitchener's sister Millie donated three pearls: '... one for Ferby, one for little Marion, and one from little Pet Evie, all the names of family pets.' Alongside these, she gave five rubies to finish off necklaces,[70] possibly in honour of Kitchener's gun-dogs.

Arriving in Mombasa in March 1911, King George V summoned Kitchener to take charge of the troops at his coronation on 22 June.[71] Kitchener travelled home on the *Feldmarschal*; the ship later to feature in 1914 as taking the German General Paul Emil von Lettow-Vorbeck to East Africa and then back to Germany as the only undefeated German general of the Great War. By then, 1919, it had been renamed

---

63   Rodd, *Memories*, pp.38-9.
64   Hodges, p.131.
65   Killett, p.27.
66   Warner, p.133.
67   Magnus, p.49; Rye, p.65.
68   Daiches, *Kitchener in Palestine*, pp.46, 49, 66.
69   Daiches, *Kitchener in Palestine*, pp.79-80.
70   Rachel Trethewey, *Pearls Before Poppies: The Story of the Red Cross Pearls* (History Press, 2018).
71   Arthur, pp.307-9.

HMS *Transvaal*, which place had other links with Kitchener. En route to England, Kitchener met the Kaiser in Venice at Lady Layard's house and then on 18 May at a lunch hosted by Haldane.[72] In England, he took an appointment on the Board of the London, Chatham and Dover Railway which paid him a salary,[73] and used his position to improve the rail services to Canterbury to save him time travelling to Broome.

Back in England, Kitchener realised he needed to befriend the Liberals if he wanted employment. He therefore approached Morley to present him to the House of Lords. Although the two men had their differences over policy in India, they had not let these affect their personal like for each other – a point which Morley noted to Minto when the Viceroyalty vacancy was being discussed. Kitchener was ambitious and competitive, but did not seem to attack individual characters to get his way. Curzon had made their differences personal. Kitchener was manipulative and worked situations to his favour but he was not vindictive. On 28 May 1911, a 'meeting of two icebergs' occurred when Kitchener met Curzon face to face for the first time since India at the dinner Haldane hosted for the Kaiser.[74]

One of Kitchener's legacies was education, although his collaboration with Milner in South Africa to introduce a staff college there failed in 1905. Kitchener not only set up education facilities in the countries in which he served, but ensured they had the necessary finance. In April 1911 he joined the Joint Committee of Education Fund for Europeans and Eurasians in India to support the college at Quetta, saving officers the need to travel to England to study.[75] He fundraised for Gordon College in Egypt and funded his niece, Frances Parker who studied at Newham College, Cambridge, from 1896.[76] For someone whose father had threatened him for poor school performance and who had not achieved highly at the military academy,[77] experience had shown Kitchener the value of formal learning. 'Education must elevate the mind, must improve your faculties of thought, must clear your vision and make you understand your place and duty in the world.'[78]

Kitchener was not known for writing orders or reports, delegating where he could; in 2019 he might well have been identified as dyslexic. Yet, when he did put pen to paper, he demonstrated a clarity of thinking and detail. His report on the fall of Khartoum was a prime example as were his reports to the Palestine Exploration Fund. For the coronation on 22 June, Kitchener's orders comprised 212 pages covering all details where the army, a total of 50,000 troops, was concerned. It was also the first

72   Cassar, *Proconsul* p.44.
73   Royle, pp.235-6.
74   Magnus, p.310.
75   Arthur, vol 2, pp.174-7; Rye, p.332.
76   Royle, p.103.
77   Lord Kitchener, *New Zealand Herald*, 28 February 1910, p.12.
78   Kitchener of Khartoum, kitchenerscholars.org.

time at a royal event where strict security control and barriers for crowd control were used. Despite civilian objection, the day passed peacefully.[79]

He then travelled to Dublin, Ireland for his investiture on 10 July as a Knight of St Patrick, but rushed back to London the following day for a meeting with Grey. On 16 July, his appointment as British Agent to Egypt was announced, although he had heard two days before the coronation that he was to be Gorst's successor.[80]

79   Arthur, vol 2, p.209; Magnus, p.311.
80   Royle, p.239; Arthur, vol 2, p.312.

8

Benevolent dictator: Egypt, 1911-1914

Following a short sojourn in England, Kitchener returned to Egypt, arriving at Alexandria on 28 September 1911; this time as British Agent following the death of Eldon Gorst. Egypt was where he felt most at home, having lived there for fourteen years before South Africa and India. It was where he had learnt the art of soldiering, and diplomacy. The Liberals had been apprehensive in employing a man with a military reputation into a civil position, but with Cromer's support, and the growing nationalist demands, a 'benevolent despot' was needed and Kitchener was appointed.[1]

The day after arriving, Kitchener was presented with just the challenge he relished. Italy and Turkey had declared war on 29 September, and he had to ensure Egyptian neutrality: his nemesis, Khedive Abbas Hilmi, schooled in Vienna,[2] supported Turkey. Rather than challenge the Khedive directly, Kitchener informed those who sought permission to support Turkey that they would find themselves on the Army Reserve List and others in their posts when they returned. None of his commanders enlisted.[3] Kitchener's presence and reputation reassured, confirmed by the press announcing on his return to Cairo that, '… the whole atmosphere of the town seemed changed. Rumours were less portentous, the word TRIPOLI could be spoken without looking round to see who might be listening […]'[4]

War averted, Kitchener turned his attention to the safety of the Empire, and Egypt. The international scene, not least events along the North African coast at Agadir and Morocco, made this imperative. Having closely followed Ottoman politics and allegiances, Kitchener was aware that if Britain went to war with Germany, Turkey would side with the latter diverting war from Europe to the Red Sea and Caucasus

---

1 Zetland, *Lord Cromer*, p.309.
2 Wilson, *Signs and Wonders upon Pharaoh*, p.68.
3 Royle, pp.241-2; Arthur, p.315, The Italo-Turkish war was fought between 29 September 1911 and 15 October 1912 in today's Libya, then Tripolitana and Cyrenaica. It was concluded with the Treaty of Lausanne/Ouchy on 18 October 1912.
4 Stewart Symes, *Tour of Duty* (London: Collins, 1946) p.22.

Mountains.[5] In May 1912, Kitchener travelled to Malta on HMS *Hampshire* for a meeting with Churchill, Asquith, and Prince Louis of Battenberg on naval strategy. Prepared as always to get his way, Kitchener provided figures proving the Navy would not have to reduce the force in the North Sea to safeguard the Mediterranean. He argued that in a European war, Egypt would need to look to India for supplies and reinforcements, hence ships would be required in the Mediterranean to protect Egypt and the Suez, and ultimately the Empire. The CID agreed, overruling Fisher at the Admiralty. During this three-day visit, Kitchener stayed with Leslie Rundle at the Governor's palace.[6]

Internally, Kitchener set about reforming conditions in Egypt. Improved well-being would mean peace. Housing and sanitation were high on Kitchener's agenda; a lesson learned in southern Africa. As with everything where he did not have someone he could trust with the task, Kitchener took a 'hands-on' approach. He '... designed model villages and gardens; he provided open spaces'; and visited medical centres. In 1913, 'a lady' reported: 'These dispensaries are very widely used now by the natives ... The nurses told me that when Lord Kitchener visited them he went into every detail and evinced the keenest interest.'[7] Eye hospitals were founded to help prevent eye disease and Public Health improved generally to prevent the spread of disease. Removing stagnant water was a challenge but with patience and education, results were achieved.[8] Where necessary, he introduced new legislation such as the 1912 Homestead Exemption Law, and had trusted others safeguard the local Bedouin from getting caught up in potentially tricky political situations.[9]

Recognising the importance of agriculture, and having an interest in farming, Kitchener paid particular attention to the plight of the cotton farmer; cotton production accounting for one-third of agricultural output. As the cotton price fluctuated dramatically, Kitchener sought ways to stabilise the situation, effectively nationalising the industry. A loan of £3 million from the British Government allowed him to develop production. This included £2 million for cotton planting and irrigation in Gezira, £100,000 for planting and irrigation at Tokar and Kassala respectively and £800,000 for railway extensions. Alongside this, the production of wheat and millet had to continue to keep Egypt self-sustaining. Later, in June 1914, as Honorary Vice-President of the International Congress of Tropical Agriculture, despite feeling he

5 Royle, p.249.
6 *The Times*, 30 May 1912; Keith Hamilton, *Bertie of Thame: Edwardian Ambassador* (London: Royal Historical Society Studies in History, 1989) p.288, John Arbuthnot Fisher, 1st Baron Fisher, born 25 January 1841, died 10 July 1920.
7 Arthur, p.329.
8 Arthur, pp.329-30; Rodd, *Memories*, p.38.
9 André von Dumreicher, *Trackers and Smugglers in the Deserts of Egypt* (London: Methuen, 1931) pp.182ff.

would not be able to contribute much, he arrived with maps and documents which he used to deliver an impromptu lecture on reclaiming waste salt-land at Biala.[10]

Ways to improve the economy were explored. Two failed attempts to locate oil did not deter Kitchener, suggesting there must have been some compelling evidence which persuaded him to take the risk.[11] Oil was eventually discovered. In 1913, Kitchener was involved in a border issue dating back to 1906 between Abyssinia and Sudan. Whilst Lake Tsana and part of Western Abyssinia fell into the Anglo-Egyptian Sudan area, he was prepared to concede the narrow strip connecting Italy's colonies of Eritrea and Italian Somaliland. Kitchener's motivation was safeguarding the water supply to Sudan. However, negotiations were put on hold with the outbreak of war in August 1914, partly to keep neutral Italy on side.[12]

Nothing escaped his attention, and although not a politician, he changed how Egypt was governed. Believing the two-house system ineffective, he passed the Organic Law in 1913 creating the Legislative Assembly with a single council. The Legislative Assembly, with 66 elected and 17 nominated members, could delay legislation and prevent taxation which had not been discussed.[13] Through this means he limited the Khedive's power. He brought Muslim charities under the control of a ministry and required that any awards the Khedive wanted to make had to be approved by the Agent.[14]

Invariably the changes, said to be more than Cromer managed in twenty-four years,[15] brought him into conflict with those who felt they were losing out. In particular, the nationalists, mostly middle class, who had been invigorated by concessions made by Gorst, started to plot against Kitchener. Fitzgerald thwarted a shooter at Cairo Railway Station in July 1912, but in April 1913, when there was another attempt on his life, Kitchener retaliated by closing newspaper offices and arresting agitators.[16] He also faced opposition from his own. During Kitchener's first week in Cairo, Ronald Storrs[17] let him know that a number of British officials planned to resign for various reasons. Kitchener tapped:

10   Arthur, vol 2, pp.322-6, Proceedings and Transactions of the Third International Congress of Tropical Agriculture held at Imperial Institute, London, 23 June to 30 June 1914, papers communicated to Congress (1915) vol 1, p.287.

11   Arthur, vol 2, pp.326-7.

12   Hugh Drummond Pearson, *Letters from Abyssinia, 1916 and 1917: With Supplemental Foreign Office Documents* (Los Angeles: Tsehei, 2004) pp.21-8. See also, Bahru Zewde, Relations between Ethiopia and the Sudan on the Western Ethiopian Frontier 1898-1935 (PhD, University of London, 1976).

13   Royle, p.245; Lord Lloyd, *Egypt Since Cromer*, vol 1 (London: Macmillan, 1933) pp.139ff.

14   Royle, p.246; Arthur, p.330.

15   Wilson, *Signs and Wonders Upon Pharaoh*, p.68.

16   Royle, p.243; Arthur, vol 2, pp.318-21; Magnus, p.334.

17   Ronald Henry Amherst Storrs, born 19 November 1881, died 1 November 1955.

a drawer in his desk and [said]: 'You'd better go down to the Club and let it be generally known that I've always kept printed acceptance forms for resignations, only requiring the name to be added to become effective.' I duly circulated this news and need hardly say that [...] not one single resignation was submitted. Next day, curious to see how the forms ran, I opened the drawer, and found it to contain a box of cigars.[18]

Contrary to popular belief, Kitchener accepted men who stood up to him. Storrs met Kitchener with trepidation the first day he was to work for him, his previous two encounters having been unfavourable. Asked how to respond to the vast correspondence congratulating him on his appointment, Storrs explained the usual practice which Kitchener dismissed saying all had to be treated equally. However, on challenging Storrs' mumbled comment about dealing with the consequences, Kitchener changed his position and Storrs was told to do 'what you damned well like.' He continued, 'From that first day's encounter followed three years of such happiness, interest and responsibility as no gratitude could repay. Many Chiefs, but by no means all, approve and reward their juniors when successful; not so many have the greatness of soul to remember positive achievements in the face of error or unsuccess. Above all, where he trusted, he trusted absolutely.'[19]

When Rundle, his Adjutant General (Chief of Staff) in Egypt, intended to resign following a disagreement, Kitchener convinced him not to and in reply to his change of mind, wrote:

I am very glad to get your letter. No two people can look at things exactly alike. I always put what I think is for the good of the Army and its success so far about all other considerations, that I frequently trample on individual feelings without it ever occurring to me that I am doing so. All I can say in extenuation is that I do not do it for my own assertion.[20]

Later in 1915, Kitchener admitted to Dawnay that he had been right about the Dardanelles, and apologised to Deedes Bey whose view he had sought in February of that year regarding the same.[21]

18   Ronald Storrs, *The Memoirs of Sir Ronald Storrs* (New York: GP Putnam's, 1937) pp.116-7.
19   Storrs, *Memoirs*, p.116.
20   Hodges, p.98.
21   John Presland, *Deedes Bey: A study of Sir Wyndham Deedes 1883-1923* (London: Macmillan, 1942) pp.225, 233-4.

Family and friends

Egypt was not all work. In his new role it was expected he host and attend official functions more than previously. Yet, when possible he was to be found in the *medina* or market mixing with the locals and looking for treasures. He travelled as much as he could, partly to get away from the pressures of administration, but also to see what progress had been made on specific projects and to meet the people where they were. His door was always open; although it did not necessarily make him more approachable.

In January 1912, on their way back from the Coronation Durbar in India, the King and Queen stopped for another at Port Sudan where they were entertained by Kitchener and Wingate. The visit, a huge success, preceded the opening of the El Obeid line which coincided with the first cinema showing in the Sudan: a recollection of the visit of the King and Queen from their arrival on HMS *Medina* through to various receptions and presentations. The showing had been timed for maximum effect with sunset prayer.[22] Kitchener continued to entertain whilst in Cairo. In February 1913 he had the Salisburys and Desboroughs to stay at the same time and was inviting Lady Ilchester and Lady Londonderry to visit the following year.[23]

In July there was the attempt on his life, but more distressing was the death in Bermuda on 6 March of his younger brother Walter from appendicitis. Later that year, his sister Millie and her husband Harry came to visit on their way to England from New Zealand. They stayed with Kitchener, and no doubt visited their son Alfred Chevalier Parker, Governor of Sinai, who purposefully kept his relationship with Kitchener quiet. Following a trip on the Nile, Harry Rainer Parker fell ill and died on 15 December. On this occasion, the two siblings could console each other, brother Arthur Buck having died on 24 February 1907 in Lucerne from pneumonia, while brother Henry was in Jamaica, having remained after retirement from the West India Regiment in 1902. Millie could also act as Kitchener's hostess at official functions.

Despite the family being spread all over the world, they regularly kept in touch by letter and in person if they happened to be near. In 1902 while Kitchener and Walter were serving in South Africa, Walter's wife Caroline, or Carrie, visited knowing she was ill with not much longer to live. She dined with Kitchener while in Pretoria where she could receive medical respite as needed without drawing attention to herself. When she could, she helped in the hospital, providing comforts.[24] Kitchener had shown no preferential treatment in Walter being called to South Africa, but when Carrie became bed-ridden he called his brother from the front and, after her death on Sunday 3 November 1901, gave him three months' leave. Previously, when Lady

22   Symes, *Tour of Duty*, pp.20-1. A copy of the film is held by the British Film Institute ID 612293 (online: http://www.colonialfilm.org.uk/node/1734).
23   BL: Add MS 51370 The Holland House Papers, to My dear Lady Ilchester, 21 February 1913, f.194.
24   Pollock, pp.197-9.

Rawlinson had to undergo an operation, Kitchener sent Rawlinson to Cairo, keeping his place open; Rawlinson returned in time to take part in the attack on Atbara.[25] Kitchener's preference was for unmarried men on his staff and as soldiers, but he understood the necessity of family and the sacrifices those who worked with him made: it was the least he could do. Carrie's death together with War Office pressure to bring the campaign to an end, resulted in Kitchener experiencing one of his lows as he complained to Methuen.[26]

Kitchener understood the value of wives, but did not appreciate the distraction some provided to officers when on duty. During the 1899-1902 war, he used Annie Botha to get a message through to Louis to start peace discussions, Mary Curzon was instrumental in easing the tensions between Kitchener and her husband in India and numerous wives, such as Evelyn Byng, acted as his hostess at official functions. Wives also made good confidants and channels to political decision makers, Alice Salisbury and Ettie Desborough being two examples, the latter also trusted with house hunting and purchasing gifts when Kitchener could not do it himself. It was partly to reduce the power of Boer wives assisting their husbands during the guerrilla phase of that war, that led to the introduction of refugee or concentration camps. However, further north, in Egypt and Sudan, Kitchener closed his eyes to the contingent of camp followers who travelled with his Sudanese troops.[27]

Although he deprecated politics, Kitchener was a political operator. He may not have played the Whitehall game but he did know how to use contacts and friendships to meet his needs and assist his career. It was Pandeli Ralli who suggested Kitchener cultivate friends to help him further his career, and no doubt assist others in the process. It was through Ralli that Evelyn came to be Kitchener's hostess in Egypt: she was Ralli's niece and probably met Kitchener on her first visit to Cairo twenty years earlier. When Byng was appointed force commander of the British garrison in Egypt in 1912 at Kitchener's instigation, Byng was invited to stay at the British Agency until his house had been arranged.[28] Many of Kitchener's connections linked to Cairo were women whose husbands held significant positions, but some were also men – Salisbury, Cromer, Charles Wilson and Asquith amongst others.

Kitchener's father, although not in England much himself, was one of Kitchener's staunchest supporters and used the networks he had to help his son. It was father Kitchener who enabled his namesake to join Chantzy's army at Loire and who liaised with the press on his behalf. Despite their differences in Kitchener's youth, Kitchener spent time with his father whenever he visited England. He was reported seen in Leicestershire after his father moved to Cossington, the manor Rothley Temple which Harry Parker had inherited, and where father Kitchener spent his last years,

25 See Kitchener's women.
26 Swindon: Methuen collection 1742/48/3, K to Methuen, 20 Nov 1901.
27 Lamothe, *Slaves of Fortune*, pp.86-8.
28 Williams, *Byng*, pp.57, 59.

Kitchener being with him during his last days of coma and death. Before returning to Egypt in 1894, Kitchener organised the winding up of the estate to ensure financial viability for the farm in New Zealand.[29]

With no place to call his own in England until 1911, Kitchener spent time with family and friends during his visits. He would always visit the Grenfells (Desboroughs) in Venice if they were there or at Taplow '... on his first Sunday back in England after his adventures abroad,' commenting that the house 'felt like home'. Kitchener had met Willy Grenfell in Egypt and the rest of the family in England, including Julian, before the South African War.[30] He told young Julian, with whom he spent many hours fishing, that he '... could not stand [...] state dinners and being photographed.' However, a photograph of Julian was the only photo to grace Kitchener's desk at the War Office.[31] Julian thought 'Modesty is one of his greatest qualities.'[32]

While in South Africa, Kitchener wrote to twelve year old Julian and his brother Billy. His letter, 13 May 1900, when compared with other letters, shows a more relaxed style appropriate of the youths he was writing to:

> My dear Julian and Billy,
>
> Many thanks for your letters which caught me up on the march here, and I read them while our guns were pounding away at the Boers who were sitting up on some hills trying to prevent our advance. However, they soon cleared out and ran before we could get round them. I wish we could have caught some of their guns, but they are remarkably quick at getting them away, and we have only been able to take one Maxim up to the present.
>
> Sooner or later we are bound to catch them, but they give a lot of trouble. The Boers are not like the Soudanese who stood up for a fair fight, they are always running away on their little ponies. We make the prisoners take a march on foot which they do not like at all.
>
> There are a good many foreigners amongst the Boers, but they are easily shot, as they do not slink about like the Boers themselves. We killed a German colonel yesterday and a Russian ditto a few days ago.
>
> Now I must get back to work, so goodbye. Mind you work hard.
>
> Your affectionate friend, Kitchener[33]

---

29   Florence E Skillington, 'Post Medieval Cossington', in *Transactions*, Leicestershire Archaeological and Historical Society, vol 20 (1938) p.227; TH Fosbrooke, 'Rothley', in *The History of Rothley* (Leicester Archaeological Society, 1921) pp.20, 61; A chimney piece in the dining room now a bedroom is from Egypt, sent by Kitchener to his sister. (https://www.le.ac.uk/lahs/downloads/1921-22/1921-22%20(12)%201-128%20Fosbrooke%20et%20al.pdf [accessed 8 July 2019]).
30   HA: D/Erv/F132/2 recollection by Julian in autumn 1902.
31   HA: D/ERv/F132/2; Trethewey, *Pearls*, p.433.
32   HA: D/ERv/F132/2.
33   HA: D/ERv/F132/2; original at D/ERv/1503/1 from Kronstadt.

Another letter, July 1901, provides further insight into the war and his stream of thinking, punctuation playing a very minor role.

> My dear Julian, I think you must send Billy out to me I will lend him a pony and he can trail his rod and line behind him. De Wet will soon be after him and get hooked like the old swan then I shall catch him, of course it may be unpleasant for Billy as he might get shamboked before we came up with relief. Give Billy my love and tell him to work hard and someday someday [sic] a long way on we have another ramble at Wrest together and I will tell you all sorts of yarns. We are catching a good many boers now I got 80 today, rather a good bag, they are not well off for clothes and their bags are generally without a seat. Goodbye awfully glad to have heard from you. ...[34]

Kitchener was comfortable with children. He was godfather to at least five.

> Children accepted him as a natural friend. I remember my little girl once meeting us, as we came in for tea from a walk, outside the tea room (she was, I may say, his god-daughter), and she immediately said to the great Lord Kitchener, 'Don't go in there, they are making such a *chatter*; come up and have tea with me,' and up he went right to the top of the house, with his lame leg, and sat down with Imogen and her nurse and had a long talk.[35]

On 23 February 1905 Kitchener wrote to Willie from Calcutta explaining that the letter telling him he was to be godfather to Imogen, had not been received. He hoped his telegram had arrived and that:

> ... your wife is [...] all right again. Please tell her I hope the infant will be another Julian. I quite think Julian better go to Oxford, whatever happens here-after it will be an advantage for him and I know he is keen to go to college. We will then work out a cavalry regiment for him and when he has done a little work with them I will take him if I am still in the service. What a grand worker he is you must be very proud of him. I only wish he was my boy – I am having rather a row with Curzon about system of army administration out here I shall be glad when it is over.[36]

---

34   HA: D/ERv/C1502/1, Letter from Kitchener to My dear Julian in an envelope dated 8 July 1901.
35   HA: D/ERv/F132/2.
36   HA: DEX/789/C31, and DEX/789/C30, dated 10 July from Calcutta.

Kitchener took his godfather responsibilities as seriously as he did his soldiering. Education was important for the solid grounding he expected, even if he was going to issue favours. A month later, he wrote:

> My dear Mrs Grenfell, I am sure Imogen[37] is all that is delightful and as charming as her name. I feel very proud of being the godfather of such a splendid young lady and all the more so because you should have thought of me to fill so important a post. Julian and I are now I suppose bound to look after the young lady and see she does not flirt. Please tell Julian I leave him in charge at present as I expect he knows more about it than I do. How splendidly your boys are getting on I am looking forward to Julian after a term at college becoming a cavalry soldier then if I am still serving I will take him on the staff and we will make a first rate soldier of him if I can help him. Love to Julian and Billy also to your husband yours always [illegible] The Godfather of Imogen[38]

Friends were important, but so was social etiquette. On 4 Feb [?] he wrote to Lady Desborough from Cairo suggesting she come and visit him at the same time as Lady Salisbury. They could organise in July when he was back in England. At the time of writing he had 'Lady Lugard and her niece, Sir F Milner, and his giant boy Ralli and one or two more staying [...] so you can see the house will be big enough for the two parties.' The Princess Royal was due to visit between 12 and 14 February. This letter ended with love to his goddaughter and Willie, the boys being at school and university.[39]

Kitchener enjoyed being with friends and staying with them in their country houses provided opportunities to meet others. At one of the gatherings at Osterley organised by the Countess of Jersey, Kitchener met up with his friend Jean Adrien Antoine Jules Jusserand when he was French Ambassador to England.[40] One Sunday returning from church, she found George Peel[41] most anxious at the heated discussion taking place next to the lake between Kitchener and Jusserand over Fashoda. '[T]hey certainly parted friends.'[42] The two men had met in Egypt in 1888 where Jusserand '... saw a good deal of Kitchener, whom I had known in London, and whom I found, with his tall stature, his steel-blue eyes, the wound which had recently broken his nether jaw,

---

37   Imogen was born 11 Feb 1905, named Alexandre Imogen Clair Grenfell, called Mog by the family, died 3 January 1969; her other godparents were Queen Alexandra, Aron Lucas, Alice Salisbury and Julian.

38   HA: DEX/789/C27.

39   HA: DEX/789/C25.

40   In 1914, Jusserand was French Ambassador to the United States of America. Born 18 February 1855, died 18 July 1932.

41   Arthur George Villiers Peel, born 27 February 1869, died 25 April 1956, writer and politician.

42   Countess of Jersey, pp.366-7.

looking even more soldierly than before.'[43] This led to a lifelong friendship with letters signed 'Kit'.[44] Another time he met Annie Botha when she was visiting Osterley, 'warm greetings' being expressed by both.[45]

During the Great War, Kitchener's social life would stagnate as he worked to get the country on a war footing. This, however, did not stop him attending work-related dinners or lunches on occasion. On 7 August 1914 he dined at Lord Granard's with the Italian Ambassador and Lloyd George, the last noting this was his opportunity to meet the Ambassador and Kitchener.[46] Again, on 13 March 1915, Lloyd George dined with Kitchener, this time Churchill joining them. No doubt the discussion centred on the huge rift which had developed between the War Office and Admiralty over the Dardanelles.[47]

Despite his paperwork being disorganised, he was himself structured in his habits. Reginald Brade[48] at the War Office, described a day:

> [...] Kitchener works hard. He arrives at the Office at 9 every morning, lunches there, and leaves about 6. His lunch is sent over from the house where he is living in Carlton House Terrace or [2] Carlton Gardens. Lady Wantage has lent it to him. The said lunch, I gathered, is a cold collation sent to the Office in a table napkin. After lunch he has a cigar. While he is smoking this he is most amenable to any request. He is very approachable and interviews a constant stream of visitors of all sorts. When he reaches home he reads the evening paper, then he has dinner, and after dinner he has a nap and then devotes himself to reading Foreign Office telegrams. Brade often goes in to see him in the evening. Brade again referred to K's habit of thinking aloud, which often causes his subordinates to imagine that he has come to a conclusion when he is merely reasoning the matter out privately with himself and ultimately may give altogether different orders.[49]

This varied little to what Desborough's brother reported from Egypt: 'Kitchener was always working, up at sunrise drilling his men, and learning Arabic, of which he knew even the dialects.' This was confirmed by a 'native' who had been with Kitchener in the advance along the Nile: 'Lord Kitchener never slept, and appeared when least

43 Jusserand, *What Me Befell*, p.115.
44 Review of *What Me Befell* – http://www.unz.com/PDF/PERIODICAL/SaturdayRev-1933dec16/1-3/ [accessed 8 July 2019].
45 Countess of Jersey, pp.366-7.
46 Kenneth O Morgan, *Lloyd George Family Letters 1885-1936* (Cardiff: University of Wales, 1973) p.168.
47 Morgan, *Lloyd George*, p.176.
48 Reginald Herbert Brade, born 1864, died 5 January 1933.
49 Riddell, *War Diaries*, p.48.

expected among every unit of the Force, and his spirit pervaded the whole.'[50] More specifically, according to Reginald 'Reggie' Barnes, Kitchener was '… up at 6 every day, and writes till 8.30; then on after breakfast till 2, and then two hours in afternoon. All his correspondence is done by his ADCs, who typewrite for him – either Fitzgerald, Victor (Brooke), or Reggie; he never gives anything to a clear so that nothing leaks out.'[51]

His increased social status meant there were fewer occasions for Kitchener to 'go native' on his travels. As Commander-in-Chief in India, he accepted the hospitality of Indian princes and magnates when travelling. Shortly before leaving the country, February 1909, he went on a shooting trip to Bhawal. 'They stayed in the European-style guesthouse known as the Baro Dalan, where they had dinner catered by a team sent out by Peliti, the famous Italian restaurant of Calcutta.'[52] The following morning the group went hunting on the back of elephant, but the shoot was regarded as unsuccessful: only one deer was shot by the Commander-in-Chief.[53] His status also meant others had to defer to him, etiquette dictating no one left before Kitchener. Hedin, recalled a dinner at the house of the German Consul General to India, Count Quadt, where he was so comfortable, he only rose to leave after midnight.[54]

Kitchener's reputation as aloof and distant was set during his early years in Egypt and as Sirdar, making him reliant on his social connections.[55] He was not popular amongst English officers as he did not mix socially, had not married and, in their opinion, worked too hard.[56] Edward Vizetelly, editor of *The Cyprus Times* said:

> … one saw little of Kitchener at the club or anywhere else where Englishmen mostly congregated, although he sometimes turned up at the gymkhana meetings to contribute his share to their success. Kitchener was always a hard worker, a gentleman with a long head who thought much but said little. It is of course easy enough to prophesy when you know, but honestly, to my mind, he looked a man who would go far if he only had his chance.[57]

Kitchener was a complex individual, a man of contradictions who was accepted for who he was by those he allowed into his circle. Lord Derby, a personal friend from South

50   HA: D/ERv/F132/2.
51   John Buchan, *Francis and Riversdale Grenfell: A Memoir* (London: Thomas Nelson, 1920) p.69.
52   Federico Peliti had restaurants in Simla and Culcatta. Federico Peliti online: http://www. peliti.org/Federico/federico.pdf [accessed 14 March 2019].
53   Partha Chatterjee, *A Princely Imposter? The Strange and Universal History of the Kumar of Bhawal* (Princeton: Princeton University, 2002) p.33.
54   Hedin, *Trans-Himalaya*, pp.16-17.
55   Royle, p.97.
56   Warner, p.71.
57   Wheeler, p.34.

African days referred to him as 'a very curious mixture of simplicity and cunning,'[58] while Hamilton expanded on an earlier description:

> Unfortunately, his character, which had grown up, so to say, 'on its own' in the desert places of the Near East, was so vitiated by streaks of ignorance, innocence, suspicion, secretiveness and, often too, by downright duplicity, that he was liable to be bowled over by any smart lawyer-like personage. So it was always on the cards that he would be scuppered before he ever reached the grand issue he had foreseen – as happened during the Great War.[59]

He was loyal, rewarding those who served him with unstinting support, even when it went against his gut feel. This loyalty trait developed as he got older. Cynics would say this coincides with Kitchener's reduced need for promotion. If this is true, other factors then influenced his loyalty to Asquith during the conscription and manpower debates of 1914-16. Contrary to Magnus' claim that Kitchener left everything to Fitzgerald:[60]

> Kitchener left £200 to each of his personal staff: Major JK Watson CVO, CMG, DSO;[61] Col EH Marker DSO,[62] Col F Maxwell, VC, CSI, DSO, Gen WH Birdwood CB, CSI, DSO, Col Oswald AG Fitzgerald, Capt GGE Wylly.[63] All his lands and estates in East Africa, about 5,000 acres, plantations, buildings etc he bequeathed to Col Oswald Arthur Gerald Fitzgerald [personal military secretary and business partner who drowned with him on the *Hampshire*.][64] His brother Henry Elliot Chevalier got £1,000 and nothing else because of the large benefit conferred on his issue [although he inherited Fitzgerald's share, it having been proved he drowned before Kitchener].[65] £20,000 went to his nephew, Henry Hamilton Kitchener, £5,000 is in trust for his half sister Letitia Henrietta Emma Kawara Kitchener for life and then equal shares for her children. £2,000 to Horatio Herbert Earnshaw. Broome went to his nephew Commander Henry Franklin Chevalier Kitchener, Royal Navy for life. And various other instructions. The will was dated 2 November 1914, the executors being Arthur Henry

58 JJ Bagley, *The Earls of Derby 1485-1985* (London: Sidgwick & Jackson) p.222; Edward George Villiers Stanley, 17th Earl of Derby, born 4 April 1865, died 4 February 1948.
59 Hamilton, *Anti-Commando*, p.165.
60 Magnus, p.309.
61 James Kiero Watson, born 18 June 1865, died 13 January 1942.
62 His father Raymond John Marker (Conk), DSO, born 1867, died of wounds at Ypres on 13 November 1914.
63 Guy George Egerton Wylly, VC, CB, DSO, born 17 February 1880, died 9 January 1962, ADC to Kitchener 7 January 1906.
64 *The People*, 2 July 1916, p.6.
65 TNA: PRO 30/57/ 99, PA 16/28 Keogh report 13 March 1917; Diane Atkinson, *Rise Up Women! The Remarkable Lives of the Suffragettes* (London: Bloomsbury, 2018).

Earnshaw of Oxford and Algernon Henry Mills. Nothing was left to his sister Mrs Parker who was a widow.[66]

Kitchener regularly advised his sister Millie about her financial affairs, and every fortnight during the 1914-18 war the two siblings 'had a ten minute chat.'[67] This accounts for him not leaving her anything in his will: he knew her to be financially secure. He had also sponsored her daughter, Frances (Fanny), to attend Newham College, Cambridge between 1896 and 1899.[68] Later, in 1908, Fanny joined the Suffragettes which Kitchener disapproved of, writing to her to 'think of her family.'[69] His issue was not equality – it was her violence against the state. Kitchener had befriended Millicent Fawcett in South Africa inviting her and associates to dinner and as early as January 1915 he was suggesting women would need to replace men in the workplace to release them for front line duties.[70] He was more likely in agreement with Ian Hamilton: women were stronger and more equal before they demanded equality and put themselves on the pedestal where their opinions could be questioned.[71] Fanny, also known as Janet Arthur, was involved in trying to blow up the Scottish poet Robert Burns' house in Ayrshire on 8 July 1914, it being revealed on 24 July that she was Kitchener's niece.[72] Kitchener, and or Fannie's brother, eventually negotiated her release from prison following which she was sent to a nursing home for examination and found to be 'in a state of collapse'. She escaped trial following the amnesty which resulted from the WSPU (Women's Social and Political Union) offering to 'put their army at the service of the government.' This had been initiated by Lena Ashwell (Lady Simson),[73] the actress sister of Roger Pocock who founded the Legion of Frontiersmen, some of whom served in Africa with the 25th Royal Fusiliers. During the war, Fanny became honorary organiser of the Women's Freedom League National Service Organisation and served in the Women's Army Auxiliary Corps at Boulogne, later being awarded an OBE for her dedication.[74]

That it was Fanny's violence he was against is supported by Millicent Fawcett who recorded in 1898 that Kitchener was 'infuriated by [the Cambridge undergraduates']

66   *Telegraph* obituary, 23 December 2011. A copy of the complete will is available at TNA: PRO 30/57/99, PA 16/1 dated 2 November 1914.
67   Trethewey, *Pearls*, p.431; Royle, p.104.
68   Royle, p.103.
69   Atkinson, *Rise up Women!*; Cassar, p.77. DNW, Kitchener's niece: The Suffragette who outraged her uncle and was abused in prison (2016), online https://www.dnw.co.uk/news-and-events/latest-news/article.php?article_id=269 [accessed 27 April 2019].
70   TNA: CAB 2/3, 27 Jan 1915 in Jennifer Margaret Gould, The women's corps: The establishment of women's military services in Britain (PhD, University College London, 1988) pp.95, 146-7. http://discovery.ucl.ac.uk/1317607/1/260868.pdf.
71   Hamilton, *Anti-Commando*, pp.26-7.
72   Glasgow *Herald*, 9 July 1914; News 24 July 1914.
73   Riddell, *War Diary*, p.7.
74   Trethewey, *Pearls*, p.441.

disorderly rowdiness' when he stayed with his cousin, Annette Peile a Suffragette and friend of Millicent, whose husband was Master of Christ's College at the time he received an honorary degree from that institution. Kitchener shouted at the students that 'he wished he had them in the Soudan' which they took to be a compliment but which he saw as an opportunity to teach them 'how to behave.'[75]

Kitchener supported family and friends but expected standards to be maintained. He helped his nephew, Alfred Chevalier Parker, to a commission in the Royal Sussex Regiment, however he expected him to serve at least four years in India before considering him for Egypt.[76] Arthur, on being appointed to Governor of Sinai however kept the relationship quiet to avoid accusations of favouritism. Walter was used to manage the camel corps[77] and to lead the hunt for the Khalifa in January 1898, the former a result of his experience in India.[78] In South Africa, Walter was appointed to lead one of four columns against de la Rey, a project Kitchener personally tried to control.[79] Being deaf did not impact on his command except as Kitchener recounted to ES May: Walter had a Boer 6-inch shell burst in his tent, not realising his camp was being bombarded at the time. 'It is a good thing sometimes in war to be deaf,' the commander concluded.[80] Walter later became Governor of Bermuda. Older brother Henry, who had remained in Jamaica following his retirement, was recommissioned and sent to East Africa in 1915 to assist with recruiting and later Kitchener's Railway Protection Unit, becoming Inspector of Railway Defences on 10 May 1915.[81] But Kitchener was not above appointing friends to positions when it supported his goal. The appointment of Edward Cecil as Financial Advisor when Agent in Egypt was a prime example. As Percival Elgood noted, Cecil was a meticulous staff officer which Kitchener needed, Kitchener looking after the financial aspects himself.[82]

It was among family and close friends that Kitchener could relax and show his human heart. As a youngster, a cousin recalled that he '... gave his treasured stamp collection to her invalid brother, Tom. As he grew older, his "grace, simplicity [...] and his total absence of guile",' was striking. Kitchener often saw his cousin's family when on leave filling the house with his 'most delightful laugh.' His dog Bang was left with them and he gave them another called Bangle.[83]

Whilst friends and family were important to Kitchener and he was loyal to them, loyalty to his monarch was paramount. It had been behind the Malta debacle and

75   Fawcett, *What I Remember*, p.78.
76   Royle, p.104.
77   Magnus, pp.38, 121.
78   Magnus, p.188, 261; Royle, p.95.
79   Arthur, vol 2, p.50; Hamilton, *Anti-Commando*, pp.164-5.
80   Edward S May, *Changes and Chances of a Soldier's Life* (London: Philip Allen, 1925) p.260. Early deafness was a family trait which bypassed Kitchener according to Pollock.
81   JG Willson, *Guerrillas of Tsavo*.
82   Egypt, p.73.
83   Trethewey, *Pearls*, p.441.

loyalty to King George V found him Secretary of State for War in 1914. On 16 November 1896, Kitchener dined with the Queen for the first time:

> Sir Herbert Kitchener is a striking, energetic looking man, with a rather firm expression, but very pleasing to talk to. He brought me back very interesting trophies, which were placed on a table in the corridor. The drum is beaten to rally or alarm the troops. The spear's head is very formidable, and the inscription on the sword, in English, is most curious, showing clearly that it was used in the Crusades. There are two flags, the smaller one of which was flying on the tower of Dongola, and was recognised by Rudolf von Slatin when they captured the place. There are some words of the Koran inscribed on them. Sir H Kitchener told me that eight hundred of the dervishes came over to him and fought against their countrymen. At Dongola it was the first time they had fled without fighting. Sir H Kitchener said it was quite true that they had found a number of quite little children, even babies, strewn on the ground near Dongola, having been dropped by the women in their flight.[84]

Salisbury recognised the significance of the monarch's approval suggesting, 'It will very much enhance the value of the proposed honour in the eyes of Kitchener if he received the announcement of it direct from your Majesty ...' which she did on September 1898: '... conferring a peerage on you as a mark of my deep sense of the services you have rendered under most difficult and trying circumstances.'[85] The Queen complained to Salisbury on 27 January 1900 that she was getting no news from South Africa especially as there had been a large loss of life at Spionkop. 'What do Lord Roberts and Lord Kitchener say? I have such faith in the latter, but we hear nothing from either.'[86]

Kitchener's close relationship with the monarchy started when he became aide to Queen Victoria on 11 June 1888 keeping her updated through letters. One, on 25 July 1899 from 17 Belgrave Square, noted he would do '... his best to obtain the finest female white donkey procurable in Egypt'. However, he would need the '... measurements of the male Egyptian donkey Lord Wolseley brought over for the Queen, so as to match it as nearly as possible.'[87] On 28 December 1899 Kitchener wrote to her from the *Dunnotar Castle* near Madeira thanking her for his appointment as Lord Roberts' second in command. The letter in tone and style is quite different to letters to friends and subordinates:

84   Queen Victoria, *The Letters of Queen Victoria* (Cambridge University Press, 2014) pp.104-5.
85   Queen Victoria, *Letters*, p.275.
86   Queen Victoria, *Letters*, pp.468-9.
87   Queen Victoria, *Letters*, p.388.

Lord Kitchener left the Soudan in complete peace. The force under Lieut-Colonel Mahon had reoccupied el Obeid, and the whole of Kordofan had willingly come under the government. The rumours of strained relations with the Emperor Menelek, started by the enemies of England, were entirely without foundation, as Lord Kitchener's relations with the Emperor were most friendly when he left.

The college at Khartoum was progressing well, the building being above the first-floor windows; it was hoped to complete the building next August or September. The teaching staff and students will be then collected.[88]

During the World War, the Prince of Wales was serving on the Western Front much to the concern of politicians:[89]

One day Lord Kitchener and the Prince met by chance at the House of Lords, the Field-Marshal inviting the heir to the Throne into a private room, and they were soon chatting over the Prince's experiences at the Front. Bearing in mind the reports he had received, Kitchener urged the need for some caution. 'It is a great responsibility for our officers,' he said. 'We admire your pluck in wanting to share the life of the ordinary soldier, but a very great deal depends upon your personal safety.' I do not propose to give the precise reply the Prince made. It was a characteristic reply, and Lord Kitchener was so overcome by it – and he was very seldom moved – that he could do nothing but grasp and hold the Prince's hand and for some moments. This incident established a great bond of sympathy between the two men – the one young and impetuous, the other old and experienced, both prepared to give their all for their country.[90]

Kitchener could phone the palace at any time and request an interview which was never denied. Similarly the King would often contact Kitchener for first-hand information. When during the India crisis and war Kitchener tendered his resignation, the King refused it; '... the reply he gave me makes it impossible that I should think of giving it up.'[91]

Kitchener's women

Mention has been made of numerous women who were significant to Kitchener. He was a 'lady's man', enjoying the company of women he trusted, but feared being alone with those he did not know or in a large group. 'He disliked them as silly havering

88   Queen Victoria, *Letters*, pp.450-1.
89   Later Edward VIII, served with the Grenadier Guards from June 1914.
90   *West Sussex Gazette*, 4 March 1926, p.6.
91   *West Sussex Gazette*, 4 March 1926, p.6.

creatures who argued emotionally, seldom troubled to inform themselves correctly and when not spreading defeatist propaganda were keeping a war going unnecessarily by their fanaticism.'[92] Edward Cecil explained, 'He placed women on a far higher level than is usual in these days, and it really hurt him to hear or see anything that touched this ideal.' Visiting England after defeating the Mahdi, '... a very proper friend of [Cecil's] spent his time in burning, after seeing there was nothing important in them, the mass of love-letters which descended on Kitchener, and which would have offended him.'[93] One will never know for certain, but the damage done to his reputation by Magnus appears long lasting, despite Magnus' admission to Winifred Renshaw in 1964 that he had 'got the man wrong'.[94] Being a gentleman, Kitchener would not kiss and tell, and neither have the women, although James Lees-Milne makes an interesting statement about the parentage of Mickey Renshaw, Kitchener's godson. Michael resembled Kitchener '... with the same large, staring, fish-like eyes. Lord Kitchener was a great *ami* of his mother, Lady Winifred, but was not Mickey's father, so Mickey assured me once. The dates did not work out. Besides, starch and stiff Lady Winifred was not that sort of lady.'[95] Another questionable relationship was that with Alice Cecil, Lady Salisbury. Ziegler records Diana Cooper following her mother allocating rooms to guests: 'Lord Kitchener must have this room and then, of course, Lady Salisbury must be here.' Later that evening she quipped, 'If you are frightened in the night, Lord Kitchener, dear Lady Salisbury is just next door.'[96] That Kitchener was close to Alice and Winifred, the latter wife of his financial adviser, was no secret. Kitchener's letters to Alice from 1888 to 1916 are all formal in address and salutation, with nothing improper or indicative of anything but a meeting of minds. His letters to Ettie Desborough, whilst also proper in format are slightly more familiar in tone. When news of Kitchener's death was received, Ettie wrote to Alice, 'How he worshiped you, and what a wonderful, steadfast, confident happiness you stood for in his life, through all those many years. I think he must have known how truly we all loved him. One always had the sense that he did.' Later that month, her husband wrote to 'My dear Alice [...] you were I suppose Lord K's greatest friend.'[97]

Two women were linked with Kitchener and marriage. The first, Hermione Baker died aged 18 in 1885, the other Helen Vane Tempest Stewart, daughter of Lord Londonderry, refused 49 year old Kitchener's proposal in 1899, but that did not stop

---

92 Margot Lawrence, *Shadow of Swords: A Biography of Elsie Inglis* (London: Michael Joseph, 1971) pp.98-9.

93 Cecil, *Egyptian Official*, p.193.

94 Lady Renshaw to Charles Kitchener, https://www.kitchenerscholars.org/kitchener-of-khartoum [accessed 19 March 2019].

95 James Lees-Milne, *Through Wood and Dale: Diaries 1975-1978* (London: John Murray, 1998) Diary note 9 March 1978, pp.237-8.

96 Philip Ziegler, *Diana Cooper: The Biography of Lady Diana Cooper* (London: Harmondsworth, Penguin, 1983) p.26.

97 Hatfield House: letter 6 June 1916 from Ettie Desborough to Alice and letter 22 June 1916 from Willie Desborough.

her corresponding and socialising with him after her marriage.[98] A third, Caroline L Hutchinson disclosed her relationship with Kitchener in *The Weekly Despatch* and *The Caledonian* in 1917, but no other information could be found.[99] The Special Remainder Kitchener had attached to the award of his Viscountcy in 1902 included a variation of the norm. Kitchener requested that if he had no sons or daughters, his title went to his brother or his brother's male heir.[100] He asked Salisbury if possible, whether '… my nephews both sons of officers in the service might be sanctioned if this could be done it would greatly enhance the reward His Majesty has been so graciously pleased to bestow upon me.' He did not want '… to have to take a permanent encumbrance,' that is, '… a wife' in order to keep the title in the family.[101] On 1 November 1910 when Archie Hunter got married, he gave his sixty year old best man, Kitchener, a £100 cheque as of the two, Archie had married first.[102]

In his younger days, Kitchener had been quite a socialite, having as good a time as any young person would. Edmonds found Kitchener '… not at all the dour, silent worker and misogynist of legend. He enjoyed good stories, good living and practical jokes.'[103] In Egypt, about 1884, he organised a party for 100 people with Taylor of the 19th Hussars, and in 1893 had a fancy dress ball.[104] On another occasion, he beat Andrew Haggard (H Rider's brother) at an eating competition, although Haggard was quick to point out that Kitchener lost the drinking competition. Kitchener knew he attracted women, often writing to his sister about the number of young ladies who sought his company at dances. However, all this came to an end when Hermione died of typhoid.

Kitchener needed to feel safe, which is evident in the women he befriended.[105] Work and pleasure were kept separate except on occasions where personal views on sensitive matters could be discretely passed to the right quarters. His conservative nature influenced by his religious background and the repercussions he witnessed in Egypt and India concerning affairs of the heart amongst the British residents, account for him not being linked with 'local' women – Mary Curzon being the exception. Many whom he befriended, being well-travelled, had links with his postings.

98   Magnus, p.187; BL: Add MS 51370 The Holland House Papers ff.163-199, letter from Kildare, Ireland undated to 22 August 1913.

99   *The Caledonian*, vol 19, 1917.

100 Cracoftspeerage, Special Remainders, http://www.cracroftspeerage.co.uk/online/Content/index22.htm; Thomas Woodcock, Garter King of Arms, College of Arms, letter to the *Telegraph*, 7 November 2011; Lord Lexden letter to the *Telegraph*, 11 November 2011, https://www.alistairlexden.org.uk/2011 [accessed 19 March 2019].

101 Hatfield House: Salisbury papers, telegram 5 June 1902 and correspondence.

102 Hunter, *Kitchener's Sword-Arm*, p.204.

103 Andrew Green, *Writing the Great War: Sir James Edmonds and the Official Histories 1915-1948* (London: Frank Cass, 2003) p.211 fn30.

104 Martin Gilbert, *Horace Rumbold: Portrait of a Diplomat, 1869-1941* (London: Heinemann, 1973) p.16.

105 Royle, p.55-6.

In Egypt, he was friendly with Princess Nzali, later introducing the Countess of Jersey to her. His years of solitude, living among the locals, made him appear abrupt and bully-ish. Kitchener had not had the opportunity to learn British socially accepted manners,[106] and as he did not mix with the British socialites in Cairo, it was assumed he had no interest in women. Once he became Sirdar of Egypt he learned to 'play the game' socially and entertained. He became competitive, trying to outdo his neighbours when camping at the durbar. 'At last in triumph he showed me a fender-seat and said, "Anyhow, Lady Northcote has not a fender-seat." But I finally crushed him with, "No, but we have a billiard-table."'[107] And he was proud of his house-keeping skills: Raymond Asquith wrote to Lady Horner on 12 January 1907 from All Souls that 'Kitchener couldn't have kept house better than Katherine [Horner, his future wife] did – consummate efficiency and no apparent effort.'[108] Following his appointment to Simla in 1902, Kitchener hosted a ball proving he could be sociable and friendly. He was '... known to have thought out every detail and taken infinite personal pains to promote his guests' enjoyment.'[109] Although Booth recalls an account at Simla where Kitchener caused offence by taking the 'pretty girl' he was speaking with into dinner on his arm rather than the 'lady with highest rank.'[110] Rodd recalled of his time in Egypt that Kitchener, '... appeared ill-at-ease in social life, and rather shy in the society of women, though it is an error to suppose that he was never susceptible to their attraction. There was certainly one who exercised a strong influence for good over his idealism [not named!]. He had in those days no intimate friends. Many admired him. Very few really liked him. He walked by himself.'[111]

During his years in France, 1870-71, he met Catherine Walters, or Skittles as she was better known. Skittles left Paris at the end of the Franco-Prussian war to set up in Mayfair where Kitchener '... was another visitor to the tea-parties in South Street and she had been delighted with the news that he had been made a peer after his victory at Omdurman.'[112] She was 'the last of the great English courtesans' and had her name linked with the Prince of Wales, who with friends, were some of the first to attend her tea-parties and evening baccarat sessions. 'She was the grande-dame of the demi-monde, [...] so respectable that in her brilliant and intellectual salons even the great WE Gladstone could happily discourse over a teacup on the classics. Thirty years later, "Skittles" [...] would daily make her queenly passage through the Park in

---

106 Smithers, p.13.
107 Countess of Jersey, p.368 (George Villier's wife); Elizabeth Taylor, *The Old World and the New: The Marriage and Colonial Adventures of Lord and Lady Northcote* (Newcastle Upon Tyne: Cambridge Scholars Publishing, 2013) has two brief mentions of Kitchener indicating the relationship continued into 1915.
108 John Jolliffe (ed.), *Raymond Asquith: Life and Letters* (London: Century, 1980) p.151.
109 Arthur, vol 2, pp.130-1.
110 JB Booth, *'Master' and Men: Pink 'un Yesterdays* (London: T Werner Laurie, 1926) p.200.
111 Rodd, *Memories*, p.37.
112 Henry Blyth, *Skittles: The Last Victorian Courtesan, the Life and Times of Catherine Walters* (London: Rupert Hart-Davis, 1970) p.230, born 13 June 1839, died 5 August 1920.

a bathing-chair, while such stirring figures as Lord Kitchener walked proudly beside her.'[113]

Accusations of homosexuality appear in the anti-Kitchener texts,[114] suggesting the epitaph was a way to discredit Kitchener at a time when homosexuality was socially unacceptable. During his lifetime, Kitchener did nothing to refute these allegations (whether they were made publicly is unknown), but his celibacy must have drawn some comment as seen by the shock on his leaving San Francisco on 7 April 1910, when he told the newspapers that 'New York should be proud of her beautiful women.'[115] Kitchener's refusal to comment on the issue was in keeping with his policy of not openly criticising people or defending himself if there was a bigger issue at stake. Not doing much to endear himself to subordinates or to colleagues, caused resentment which fuelled such sentiments. Esher claims Kitchener '... was never seen to address or even notice a private soldier.'[116] But he did care. Harold Hartley recalled Kitchener appointing an over-age soldier to the War Office so he could access his pension, all his previous officers having died.[117]

His reputation for not employing married men is often used as evidence to prove his homosexuality. However, unmarried men did not need to be paid the married person's allowance which was important for balancing budgets. Unmarried men did not worry about wives back in England or in Cairo, a point reinforced when, on his first posting to Cairo, a few officers had attempted suicide due to unfaithful wives. Married men would not take as many risks which could be problematic on the battlefield, especially leading Indian and African troops where commanders were expected to be at the front. Wolseley agreed with Kitchener.[118] Kitchener was not against marriage, all but one of his 'band of boys' married, and at a staff dinner when Kitchener marrying was discussed, Maxwell, 'from the end of the table [said] "If you marry sir, I shall resign".'[119] Kitchener's friends could joke about the misconceptions others had. When Marker announced he was to get married on 30 October 1906, Kitchener wrote from Simla, 'I had no idea you would get married so soon please give Miss Jackson my best regards and best wishes for the future.'[120] He then asked Maxwell if he would,

---

113 Tisdall, *Unpredictable Queen*, pp.98-9; Henry Blyth, *Skittles*, pp.235-6.
114 Bosie, or Lord Alfred Douglas (22 October 1870-20 March 1945), the lover of Oscar Wilde claimed a 'romantic meeting' with Kitchener in 1894 in Cairo according to Neil McKenna, *The Secret Life of Oscar Wilde* (Random House, 2011) p.375. However, no other biographers mention it and neither does he in his memoirs. That Bosie was found guilty of libelling Churchill for organising Kitchener's death suggests Bosie might have made advances but was rejected.
115 Royle, p.232.
116 Warner, p.13.
117 TNA: PRO 30/57/1 newspaper cutting.
118 Arthur, *Wolseley Letters*, December 1896, p.355.
119 NAM: 7807-25-45, Maxwell-Kitchener correspondence 4, 19 October 1933, K of K, Holly's Bridge, Kenya.
120 BL: Add MS 52976A, Marker papers, 30 October 1906, Kitchener to Conk.

… come back to the family and see me through my last year of office. It is perhaps a little premature to settle, but as I have been asked for the app I should like to be able to say that notwithstanding my drinking habits [a topical issue then] you were going to come back to me. I do not think it would do you any harm as it would not be for long, but if you do think you could do better elsewhere do not for a moment consider my wishes in the matter.[121]

In 1906, Kitchener became aware of rumours about his drinking. He received '… letters from old ladies begging me to give up my drinking habits. What disgusting people there are at home going on spreading such lies.'[122] Maxwell was sent to deal with the situation and to pacify Royal circles. Kelly-Kenny's rapid departure for the Nile[123] suggested he was the rumour source, but Kitchener never said anything publicly. In fact, Kitchener did not consume much alcohol generally. He would have a wine glassful of brandy when, during the 1899-1902 war, his ADCs felt he needed it and occasionally a whisky and soda at night. In Cairo, Lord Calumn Critchlow-Tenant noted that, 'To close the day there was a light supper, an exact and unchanging ration of alcohol, and a last cigar.'[124] During the Great War when he gave up alcohol as part of the national initiative to improve productivity, his temper became 'very trying'. Dinners at the palace were noticeably quieter.[125]

Maxwell's return home achieved more than suppressing the drink rumours. He was to marry on 22 December the same year, Kitchener writing, 'I wish I was at home to be present. Hammy [Hamilton] tells me he is to represent me as best man.'[126] Later in 1908 when Marker/Conk's first son was born, Kitchener became godfather and took his task seriously, regularly sending wishes to 'Mrs Conk' and asking after the boy.[127] He also became godfather to Maxwell's two daughters, and proposed the health of the bride when Minto's daughter married Charles Fitzmaurice in India in 1908. His sword was used to cut the cake.[128]

Kitchener's preference for unmarried men was short-hand for 'men (and women) focused on the task at hand'. If a married man could put aside complete concern for family and attend military matters, Kitchener would work with him. Rawlinson,[129] appointed Grenfell's DAAG when he accompanied his wife to Egypt, her having

121 NAM: 7807-25-37, Kitchener to Frank 14 June 1906.
122 NAM: 7807-25-41, Kitchener to Frank 25 October 1906.
123 King, *Fall of the Viceroy*, p.145.
124 Hatfield House: Lord Calumn Critchlow-Tenant, A day with Lord Kitchener with letter from Lord K-3, 9 March 1952, 23 Charles Street, Berkeley Square to My dear Lady Salisbury.
125 Mark Pottle (ed.), *Champion Redoubtable: The Diaries and Letters of Violet Bonham Carter 1914-45* (London: Weidenfeld, 1998) p.36.
126 NAM: 7807-25-42, Kitchener to Frank 13 November 1906.
127 BL: Add MS 52276B Marker papers, April 1908.
128 Buchan, *Minto*, p.284.
129 General Sir Rawlinson of Trent.

been ordered there by her doctor, was sent to Kitchener when the latter asked for 'another staff officer'. His first impressions of Kitchener were:

> I think that I get on all right with K. I was told that he was a queer customer, but I have never failed to hit it off with anyone who means business, as he certainly does. His is a curious and very strong character. I both like and admire him, but on some minor points he is as obstinate as a commissariat mule. He is a long-headed, clear-minded man of business, with a wonderful memory. His apparent hardness of nature is a good deal put on, and is, I think, due to a sort of shyness. It made him unpopular at first, but, since those under him in the Egyptian Army have come to realize what a thoroughly capable man he is, there is a great deal less growling than there used to be.[130]

One sad consequence of the rumour was the suicide of Hector MacDonald. A tribunal found the accusations of homosexuality false and his body was claimed by a wife. The relationship had been kept quiet partly because of Kitchener's position on married men.[131]

Sensitivity

Beneath the detached, hard and on occasion ruthless façade, was a shy and sensitive man. Recorded as having approved 51 executions by the time he was 51, many more soldiers and officers had suffered a tongue lashing for incompetence.[132] In August 1914, Margot Asquith recorded the incident of a young soldier who returned wounded from the front and asked to speak to Kitchener. Learning the soldier had not been sent by French, Kitchener ordered his arrest: military discipline had been broken, and he could ill afford setting a precedent if the war was to be won. The politicians, however, were angry at the lost opportunity to find out what was happening on the Western Front.[133]

Kitchener did not take a life without due consideration. He set up a special commission in South Africa and in early 1916 approached FE Smith, Lord Birkenhead, the UK Attorney General to take over the court martial cases he had pending as he did not have sufficient time to 'give any real attention to them.' Birkenhead continued to review such cases until Kitchener's death, following which he did so for subsequent Secretaries of State until his appointment as Lord Chancellor. 'Finding a soldier of

---

130 Atwood, *Rawlinson*, p.30.
131 Woodliffe medals (dnw.co.uk), p.57. TNA: WO 138/24 names only a son as heir to MacDonald.
132 Royle, p.166.
133 Michael & Eleanor Brock, *Margot Asquith's Great War Diary 1914-1916: Views From Downing Street* (Oxford: Oxford University Press, 2014) 28 August 1914.

his experience and eminence thus open-minded in accepting expert civilian help, I seized the opportunity to press most urgently upon him my views as to the need of the Army in France of similar help. He welcomed the idea, and after that the obstacles to the scheme diminished.'[134] Magnus noted that Kitchener 'had a reputation for brutality' and was 'filled with a ruthlessness which took no account of personal feelings.' At Nablus on 1 November 1877, Kitchener recorded that he was '... compelled to have a number of boys tied to posts and publicly flogged for throwing stones'.[135] However, Anthony Babington found no significant increase in corporal punishment once Kitchener took command of the British forces during the 1899-1902 war in southern Africa.[136]

As a child, Kitchener had learnt not to show emotion which meant only those close to him were privy to his expressions of sorrow. His Chief of Staff 1901-02, Hamilton, noted that Kitchener was '... impassive as a rock in appearance, [but] he was really a bundle of sensitive and highly strung nerves kept under control 999 hours out of 1000 by an iron will.'[137] When Kitchener returned to England after Fashoda (Kadok) on 27 October 1898, his brother Walter observed he '... was "not in the least swollen-headed"; but that he was occasionally liable to "behave abominably" through "shyness".'[138]

Kitchener shed a tear on occasion. In addition to those already mentioned, the death of Billy Desborough presented another occasion. Kitchener felt personally responsible, writing, 'We all wish sometimes that the trumpet would sound for us, but we have to stick it out and do our very best until the release comes. I only wish that I could do more, or rather that what I do was better work.'[139] On 9 August 1915, Lady Desborough told Kitchener not to grieve for the boys: 'Death I saw as a gateway; not a barrier.'[140] Julian was buried on 28 May 1915, two days after his death, and Billy on 30 July 1915.[141] 'Lord Kitchener knew the boys ever since they were quite little, and was more than kind to them, and would get up early to go fishing with them, an occupation for which I do not think he had much natural taste! Julian was especially devoted to him.'[142] When Julian died, Kitchener wrote to Willy Grenfell: 'I grieve with you both − I loved poor Julian and feel his loss badly − He was a splendid soldier

---

134 Earl of Birkenhead, *Points of View* (London: Hodder & Stoughton, 1922) vol 2, p.8.
135 Magnus, pp.37-8.
136 Anthony Babington, *For the Sake of Empire: Capital Courts Martial 1914-18: The Truth* (New York: St Martin's, 1985) p.3.
137 Arthur, vol 2, p.73.
138 Magnus, p.174.
139 Magnus, p.144; HA: D/ERv/F132/2.
140 TNA: PRO 30/57/108/13, Lady Desborough to Kitchener, 9 August 1915.
141 HA: D/ERv/C1174/2, Desborough letter, 3 August 1915, Billy born 29 March 1890; CWGC, Julian Grenfell died age 27, buried Boulogne Eastern Cemetery, Pas de Calais, France; his brother Gerald William died age 25 is commemorated at Ypres (Menin Gate) Memorial, West-Vlaanderen, Belgium.
142 TNA: PRO 30/57/91/25, Lady Desborough to Arthur, 1 January 1916.

and served his country right well.'[143] Despite the feelings of loss many experienced, Margot confided to her diary: 'I felt like cancelling all engagements, but fearing this would inconvenience my guests I went down to dinner with a heavy heart.'[144] Kitchener was one of the guests but there is no mention of his relationship to the two boys, despite Margot's family and social network connections. Margot had recorded Kitchener's concern for the King at a lunch she hosted in 1909. And despite being on tour on the Indian Northern Frontier in 1903, Kitchener sent telegrams to ascertain how Salisbury was when he was gravely ill, receiving a reply within four hours from Hatfield House.[145] 'When the news of Neuve Chapelle [10-13 March 1915] reached London, and the heavy tale of the losses became known to him, he was moved as none ever imagined him. "My poor soldiers!" he repeated, "My poor soldiers!" and for hours he paced his room at the War Office alone [...]'[146] One third of the 11,200 lives lost had been Indian.

His most eccentric breakdown was when he captured two injured birds. He refused to let them go even after one had died. The other managed to escape whilst he was away causing his staff eventually to undertake a search to no avail. A few days after Kitchener's return, he found the bird and is recorded as dancing around in great joy.[147] Again, by this point, Kitchener had not had leave for some time, since July 1899, and had suffered the loss of good friends and colleagues through capture or death. These behaviours were clearly evident on the battlefield. When things got too much in India and he was refused leave, Kitchener withdrew to Simla where he concentrated on growing his flowers. By then most of his systems were already in place and his withdrawal from work was not as noticeable.

In 1915 Hamilton felt '... the forcing of Sir William Robertson upon him as a Chief of the Imperial General Staff gave him so great a shock that it took the heart out of his work, leaving him transformed into the mere shell of the K of K that was.' This was not the case when it was suggested to Kitchener in 1901 that Hamilton join him. 'I am extremely grateful: there is nothing I should like better. He is just the man I want, Hamilton will be a great help to me ...'[148] Kitchener quite clearly trusted Hamilton whom he knew personally having worked with him before, whereas Robertson had not. Robertson's appointment was suggested by politicians Kitchener did not trust, whereas it was a fellow officer, Roberts, who suggested Hamilton.

For all his reputation of being a hard, cold man, Kitchener regularly won the admiration and respect of his men when he visited and especially when he joined in, for

143 HA: D/ER/D1170/3, 30 May 1915 from Hardelot to My dear K, also DEX/789/C26; Trethewey, *Pearls*, p.435 (not brother as Trethewey has).
144 Bonham Carter, *Margot Asquith*, diary entry 3 August 1915, pp.312-3.
145 Arthur, vol 2, p.128.
146 Grew, p.16.
147 Royle, p.165.
148 Hamilton, *Anti-Commando*, p.147.

example, mucking in with a shovel to help rebuild the railway line from Wadi Halfa.[149] They might not have liked him, but they trusted and respected him.

He also cared. Many of Kitchener's letters contain messages for men who had served with him. A letter to Maxwell in August 1906 ended with 'Love to Rawly write and tell me how Victor is and if the operation was a success.'[150] In September he was telling Maxwell that Victor had to get well before coming out, there was no rush as he was only needed in December for when the Amir visited. On 11 June 1916, Desborough publicly shared an intimate letter from Kitchener: 'Nothing struck me more in visiting the many hospitals abroad than the spirit in which officers and men faced death, and the fervent confidence they had in the life to come. This to me is the most remarkable feature of the war; the true religious confidence underlying both officers and men.'[151]

Kitchener's preference was to be with a select group of friends, in the open, or working in his garden. He grew orchids, winning a competition for the 'best display of *Dendrabium Orchis* at the Orchid and Floral Exhibition, Victoria Nursery, Calcutta'.[152] When required to entertain, such as at Simla and in Cairo, Kitchener took a hands-on approach, including organising the flowers himself. In April 1916, Winifred Portland congratulated him as, '[York] House looked so nice with your glorious flowers and I liked both my dinner neighbours immensely.'[153]

---

149 Royle, p.108; Magnus, p.125.
150 NAM: 7807-25-39, Kitchener to Frank 2 August 1906.
151 HA: D/ERv/F132/2.
152 Rye, p.262.
153 Pollock, p.464.

9

Test of a lifetime: Britain, 1914-1916

On 19 June 1914 Kitchener left Cairo on annual leave, having been made an Earl two days prior.[1] Staying with the Desboroughs, 29 June, he heard of the assassination of the Archduke in Sarajevo and knew instinctively it meant war. This was confirmed when, on 21 July, Kitchener met the German ambassador in London. The same day, Kitchener told Asquith and Churchill that Britain should stand by France.[2] This was quite a turn-around from 1909 when he had objected to Haldane talking to the French about military planning. At that time, Kitchener was concerned that as Britain had no plans, any military agreement would result in Britain being tacked onto whatever France determined.[3] He was not far wrong given how things worked out in 1914. Ten days later, all the heads of overseas missions were instructed to return to their countries and Kitchener planned accordingly.[4] In the meantime, 28 July, Churchill told Kitchener at lunch that 'If war comes, you will not go back,'[5] supplemented the next day at lunch with Daisy, Princess of Pless, and Prince and Princess Lichnowsky at the German Embassy, who sitting next to Kitchener, implored him not to go: '… you are wanted in England; there is no one.' He needed to help with home politics, the Irish Question and other things. 'I did not think of war then; I even begged him to stay in England and marry, and he looked at me through his dear bright but strange eyes, as one didn't match the other, and laughed.' Daisy left London on 1 August, recording her last encounter with Kitchener the night she heard he had drowned.[6] Kitchener,

---

1   Arthur, p.345.
2   Royle, p.251.
3   Royle, p.225.
4   Royle, p.253.
5   David Fromkin, *A Peace to End All Peace: The Fall of the Ottoman Empire and the Creation of the Middle East* (New York: Henry Holt, 1989) p.79.
6   Daisy Princess of Pless, *Daisy Princess of Pless* (New York: EP Dutton, 1920) p.406. Mary Theresa Olivia, nee Cornwallis-West married Hans Heinrich XV von Hochberg of Silesia. Born 28 June 1873, died 29 June 1943.

however, was anxious to return to Egypt where he could protect the Empire and control the Suez Canal.

On 3 August 1914 with war declared, Kitchener rushed to get the last boat to Egypt, but following delays which he could not control, a message was delivered instructing he return to London. Asquith wanted him available for 'personal consultation and advice'.[7] On 5 August, Kitchener finally accepted the post of Secretary of State for War when it was made clear the King had requested compliance. Kitchener acquiesced on condition that his appointment be on the same terms as the enlisting men: the duration of the war or three years.[8] Further, he would have no parliamentary duties,[9] but would be a participant at the eventual peace conference.[10] His comment to Girouard was, 'May God preserve me from the politicians.'[11]

Broderick's 1905 prediction had come true: 'After every one has failed [at the War Office] there will be a call for some one, and you will not be able to avoid the War Office for ever!'[12]

For all the negative press Kitchener attracted, a number of people claim to have influenced his appointment in 1914, not least Haldane who had overseen the army reforms. Austen Chamberlain recorded that 'affairs at the War Office were in some confusion owing to the fact that the Prime Minister had no time for his departmental duties as Secretary of State.' This had been reported by Leverton Harris who had been told by Girouard:

> ... that Kitchener, who left London at 11.30 this morning, might well be kept and used at the War Office. The idea was taken up, and Balfour sent an immediate note to Winston, then at the Cabinet, asking if it had occurred to the Prime Minister that Kitchener might be more useful in organization at the War Office at this moment than in Egypt. If the Prime Minister approved the idea there would be time to stop Kitchener at Dover.[13]

Given this is the only entry about Kitchener in Chamberlain's published memoir, it has a strong element of validity about it. Others responsible for Asquith appointing Kitchener to the War Office were Alfred Milner[14] and Leo Amery. Hearing from

7   Peter Simkins, *Kitchener's Army* (Barnsley: Pen & Sword, 2007 reprint) p.35.
8   Arthur, vol 3.
9   Royle, p.254.
10   Marie Belloc Lowndes, *A Passing World* (London: Macmillan, 1948) p.223. Marie had been friends with Margot Asquith since 1894. She published an anonymous biography on Kitchener which her husband wrote. Mrs Belloc Lowndes, *The merry wives of Windsor* (London: Macmillan, 1946) p.100.
11   Simkins, p.35.
12   Arthur, vol 2, p.120.
13   Austen Chamberlain, *Down the Years* (London: Cassell, 1935) p.104.
14   Vladimir Halperin, *Lord Milner and the Empire* (London: Odhams, 1952) p.113.

Henry Wilson that Asquith was looking to appoint Haldane, Amery felt Kitchener would be better and discussed it with Milner:

> My impression is that [Milner] had not actually seen Asquith at all, because what I am quite clear about is that Milner, having elucidated from K that he had no views at all about the Expeditionary Force, worked up K on the other question to the point of putting him into a taxi there and then to go to Downing Street and tell Asquith that things in Egypt were serious and that he must go off at once, unless Asquith wanted him to stay for some more definite and important work. I don't think, however, that you can quote this, because it was told me by Milner at the time and of course he could be the only source of information, and that would embarrass him in his present position. But I put it down to confirm you in the view that up to that moment Asquith, whatever vague ideas he may have had as to utilising K in some capacity ... had certainly not decided to make him Secretary of State and had not in fact offered K anything at all.[15]

Amery's position resonates with Crawford's account of a discussion at the Carlton on 4 August. 'Much fear is expressed lest Haldane may return to the War Office. In point of fact there is no real danger of this: all Haldane is working for is to prevent Kitchener going there, for the Lord Chancellor fears the inevitable exposure of his follies which would ensue.'[16] Haldane had been responsible for the War Office reforms after the 1899-1902 war, and the introduction of the Territorial Army. He had also seen how Kitchener had dealt with Curzon in India over army reform.

Kitchener's reluctance to accept the post was not one of modesty. He had no faith in the War Office having done everything to avoid being sent there or to do what he considered routine duties.[17] Reportedly on arrival at the War Office, he discovered his pen 'did not function,'[18] which did nothing to boost his confidence in the organisation. Kitchener's concerns about the War Office dated to the early days of his military career. He had received a note of objection and censure from the War Office for trying to change the way transport in South Africa was organised in 1900, but he could not see why he was being reprimanded by the 'old red-tape heads of department' who quoted regulations which were 'generally dated about 1870 and intended for Aldershot

---

15   Gollin, pp.240-1.
16   John Russell Vincent, *The Crawford Papers: The Journals of David Lindsay, Twenty-Seventh Earl of Crawford and Tenth Earl of Balcarres (1871-1940), During the Years 1892 to 1940* (Manchester: Manchester University, 1984) p.340.
17   Magnus, pp.91-2; For a relatively balanced assessment of the War Office at the start of the twentieth century, see R McGregor Dawson, 'The Cabinet minister and administration: The British War Office 1903-16', in *The Canadian Journal of Economics and Political Science* (November 1939) vol 5, no 4, pp.451-78.
18   Cassar, p.184.

manoeuvres.'[19] For Kitchener, the men in the War Office had little practical experience of the field evidenced in the instructions and weapons they sent. When he asked for breaching guns for his action in Omdurman, the War Office sent him something else. He kept objecting until he got what he wanted, the incident eventually being reported in the press.[20] By 1914 his view had not changed.

Politically, Kitchener's appointment was a great achievement. The Dominions, India, and Egypt were in accord, and the British public was confident: the man who avenged Gordon and defeated the Boers was in charge. However, it was not without difficulties. Kitchener was a soldier, one who commanded, in control of a civil department running things as he had previous campaigns, causing subordinates and colleagues, political and military, to despair. He saw his role as Secretary of State in the same way he saw being Commander-in-Chief. He was ultimately responsible for Britain's military success and would therefore run the War Office in the same way he did a campaign: hands on and in complete control. However, having to explain and defend his every move before he made it was new to him. In spite of his anomalous position as head of the War Office and as a/the senior military officer, he recognised he had to leave the fighting, strategy and tactics to those on the ground. For a man of Kitchener's calibre, this was not easily done, especially when he saw mistakes being made or had an alternate approach. But he also understood issuing an instruction and then leaving those at the coal face to deliver as they thought best. This had been his practice in Egypt and South Africa providing he trusted those in command. The tension caused between these two positions, soldier and statesman, played out most notably during the 1914-18 war in his relationship with sixty-two year old John French.

Although he had been back to England regularly on leave, and to sort out business face to face, Kitchener was effectively out of touch with British society and military planning. Membership and attendance at the Committee of Imperial Defence (CID) meetings when in London would have given him some insight into Britain's preparedness for war. But considering the advice he had given Australia and New Zealand on preparing for war only four years before, he must have despaired when on 14 July 1914, less than a month before war broke out, the 128th meeting of the CID discussed the pros and cons of building a channel tunnel, and a report on the Dominion War Book. This was the 'first time [Maurice Hankey] ever saw Kitchener strongly moved' – Kitchener called on Hankey '... and for at least half an hour inveighed against the construction proposal' on security grounds. The final agenda item, 'Coordination of Departmental action upon the outbreak of war', had no reference to the tensions then

19   Magnus, p.196.
20   Groser, p.130; Waimate *Daily Advertiser*, 21 April 1900.

already present about a possible outbreak of war.[21] Concerning the CID, he 'doubt[ed] they know what a fuse is!'[22]

Kitchener had worked to improve the Empire's security. He knew there were different ways of waging war and managing armies, all with three common basic requirements: men, material and money.[23] Knowing his experience of warfare was 'prehistoric', or less technical, when it came to battle in Europe, he supplemented his knowledge by observing and studying European war when possible. His experiences in Africa and on the Indian frontiers had played their part in broadening his under-standing of conducting military operations. Charles Callwell,[24] Director of Military Operations between 1914 and 1916, who served with Kitchener, wrote in 1919 that, 'Some day, no doubt, an illuminating record of what the War Office achieved in trans-forming this country into a great military power under the inspired, if unorthodox, leadership of Lord Kitchener, will make its appearance.'[25] This is quite a statement coming from Callwell whose official papers on the First World War in Africa repre-sented the traditional War Office school of thought, differing from Kitchener in his advice to the Cabinet. Here, Callwell focused on the immediate battle and how that was conducted, while Kitchener took a longer, more holistic view.[26]

Manning the war

Quickly grasping what he thought was needed, creating an effective army or military machine, Kitchener began to recruit, arm, and supervise the conduct of the general war. Birkenhead claims that when the British Expeditionary Force departed for France, Kitchener had no officer 'of the General Staff of high rank and continuous employ-ment at the War Office capable of working out a Staff plan for [his] consideration.'[27] On arrival at the War Office, there were eight unemployed General Officers on the

21 MP Hankey, *Supreme Command*, vol 1 (London: George Allen & Unwin, 1961) p.109; Cassar, p.19; TNA: CAB 38/28/35, 128th meeting of the CID 14 July 1914.
22 Riddell, *War Diary*, p.75.
23 Rye, pp.267, 529.
24 Born 2 April 1859, died 16 May 1928, 2nd Anglo Afghan war, 1st and 2nd Anglo-Boer wars, left the army 1909, recalled August 1914: DMO 1914-23.12.1915, DMI 23.12.1915-3.1.1916, special mission to Russia.
25 CE Callwell, 'Good old times at the War Office', in Littell's *The Living Age*, vol 300 (1919) p.224.
26 The contrasts between the approach by the two men based on their official papers to the War Cabinet regarding the war in East Africa 1915 needs more detailed investigation, especially as Daniel Whitingham's forthcoming biography on Callwell suggests he and Kitchener had a similar outlook. Daniel E Whittingham, *Charles E Callwell and the British Way in Warfare* (Cambridge: forthcoming), Charles Edward Callwell, *Small Wars: Their Principles and Practice* (London: HMSO, 1896), *Experiences of a Dug-Out 1914-18* (London: Constable, 1920); Samson, *Britain, South Africa and East Africa*.
27 Birkenhead, *Points of View*, p.24.

Army List. However, many of them were of a different era and unsuited to an active post in modern warfare. A few were able to train new recruits.[28]

Kitchener had his work cut out for him. The Chief of Imperial General Staff (CIGS), Charles Douglas, was not coping and died on 25 October 1914 from stress. He was replaced by James Wolfe Murray, recently returned with the South African Imperial Service Garrison troops. Murray soon became known, particularly amongst the Admiralty as 'Sheep Murray' and 'attracted little praise'.[29] His succession as CIGS did little to ease Kitchener's burdens, the latter absorbing the functions into his own workload. Others, although not outstanding, were able to do Kitchener's bidding with instruction. One such was Henry Sclater, the Adjutant-General who was eventually replaced by Neil Macready in December 1915 during the War Office staff shuffle.[30] '[Kitchener] was a very hard worker, and he mercilessly exacted the maximum of effort from his subordinates. He seldom bestowed praise, or even approval. And yet men worked for him as for no other.'[31] The men Kitchener trusted were left to get on with the job. Simkins notes Kitchener 'rarely saw his senior advisers as a body', leaving them to act on his instructions.[32] Men like John Cowans, Quartermaster General, were given free reign. Cowans had seen war coming and had started planning as far as he could. He introduced food magazines and constantly found ways around problems to ensure the armed forces were fed, watered, and supplied with the necessary equipment.[33] Kitchener had Cowans press commanding officers regarding the importance of light railways.[34] But in 1916 his position was threatened because of an accusation of favouritism levelled by the new Secretary of State for War, Lloyd George.[35]

Habits are hard to break and the sixty-four year old Secretary of State for War was no exception. His appointment was 'a hazardous experiment.'[36] Although Kitchener's appointment was not the first since 1660 that a serving soldier was a member of cabinet, he was the first with political power,[37] effectively becoming the equivalent of the Military Member in India; a position which would conflict with that of the

---

28   Smithers, p.113.
29   Smithers, p.118. James Wolfe Murray, born 13 March 1853, died 17 October 1919, Ashanti and 1899-1902 wars, Chief of Imperial Garrison South Africa and Acting High Commissioner South Africa August 1914.
30   Smithers, p.118.
31   Rodd, *Memories*, p.37.
32   Simkins, p.38.
33   Smithers, p.119.
34   Arthur, p.263.
35   Jennifer Anne Pauley, The social and political roles of Edith, Lady Londonderry 1878-1959 (PhD, University of Ulster, 1994); Chapman-Huston & Rutter, *Cowans*, vol 2, pp.142ff. How much this had to do with Lloyd George making his mark vis a vis Kitchener requires further investigation.
36   Royle, p.254.
37   Gordon Corrigan, *Mud, Blood and Poppycock: Britain and the Great War* (London: Cassell, 2004) p.308.

Commander-in-Chief of the British forces, John French. Asquith recognised, with backing from the Northcliffe press, this would be a war requiring extraordinary measures, but he did not reckon on the personalities.

Kitchener's task was huge. On 11 October 1914, the Earl of Crawford reflected:

> Kitchener isn't well – he gets no exercise, his old headaches are returning. He is worried and overwrought. He has not the faculty of delegating work. Is it that he overtrusts himself, or that he distrusts mankind? Anyhow, work is not being done because he won't dissolve responsibilities. The other day there were 2,000 unopened letters at the WO so Cecil Smith told me. The work of the Education Department has fallen off, and Smith very properly offered some of his staff to carry out the ordinary work of the WO, such as opening, sorting, registering, and acknowledging correspondence, keeping accounts and so forth, all of it work for which his men are quite well qualified – not a bit! The WO doesn't want any extra help: yet they admitted to him that at that moment there were those 2,000 envelopes.
>
> Kitchener has done much. Nobody living could have done more in these two months: but he was amazed at the criminal neglect of his predecessors. His fault is that he won't enlist the voluntary help which is longing to give competent assistance. Hence the state of confusion in Whitehall. He is called Lord K of Chaos ...[38]

That Kitchener was over-controlling confirms the poor state of British preparedness for a European war. A year after the outbreak of war, on a visit to Edinburgh to see an aunt and inspect the defences at Cromarty Leith, he discovered the local 'fishing fleet with some scores of Germans on board' was still operating with no restrictions. He naturally saw to it that the area was better protected but the authorities, according to Archibald Sayce three years later, remained in a 'fool's paradise so far as aviation was concerned' having done little to divert zeppelin raids.[39] Cowans called Kitchener: '... a truly magnificent man [...] He said what he wanted, and if he found a Staff Officer an incapable creature he applied Lord Fisher's three R's – Ruthless, Remorseless, Relentless – and rightly so. Never whilst either in the East or in the War Office did I know Lord Kitchener interfere with any work in any department unless it was shaky.'[40] This was no different to Millicent Fawcett's observation in a previous war. Visiting South Africa between July and December 1901, she observed:

38   Vincent, *Crawford Papers*, pp.343-4.
39   Archibald Henry Sayce, *Reminiscences* (London: Macmillan, 1923) pp.419-20, born 25 September 1845, died 4 February 1933.
40   Chapman-Husten and Rutter, *Cowans*, pp.294-5.

Later we had many talks about [Kitchener] with men of his staff and others. We were told that on his journeys up and down the line or on horseback his keen eye saw everything and everybody, noting which men were doing their work well and which were slack or indifferent; the first were promoted, the latter were, in the phrase of the day, "Stellenbosched," i.e. sent where they could do no harm.[41]

One can imagine that Kitchener's first meeting as Secretary of State for War was 'Hell with the lid left off.'[42] Mobilisation had been ordered on 4 August. On 5 August a three-hour debate, including Wilson, French and Kitchener, took place to determine where the Force should go. Not being officially in post, nor having been privy to pre-war discussions, and with insufficient time once appointed to master the position, Kitchener gave way allowing Asquith to make the final decision whether to attack Mauberge or Amiens.[43] However, it did not all go French's way when the War Council accepted Kitchener's view concerning the number of divisions to be sent.[44] Kitchener's gut reaction proved right, George Arthur absolving him of complicity in the defeat which followed. Arthur had only worked with Kitchener from the outbreak of war and according to Fitzgerald, his lack of military knowledge and experience caused Kitchener great anxiety.[45]

Kitchener believed the war would last between three and five years and that the United Kingdom would or should be able to furnish about seventy Divisions. At the time of his death, sixty-seven were in the field with three in training.[46] More alarmingly, it would take until 1917 for Britain and the Empire's impact to be really felt, although he could put men into the field as early as spring 1915 once they had been trained.[47] Before then, Britain would be planning and assisting the French with holding actions. However, this required a careful balancing act which he was ultimately to lose. Politics, and the politicians, got the better of strategical insight and would continue to do so for the remainder of the war, yet the soldiers were held responsible.

His experience in 1870's France, and later South Africa, and studies of the American Civil War made him wary of using volunteers, but the reality of the situation dictated otherwise. For Kitchener, the army, including its support systems, '... would have to be raised from scratch.'[48] Experience told him that the army which controlled all aspects of its service operated best – with no political interference,[49] but that was not

41   Millicent Fawcett, *What I Remember*, p.171.
42   Royle, p.303, Charles Harris, Director of Finance, War Office.
43   Royle, p.307.
44   Royle, p.269.
45   Hatfield House: 2 September 19?? Fitzgerald to Lady Salisbury.
46   Arthur, pp.307-8.
47   Royle, pp.258-9.
48   Smithers, p.92.
49   Royle, p.214.

to be. In Britain, politics controlled the military; a factor Kitchener resisted despite being in a civilian-political role. He remained first and foremost a soldier insisting that his term as Secretary of State be on the same conditions as if he had enlisted into the army. It was this juxtaposition of civil versus military power that led to the later conflict between Kitchener as Secretary of State for War and other Cabinet members.

Within hours of his appointment, Kitchener called for volunteers to join the army and within days, 500,000 had flocked to the colours,[50] in addition to those already enlisted in the Territorial Army which had been formed for just such an occasion. Kitchener's decision to create the New Armies was to have a force trained specifically to serve in Europe which would allow the Territorial Army to do what it was trained for: protect England in case of an invasion. However, Esher thought otherwise. He complained that Kitchener 'knows nothing of the organisation of our home armies' and so created something he understood.[51] In contrast, Walter Long explained:

> [Kitchener] had just gone up to dress for dinner [5 August 1914], and had left word that I was to see him in his bedroom. I vividly remember the impression made on me [...] as cool and collected as if nothing at all had happened.
>
> He had sent for me to ask some questions about the capacity of the country to provide the necessary number of men, and he proceeded [...] to put a series of clear, concise questions to me. I found the greatest difficulty in convincing him that the Territorials could be relied upon to form a very useful force if certain steps were taken. I always believed that he thought he could not calculate upon them being sufficiently trained to be relied upon as a fighting force. However, his complete command of the situation, and his unhesitating decision as to the numbers he would require, all served to add to the confidence I had always felt in him, and to make me feel certain that we had the right man in the right place.[52]

Use of the Territorial Army vexed Kitchener as he explained to Alice over dinner on 13 August.[53] Despite his decision to raise the New Armies, the Territorials could, and would with more training and better skilled officers, be used overseas if those who did not want to serve outside of England were removed from units which expressed a desire to do so. In the words of GW Steevens, the 'Sudan machine' had to be created. Another consideration was that the Territorial Force was armed with the 'old

---

50   Lee and Starling, p.22; Hankey, *Supreme Command*, vol 1, p.225.

51   KW Mitchinson, *Gentlemen and Officers: The Impact and Experience of War on a Territorial Regiment 1914-18* (Andrews UK, 2012) p.32; see also Peter Eric Hodgkinson, British Infantry Battalion Commanders in the First World War (PhD, University of Birmingham, 2013) for an analysis of the Kitchener Army.

52   Walter Long, *Memories* (London: Hutchinson, 1923) p.216. Long's views of Kitchener vacillated as did many others. This is one of his few favourable comments concerning Kitchener.

53   Hatfield House: Alice Salisbury papers, letter 13 August 1914.

long rifle' which had limited reserves of ammunition. Current arms production was focusing on the 'new short rifle' which the Regular Army used, and which Kitchener's armies would also use.[54]

Having recommended conscription to Australia and New Zealand, Kitchener did not push for it in England as he knew there was no united political support for it. Asquith was loathe to introduce conscription despite significant others believing the public would have condoned it if Kitchener had asked.[55] It would be the final resort. Kitchener was further motivated not to encourage conscription because it was '… inconvenient to get the men before he could arm them,' and more significantly, as '… the secret of storming trenches had not yet been discovered, [hurling] men against a trench system defended by barbed wire and machine guns was pure butchery.'[56] Although Kitchener took risks, he only did so once he was confident of success. The nature of the war on the continent meant Britain had to develop 'an army on a continental scale' and to fight in a continental manner; a situation he grasped but which French did not. Such armies technically could not be created in war time: 'I felt myself that though there might be some justice in this view, I had to take the risk and embark on what may be regarded as a gigantic experiment.'[57] The outcome was the New Armies, which for some time suffered from shortages of training material, uniforms, and poor administrative systems.

As Kitchener became aware of situations, he acted. By 11 August, Leo Amery was Director of Civilian Recruiting for Southern Command having sorted out the blockages affecting recruitment in Birmingham South.[58] However, receiving little support from the Cabinet system which was totally inadequate to deal with a war time situation, many men were taken away from vital war work causing other problems.[59]

Within the New Army, the formation of the pals battalions was encouraged. They were 'one of Lord Kitchener's numerous inspirations':[60] men would fight better and in a more coordinated fashion if they knew each other and had something in common, for this reason a commander needed to train with their rank and file. For the remainder of 1914 Kitchener had his hands full with the British Expeditionary Force settling into a routine in Europe and getting the New Armies organised in a way which would allow the best training in the shortest time he believed possible; six months.

54   Hankey, *Supreme Command*, vol 1, p.194; GW Steevens, *With Kitchener in Khartoum* (Edinburgh: William Blackwood, 1901) p.48.
55   Callwell, *Dug-Out*, p.73.
56   Hankey, *Supreme Command*, vol 1, p.426.
57   Kitchener to House of Commons as reported in Times Literary Supplement, *The real Lord Kitchener* (1920) vol 305, p.548.
58   Simkins, pp.52-3.
59   Hankey, *Supreme Command*, vol 1, p.225.
60   *Rand Daily Mail*, 31 August 1914.

In the meantime, the Territorials, not ready for the battle front but who had some training, could be used to release troops for the front. This was 'a calculated risk',[61] however, Kitchener was confident the Navy could protect and dominate the seas preventing an invasion. The Territorials could also relieve British officers in India, territory he saw as expendable in order to save the motherland. Kitchener had foreseen that the men would return to Europe before the end of the war, but they first had to see action in Mesopotamia and Palestine, whilst one, the 42nd (East Lancashire) Division would see action at Gallipoli.[62] With losses on the Western Front and the retreat to Mons on 23 August 1914, Kitchener was forced to send units of Territorials to fill gaps in French's forces, seventy battalions having volunteered to serve abroad. They were to prove their worth.[63]

The developing stalemate on the Western Front, the resultant need for replacements, as well as pressure from the French that Britain did more, meant recruitment and conscription remained high on the agenda. On 2 January 1915, Kitchener wrote to French about the possibility of operations elsewhere, but French believed only a Western Front breakthrough would determine the outcome of the war.[64] Kitchener was, therefore, forced to play a waiting game as his forces were neither sufficient, nor sufficiently trained, to join either the British Expeditionary Force in France or elsewhere.[65] French's limitations were becoming known, and at a dinner on 22 January 1915 when the discussion turned to who was to the command the New Armies, Brade responded: 'Ah, that is the question! I don't think French will be equal to the task.' He did not know whether Kitchener would go, '... but thought he might like to.'[66]

Offers of assistance flooded in creating dilemmas: how to accept help from irregular forces without undermining discipline and other requirements Kitchener knew winning the war would entail. Everything had to conform to an overall plan and place within the 'military machine',[67] and again, previous experience urged caution: volunteers under Basil Spragge and the 13th Imperial Yeomanry had surrendered at Lindley during the 1899-1902 war. 'Amateur soldiers were not merely useless but a liability.'[68] Most offers were declined.

Some were persistent such as the Legion of Frontiersmen. The Legion formed in 1905 under Roger Pocock aimed to help the Empire in time of need. Many had honed their skills in the 1899-1902 southern Africa war and other frontier encounters. The outbreak of war in 1914 provided their opportunity and on 4 August some of the Manchester Squadron had gone across to support Belgium becoming part of

61   Smithers, p.93.
62   Smithers, p.93.
63   Smithers, p.97; Simkins, p.45.
64   Royle, p.300.
65   Royle, p.301.
66   Riddell, *War Diary*, p.48.
67   Arthur, p.310.
68   Smithers, p.31.

the 3rd Belgian Lancers. But they wanted to do more and offered their services to the Colonial Office which were declined, it being suggested that they provide support to the armed forces.[69] Based at Southampton and Avonmouth, they broke in horses for the cavalry and transport. This was still not enough and under the leadership of Daniel Patrick Driscoll,[70] they continued to lobby for armed service. Eventually, in 1915, Kitchener authorised their going to East Africa under the auspices of the 25th Royal Fusiliers. Sending the Frontiersmen to Africa solved a number of problems for Kitchener. It gave this experienced, ill-disciplined, and mainly untrained motley group of men, who did not meet enlistment criteria, an opportunity to do what they could in a theatre which was deemed less important to the greater war. It would reduce pressure from the Colonial Office pressing him for troops to safeguard the colony. The Germans were occupying the only British territory they would of the war, Tsavo. The Indian Expeditionary Forces which had been sent out in 1914 had been decisively beaten at Longido and Tanga in early November 1914, and attempts to regain the upper hand at Jasin had failed in January 1915. The Germans were also impacting on trade by raiding the Uganda railway. This was work ideally suited to the Frontiersmen and on 10 April 1915, 1,116 men set sail to do their duty in a theatre Kitchener did not want escalated.

Having sorted out the Legion of Frontiersmen, the Canadians provided another challenge. They sought to have Sam Steele[71] made commander of the 2nd Canadian Division to serve in France. Kitchener was prepared to have Steele command the Canadians generally but in France they would have a British commander. Protracted and heated discussion followed until eventually on 26 July 1915, Steele was persuaded that command of Shorncliff District where the Canadians were based was the best option for the sixty-six year old who had never even commanded a force the size of a battalion. French was also against Steele's serving in Europe. Age was a factor – some thought Kitchener at sixty-four was too old for the War Office. More significantly having senior officers trained or experienced in the same way ensured better under-standing of orders which could then be explained and adapted to local conditions, subordinate officers translating for their men. This was common practice as seen with the Indians serving alongside British units, the South Africans under Lukin with the 9th Scottish Division and the Cape Corps with the Welsh in Palestine. It was a fine line ameliorating national identities and winning the war.

Nationalist interests impacted on recruitment in Britain too, bringing Kitchener into conflict with Lloyd George who wanted a separate Welsh division and to provide for Non-Conformist chaplains. Kitchener clearly did not understand Welsh politics or Lloyd George's position and it was left to Asquith to mediate and resolve.[72]

---

69   TNA: CO 323/63/10, letters 20 and 15 September 1914; CO 323/64/7, 25 September 1914.
70   Daniel Patrick Driscoll, born 11 May 1862?, died 6 August 1934.
71   Samuel Benfield Steele, born 5 January 1849, died 30 January 1919, Canadian.
72   Royle, p.270.

Kitchener and Lloyd George were bound to clash. Two strong men with different approaches, both ambitious, and loyal to their country. The one secretive, the other expressing his feelings as they arose. Yet, from comments recorded by others and the advice Lloyd George gave Edwin Montagu,[73] it appears the two men understood each other, gave as hard as the other and respected the others' skills. A perusal of Riddell's *War Diary* gives an indication of Lloyd George's vacillating moods and feelings towards Kitchener, and provides an insight into the 'hidden' Kitchener.

Lloyd George was annoyed with the way the War Office was treating Dissenters and the Welsh Army Corps. The reason was language. The Welsh wanted to speak Cymraeg in their units, but this would not work where most officers and others did not speak the language. Military orders had to be in English. As far as Lloyd George could see, this was killing recruitment. On 28 October 1914, Lloyd George informed Riddell '... that he had had an argument with Kitchener' regarding the issue. No further details are recorded until 31 October when Lloyd George was

> ... full of his interview with Kitchener. He greeted me with: 'Look here! Kitchener is a big man. Nothing small or petty about him. Yesterday he sent for me.' He said, 'I have thought over what you said. There is a good deal of justification for these complaints. Tell me exactly what you want.' Having been told, 'K wrote an appropriate order against each item. He really acted extraordinarily well.' [A favourite phrase with LG.]

On being asked who he wanted in command in North Wales, Lloyd George said,

> I really don't know, but I have a very clever Welsh officer with me now. He is outside. Colonel Owen Thomas.[74] Kitchener said, 'Have him in!' and rang the bell. Thomas came in. K said, 'I remember you in South Africa. As from today you will be Brigadier-General Owen Thomas, but go and put on your uniform. Never let me see you in mufti again during the war!' Very dramatic! added LG.[75]

This encounter is enlightening, especially by a man who was not scared to be confrontational and work behind the scenes to have Kitchener's power curtailed. Kitchener was open to advice, but was not a quick decision maker as shown at Paardeburg and on occasion in the Sudan. The 'stand up fight' with Lloyd George on 28 (25) October was sufficiently intense for Kitchener to '... retire – from the room, from the government, and [cause] a terrible crisis.' Jack Pease[76] stopped him leaving the Cabinet meeting repeatedly telling him, 'You can't leave the cabinet room' and eventually 'Kitchener

73   Edwin Samuel Montagu, born 6 February 1879, died 15 November 1924.
74   Owen Thomas, born 18 December 1858, died 6 March 1923.
75   Riddell, *War Diary*, pp.36-8.
76   Joseph Albert 'Jack' Pease, 1st Baron Gainsford, born 17 January 1860, died 15 February 1943.

with the slow subconscious movements of the somnambulist moved silently back to his seat,' the issue being tactfully dropped for the remainder.[77] He had to think things through and if the new information proved a change was required, he made it. His immediate appointment of Thomas to the North Wales command, although a spur of the moment decision, was based on prior knowledge and experience of the man in South Africa. He had proven his worth then and was trusted to do what was needed in Wales. Kitchener had learnt to compromise and bargain, he was a master at it. And, he never forgot his first encounter with the Duke of Cambridge back in 1871, reminding a soldier what he was about whilst recognising the human side.

Kitchener's treatment of the Welsh contrasted with that of the Irish. Maurice Headlam,[78] Paymaster for Ireland, recognised Kitchener was too busy to understand the Irish situation himself, defaulting to the government's position. This exacerbated the divisions with Ulster. Despite Edward Carson[79] and John Redmond[80] meeting with Kitchener on 7 August 1914 to suggest Ulster and Irish volunteers be kept separate within the British Army, Kitchener refused in line with his policy of not engaging private militias. When Redmond continued pushing to have Irish volunteers recognised, Kitchener held his ground for fear of allowing politics to enter the army, a fear fuelled by the government's position as Joseph Devlin[81] noted after meeting with Asquith. Eventually, an agreement on Home Rule was achieved in September to encourage recruiting but other issues were soon to impact, such as the military emblem for the Ulster regiment; the nationalist Shamrock.[82] One wonders if the Irish experience would have been any different had Kitchener had time to better understand Ulster given his record in South Africa and the perceived political similarities between the two peoples.[83]

Margot Asquith rated Kitchener's 'muddling' of the Irish as his second blunder of the war; the first was rejection of the territorials. Both were politically sensitive in the British context; a position Kitchener was ignorant of and reliant on the politicians for guidance. Despite having spent his early years in Ireland, Kitchener apparently regarded the Irish as idle, and nationalists were '... a danger to the stability of

77   Morgan, p.174; Vincent, *Crawford Papers*, pp.613-4 reporting Churchill, 15 February 1940.

78   Maurice Francis Headlam, born 19 October 1873, died 2 November 1956.

79   Edward Carson, born 9 February 1854, died 22 October 1935.

80   John Edward Redmond, born 1 September 1856, died 6 March 1918.

81   Joseph Devlin, born 13 February 1871, died 18 January 1934.

82   B Grob-Fitzgibbon, *Turning Points of the Irish Revolution: The British Government, Intelligence and the Cost of Indifference, 1912-1921* (Springer, 2007) p.83; Christopher M Kennedy, *Genesis of the Rising 1912-1916: A Transformation of Nationalist Opinion* (Peter Lang, 2010), pp.153-5.

83   Anne Samson, *Jan Smuts and the British War Cabinet 1917-1919* (MA Dissertation, University of Westminster, 1998)

the British Empire for which he had fought all his life.'[84] Charles Townsend claims Kitchener had been influenced by Conservative concern of Home Rule and that Asquith had failed to explain to Kitchener the importance of pacifying Ireland for political reasons.[85] Kitchener had his own thoughts on the matter as he expressed in 1912 in a letter to Marker from Cairo. Although '... officers have no politics, [...] I suppose they have religious feelings and the bringing of a Protestant community under [Roman Catholic] domination by force would probably be very distasteful to them at least that is how some of them seem to feel about the matter.' It would '... be very serious for the army if officers leave the service on conscientious grounds and that it may have far reaching results in the future.' The next week he asked Conk not to make his views known as he did not want to get mixed up in the matter.[86] In December 1915, Kitchener replaced the officer commanding 16th Irish Division with a Roman Catholic as many of the men in the Division were likely to be Catholic.[87]

Tensions in Ireland continued to develop and eventually Maxwell was appointed military governor on 28 April 1916[88] after the Irish Easter Rising as he had 'no past record' with Ireland and so would be neutral. Townsend suggests the appointment related to Kitchener's view of Maxwell's efficiency and 'insight into and sympathy with racial characteristics', 'strong common sense' and 'imperturbable good humour'. Instructed to '... take such measures as may in your opinion be necessary for the prompt suppression of the insurrection,'[89] Maxwell was placed in an unenviable position and naturally made some controversial decisions. Maxwell's previous experience had been Egypt, a post he left in March 1916 after Archibald J Murray had been appointed above him. Little knowing how much Kitchener's power had been eroded, he was berated by Maxwell's wife for not defending Maxwell after all their years of friendship.[90] With Kitchener no longer on the scene after June 1916, Maxwell moved to Northern Command, York and his military career stagnated.

Various volunteer groups were to come into operation, all seeking sanction from the War Office, if not Kitchener himself. Already in August 1914 the Volunteer Training Corps (VTC), '... an organisation wh[ich] Lovat[91] & Desborough are promoting for

84 Jérôme van de Waal, *The Catholic Church in Ireland 1914-18: War and Politics* (Dublin: Irish Academic, 2003) p.13.
85 Charles Townsend, *Easter 1916: The Irish rebellion* (London: Penguin, 2006) pp.63-4.
86 BL: Add 52276B, 22 March 1912 & 29 March 1912, letters from Kitchener to Conk.
87 Martin Purdy, *Roman Catholic Army Chaplains During the First World War: Roles, Experiences and Dilemmas* (MA thesis, University of Central Lancashire, 2012) p.32.
88 Maxwell's appointment to General Officer Commanding Northern Command, York was temporary 27 April 1916 and substantive 1 November 1916.
89 Townsend, *Easter*, p.208.
90 Letitia Wufford, 'Imperialists at work and play: The papers of General Sir John and Lady Maxwell', in *The Princeton University Library Chronicle*, vol 51, no 2 (Winter 1990) pp.141-82.
91 Simon Joseph Fraser, 14th Lord Lovat and 3rd Baron Lovat referred to as 16th Lord Lovat, born 25 November 1871, died 18 February 1933.

drilling middle-aged breadwinners,' had been unofficially formed. Many, including Raymond Asquith volunteered. Following a forty-five minute discussion on 11 February 1915 with representatives of the Association of Lieutenants of Counties, Kitchener determined that the VTC '... seemed to be the most suitable organisation for the employment of persons who could not serve in the Army, and the War Office agreed to accept it for the whole country.' The '... Volunteer Training Corps were only to be organisations for persons to perform useful services such as the removal of stock etc. in case of invasion.' There would be huge objection from '... the War Office if the 'Territorial Associations, which work closely in conjunction with the War Office, should alienate their energies to a purpose for which they were not created.' He would also 'greatly object to give official rank' to officers of the VTC unless the War Office was prepared to arm the corps.[92]

Women also looked to do their bit, Raymond Asquith noting that '... the crisis has brought out all that is best in British womanhood.'[93] Kitchener, aware that women would need to be mobilised to relieve men for war duties, was amenable to requests. The Women's Army Auxiliary Corps was set up at Boulogne, an organisation in which his niece Fanny was involved. Diana Manners,[94] whom Raymond Asquith thought should be at the War Office, had been instrumental in its formation and the actress Lena Ashwell created an offshoot to provide men with theatre entertainment.[95] Lord Burnham, proprietor of the *Daily Telegraph*, suggested Kitchener be approached. He 'readily gave his approval' to take performances to the front, although he had to get permission from French who agreed to shows behind the lines, in training and rest camps and at hospitals.[96] In May 1915 there was concern about women at the front. 'Kitchener wanted something done about clearing ladies out of Boulogne'. Ever concerned about the reputation and safety of the army, he was responding to 'a good many comments made to him on the subject' and was 'rather anxious' concerning the 'good many stray ladies who have no business in Boulogne.'[97] FT Clayton,[98] Inspector General of Communications, British Army in the Field, replied on 17 April that '... there [was] a lot of nonsense talked about ladies being at the various Base ports'. He had not heard any scandal. The accounts getting back were due to 'too many people who come out to this country on what we call "joy rides", and who take back with them extraordinary stories for which there is not the slightest foundation.'[99] Officers'

92   PA: ALC/1/7 file 7/117b, Note of interview at War Office by a Sub-committee of the Association on the subject of Volunteer Training Corps, 11 February 1915.
93   Jolliffe, *Raymond Asquith*, pp.190-2.
94   Diana Olivia Winifred Maud Manners, later Viscountess Norwich, born 29 August 1892, died 16 June 1986.
95   Trethewey, *Pearls*, p.441.
96   LJ Collins, *Theatre At War, 1914-18* (Basingstoke: Macmillan, 1998) p.145.
97   TNA: WO 107/14, 10 April 1915, Cowans to RC Maxwell, no.270.
98   Frederick Thomas Clayton, born 7 October 1855, died 6 December 1933.
99   TNA: WO 107/14, 17 April 1915, Clayton to Cowans, no.276A; 12 April 1915, Maxwell to Cowans, no.275.

wives were not allowed to live on the Lines of Communications and as far as he was aware this had been strictly adhered to, including claims of women working with the Red Cross. The French were enticing people to visit France and with Boulogne under French control, unless a woman was under military command, there was nothing that could be done; the Foreign Office issuing passports. The suggestion of setting up a club such as an 'Indian club, with lady members' would soon lead to complications, it would be better to issue permits.[100]

Children and young people also had their role to play, most notably the Scouts. Kitchener had been introduced to the scout movement when he stayed with the Byngs at Newton Hall after his return from East Africa in 1911.[101] The movement, started by Robert Baden-Powell[102] after his experiences in the 1899-1902 war and based on ideas set out by Roger Pocock of the Legion of Frontiersmen,[103] aligned somewhat with the cadets Kitchener had been promoting in the southern hemisphere. In summer 1911, Kitchener was appointed president of the 1st North London Boy Scouts in which capacity he hosted the youngsters at Broome for camping expeditions.[104] During the war, the Scouts provided valuable assistance as messengers and assistants in Voluntary Aid Detachment hospitals and other similar organisations. When one young nine year old Irish lad offered to be a despatch rider on the Western Front, Kitchener instructed his War Office Private Secretary, Herbert James Creedy,[105] to reply, '[Kitchener] is afraid that you are not quite old enough to go to the front as a despatch rider.'[106]

Another issue Kitchener grappled with, a decision only made after his death, was that of conscientious objectors.[107] The *Derby Daily Telegraph*, reported Reverend FB Meyer:[108]

> Four days ago [2 June 1916] Lord Kitchener was good enough to give a prolonged interview to Dr Clifford,[109] the Rev JH Shakespeare,[110] Dr Garvie,[111] and myself on the subject of the conscientious objectors, and the memory of that interview will be one of our most treasured memories. We may not make public his utterances except that they showed he had bestowed large consideration on

100 TNA: WO 107/14, 17 May 1915, from Clayton to Cowans, no.295.
101 Williams, *Byng*, p.56.
102 Robert Stephenson Smyth Baden-Powell, 1st Baron Baden-Powell, born 22 February 1885, died 8 January 1941.
103 Anne Samson, 'Origins of the Legion of Frontiersmen and the formation of MI5/6', in *SOQT: Soldiers of the Queen*, issue 172 (2018).
104 Williams, *Byng*, p.55.
105 Herbert James Creedy, born 3 May 1878, died 3 April 1973.
106 Richard van Emden, *Boy Soldiers of the Great War* (London: Bloomsbury, 2012) p.25.
107 Lee and Starling, Hansard 21 March 1917, pp.26, 209.
108 Frederick Brotherton Meyer, born 8 April 1847, died 28 March 1929, Baptist Minister.
109 John Clifford, born 16 October 1836, died 20 November 1923, Baptist Minister.
110 John Howard Shakespeare, born 16 April 1857, died 12 March 1928, Baptist Minister.
111 Alfred Ernest Garvie, born 29 August 1861, died 7 March 1945, Congregational Minister.

the problem, and had already devised a treatment of various aspects of it which augured a satisfactory solution. He was an uncrowned king of men.[112]

In May 1916, Kitchener put Adjutant General CFN Macready's paper on the topic to Cabinet. He did not add any comment,[113] however, on 24 May 1917 in a Lords' discussion, Kitchener's view was presented by Lord Parmoor:[114] 'He took a very wide and tolerant view [...] "The genuine conscientious objectors will find themselves under the civil power."' Kitchener's view was taken to be in connection with religious objectors, a point he had made to Conk a few years earlier.[115]

The big challenge remained conscription. Kitchener believed Britain's military could only be reformed if conscription was introduced, preferably in peacetime. With the British civilian population not in favour, and Asquith against it and upsetting the nation, Kitchener was convinced the time was not yet ripe for conscription. Amery informed Milner, head of the National Service League, that at the 11 August 1915 Cabinet, 'Curzon, Ll G & Winston all pushing hard ... K even went so far as to say he thought we should have to resort to NS before an end with this war! But Squiff will probably get at him alone and frighten him with logic. It is K that must be battered down ...'[116] Had Kitchener voted with Churchill, Curzon and Lloyd George on 11 August, conscription may well have been introduced.[117] The situation became so tense that the King called a conference on the issue at Buckingham Palace on 28 August, supporting the outcome which was against National Service.[118] Milner, however, did not give up and spent an hour with Kitchener on 1 September 1915.[119] The following day, Henry Wilson shared with Amery:

> It is amazing to me why K won't face compulsion. The arguments against it are purile, & for it overwhelming ... I don't think you can make K a C in C of all the Armies ... his idea of strategy simply *terrify* me ... K as PM and Milner at WO would do, but I suppose it is not practical politics to kick out Squiff altho' I honestly believe that unless we do we run a serious chance of losing the war ...[120]

112 Derby *Daily Telegraph*, 7 June 1916, p.2.
113 TNA: WO 32/5491 Conscientious Objectors and military service, 15 and 16 May 1916.
114 Charles Alfred Cripps, 1st Baron Parmoor, born 3 October 1852, died 30 June 1941.
115 Margaret Heyworth Hobhouse, *I Appeal Unto Caesar: The Case of the Conscientious Objector* (London: George Allen, 1917); Lord Sandhurst, Military Service, House of Lords, Hansard, 4 July 1916; Lord Parmoor, Conscientious objectors, House of Lords, Hansard, 11 November 1917.
116 Gollin, pp.277-8.
117 Gollin, p.280 Milner to Philip Gell 20 August 1915; see RJQ Adams, 'Asquith's choice: The May coalition and the coming of conscription, 1915-1916', in *Journal of British Studies* (July 1986) vol 25, no 3, pp.243-63.
118 Gollin, p.283.
119 Gollin, p.285.
120 Gollin, p.294 (Amery papers, Wilson to Amery, 2 Sep 1915).

Wilson had revealed why Kitchener would not back conscription: Asquith would be overthrown as Prime Minister. As much as men were needed, Kitchener remained loyal to Asquith, who had appointed him and continued to back him despite growing dissatisfaction with his idiosyncratic ways.

Not surprising, it was all starting to take its toll. On 15 October 1915, Maurice Bonham Carter[121] recognised Kitchener was 'rattled & tired & in need of a holiday' but the only person who could fill his position as Secretary of State for War was Asquith.[122] Two days later, Asquith warned Kitchener of a plot against him by Curzon and Lloyd George, amongst others:

> We are (as you realise) in a most critical situation. You and I have since the war began worked in daily intimacy and unbroken confidence. And you know well that, in every exigent crisis, I have given you – as you have given me – loyal and unstinting support.
>
> I should like you to know that what is now going on is being engineered by men (Curzon, Lloyd George and some others) whose real object is to oust you. They know well that I give no countenance to their projects, and consequently they have conceived the idea of using you against me. God knows that we should both of us be glad to be set free. But we cannot and ought not. So long as you and I stand together, we carry the whole country with us. Otherwise the Deluge! …
>
> … I do not appeal to personal considerations, but I am certain, in the interests of the Country, and of the effective prosecution of the war, that it is essential that you and I should stand together, and that the intrigue, which has for its main object both to divide and to discredit us both, should be frustrated.[123]

By the end of the year it was evident that insufficient men were coming forward and some form of conscription would be needed. The result was Derby's appointment as Director General of Recruiting. His task was to ensure one last effort for voluntary recruiting which became known as the Derby Scheme. Finally, on 5 January 1916 an element of compulsory service was introduced to Parliament becoming law on 27 January. Asquith still vacillating,[124] the press took advantage.

Reporting

Kitchener was not fond of journalists and did not want them on the battle front. His dislike and mistrust of journalists began at Suakin where journalists who did not

---

121 Maurice 'Bongie' Bonham Carter, born 11 October 1880, died 7 June 1960, married Violet Asquith.
122 Pottle, *Champion Redoubtable*, p.82.
123 Royle, pp.335-6, 17 October 1915.
124 Gollin, pp.336-7.

approve of his decisions, accused him of encouraging raids to win 'cheap laurels'.[125] They were quick to spread rumours, contributing to the myths which built up around him. Concerning Suakin, Kitchener silenced his critics by his actions.[126] While preparing for the attack on Omdurman, Wingate alerted Kitchener to complaints that *The Times* indirectly had an unfair allocation as one of their reporters was ostensibly working for the *New York Herald*. To overcome the issue, Frank Rhodes, by now a friend and the second reporter, withdrew his reports.[127] Having to resolve such minor and peripheral issues whilst planning a major offensive could only have led to frustration and annoyance. Ironically, the reporter in question, Hubert Howard,[128] was killed when Rhodes was shot through the shoulder.[129]

For a time, Kitchener was himself a journalist, anonymously contributing *Notes from Cyprus* (August 1879) and *A visit to Sophia and the Heights of Kamerleh – Christmas 1877* (February 1878) to *Blackwood's*, and was listed as a 'war correspondent'.[130] In the first, he expressed his dislike for the Bulgarians, thereby supporting the Turks, and in the second suggested British involvement in Cyprus. This included raising a Turkish regiment in Cyprus and setting up a training school for Turkish officers.[131] In addition, he published a book on Biblical sites in Palestine using his photographs of the surveyed area.[132] Kitchener clearly understood the value and impact of the image, and these he banned from the war front. He was also not averse to using the press when it suited him. Ready to launch his Sudanese campaign in 1893, Kitchener suggested to his father that the press be stirred up.[133] Later, during the 1899-1902 war, his ADC Marker would leak news to Amery and Repington, friends and correspondents for *The Times*.[134]

Yet, not all journalists were anathema to him. Following the death of George Warrington Steevens[135] of the *Daily Mail* on 15 January 1900 from enteric during the siege of Ladysmith, Kitchener disclosed: 'He was such a clever and able man. He did his work as correspondent so brilliantly, and he never gave the slightest trouble. I wish all correspondents were like him.'[136] Steevens' philosophy as a war correspondent was that he would '… state nothing on any authority unless he had seen it himself or had

125 Smithers, p.9.
126 Royle, p.80.
127 Burleigh, p.109.
128 Hubert George Lyulph Howard, born 3 April 1871, killed Battle of Omdurman, 2 September 1898.
129 Burleigh, p.199.
130 Warner, p.25; Magnus, p.41.
131 Magnus, pp.41-2.
132 Warner, p.21.
133 Royle, p.97.
134 Royle, p.201.
135 George Warrington Steevens, born 10 December 1869, died 15 January 1900.
136 Rye, p.160, 25 January 1900; F Lauriston Bullard, *Famous War Correspondents* (Boston: Little, Brown & Co, 1914) p.304.

heard it from a European who had seen it, and he declares that, although the resolution cost him some excellent stories, on the whole he did not regret it.'[137] Steevens recognised Kitchener as someone who would bring order to things; he would be 'a splendid manager of the War Office' and there were some who '... nurse a desperate hope that he may some day be appointed to sweep out' that office.[138] It was the one place Kitchener did not want to go; because he knew what a sweeping out it required and that it would be the end of him. On Sudan, Steevens reflected: 'The ripe harvest of fifteen years is that he knows everything that is to be learned of his subject. He has seen and profited by the error of others as by their successes. He has inherited the wisdom and achievements of his predecessors. He came at the right hour, and he was the right man.'[139] The same could be said about his arrival at the War Office in August 1914. Steevens was a shrewd observer: 'Other generals have been better loved; none was ever better trusted' which had 'every man go forth with a tranquil mind' when he asked.[140] Kitchener's one weakness was ambition – he was commanding '... armies at an age when most men are hoping to command regiments.' Aged 46 he was entrusted with '... an army of six brigades, a command such as few of his seniors have ever led in the field.' This no doubt, 'awakened jealousies.'[141]

During the 1899-1902 war, Kitchener had double the press to deal with – that in South Africa owned by the mining magnates, and that in Britain. Of the two, he had more control over the South African press as President Steyn complained that a letter he sent to Kitchener had been mistranslated and adapted by the time it got to the papers. In Britain, Kitchener had to deal with the Liberal Press which was anti-war and, following Hobhouse's visit, took up the issue of the concentration camps with great fervour. The uneasy relationship between Kitchener and Milner, replicated between the War and Colonial Offices, did little to provide a balanced counter-news flow to the British press.

From the outbreak of the war in 1914 until May 1915, the press was not allowed at the front. However, when a journalist managed to have an article on the retreat of the British forces published on Sunday 30 August despite the ban,[142] Kitchener reacted. Recognising '... the nation ought to have more news about the war than it was getting', he instructed ED Swinton,[143] who had served with him in South Africa to prepare 'eye witness' accounts.[144] His instructions, issued on 7 September 1914, were '... to report to the Commander-in-Chief for the duty of writing articles on the

137 Bullard, *Famous War Correspondents*, pp.305-6.
138 Steevens, p.46.
139 Steevens, p.47.
140 Steevens, pp.50-1.
141 Steevens, p.51.
142 Swinton, *Eyewitness*, pp.20, 31.
143 Ernest Dunlop Swinton, born 21 October 1868, died 15 January 1951.
144 ED Swinton, *Eyewitness: Being Personal Reminiscences of Certain Phases of the Great War, Including the Genesis of the Tank* (New York: Doubleday, Doran & Co, 1933) p.19.

operations of the Army. These articles, after whatever censorship was deemed necessary in France, were to be sent direct to the Secretary of the War Office for Lord Kitchener's personal approval before publication.'[145]

Kitchener's dislike of journalists may well have been linked to ensuring his version of events were received by the authorities before those of the press, but he was also conscious of the press releasing military secrets which could damage proposed action. On 26 November 1914, he explained his position on press censorship to the House of Lords. The need for information and news from the front was not to be to the detriment of military activity, and, therefore, asked that the public be patient in waiting for information.[146] Kitchener had refused to let it be known on what days the British Expeditionary Force was sailing, much to the annoyance of family members, but when the force arrived safely without incident, Kitchener was vindicated.[147]

This reluctance to provide information, however, caused problems and was one of the reasons for his downfall. In November 1914, Kitchener informed Edmund Talbot,[148] Chief Whip that, 'There is not a member of the cabinet I would trust, unless it is Asquith, whom I trust – a little.'[149] His concern was that politicians would share information with their 'pillow talk'. This did not extend to him sharing Cabinet information with Margot Asquith as her husband pointed out. Perhaps Kitchener was sharing what he thought she already knew, but as Warner points out, he did not include military details.

There was no question, however, over news being managed. Previous wars had shown the need. The day the ultimatum was handed to Germany, FE Smith (Lord Birkenhead) was appointed Director of the Press Bureau in a joint meeting between Kitchener and First Lord of the Admiralty, Churchill. The Press Bureau was established on 7 August 1914,[150] two days after Kitchener accepted his post at the War Office. The meeting referred to was dinner at the 'Other Club' on the evening of 6 August, Kitchener's first day in office. George Riddell of *News of the World* was in attendance as was Lord Stamfordham,[151] the King's Secretary and others. Kitchener, in the chair, announced the appointment of a Press Censor, '… and pointing to FE [Smith], said, "There he is. Come and see me in the morning and I will tell you all

---

145 Magnus, p.124; Henry Woodd Nevinson, *Fire of Life* (London: James Nisbet, 1935) p.302 has March 1915 for journalists being permitted to the front.

146 Rye, p.491.

147 Arthur, vol 3.

148 Edmund Bernard FitzAlan-Howard, 1st Viscount FitzAlan of Derwent, known as Lord Edmund Talbot 1876-1921, born 1 June 1855, died 18 May 1947.

149 Vincent, *Crawford Papers*, p.345.

150 *Hansard, HC Deb 07 August 1914 vol 65 cc2153-6, Mr Churchill and the Press*, FE Smith was Member for Walton Division of Liverpool. Online: https://api.parliament.uk/historic-hansard/Commons/1914/aug/07/mr-churchill-and-the-press [accessed 14 January 2019].

151 Arthur John Bigge, 1st Baron Stamfordham, born 18 June 1849, died, 31 March 1931.

about it".[152] In post, Smith would meet with Kitchener every day, including Sundays, for at least thirty minutes for the first six weeks of the war, unless he was in France. The two men would discuss '… at length the form of the public announcement which it was proper to make. [Kitchener] was entirely free from the paltry imbecility which marked every decision of the censorship at GHQ in France. His criterion was a simple one. Will the publication of that which is true aid the enemy by giving him information otherwise unattainable or at least difficult of attainment? He laughed at the apprehension that bad news would dismay the people of England.'[153]

Riddell also visited Kitchener on 7 August 1914 with Brade. He,

> … found him with the door open, surrounded by Generals and maps – everyone coming and going in a state of great excitement. I asked Kitchener what the duties of the Press Censor were to be. His reply was, 'He will see that nothing dangerous goes into the newspapers. Go away with Brade and settle the matter now. We must make the English people understand that we are at war and that war is not pap. At the present moment they do not understand the situation. They ought to act as if we were at war.' We went to Brade's room to discuss matters. The great difficulty was to find premises adjacent to the Admiralty and War Office. Ultimately we arranged to install FE with a scratch staff in a disused, rat-infested building in Whitehall.[154]

In April 1915, after consulting Riddell, Kitchener allowed six accredited press correspondents to join GHQ in France. Initially there for a limited time, they remained for the duration. Riddell thought either Kitchener had forgotten about them or it was a '… convenient subterfuge that would enable him to appease the Press and simultaneously placate the French should questions arise.'[155] Two months later, the decision was made to do away with the War Office appointed correspondents and allow select war correspondents to operate under a special 'Press Conducting Officer', but to appease the French Commander-in-Chief, no journalist would accompany the troops.[156] Although an American journalist, Beach Madham, wrote contrary to St Loe Strachey, that the French were allowing journalists with the troops.[157]

Discovering Repington at the front visiting French in May 1915, Kitchener expressed great displeasure. French argued Repington was there having been an officer, however, Kitchener was fully aware of the information being sent from the front to *The Times* which was damaging the war effort providing the enemy with information about the shell shortages and other issues in the British Army. Repington

152 Riddell, *War Diary*, p.9.
153 Smith, pp.2-3.
154 Riddell, *War Diary*, p.10.
155 Riddell, *War Diary*, p.23.
156 Swinton, *Eyewitness*, p.104.
157 PA: STR 26/2/13, Beach Madham, 11 April 1915.

was eventually removed and lost his job. He had burnt his bridges when on 15 August 1914 Kitchener gave Repington an interview regarding his plans. In doing so, Kitchener broke the unwritten rule that the Liberal Party provided 'insider information' to Liberal editors before *The* (Conservative) *Times* received the news. Kitchener, not being a party man, was unaware of this political protocol when he gave the interview and felt, when made aware of the situation, that he had been manipulated. He 'refused to see Repington again.'[158]

Apart from Repington, Kitchener only gave one other interview to a journalist, after which he 'absolutely refused to see any journalists at all,'[159] the event referred to as the 'Cobb fiasco.' The neutral American journalist had realised within weeks of war breaking out that the war correspondent if 'not dead [...] must be described as moribund' and that 'never again will army commanders give a free run of their headquarters to "chiels" taking notes to be incontinently printed.'[160] Northcliffe had managed to organise for leading American journalist Irvin Shrewsbury Cobb[161] to interview Kitchener on 21 October 1914. If Cobb's report is as accurate as he claims, the discussion had been rather frank. Kitchener questioned Cobb regarding his recent visit to Germany which Cobb repeated in the press, breaking Kitchener's rule of not giving anything away which would assist the enemy. The understanding he had with British newspaper men in general did not extend to America.

Kitchener's questions reveal he was most concerned about German morale, in particular, that of the rank and file. 'If Generals win battles, soldiers win wars.' He also gave insight into his confidence that Britain and the allies would win despite Germany appearing the stronger: 'When an army of invasion ceases to invade, that army has lost its principal function and has failed in its principal object [...] it is doing nothing except waste itself. And on the ethics of war, a soldier had to do as told, and not be judge and jury over civil actions. If that happened, armies would no longer be necessary, it would be better to employ executioners. He also saw no point in dropping bombs on cities whether or not they were defended. 'It is not war. It is a costly, spectacular by play, which counts for nought in the final result.' In his assessment, Cobb did not see Kitchener as 'the typical soldier. Rather he seemed to me the typical man of affairs.' He also thought Kitchener quite similar to the German General Josias von Heerigen[162] – masterful, competent and 'born to have power and to hold dominion over lesser men.' Cobb's interview was printed on 5 December 1914 in the Philadelphia *Saturday Evening Post* which led to the fiasco, a denial by the Press Bureau that the interview had taken place and that Cobb was 'drawing on his

158 Ballard, p.250; King, *Fall of the Viceroy*, p.147.
159 PA: STR 5/9/1, Eric Drummond to St Loe Stratchey, 2 Jan 1915.
160 *The Literary Digest*, 15 August 1914, p.271.
161 Irvin Shrewsbury Cobb, born 23 June 1876, died 11 March 1944.
162 Josias von Heeringen, born 9 March 1850, died 9 October 1926.

imagination.'[163] Having been burnt twice by journalists in as many months, it was safer to avoid them.

There were, however, journalists favourable to Kitchener. These included Pearson, owner of *The Standard* (edited by Gwynne),[164] *St James' Gazette* and *Daily Express*, Edward J Buck of Reuter's India and Lovet Fraser of *The Times of India*.[165] Despite his tense relationship with the press, Kitchener recognised how tough their job was. At the end of the 1899-1902 war, he thanked the correspondents and hoped 'we would understand how necessary his recent strictness in the Censorship had been.'[166] He did not live to do the same in 1918.

Mobilising

In Kitchener's scheme of the war, 1914 was a holding year. The battles fought aimed to prevent Germany breaking through but there was not enough force – manpower or material – to hit back in 1915 which meant holding actions would again be required whilst all combatant countries restocked and trained fresh troops. In addition to preparing to retaliate against Germany, Kitchener was already looking forward to demobilisation.[167] In line with this, the South Africans set up a vocational training centre at Richmond Park in 1916 for men unfit to return to the front.[168]

Despite predicting a long war and the need for bombardments, Kitchener underestimated the need for shells. When he arrived at the War Office, arrangements had been made to ensure that seven Divisions could be maintained at all times for a limited campaign. This was in accordance with the post-1899-1902 war recommendations, however, it was not enough. He admitted to French:

> The supply of ammunition gives me great anxiety ... Do not think that we are keeping munitions back. All we can gather is being sent, but at the present rate of expenditure we are certain before long to run short, and then to produce a small daily allowance per gun will be impossible. I hope to increase the ammunition being sent today.[169]

He received permission from Chancellor Lloyd George to supply weapons without obtaining quotations to speed up supply. This helped, although Master General

163 New Zealand, *Dominion*, vol 8, issue 2325, 7 January 1915.
164 Howell Arthur Keir Gwynne, born 3 September 1865, died 29 June 1950.
165 King, *Fall of the Viceroy*, pp.150, 156.
166 Nevinson, *Fire of Life*, p.133.
167 Grey in Arthur, p.80fn.
168 John Buchan, *The History of the South African Forces in France* (London: Thomson Nelson & Son, 1920) pp.330-1.
169 Royle, p.281.

for Ordnance Stanley von Donop[170] continued to be conservative in allowing the £20million available for weapons. This led to Kitchener taking on more until Girouard and George Booth[171] were able to develop a large-scale armaments industry and centralised military supply, essential for winning the war. As with various initiatives Kitchener had, this fell foul of politics. Many systems, such as the Ministry of Munitions, were later introduced without reference to Kitchener, having been prevented earlier in the war. Royle suggests this was because so few politicians and soldiers understood the scale of the war.[172] Being a perfectionist did not help matters. Kitchener refused to enter into a contract despite the great need for weapons if he could not guarantee the company was legitimate. His cautious approach was to ensure that the men using the weapons were kept as safe as possible and not harmed unnecessarily. Here, von Donop aligned with Kitchener. He had an ability to determine the success of manufacture; turning down high explosive which, when the French used them, proved to be defective. Kitchener backed von Donop. He:

> ... has worked hard to supply the Army with the guns and ammunition needed in these days of enormous expansion ... Above all, he has by the application of technical knowledge of the highest order secured that the guns and ammunition supplied are of a quality to ensure adequate safety, and he has enabled us to avoid the dangers – from which we know some of our Allies have suffered – arising from the use of material which has been hastily constructed and allowed to fall too far below the accepted standards.[173]

The existing weapon manufacturers had not modernised before the war and alternative suppliers of German material, such as nitrate, had not been sourced.[174] To increase armament output, Kitchener needed labour, but many had already enlisted and others were doing so to avoid accusations of cowardice. He therefore authorised that labourers working on military aspects wear a war service medal to show their commitment to the country.[175] However, this was not enough. To obtain labour for munitions factories, Kitchener agreed with Union leaders he would not introduce conscription. He '... recognised that no section of the nation contributed more in human wealth than did the working classes. [Arthur Henderson][176] found him free from all prejudice and frankly and sincerely sympathetic in his attitude towards labour.' Realising that drunkenness was impacting on munitions production, Kitchener lobbied for limited drinking hours. This led to a clash with Lloyd George on 30 October 1914 when

---

170 Stanley Brenton von Donop, born 22 February 1860, died 17 October 1941.
171 George Macaulay Booth, born 22 September 1877, died 10 March 1971.
172 Royle, pp.281-2.
173 Arthur, p.279; Riddell, *War Diary*, p.110.
174 Royle, p.283.
175 James Edmonds, *A Short History of World War I* (London: Oxford UP, 1951).
176 Arthur Henderson, born 13 September 1863, died 20 October 1935.

the latter observed that '... he [Kitchener] was only one among 19, and must stand criticism in the same way as any other member of the Cabinet.' Kitchener wanted complete control of labour and industry and so did Lloyd George.[177] Politics conflicted with winning the war.

By 14 September 1914, Lloyd George wanted a committee to investigate the armament situation, but Kitchener refused claiming it would increase his workload. He had no time for committees. On 12 October, a Shells Committee was formed by Asquith, with Kitchener as chair. Lloyd George, Churchill, Haldane, Reginald McKenna,[178] Walter Runciman,[179] and Lord Lucas[180] were members. Kitchener, however, refused to attend but the group did manage to persuade von Donop to increase the number of 18 pounder guns on order and to speed up delivery dates. Finance was made available to expand private production. The committee met six times in total and showed some awareness of Kitchener's difficulties in obtaining ammunition for the front.[181] It was easy to make decisions, but not necessarily to have them fulfilled. It was a juggling game. The Dominions, too, required weapons, and as early as 20 December 1914, Kitchener was organising weapons for the Russian front as he recognised this would ease pressure on the British Expeditionary Force. UF Wintour,[182] co-ordinating the Russia Supply Committee, looked to the United States of America for supplies, while Portugal was encouraged to remain neutral to save Britain having to find more supplies.[183]

Kitchener's methodical approach was not fast enough for his colleagues who started to take matters into their own hands more forcefully. Following a meeting between Asquith, Lloyd George, and Kitchener on 5 March 1915, a Munitions Committee with executive powers was agreed, with details finalised on 23 March. The committee would report to Cabinet and not to the War Office. Significantly, Kitchener was not invited to the final meeting. In the meantime, 15 March, Kitchener announced to the House of Lords that the workforce size and a minority of slackers were causing the shortage of ammunition and the following day he would be creating an Armaments Output Committee to deal with manpower problems. George Booth – a relative, and successful industrialist – would oversee the committee, which would also include Girouard, Managing Director of Armstrong's armaments.[184] Both men were '...

177 Royle, p.284.
178 Reginald McKenna, born 6 July 1863, died 6 September 1943.
179 Walter Runciman, 1st Viscount Runciman of Doxford, born 19 November 1870, died 14 November 1949.
180 Auberon Thomas Herbert, 9th Baron Lucas and 5th Lord Dingwall, born 25 May 1876, died of wounds 3 November 1916.
181 Royle, pp.284-5.
182 Ulrick Fitzgerald Wintour, born 1877, died 1947.
183 Royle, p.314.
184 Royle, p.285.

authorised to act without further reference to the Secretary of State,'[185] again demonstrating Kitchener's willingness to delegate to men he trusted. Booth had advised Kitchener since the outbreak of war, believing orders should be widespread – by October 1914, 3,000 firms were working on munition production of some sort, yet orders were well behind delivery date.[186] Girouard's appointment, 28 April, although suggesting state control of munition manufacture helped Kitchener see the value in a department solely responsible for munitions.[187] However, it was too late. By the time Kitchener began to widen production, Lloyd George had taken up the mantle and complained to Balfour. Hearing of Lloyd George's committee on 26 March, Kitchener threatened to resign if any more committees were set up to interfere with the work of the War Office. As far as Kitchener was concerned, politicians provided a framework in which military men could work. They were not to dictate how it was done.[188] Kitchener clearly saw himself as a soldier and not a politician.

On 7 April, the Armaments Output Committee was made public. With Kitchener having earned the wrath of *The Times* and Lloyd George threatening to resign and go to the papers, Asquith was forced to act. The next day, he announced the new Munitions Committee under Lloyd George '... to ensure the promptest and most efficient application of all available resources of the country to the manufacture and supply of munitions for the army and navy.'[189] The Armaments Output Committee would be subordinate, and Booth would attend both meetings to supply technical information. Lloyd George angered Kitchener when he made public the number of men sent to France that month. This was giving information to the enemy.

The following month, 26 May 1915, the Ministry of Munitions was created, opening its doors on 9 June 1915 with Lloyd George in the driving seat. This coincided with the formation of the coalition government, during which discussions Walter Long had suggested that Kitchener be made Commander-in-Chief Home Force with responsibility to determine which forces were sent overseas.[190] Despite their differences, Kitchener congratulated Lloyd George and suggested they work together: there was a job to do – win the war. Kitchener was also the only person to say farewell to Churchill and Haldane, the two ministers to lose their posts in the reshuffle.[191]

When French lost the battle of Aubers Ridge, 9-10 May 1915, he blamed the shell shortage and joined forces with Lloyd George and Northcliffe, owner of *The Times*, to get rid of Kitchener. They were aided by Repington, who was angry with Kitchener for

185 Royle, pp.285-9; Riddell, *War Diary*, pp.88-9 provides interesting background to the formation of the Ministry of Munitions and the role of Brade, Permanent Under Secretary for the War Office.
186 Edmonds, *A Short History*, p.97.
187 Simkins, pp.130-3.
188 Royle, p.287.
189 Royle, p.289; Edmunds, *A Short History*, p.97.
190 PA: BL 117/1/12, Walter Long to Bonar Law.
191 Royle, p.295.

his attitude towards the press,[192] and John Buchan, *The Times* special correspondent in France. When Northcliffe's *Daily Mail* got involved in the shell debate, Asquith too blamed Kitchener for the shortage, but the public remained firmly behind him, burning the newspapers which called for his removal.[193]

Kitchener's paper, 'The state of the war', provides a different picture of the shell issue. On 2 May 1915, French sent Kitchener a letter noting 'the ammunition will be alright'. However, Kitchener did not say anything publicly as he was fighting the Germans and not John French. Getting into a personal fight with the Commander-in-Chief of the British Expeditionary Force over who was responsible for the shortage of shells would not help defeat the Germans, 'Our job is to get on with the war – it will be quite enough time to answer these [venomous attacks] when we have won it'.[194] In the meantime, his only response was to ask French why Repington, a journalist, was allowed at the front and given access to GHQ.[195] Yet, as serious as what the shell shortage was, it was not enough to bring about a change in Cabinet. The deciding factor would be Fisher's resignation over the Dardanelles.[196]

It was soon shown that the Ministry of Munitions needed the War Office when Eric Geddes[197] asked Kitchener for information on the '... proportion of rifles to machine-guns that would be required nine months hence.' Kitchener replied, 'I want as much of both as you can produce' and when pressed, noted that 'two machine-guns was the minimum and four the maximum.' Although his first response seemed flippant, his second was to prove all that could be supplied. This was despite Lloyd George instructing Geddes to 'multiply that by four, double that for luck, and double that again for contingencies. The sum of four, multiplied by four, multiplied by two, equals sixty-four, and provide that per battalion.' According to Royle, '... no infantry battalion was ever to be equipped with the number of machine-guns promised by Lloyd George. Four was to remain the maximum number allotted to infantry battalions and the only unit ever to receive the much-vaunted 64 was the Machine Gun Corps.'[198]

AJ Sylvester,[199] confidential shorthand writer to Hankey, recalled that the '... contracts which [Lloyd George] had placed for munitions had in their size and complexity staggered not only Lord Kitchener and the "experts" in the War Office, but every member of Cabinet.' A later, overheard conversation between Lloyd George and Asquith had Lloyd George scornfully ejaculating, 'To hear Kitchener and some of the others talk, one would imagine we were fighting a host of savages and not the most

192 Royle, pp.290-1.
193 Royle, p.294.
194 Royle, p.295.
195 Royle, p.294.
196 Royle, p.292.
197 Eric Campbell Geddes, born 26 September 1875, died 22 June 1937.
198 Royle, pp.298-9.
199 Albert James Sylvester, born 24 November 1889, died 27 October 1989.

efficient military organisation in the world.' Lloyd George had visited France '... and seen for [him]self what the troops need[ed]. I've promised them they shall have what they need.'[200] This was a clash of reality versus idealism. Kitchener representing the former, Lloyd George the latter. An order for the two hundred 18 pounders placed in November 1914 with the only company in Britain to manufacture high quality guns, the Bethlehem Steel Company, for delivery a year later, had delivered six by August with the remainder arriving in March 1916.[201] The company never seemed to keep up with demand even once the Ministry of Munitions had been formed.

Yet, these two antagonists worked together for the greater purpose as Lloyd George informed Montagu in 1916. Personal views had to be put aside in war and hierarchy had to disappear as there was too much work to be done for the Secretary of State to be involved in everything. This was something he and Kitchener had agreed when the Ministry of Munitions came into being.[202]

When Lloyd George took over the War Office in 1916 he asked H Leith Lewis at the Paris Embassy to write to him with news of the 'politico-military situation'. Lewis was:

> ... only too pleased to [...] more especially as I shall not be breaking any new ground for [he] was in the habit of writing constantly to Lord Kitchener at his request. [...] Lord Kitchener expected me to write freely, but he was in the habit of keeping his letters to himself, and did not communicate their contents to anyone, as far as [Lewis knew].[203]

The month Kitchener died, saw the 13,995,360th round of ammunition delivered. Between June and December 1916, a total of 35,407,193 rounds were delivered. These figures compare to the 1,363,700 which Kitchener sourced in the first five months of war.[204] In the words of Warner, Kitchener had orchestrated a fifty percent increase in shell production.[205] Edmunds contributes that most of the munitions sent to France in 1916 were defective 'owing to lack of sufficient expert inspection.'[206]

When Riddell commented that 'K always looks well after the soldier,' Lloyd George concurred,[207] but did not grasp what this entailed. Kitchener also insisted on inspecting the New Armies before they left for France, demonstrating his concern and interest.[208] He encouraged officers to ensure the safety of as many lives as possible

200 AJ Sylvester, *The Real Lloyd George* (London: Cassell, 1947) p.3.
201 *History of Munitions*, vol 10, p.64.
202 PA: LG/E/2/19/4, letter 19 July 1916 to Montagu.
203 PA: LG E/3/14/4, 18 Aug 1916 Private and Personal to Lloyd George.
204 Royle, p.299.
205 Warner, p.191.
206 Edmonds, *A Short History*, p.98.
207 Riddell, *War Diary*, p.50.
208 Royle, p.268.

when they were evacuating Gallipoli, yet according to Byng sulked with him when he evacuated everyone without loss. Kitchener's approach suggested a humanitarian element, but also made economic sense. The cost of replacing manpower was expensive, so logically, the most valuable resource of the army had to be kept alive and functioning healthily for as long as possible. In India he looked to reduce the percentage of men hospitalised from fifteen per cent to the 'normal 5 per cent.'[209] In the 1880s, there had been a scandal when it came to light that defective weapons had been issued to the army. This was due to official negligence and corruption on the part of the contractors. Kitchener's men had been on the receiving end of these defective weapons and he vowed it would never happen again if he could help it.[210] Less than a month after Kitchener's death, the battle of the Somme was to begin with all its slaughter. In addition to those killed and maimed by the enemy, it was found that the British were working with defective guns, faulty fuses and insufficient high explosive.[211]

Innovation

Politics aside, the Dardanelles campaign gives insight to Kitchener's approach to war: use all available means, not only the armed forces. His early experiences of war demonstrated the value of the collaborative approach and where he could, he did. He could also be innovative, having observed those around him. When it came to transporting wire, he demonstrated how effectively it could be done by wrapping the wire around a donkey: you needed to lift its back legs to fit the role of wire.[212] In 1903, the year the British Ski Club was formed, Kitchener was exploring the military use of skis and snowshoes in the Himalayas but concluded in 1905 'there is little probability that ski will be of use.'[213]

His time in France in the 1870s introduced him to the value of the air balloon and hence the plane for spotting and intelligence. Smithers believes Kitchener was the 'only officer of General rank who had seen a battlefield from the air': he had flown over the pyramids. Whether or not he was the first British General to go up in a balloon or in a plane is immaterial, what is significant is Kitchener's appreciation of seeing the whole battlefield from above and being able to translate that into the limited view from ground level. On 25 January 1917, William Sefton Brancker,[214] Director of Military Aeronautics, told his audience:

209 Beauvoir de Lisle, *Reminiscences of Sport and War* (London: Eyre & Spottiswood, 1939) pp.235-6.
210 Warner, p.82.
211 Nicholas van der Bijl, *Intelligence*, p.120.
212 Sandes, p.105.
213 Arnie Wilson, *Snow Crazy: 115 Years of British Ski History* (Rickmansworth: TSL, 2018) p.61.
214 William Sefton Brancker, born 22 March 1877, died 5 October 1930.

I do not think that anyone will ever realize how much Lord Kitchener did for aviation in the early part of the war. From the very first he realized its importance and its possibilities and he was always urging me to push on, place more orders and do more ... I well remember that when I was rejoicing over a very feeble output of partially trained pilots, he was telling me that they should be trained to fly in groups of 60 to 100 with a view to bombing Essen. I remember how one day he explained to me his ideas of how it should be done and what formations[215] should be adopted ... More than a year later ... Lord Kitchener came and visited St Omer aerodrome. Just as he got out of his car, about 12 aeroplanes in beautiful formation flew over his head. He smiled and turned to me saying, 'There you are. I told you to do that a year ago, and you said that it couldn't be done'.[216]

At his request on 3 September 1914, David Henderson was given control of the air services in Europe whilst the Admiralty took control of home air defence, ostensibly because the army did not have sufficient planes.[217] In October, Hugh Trenchard,[218] who had successfully completed challenging tasks during the 1899-1902 war, was given two days to supply a 'battleworthy air squadron' for an attack on Antwerp.[219] To what extent Churchill's eagerness to be involved in everything led the Admiralty to take on the air defence of London is not clear, but from Balfour's contributions to the air committee which met between late 1915 and early 1916, it is clear that this arrangement was meant to be temporary.

Both Kitchener and Douglas Haig were keen to have cavalry units on the front despite the change in fighting formation. Already in 1903 when restructuring the Indian Army, Kitchener had recognised the impact the carbine would have on the cavalry and organised training in this regard. He continued: the '... dash which has very rightly done so much to make our cavalry famous throughout the war,' should not be lost. 'Opportunities will still occur on the modern battlefield when a well-delivered charge may turn the fortunes of the day [...] [b]ut these occasions will be few and far between'. The modern cavalry soldier would be required to '... work in entire rank; to mount and dismount with the greatest rapidity and with the least confusion; to provide for the safety of their horses while bringing the greatest number of rifles into the firing line; to become proficient in dismounted field duties.'[220]

---

215 He instructed Trenchard similarly: Eric Ash, *Sir Frederick Sykes and the Air Revolution, 1912-1918* (London: Frank Cass, 1999) p.71 fn74.

216 Smithers, pp.152-3.

217 James Pugh, *The Royal Flying Corps, the Western Front and Control of the Air, 1914-1918* (London: Routledge, 2017) p.165.

218 Hugh Montague Trenchard, later 1st Viscount Trenchard, born 3 February 1873, died 10 February 1956.

219 Andrew Boyle, *Trenchard* (London: Collins, 1962) p.121.

220 Rye, p.213.

Kitchener was a renowned horseman having learned to ride in Ireland. In Egypt, 1883, serving as second in command to Taylor of the 19th Hussars, he selected the officers to undergo training in the Egyptian Cavalry. Taylor wrote, 'It would be impossible for me to speak too highly of the assistance which this officer has given me. The facility with which he has mastered the details of cavalry drill, and his capacity for imparting instruction are remarkable. His energy is untiring.[221]

In India and Cyprus, he owned and trained his own race horses.[222] He was a firm believer that polo and other sports helped keep a man fit for military service. A fall from his horse whilst travelling the narrow streets of Simla without a companion resulted in a severe broken leg, which did not stop him riding.[223] On 15 November 1903, his horse had shied at the sudden appearance of an Indian appearing out of a hidden doorway and with little room to move, Kitchener's leg was crushed. 'Some natives saw the accident, but were too terrified to go near him; at last they summoned up courage to bring the news that the "Lord-of-War" as they called him was lying seriously hurt.'[224] The doctors failed to set the leg properly resulting in a permanent limp which did not seem to affect his work much.[225] Doctors in England refused to rebreak and set his leg,[226] although his injury featured in the *British Medical Journal* as the author, using the information to hand, tried to determine the extent to which Kitchener would be impacted.[227] He recovered, but four years after the break, complained to Alice that he still could not walk far; he had just completed a ten mile walk.[228]

During the 1899-1902 war, Kitchener successfully created a Mounted Infantry of 80,000 men who were used in conjunction with the cavalry and moved in similar fashion to the Boers. They were colonial irregulars and excellent horsemen, although 'the new yeomanry are rather peculiar riders otherwise they are not too bad though some of them have evidently not passed a medical exam.'[229] However, he failed to get permission to have Sudanese and Indian troops supplement the white troops considering it was a 'white man's war'.[230] Kitchener would ride with the Mounted Infantry in front of the columns giving commands and seemingly unaware of the danger. In Omdurman, he had done the same sitting on a white horse. This action endeared Kitchener to the Boers, 'a strong man', but was deprecated by British officers.[231]

221 Magnus, p.71, 28 June 1884.
222 Hook, p.236.
223 Jerrold, p.211.
224 HA: D/ERv/F132/2.
225 Royle, p.219; Arthur, vol 2, p.138.
226 HA: D/ERv/F132/2.
227 British Medical Journal (21 Nov 1903) *The Accident to Lord Kitchener*, p.1357.
228 Arthur, vol 2, p.129.
229 HA: DEX/789/C24, Kitchener to Lady Desborough for Julian; Royle, p.163.
230 Royle, p.177.
231 Royle, p.173.

At the coronation of King George, Kitchener rode *Moifaa*, which King Edward bought after its 1904 Liverpool win.[232] It was not the first royal horse Kitchener had ridden. On leaving India, he wrote to the King's horse trainer to ascertain what should happen to *Democrat*.[233]

> One day the late Lord Kitchener was going round the stable, and I think I am right in saying King Edward VII was there at the time; when they came to Democrat Lord Kitchener remarked on his good looks, and that he was the size and make for a man like himself with long legs. 'Yes, my lord,' said Mr Marsh, 'he would suit you to take out to India as a charger if you would accept him as a gift.'
>
> Lord Kitchener was not a great horseman at any time, and liked something quiet so that he need pay no attention to his mount and devote it all to the business in hand [...] this great winner of races after landing £12,939 in stakes became Lord Kitchener's favourite charger, and was ridden by him at the Delhi Durbar and Coronation Procession of King Edward.[234] Democrat bore himself very proudly in India, winning several prizes at the Indian Horse Shows. Lord Kitchener's and Democrat's name will go down to history together, for in Calcutta there now stands a statue of them sent out from England in 1913. A good and honourable man on a good and honourable horse. I have been told that Democrat died in India shortly before Lord Kitchener left the country.[235]

The first battles of the war, Mons and the Marne, were to feature cavalry divisions on both sides – the war appeared to be progressing along the lines of previous wars with some entrenchments being embarked upon. In 1915 Kitchener changed his mind, the barbed wire was a deterrent for cavalry charges. However, the cavalry was to see service in East Africa, where large numbers died from tsetse fly, and in Mesopotamia, while the desert equivalent, the camel, saw service in Egypt. In place of the cavalry, were tanks.

When the idea of a 'machine gun destroyer' was first explained to Kitchener, 'he made it clear that it would have no backing from him.' ED Swinton suggests this was because Kitchener had no real awareness of 'the problem confronting the forces in the field.' Military protocol prevented Swinton from raising the issue with Kitchener directly despite having almost direct access to the Secretary of State. Fear that others at General Headquarters would reject the idea meant Swinton failed to discuss it with them too. In May 1915, when Swinton submitted an appreciation to GHQ, the Engineer in Chief suggested he 'descend from the realms of imagination to solid

232 Mrs Stuart Menzies (Amy Charlotte), *Lord William Beresford VC: Some Memories of a Famous Sportsman, Soldier and Wit* (London: Herbert Jenkins, 1917) p.324.
233 BL: Add MS 52276B, Marker papers.
234 Democrat is named in the *History of the Delhi Coronation Durbar*, p.45.
235 Stuart Menzies, *Beresford*, pp.320-4.

fact.'[236] There was 'no necessity for complicating matters by the introduction of a new weapon and a new method of fighting.'[237] Meanwhile, Hankey had been moving things forward despite the War Office and Kitchener's views. Churchill adopted the idea.[238]

Within five days of becoming aware of progress on the caterpillar, 24 December,[239] Kitchener wrote, 'As soon as the machine can be produced, the first thing the Secretary of State for War considers necessary would be to test its practical utility under field conditions: without such a test we may be wasting material and men uselessly.' Swinton helpfully briefed Fitzgerald, but Kitchener remained concerned about life and costs. Following the testing of the caterpillar on 2 February 1916, Kitchener 'was entirely sceptical. In [Swinton's] hearing he said that the war would never be won by such machines, which would be knocked out by the enemy's artillery.' Kitchener had earlier discussed the tank during a surprise visit to Hatfield the morning of the trial, but would leave GHQ to make the final decision. The initial failure of the tank was attributed to their not being used correctly. Swinton, though, remained convinced Kitchener's approval would eventually have been forthcoming had he been able to see the tanks in action when they were tested at Elveden in July 1916.[240] But, all was not as it appeared.

> … Kitchener was so much impressed that he remarked to Sir William Robertson that it was far too valuable a weapon for so much publicity. He then left the trial ground before the trials were concluded, with the deliberate intention of creating the impression that he did not think there was anything to be gained from them. Sir William Robertson followed him straight away, taking me with him, to my great disappointment as I was just going to have a ride in the tank! During the drive back to London, Sir William explained to me the reason of Lord Kitchener's and his own early departure, and impressed on me the necessity for maintaining absolute secrecy about the tank, explaining that Lord Kitchener was rather disturbed at so many people being present at the trials as he feared they would get talked about and the Germans would get to hear of them. It is a matter of history that after these trials fifty tanks were ordered and that Lord Kitchener went to his death before they were ready for the field. I do know, however, that he had great expectations for them, for he used to send for me pretty frequently while he was S of S and I was DCIGS, and he referred to them

236 Swinton, *Eyewitness*, p.111.
237 Swinton, *Eyewitness*, pp.73-4.
238 Kellett, p.88.
239 Hankey, *Supreme Command*, vol 1, p.252.
240 Swinton, *Eyewitness*, pp.161-2, 170-1, 211-2, 222.

more than once in the course of conversation. His one fear was that the Germans would get to hear of them before they were ready.[241]

So reported Robert Whigham to Lloyd George who expressed regret that Kitchener never told him, but he does note an order for 100 tanks was placed by the War Office on 12 February 1916.[242] Kitchener's sanctioning of the tank trials followed closely on his approval of the Machine Gun Corps where he had called Christopher D'Arcy Bloomfield Saltern Baker-Carr to London to explain his idea. On being convinced that the weapon would 'be a great saving of man-power if used properly,' he authorised the diversion of 40,000 men to the corps.[243]

Kitchener was not averse to experimenting providing there was a financial and military case, including life-saving, for doing so. Following a visit to the Creusot works in France, on 17 December 1914, he 'gave instructions for experiments' to be made in filling shells with TNT and Schneiderite 'in view of the shortage of piric acid and TNT.'[244] In January 1916 authorisation was given to test Schniederite in Faversham.

On 6 January 1915, Kitchener formed a small committee to determine the allocation of explosives to allies using British resources.[245] He was looking to create a new department which would focus solely on the production of high explosives. A procedure was agreed six months later, 30 July 1915, which came into operation on 13 October under Lord Moulton.[246] In addition to Moulton being an authority on patents, he was 'a brilliant scientist', director and organiser.[247] These arrangements changed in 1917 when America entered the war.

Kitchener's concern for the well-being of his soldiers extended beyond good quality weapons and training. He is credited with the Kitchener stitch, a way of stitching the toes of socks to ensure they do not rub against the toes and cause blisters. He asked the Marchioness of Tullibardine to organise hose-tops for Highland regiments serving in France. These were to fit a specific pattern allowing them to be pulled up over the knee in the cold, greatly assisting those in kilts. Needed by 14 November, the Marchioness organised the 'many fisher girls who have been deprived of their main source of livelihood by the war' to knit.[248] Her husband, Duke of Atholl, had been responsible for

241 Lloyd George, *Memoirs*, vol 1, Robert Whigham, Army Council member 1916, and Deputy Chief of Imperial General Staff, accompanied Kitchener to the trials at Hatfield Park, pp.384-5.
242 Warner, p.205.
243 CD Baker-Carr, *From Chauffer to Brigadier* (London: Ernest Benn, 1930) pp.134-41; born 1878, died 1949.
244 *History of Munitions*, vol 10, pp.9-12.
245 *History of Munitions*, vol 10, p.27.
246 John Fletcher Moulton, Baron Moulton, born 18 November 1844, died 9 March 1921.
247 *Derby Daily Telegraph*, Wednesday 7 June 1916 p.2.
248 *Glasgow Herald*, 24 October 1914.

raising the Scottish regiments during the 1899-1902 war which saw the Transvaal Scottish serve in the Atholl tartan at Delville Wood in July 1916.[249]

Medical aspects received attention too. He was a great supporter of inoculation to prevent disease.[250] In September 1914, having annoyed politician Arthur Lee's attempts to enlist by saying he 'did not want politicians in the Army,' Kitchener appointed him his personal medical advisor for the Western Front.[251] By 8 October 1914, Lee was visiting the front lines, where together with Director General of the Army Medical Service Alfred Henry Keogh,[252] advances were made to meet the changing demands of war.

Lee's description of the slaughter at Neuve Chapelle received 'a tirade against what [Kitchener] called the "preposterous waste of ammunition",' and was aghast that the 'British soldier could not be relied on to advance and attack with the bayonet unless the enemy has first been battered into a state of insensibility.' Lloyd George on being told reacted similarly but, rather than at the wasted 48 hours of attack, that it was only 48 hours of bombardment. Lee eventually joined Lloyd George in Munitions.[253] No doubt had Kitchener been Commander-in-Chief instead of French or Haig, he would have found another way to overcome the stalemate the entrenchments presented. According to Victor Wallace Germains, Kitchener was critical that the element of surprise had been lost, and it was this that resulted in the war of attrition.[254] The drive for economy and to save lives would have been his motivation. However, as Secretary of State, he left the men on the ground to do what they felt best.

Kitchener had learnt much at the War Office, one lesson being the value of dedicated departments to look after specifics. When it was suggested that another department take over the management of men returned disabled, Kitchener much to Brade's surprise acquiesced.[255] He realised the enormity of the task, especially in rehabilitating the men to civilian life.

249 The Marchioness (Katharine Marjory) of Tullibardine (ed.), *A Military History of Perthshire, 1899-1902* (Perth: RA & J Hay, 1908) p.30. Katharine became the first female Scottish MP in 1923, born 6 November 1874, died 21 October 1960; John George Stewart-Murray, 8th Duke of Atholl, born 15 December 1871, died 16 March 1942.

250 Ian R Whitehead, *Doctors in the Great War* (Barnsley: Pen & Sword, 2013) p.28.

251 Alan Clark (ed.) *A Good Innings: The Private Papers of Viscount Lee of Fareham* (London, John Murray, 1974), pp.136-7; Arthur Hamilton Lee, 1st Viscount Lee of Fareham, born 8 November 1868, died 21 July 1947.

252 Alfred Henry Keogh, born 3 July 1857, died 30 July 1936.

253 Clark, pp.140-1, 147. Medical developments explained in Ana Carden-Coyne, *The Politics of Wounds: Military Patients and Medical Power in the First World War* (Oxford: Oxford University, 2014) shows how Kitchener tried to manage medical aspects of the war.

254 Victor Wallace Germains (A Rifleman), *The Truth About Kitchener* (London: John Lane, 1925) p.331ff.

255 Riddell, *War Diaries*, p.55.

Managing the war

At the start of the war, the relationship between Kitchener and French was friendly. Kitchener had approved French's appointment to Aldershot after the 1899-1902 war where fresh ideas were introduced to the army. On French's appointment to the BEF, Kitchener had full confidence and correspondence between the two men showed the admiration they had for the other,[256] or perhaps they were both trying to convince themselves of the other's suitability. Irrespective of what he really thought about French, Kitchener was firmly of the opinion that the senior officer on the ground had to progress things as he saw best. He therefore refused to move officers unless absolutely necessary. This caused a problem in Gallipoli when Kitchener refused to send Byng and Rawlinson at Hamilton's request. When Byng was eventually sent, it was too late.[257]

The split between the two men developed with French's decision to withdraw his troops to preserve them for a future attack. This would cause political ructions with the French which the Germans could exploit. The difference between the local position and wider perspective was ultimately the cause of the two Field Marshals falling out with each other. That Kitchener held military rank and was in a civilian position of authority was both positive and negative. He could see the military implications and understood the decisions French was having to make. With his natural ability to see the wider picture, he foresaw difficulties.

Before the end of August 1914, communications with French led Kitchener to conclude that he needed to travel to France and meet with French. Believing French too depressed to give an objective view, he made a spur of the moment decision to talk rather than rely on the written word to resolve the sensitivities between the BEF and the French. However, in keeping with disasters attendant with Kitchener's spur of the moment decisions, his visit to France on 1 September did more harm to his relationship with French than with the French. His fatal error was going in uniform, asking to inspect the troops and how this was interpreted. Kitchener saw nothing wrong, as far as he was concerned his appointment as Secretary of State for War was on war service, on the same conditions as the BEF: he was a soldier fulfilling a given task. This contrasted with India where Edmond Elles, Military Secretary and a civilian, used to wear military uniform to the Viceroy's Council and was allowed to vote on military matters which the Commander-in-Chief was not.[258] However, Kitchener's objective was met in that French pulled himself together.

Kitchener's appointment, a soldier, as Secretary of State, was unusual, as was Britain's position. Kitchener told Birkenhead soon after his appointment that '... of

---

256 Arthur, p.26.
257 Williams, *Byng*, p.92.
258 Brice, Henry Brackenbury, p.216; Edmond Roche Elles, born 9 June 1848, died 6 January 1945.

his colleagues, no one at least can deny them courage. They have no army; and they have declared war against the mightiest military nation in the world.'[259] They needed someone who could build an army, who knew something about strategy and directing forces over vast distances. For the country's sake a soldier was required in the highest position, but for those running the country they needed an administrator. Kitchener was both, but he was foremost a soldier. The confusion over his role as Secretary of State for War was evident, most noticeably in the discussion of who was to replace Kitchener after his death. Three senior officers were mentioned, French, Robertson and Smith-Dorrien, alongside Lloyd George and Milner.[260]

Arthur suggests Kitchener and French remained friendly all through French's time in Europe and that Kitchener had no input in French moving to command the Home Front, because the public had made a hero of him 'after his ride to Kimberley.'[261] Yet, Prior, Wilson[262] and others imply the relationship was not healthy, with French blaming Kitchener for the 'shell scandal' which erupted after the battle of Aubers Ridge in May 1915. Once French leaked information to the press, via Repington of *The Times*, and Fisher's resignation, Asquith felt the need to form a coalition government to remain in power. Despite Bonar Law's view that 'none of his men will stand K,'[263] he survived the change.

Kitchener's philosophy was to save lives where possible and acted quickly. He was also conscious of the rules of war, so when the Germans attacked with gas at Ypres on 22 April 1915 his initial reaction was outrage. However, he refused to respond in kind as requested by French until the matter had been submitted to the government, as he did not want to 'fall to the level of the degraded Germans.' He made a speech to the House on 24 April, following which 'the employment of similar weapons by our troops was agreed on.' On Monday 26 April, Kitchener saw John Scott Haldane, and Keogh questioned Herbert Brereton Baker, both scientists who were to investigate the matter.[264] Within days the scientists were in France. Neither liked what they were doing but saw the necessity. On 2 May, Haldane and Baker were designing respirators at Kitchener's request and on 3 May Jackson was 'entrusted [with] the task of preparing a reply to the German gas offensive.' Having organised investigations into Britain's chemical warfare capabilities, and ways to protect his troops from attack, Kitchener left the experts to get on with it.[265] A Scientific Advisory Committee was

259 Birkenhead, *Point of View*, vol 1, p.21.
260 *Rand Daily Mail*, 8 June 1916, p.6.
261 Green, p.211; Edmonds, *A Short History*, fn30.
262 Robin Prior & Trevor Wilson, *Command on the Western Front, The Military Career of Sir Henry Rawlinson, 1914-18* (Oxford: John Wiley, 1992) p.94.
263 Brock, *Margot Asquith Diary*, 17 May 1915.
264 Herbert Brereton Baker, born 1862, died 1935; John Scott Haldane, born 1860, died 1936, his brother was RB Haldane. Hannah Gay, *The History of Imperial College London, 1907-2007: Higher Education and Research in Science, Technology and Medicine* (London: Imperial College, 2007) pp.139, 179.
265 TNA: WO 142/281 diary of Baker, pp.34-5; WO 142/240.

set up on 23 June 1915 which oversaw developments, but French continued to apply pressure. When Hamilton asked to use gas in Gallipoli, Kitchener initially refused because the wind favoured the Turks. With Churchill in disagreement, Kitchener gave in warning Hamilton that he used it purely at his own discretion. The Turks had refused its use despite receiving supplies from the Germans.[266]

The failure of both commanders to communicate their plans with each other led to problems, as did the 'messenger' service. Rawlinson, in charge of IV Corps, fed information to Kitchener,[267] while Brinsley Fitzgerald, French's military secretary, fed information to Lloyd George.[268] Rawlinson and French had no liking for each other and when news came through 'that Joffre and French HQ were much put out with Sir J French for his stupidity and obstinacy', this was passed to Kitchener. Rawlinson was letting the King, Derby (Director of Recruiting), and Walter Bagot (Director, Ministry of Munitions) know his feelings about French too. Haig was doing the same, writing to the King, Asquith and others.[269] The result: 'A new Commander-in-Chief was felt to be necessary in order to win battles.'[270]

Before the battle of Loos, planned as a limited action, Kitchener arrived on 18 August 1915 to meet with GHQ. With the collapse of the Russians and pressure on the French, he '... *had decided that we must act with all our energy and do our utmost to help the French, even though, by so doing, we suffered very heavy losses indeed ... All we wanted was ammunition.*'[271] Politics was driving the war, but the soldiers made no suggestions. The colonial-establishment divide of the late 1890s was wrecking Britain's chances in 1914-18.

In November 1915, Rawlinson took leave in London and met with Lloyd George about French. When asked his opinion on Haig, Rawlinson felt he was 'the best soldier we had in France'. On 12 November 1915, Rawlinson wrote to Derby about 'strengthen[ing] the General Staff at home and to change the Command of the Army in France.' Robertson should be appointed 'to a supreme position at the War Office' and Haig replace French.[272] By 4 December, Rawlinson's suggestions were being implemented.[273]

266 TNA: WO 142/240, pp.41-2, 54.
267 Brinsley FitzGerald, born 25 September 1859, died 9 February 1931.
268 David French, *British Economic and Strategic Planning 1905-1915* (London: George Allen, 1982) p.166.
269 Gollin, p.494; Walter Lewis Bagot, born 22 April 1864, died 26 March 1927.
270 Prior and Wilson, pp.132-3.
271 Prior and Wilson, p.105; emphasis in original.
272 Prior and Wilson, p.133.
273 Prior and Wilson, p.133.

A diversion

Kitchener's time in Sudan gave him first-hand experience of working jointly with the navy;[274] his first encounter being on HMS *Invincible* from which he observed the bombardment of Alexandria. In his campaign against the Dervishes, he had worked closely with the navy, developing a high regard for David Beatty. So, when naval action was proposed against the Dardanelles, he was in favour.

Having seen Turkish soldiers in operation in 1913, Kitchener was hesitant to attack the Dardanelles direct.[275] Kitchener had realised by February 1914 that Turkey would most likely side with Germany, but continued to do what he could to keep Turkey on side. However, Egypt, the key to protecting Britain, had to be protected.[276] Believing the Ottoman Empire corrupt and harsh on its people, he was not against undermining it providing there was minimum military input.[277] Maxwell, commanding the British forces in Egypt, trusted Kitchener:

> ... he knew what risks to take, and took them. Few saw as clearly as Lord Kitchener did, the German designs on the East [...] had it not been for pressure at home, I know that he saw the necessity, once Turkey declared war against us, to strike at her and Germany, by an attack on her sensitive lines of communication to Mesopotamia, Syria, Palestine and the Hedjaz.[278]

Kitchener supported an attack on the Dardanelles to protect Britain, India, and Egypt from the East feeling that if a sufficient show of force could be made, the Turks would collapse. Ambassador to Egypt, Henry Morgenthau believed Kitchener was right. 'As soon as the guns began to fire, placards appeared on the hoardings denouncing Talaat and his associates as responsible for all the woes that had come to Turkey.'[279] The question was how best to effect the attack. Kitchener, unable to release the estimated 150,000 men calculated to take the Dardanelles, backed Churchill when he announced the Admiralty could do it alone.[280] Within the month, things began to unravel with differences between Churchill and Fisher becoming apparent. The situation was further complicated when Kitchener announced, 24 January 1915, that if the Navy could not breech the straits unaided, '... the Army ought to see the business

274 See the Melik Society: www.melik.org.uk.
275 Rye, p.351.
276 Arthur, p.95; Jukka Nevakivi, 'Lord Kitchener and the partition of the Ottoman Empire, 1919-1916', in K Bourne & DC de Witt (eds.), *Studies in International History* (London: Longmans, 1967) pp.316ff.
277 Henry Morgenthau, *Ambassador Morgenthau's Story* (New York: Doubleday, Page & Co, 1919) p.13. American Ambassador to Turkey, born 26 April 1856, died 25 November 1946.
278 George Arthur, *General Sir John Maxwell* (London: John Murray, 1932) p.148.
279 Morgenthau, p.49.
280 Royle, pp.316-7.

through. The effect of a defeat on the Orient would be very serious.'[281] As it turned out, the fleet's failure to break through, strengthened the position of the Young Turks.

Kitchener's apparent dithering over what troops to send, if he could, is evidence of him having to make decisions under pressure where he had little control, the mixed messages from the Admiralty not helping. By 13 March, Kitchener felt the situation elsewhere was sufficiently settled to allow the 29th Division to go to Gallipoli.[282] He was committed and prepared to take responsibility for his actions; as with Paardeburg, not doing anything would be worse.

When Violet Bonham Carter commented to Kitchener that Churchill would get full credit for the success of the Dardanelles due to his courage and usurping the experts, Kitchener 'indignantly' replied, '... not at all, I was always strongly in favour of it. No one who has seen as much of the East as I have [could] fail to appreciate its importance.' However, she could not see Kitchener standing by Churchill if things went wrong.[283] It was a love-hate relationship. Marie Belloc Lowndes reported a dinner guest telling 'how he had reason to go into a room at the War Office, where he found, to his boundless astonishment, Churchill hobnobbing with Lord Kitchener, though when they were in the Cabinet together Kitchener was regarded as Churchill's deadliest enemy.'[284] As with Lloyd George, Kitchener put personal issues aside to win the war.

By April, the situation in Gallipoli had deteriorated to such an extent that Amery, near Lemnos, wrote to Milner, 'I think the storm will come and even the splendid Kitchener Umbrella (which you were largely instrumental in forcing into Asquith's reluctant hand) will not save them [the government].'[285] In June 1915, Bonar Law questioned Kitchener's confidence that 'the man on the spot thought the work could be done with the additional troops', and 'that K as a soldier believed there was good reason to think that Hamilton was right'; but being 'ignorant on military matters' did not push his enquiry.[286]

Pressured by his party and the press, on 3 November, Asquith felt he had little choice but to send Kitchener out of the country, where 'his very presence caused offence.' He told Lloyd George, 'I am confident that in the course of the next month, I can put things on a better footing. We avoid by this method of procedure the immediate supersession of K as War Minister, while attaining the same result.'[287] Bonar Law had threatened to resign but was the only dissenter. He thought it a waste of time sending Kitchener to 'do over again the work which had already been done by General Monro' which had been accepted by Cabinet. The decision was 'wrong [and]

281 Dardanelles Commission Report, p.120.
282 Dardanelles Commission Report, p.124.
283 Mark Pottle (ed.), *Champion Redoubtable*, p.34.
284 Marie Belloc Lowndes, *A Passing World*, p.73.
285 Gollin, p.253.
286 PA: Dav 19, Bonar Law to Selbourne, 8 June 1915.
287 Royle, p.338; Magnus, p.427.

altogether indefensible' and needed a more complete discussion and definite decision. That he did not resign was the result of men such as Austen Chamberlain encouraging him not to. Instead he was offered a role on the War Cabinet.[288]

Kitchener left for the Dardanelles on 4 November 1915:

> Not a word spoken! He might have been going out to lunch. He knew as well as anyone that it was good he was leaving, but not a sign of his countenance or demeanour gave evidence of this. D [Lloyd George] says that he felt a lump in his throat, and he thinks many other members of the Cabinet were touched also. Crewe passed a rather significant note across to D. Personally I think it is rather a cowardly thing the PM has done.[289]

The media speculated over Kitchener's tour of duty and Asquith taking over the War Office. This ranged from the opportunity to change the way the War Office functioned which would mean a change in the War Secretary's role through to Kitchener setting up an Eastern Command to coordinate Gallipoli, Macedonia, Egypt and Mesopotamia or focus on India. On 12 November LJ Maxse (*National Review*) wrote that when he saw the '... original announcement in the *Daily Express* [he] knew that the intrigue against Lord Kitchener had been successful and that on one pretext or another he was being ejected from the Cabinet. [...] Did any man ever pack so many lies into such a short space of time as Asquith last night?'[290]

The underlying message was that the work Kitchener had been brought in to do, namely get Britain on a war footing, was complete and he was no longer needed at the War Office.[291] That his work in organising the army was done was a repeated theme through the memorial services and reassurances after his death. Officially, Kitchener's visit to Gallipoli was to ascertain whether withdrawal was feasible, despite Monro having been to Gallipoli for the same purpose.[292] He felt it was, providing Egypt's safety could be assured and to do so, proposed an attack on Alexandria, the Alexandretta Project.[293] The General Staff objected, believing it impossible. Kitchener, however, reminded the Prime Minister that it had been discussed before he left England and

---

288 PA: BL 50/3/9 and others Austen Chamberlain wrote to Bonar Law that if his view was accepted, it would appear Kitchener's removal was a result of 'sordid and cowardly intrigue'. Charles Carmichael Monro, 1st Baronet, born 15 June 1860, died 7 December 1929.

289 Royle, p.338.

290 PA: BLU 1/MAXS/5, Leopold 'Leo' James Maxse, born 11 November 1864, died 22 January 1932.

291 *Rand Daily Mail*, 8 November 1915, p.6.

292 Gollin, pp.312, 316; Royle, pp.337-338.

293 Yigel Sheffy, *British Military Intelligence in Palestine* (London: Routledge, 2012) p.113.

that McMahon,[294] Maxwell[295] and himself '… who were expert in the field in Egypt had considered the plans. The move was vital, if nothing else, from a political perspective in order to keep the Mohammedans loyal to Britain.'[296]

It is not the intention of this book to comment on the decisions made or pass judgement, but rather to provide insight into the influences Kitchener had to manage when making his decisions. Kitchener was making decisions based on only part of the story and pressures coming from different fronts. As seen at Paardeberg and Abu Hamid he was not good at these spur of the moment decisions, but he stood little chance of making the right decision if he did not have the right information to begin with. EF Aspinall claims Kitchener pressured French to undertake the operations at Loos because of 'Joffre's threats of insurrection, although these concerns were not shared by "responsible French statesmen".'[297] Had the French learnt this was the trigger to get Kitchener to authorise British action: threaten insurrection or a split in the relationship?

Hamilton's apparent deference to Kitchener provides an opportunity to consider the relationship. Kitchener was his Commander-in-Chief, '… to be defended against the demands of alarmist politicians [and] to be revered for the power of summary dismissal he held over his generals.' Aware that Kitchener had removed reinforcements when asked for additional troops in the 1899-1902 war, Hamilton held back in directly asking for more men.[298] Was Hamilton that awed by Kitchener? Having worked with Kitchener, Hamilton was one of the inner circle. Knowing the pressure Kitchener was under, he would have naturally done all he could to prevent adding further to his burden, but to the extent of putting his own force at risk? If this is the case, Aspinall's question about the lives of so many being lost for such a reason must remain and reflects why Kitchener did not favour married men on his staff – they would not make clear decisions for personal reasons.

Nevinson claims Kitchener was 'won over by Monro's report and the persuasion of Staff officers upon the *Aragon*, one of whom proudly boasted to me that, "We soon brought Kitchener round to our way of thinking".'[299] It was Kitchener's seeing the peninsula himself that confirmed his decision to withdraw the troops. Byng tasked with the withdrawal managed it without loss of life. His biographer, Jeffery Williams claims Kitchener refused to see Byng on his return to England in March 1916 because Kitchener had not 'forgiven' him for his achievement.[300] It is more likely Kitchener was in one of his depressed states, anxiety over Townsend in Kut, the removal of Duff

---

294 Vincent Arthur Henry McMahon, born 28 November 1862, died 29 December 1949.
295 John Maxwell, Chief British liaison officer to Joffre before being posted to Egypt as General Officer Commanding British Force.
296 Arthur, p.192.
297 Green, p.136, Cecil Faber Aspinall, born 8 February 1878, died 23 May 1959.
298 Green, pp.142-3.
299 Nevinson, *Fire of Life*, p.320.
300 Williams, *Byng*, p.109.

in India from managing Mesopotamia, uncertainty of his own role with parliament discussing his salary, and the unnecessary loss of life in East Africa in early February 1916. His self-abrogation lost him a friend.

The day he sailed from Gallipoli, a request arrived for him to see the Italian King in Rome, a request Kitchener fulfilled with Cabinet consent. Awarded the Grand Cordon of St Maurice and St Lazarus, he then went to Greece to convince that king to support Britain or at least remain neutral. A stop in Egypt determined what actions were needed there to support the evacuation of Gallipoli and to ensure the safety of Egypt itself and the canal. He wanted to return to London to explain the situation, but it was recommended he remain in Egypt to help manage the morale of those evacuated. Kitchener felt this unnecessary and that his presence would do more harm. He returned to England, arriving on 30 November to discover exactly how his position had changed and been undermined.

European 'Sideshows'

While French was preparing for the Western Front in August 1914, Kitchener was studying the maps and information he had to hand to enable him to advise colleagues about the wider war. He had commandeered the 275 Indian Service British officers on leave in summer 1914,[301] and did the same to the African officers. This move, although helping the Western Front did not bode well for the areas concerned. India lost ten per cent of its officer force while Africa lost commanders who knew the territory as well as the people. However, having been appointed on 5 August and assuming his position the following day, many decisions had already been made. One of these concerned East Africa.

The Cabinet decided on 5 August that an Indian Brigade would be sent to East Africa to help protect the border with German East Africa and another Expeditionary Force would launch a coastal attack on the German colony. After various vacillations, the troops were eventually despatched, only to be defeated at Longido and Tanga respectively. On 22 November 1914 the War Office took control of the campaign from the India Office, the latter remaining in control of material supply, the result of Kitchener's drive to make India self-sufficient. Kitchener, however, refused to sanction any action in the theatre unless there was a clear chance of victory and that troops would not be required from elsewhere.[302]

It could cynically be argued that Kitchener was trying to avoid war as he owned a struggling coffee farm on the Uganda Railway, however, significantly, he knew the

---

301 George Morton-Jack, *The Indian Army on the Western Front: India's Expeditionary Force to France* (Cambridge: Cambridge Military History, 2014) p.160.

302 Samson, *Britain, South Africa and East Africa* for the rest of this section unless otherwise specified.

terrain. Having fought successfully in Egypt and the Sudan, he knew what preparation and precautions were needed in hostile African territory. Added to this, were his experiences against the Boers in southern Africa, and having travelled some of the land in East Africa, he knew its challenges. He had also been involved in the decision to give Mount Kilimanjaro to Germany in 1885 and so could not see any reason to fight for something Britain had determined to give away. However, in November 1915, his colleagues both in the War Office and Cabinet decided otherwise, and in contrast to the 1914 decision that action in Africa would not be for territorial gain. As complaints about Kitchener increased, Asquith was forced to take action, which he did by sending Kitchener to the Dardanelles, and the decision was made to re-launch the campaign in East Africa.

In terms of the wider war, East Africa consumed unnecessary time. Ostensibly under Colonial Office control with the India Office responsible for supplies, the Foreign Office and Admiralty needed to be consulted to ensure Belgian, French and Portuguese allies were pacified and that necessary shipping was available. Kitchener's authorisation of offensive-defensive actions only if there was a clear chance of success meant he had to consider proposals on occasion. Despite these safe-guards, the attack in December 1914 and January 1915 against Jasin failed. However, the timing coincided with offers of assistance by the Legion of Frontiersmen under Driscoll and with the majority of the Legion not meeting army recruitment standards, but having frontier experience, Kitchener sent them to Africa where their independence and specialist skills would be more suited than in the disciplined and stalemate trenches. To regularise the unit, they were allocated to the 25th Royal Fusiliers. The only unit to be deployed without undergoing training, they obtained weapons at Malta on route and trained in their use on ship. Along with the 2nd Loyal North Lancashires, who had been in India on the outbreak of war, these were the only two British units which served in the theatre. The Indians, local East African Mounted Rifles, and King's African Rifles along with white volunteer units in Nyasaland and Rhodesia faced the Germans until December 1915, during which time, the Germans occupied the only British territory they did of the war; Taveta in Tsavo British East Africa from 15 August 1914. This irked the Colonial Office and by 1915, the politicians had moved from safeguarding shipping and existing possessions, to wanting additional territory.

The Colonial Office wanted more troops, which Kitchener would not supply if they could be better utilised on the Western Front. When he offered troops from French Madagascar, the Colonial and Foreign Offices objected as they did not want to complicate international involvement in the area. Who would pay for the troops was another consideration the Colonial Office pondered before accepting Kitchener's preferred troops. With recruitment ostensibly exhausted, Kitchener sent older brother Henry to East Africa to investigate. This caused suspicion, those in Africa suspecting he was spying for the Secretary of State, but there is no evidence, yet, of this having happened. Later in the war, HEC worked with the Railways and after his brother's death, remained in the country until his own death in 1937.

It was the conclusion of the campaign in South West Africa which provided an opportunity for a relaunch of the war in East Africa. Kitchener, however, thought differently preferring to have the South Africans in Europe. Discussions ensued and a difference between Kitchener and his War Office colleagues became apparent. Charles Callwell, brought back from retirement and who remained in post following various reshuffles, had a fundamentally different view of the campaign in Africa to Kitchener. His experience of African warfare had led to his book *Small wars* setting out the principles of subjugating tribes which directed his thinking. He also supported the politicians in their desire for territorial expansion. Kitchener's departure to the Dardanelles gave Cabinet the opportunity to sanction the use of 10,000 South African whites in the theatre, Horace Smith-Dorrien being appointed Commander-in-Chief. On 10 and 12 December, Kitchener made a last attempt to prevent the action, but was overridden.

Smith-Dorrien, confirmed as going to East Africa, wrote to Kitchener requesting an increase in his entertainment allowance, Nairobi known to be more expensive than Europe, and to arrange additional military equipment. As much as Kitchener respected Smith-Dorrien and had supported him after his dismissal by French,[303] he remained true to his principle. After two 'most unsatisfactory interview[s]' on 6 and 13 December respectively, with Kitchener 'who is very cussed about my expedition because it was agreed by Asquith and Bonar Law in his absence,' and 'who is quite impossible and throwing every difficulty in the way of my command in East Africa,'[304] he finally wrote to Asquith on 20 December:[305]

> I really am ashamed to trouble you, but the fact that if the two matters [troops, emoluments and equipment] I am referring to are satisfactorily settled I must embark for Africa on Thursday, makes it necessary for me to appeal to the fountain head. [...]
>
> Since Lord Kitchener refused these Howitzers, 140 guns have been safely got away from Gallipoli, and I am told by the General Staff that now there should be no difficulty about letting the Howitzers go to East Africa.
>
> I regard this Brigade as of vital importance.
>
> Lord Kitchener's attitude is that you were the SoS who decided on the campaign, that he does not approve of it, and does not consider himself bound by the conditions under which I accepted the command.
>
> Re pay [...] Today, I asked Lord Kitchener to give a ruling confirming this, but he told me that I must refer the matter to you, as he had no idea what was in your mind at the time you made the appointment, but that, if you would let him know what your wishes on the subject were, he would carry them out.

303 Ian FW Beckett & Steven J Corvi, *Haig's Generals* (Casemate, 2006) p.118.
304 IWM: Smith-Dorrien papers 87/47/3, diaries.
305 IWM: Smith-Dorrien papers 87/47/8, 20 Dec 1915 Smith-Dorrien to my Dear Asquith.

I would remark that I hear Nairobi, where my Head Quarters will be, is a very expensive place and that I shall have to do a considerable amount of entertaining there, which points to the desirability of a special entertaining allowance.

Smith-Dorrien sailed on 26 December but falling ill on route, was replaced as Commander-in-Chief by South African Jan Smuts. Kitchener's concerns were realised when the first attack, Salaita Hill, the South Africans were involved in failed. They followed a battle plan Smith-Dorrien had drawn up and which was approved on 23 December by Robertson on his first day in the office. The loss of manpower due to illness and malnutrition meant the South Africans were withdrawn at the end of 1916, to be replaced with regiments from the Gold Coast, Nigeria and West Indies and the King's African Rifles rapidly expanded to deal with the fragmented mobile warfare the theatre had adopted. The situation created by the Cabinet decision to increase action in a theatre which would have no impact on the outcome of the war in Europe was anathema to Kitchener and was to have significant long-term repercussions for the countries involved. For the inhabitants of those countries, this was no sideshow.

Similarly, although he was happy to see the overthrow of the Ottoman Empire, Kitchener did not believe Mesopotamia should be drawn into the war. In March 1915, despite the India Office being of the same mind, the War Cabinet, or Dardanelles Committee as it was then known, not fully understanding the local situation, overrode the experts. The outcome was Townsend's surrender at Kut-el-Amara on 29 April 1916 after a five-month siege, the sending of more troops and the change in control from the India Office to the War Office,[306] the same as had happened in East Africa post-Tanga in November 1914. Kitchener had also withheld permission to raise a Zionist unit to fight for control of Palestine because the diplomats had already determined who would control what territory, removing any need for 'fancy' units. As he foresaw, British forces became involved in another long drawn-out campaign with unnecessary loss of life.[307]

All part of the plan

By November 1915, Kitchener's star had faded amongst his colleagues but not amongst the people. Rather than replace Kitchener as Secretary of State for War which would have caused difficulties with the public, Asquith sought to reduce his

---

306 Arthur, p.205; NS Nash, *Betrayal of an Army: Mesopotamia 1914-1916* (Barnsley: Pen & Sword, 2016) pp.177-8.
307 AJ Barker, *The First Iraq War – 1914-18: Britain's Mesopotamia Campaign* (Enigma, 2009); Vladimir Jabotinsky, *The Story of the Jewish Legion* (New York: Bernard Ackermann, 1945) pp.58ff; John Fisher, *Curzon and British Imperialism in the Middle East, 1916-1919* (London: Routledge, 2012).

power and influence. Returning on 30 November 1915, Kitchener handed in his resignation as Secretary of State for War, although on 8 November *The Globe* reported he had done so the Friday before and then 'reasserted'.[308] Close friends had warned before he left for Gallipoli that Cabinet colleagues were hoping he would not return, and no doubt with all the attempts to delay his return, he felt it time to go. The Prime Minister, however, declined his resignation and Kitchener returned to the War Office.[309] He also learnt of the Cabinet's decision to replace French with Douglas Haig as Commander-in-Chief.[310] Haig took over on 10 December 1915, thirteen days before Robertson became Chief of Imperial General Staff. French had commanded for sixteen difficult months, building a fighting force where none had existed before in conjunction with France, which had a long-standing large army, and Belgium whose input was small but whose feelings were strong.

An enquiry in 1917 into the Dardanelles episode was sensitive to the fact Kitchener was not there to defend himself and that the other most significant person who could, Fitzgerald, had drowned with him. Kitchener's tendency to secrecy, not writing down his thoughts or confiding in others, meant the Enquiry team was in the dark regarding his views. Despite the caution the Enquiry felt it should exercise, it naturally fell to piecing together the events and scenarios as presented to them and it is only with the wisdom of insight provided by hindsight that missing pieces of the puzzle create a different picture of the time.

The Enquiry, headed by Cromer, determined that Kitchener centralised too much in himself. This was true in the early days of the war as he tried to get control of a system acknowledged to be chaotic. Decisions had been made before Kitchener was appointed and many of the senior War Office officials had left to take up roles on the Western Front. This left a largely inexperienced and young staff behind to support the Secretary of State for War. Kitchener had little faith in the War Office and strongly believed that those supporting soldiers should be experienced in leading men in the field. As few people met these minimum requirements, he took their responsibility upon himself. Those who met his criteria were left to 'get on with the job' and where he could he supported. The Dardanelles Commission concluded that Kitchener did not listen to experts and subordinates as he did not trust them, whereas Churchill seemed to ignore the advice of his experts when they had reservations about an action he felt passionately about.[311]

The political games Kitchener had to deal with caused him to lose touch with his war aims.[312] He had reluctantly sanctioned the battle of Loos in September following strategic losses elsewhere. Similarly, he sanctioned troops for the Balkans; against

308 *Rand Daily Mail*, 8 November 1915, p.6.
309 Arthur, pp.208-9; Magnus, p.433.
310 Arthur, p.293.
311 Dardanelles Commission Report.
312 Royle, p.333; Magnus, p.46.

his better judgement but felt politically trapped.[313] In the words of Royle, 'We had to make war as we must, not as we would like to.'[314]

Arthur claims Robertson's appointment as CIGS was part of Kitchener's plan.[315] Kitchener had planned for an assistant to be appointed when it was opportune without undermining French's arrangements. Thus, the Cabinet decision to appoint French to command the Home Forces, enabled Kitchener, with Asquith's blessing, to effect changes at the War Office.[316] The result was the replacement of James Wolfe Murray as CIGS with Robertson. Wolfe Murray had become CIGS in 1914 on his return to Britain from South Africa where he had commanded the Imperial Garrison and, following the resignation of Herbert Gladstone,[317] assumed the role of acting High Commissioner until the arrival of Sydney Buxton[318] in early September. With all the other senior officers already on the Western Front, when CIGS incumbent Charles Douglas died in office, Murray was in the right place to fill his shoes.

Robertson, appointed CIGS on 23 December 1916, having heard of Kitchener's reputation before meeting him, insisted on various powers to counteract the Field Marshal if required. A month after his appointment, the two men met and agreed a working relationship on 27 January 1916.[319] Robertson later reported that his special powers were not needed. Kitchener obviously trusted Robertson and left him to focus on the military aspects.[320]

As Kitchener's workload diminished, the result of new appointments and the systems he had successfully implemented over the previous year, so he was able to get out and about and focus on things where he could make the most impact. This was as mediator between the military and foreign politicians; it was on just such a mission that the ship he was travelling on went down. He visited munitions factories to encourage and cajole production, his comment on Bernard Oppenheimer's factory in Letchworth Garden City being favourable.[321] Ten days before his fatal trip, on 25 May 1916, a visit to Woolwich was his last official military appearance.[322]

Opposition to Kitchener being in the War Office remained and on 31 May 1916 a move was made in the Commons to reduce his salary. Asquith objected,[323] explaining

---

313 Royle, p.337.
314 Royle, p.327.
315 Arthur, pp.296-300.
316 Royle, p.333.
317 Herbert John Gladstone, 1st Viscount Gladstone, born 7 January 1854, died 6 March 1930.
318 Sydney Charles Buxton, 1st Earl Buxton, born 25 October 1853, died 15 October 1934.
319 Royle, p.347, 27 January 1916.
320 Arthur glosses over the conflict between Kitchener and French; Steven J Corvi & Ian FW Beckett (eds.), *Victoria's Generals* (Barnsley: Pen & Sword, 2009) p.212.
321 Andrew Hocking, *Oppenheimer and Son* (Maidenhead: McGraw-Hill, 1973) p.69, Bernard Oppenheimer, 1st Baronet, born 13 February 1866, died 13 June 1921.
322 Royle, p.27.
323 Rye, p.576; Davray, p.68.

how reluctant Kitchener had been to take up the post of Secretary of State for War. Two days later, 2 June, Kitchener addressed the politicians in a secret session to answer questions about the administration of the war. Despite his refusal to discuss military strategy, the meeting ended with a vote of thanks.

Having worked as a spy in environments where news quickly spread, Kitchener had learnt to be secretive and tended to keep to himself having little in common with most of his compatriots. Rodd suggested, '... his mentality had been affected by long communion with men whose minds worked on Oriental lines ...'[324] He was aware of the gossip-mongers in Egypt and the damage they could do. His time spent in Egyptian markets and other local settings would have made him wary of trusting even those who appeared trustworthy. Spies abounded and as Kitchener was a white man working in areas where the white man obviously stood out, he needed to keep his counsel. His later encounters with Milner and Curzon only served to exacerbate this perceived need for secrecy – not necessarily because he did not trust them (at least initially) but because he was shy and felt they would not understand what he was trying to do. Their allegiances were elsewhere. His earlier seniors seemed to have had quite a good grip on who or what Kitchener was; Cromer picked up on his depressions and Biddulph on what motivated him. Kitchener's tendency to greater secrecy seems to have developed with age and who he could trust. Henderson commenting of Kitchener before his death: 'I have never dealt with a Senior Officer who took me so much into his confidence and gave me his opinion so frankly as Lord Kitchener.'[325]

324 Rodd, *Memories*, p.36.
325 Birkenhead, *Points of View*, p.14.

10

The private Kitchener

Kitchener was a private man who lived in the limelight. His austere nature meant few penetrated the real Kitchener. Those who did found a loyal friend, and it was only with his death that the inner man became better known.

Beliefs

Kitchener had a strong religious faith; his favourite book the Bible.[1] It had developed working with Claude Conder who was studying Hebrew as part of his work on mapping Palestine, and through their studies both became interested in Anglo-Catholicism.[2] In 1874, the year the Public Worship Regulation Act was passed, Kitchener joined the English Church Union and on 1 January 1876, after his first visit to Palestine, enrolled into the Army Guild of the Holy Standard. He remained a 'silent member till the day of his lamentable death.'[3] At Aldershot, Kitchener's padre was JC Edghill who founded the Guild of the Holy Standard in 1873 which aimed to support Anglican communicants and encourage them to work with chaplains.[4] In 1911 on leaving a church service Kitchener revealed to Byng, '[…] when I hear that response "because there is none other that fighteth for us, but only Thou, O God," I rather wonder where we generals come in, don't you?'[5]

Kitchener's idea of faith was such that he was able to relate to his Hindu and Islamic subjects without causing offence. His knowledge of the Mahdi's religion enabled him

---

1   Samuel Daiches, 'Lord Kitchener: In memoriam', in *The Zionist Review*, vol 1, no 2 (June 1917) p.25.
2   Royle, p.26.
3   Arthur, vol 1, p.14; Pollock, pp.36-7.
4   Michael Snape, *The Redcoat and Religion: The Forgotten History of the British Soldier from the Age of Marlborough to the Eve of the First World War* (London: Routledge, 2005) p.135 using Pollock. John Cox Edghill, born 1835, died 1917.
5   Williams, *Byng*, p.56.

to explain his actions satisfactorily to Queen Victoria when she expressed concern at the treatment meted out on the Madhi's grave.

After his successes against the French at Fashoda and the Boers, Kitchener had thanksgiving services which helped win over the vanquished. In contrast, when he defeated the Madhi, he had the Mahdi's body thrown into the Nile and on another occasion had one of the Madhi's generals paraded in humiliation.[6] The battle for Ras el Hudi was fought on Good Friday, 8 April following a consultation conducted under a tree in Arabic with Khulusi Bey, the Egyptian Commanding Officer of the 8th Fellahin Battalion. With his Muslim soldiers not likely to protest at fighting on a Friday, the prophet Mohammed having himself fought a battle on that day, and Maxwell reassuring Kitchener that liberating others on Good Friday was appropriate, Kitchener gave the order to advance.[7] In preparing for the attacks on Dongola and Omdurman, with irregular forces composed of local tribesmen, Kitchener noted on an undated letter, 'The Shaigia are now very well I have said Muslim prayers with their [illegible] and we are to be great friends.'[8] The outcome was 2,000 men who did not need to be paid for.

Kitchener's awareness of religions and spirituality allowed him to integrate different aspects of his life. There is evidence from diaries of subordinates in India that he attended church services as often as travel and other commitments allowed. He saw no conflict becoming a Freemason, even introducing the Amir of Afghanistan to the fold, the Amir's vows being made on the Qu'ran.[9]

The appointment of non-conformist chaplains to the army led to Kitchener's first conflict with Lloyd George: 'Tremendous row with Kitchener today about non-conformist Chaplains. Spoke out savagely, Carried Cabinet and got my way.'[10] The outcome was Kitchener asked '... for the names of these sects for which you want padres. Is this list right? Primitive Baptists, Calvinistic Wesleyans, Congregational Methodists ...?' The spirit with which this was done indicated that Kitchener 'had simply never heard of these great religious bodies.'[11] Kitchener's lack of awareness was the result of spending so much time away from Britain and, when Secretary of State for War, completely engrossed in the task of sorting out the army as he appeared oblivious of being 'surrounded by representatives of [...] "superfluous and eccentric sects" in Cabinet.' Asquith, John Simon, Attorney General, and T McKinnon Wood, Secretary of State for Scotland, were Congregationalists; Lloyd George and Percy Illingworth, Chief Whip, were Baptists; Runciman, President of the Board of Trade,

6   Rye, p.146.
7   Arthur, *John Maxwell*, pp.55-6.
8   TNA: PRO 30/57/3 G2.
9   Henry McMahon, *An Account of the Entry of HM Habibullah Khan Amir of Afghanistan into Freemasonry* (for private circulation, 1936).
10   Morgan, p.173; in JH Thompson, The Free Church Army Chaplain 1830-1930 (PhD, University of Sheffield, 1990) pp.294-5.
11   Lloyd George, *Memoirs*, vol 1, p.451.

was Wesleyan;[12] and Pease, President of the Board of Education, was a Quaker. In 1914, 126 Members of Parliament, excluding Unitarians, were non-conformist.[13] Once he understood the position of non-conformists in relation to the army and the other religions, Kitchener ensured appropriate religious leadership despite War Office concern that it would lead to splits and unnecessary additional costs.[14] Cabinet approval for the appointment of non-conformist chaplains was obtained on 28 September 1914. In November 1914, the United Navy and Army Board was formed to advise on the appointment of chaplains, in the same way the Presbyterians had their own board and later the Anglicans would have theirs.[15]

In August 1915, the Right Reverend LH Gwynne, brother of HA Gwynne editor of the *Morning Post*, was appointed to represent the Chaplain General with the Army in the Field. This was to balance the criticism being levelled against Bishop Taylor Smith,[16] head of the War Office Chaplain's Division directly responsible to the Secretary of State. Gwynne had been Bishop in Khartoum and had dined with Kitchener in June 1914. When Gwynne objected to the role, for fear of becoming an administrator, Kitchener informed him that 'you are now in uniform and under my orders for the duration of the war. If I order you to go to Timbuctoo that is where you will go ...'[17] He would only be responsible for the chaplains and troops of the Church of England, the other denominations remaining under the watchful eye of Dr John Simms,[18] the Principal Chaplain who was Presbyterian. Simms, too, had known Kitchener before the First World War. He had been in the Chaplains' Department in the Sudan in 1887 and then in the column which relieved Mafeking in May 1900.[19]

However, Kitchener would not have the church obviously used for recruiting. Esher informed Randall Davidson Archbishop of Canterbury on 10 September 1914 that 'Lord K does not wish for any "Campaign" on behalf of recruiting under the auspices

12   Rodd says, in *Memoirs*, of Runciman after a visit to Italy in August 1916: 'I now understood why Kitchener, speaking of the political associations in which he never felt at ease, had told me that he felt more drawn to Runciman than to any other member of the Cabinet.' John Allsebrook Simon, 1st Viscount Simon, born 28 February 1873, died 11 January 1954; Thomas McKinnon Wood, born 26 January 1855, died 26 March 1927, Percy Holden Illingworth, born 19 March 1869, died 3 January 1915.
13   Thompson, Free Church Army Chaplain, p.295fn.
14   Thompson, Free Church Army Chaplain, p.320.
15   Michael Francis Snape, *The Royal Army Chaplains' Department, 1796-1953: Clergy under fire* (Boydell, 2008) p.199; TNA: WO 32/5636 in Thompson, Free Church Army Chaplain, p.322. The Advisory Committee on Anglican Chaplains was formed with Salisbury, Grenfell and Brade, amongst others. The Bishop of Winchester noting, 'No call from yourself for assistance should be met by anything but consent. I therefore at once accept ...' The committee continued to meet until 1920.
16   John Taylor Smith, born 20 April 1860, died 28 March 1938.
17   HC Jackson, 'Pastor on the Nile', p.150 in Thompson, Free Church Army Chaplain, p.317.
18   John Morrow Simms, born 23 November 1854, died 29 April 1934.
19   Thompson, Free Church Army Chaplain, p.319; Alison M Brown, Army chaplains in the First World War (PhD, University of St Andrews, 1996).

of the Church. He would "intensely dislike it" – his words.' Kitchener's private secretary Arthur clarified on 1 October: 'I think these referred to the Church – as such – being made a vehicle for military purposes and especially to pulpit pronouncements. One may be quite certain that the Archbishop – if he writes – will use words as felicitous as they will be useful.'[20] There was a place for religion in the armed forces, but the army needed to be independent of religion to avoid divisions. Something he feared might happen in Ireland in 1913.

On occasion, he was critical of the clergy during the war, and appeared contradictory:

> The clergy are the most conservative, tiresome, unimaginative men to deal with that I have ever come across; I suggested all sorts of things to them: proper hymns like 'Eternal Father Strong to Save', and 'Onward Christian Soldiers', but they would not listen to me: I want this service to be a great recruiting occasion. The Archbishop could, in a short sermon, stir up the whole congregation [to do their duty], which would be a far better way doing things than all this intrigue about Conscription.

Margot Asquith in whose company this comment was made, 'was surprised to find that Lord Kitchener not only disliked intrigue but was averse to Conscription.' The result 'was a disappointing service [at St Paul's], and a great occasion missed.'[21]

Freemasonry

Being a Mason for Kitchener was more than upholding the code. It allowed him to combine his religious beliefs with his duty to monarch. The centenary booklet for the formation of Kitchener Lodge explains:

> The purpose of Freemasonry is to make men good and good men better … Its fundamental principles are those of Peace and brotherhood throughout the World. The basic qualification is a belief in God (the Supreme Being). It is not a Religion. It does not teach Religion but joins with Religion for the moral betterment of mankind. Freemasonry does not permit a Mason to replace Faith but to reinforce it.
>
> Live for something. Do good and leave behind you a monument of virtue that Time cannot destroy. Write your name in Kindness, Love and Mercy, on the

20   GKA Bell, *Randall Davidson Archbishop of Canterbury*, vol 2 (London: Oxford UP, 1935) p.740, Randall Thomas Davidson, 1st Baron Davidson of Lambeth, born 7 April 1848, died 25 May 1930.
21   Bonham Carter, *Margot Asquith*, pp.313-4.

hearts of hundreds you come in contact, year in and year out and you will never be forgotten your deeds will shine as the stars. [sic][22]

Membership was a tool to be used for Imperial purposes. On Queen Victoria's birthday in 1900, a brother Mason observed that Masons had 'proved to be the bulwark of her throne' and were responsible for 'building up the British Empire to its present grand position.' It had been '… welded and is being more tightly welded together by men who have been reared and trained amidst Masonic influences.'[23] Kitchener's involvement was political, a situation the District Grand Lodge of the Punjab recognised when it recorded him being '… deeply engaged in a work of construction that cannot but appeal to us as Freemasons – the repair and strengthening of the defences of this great Empire.'[24]

At the invitation of the British government, the Amir of Afghanistan visited India. Aged thirty-four he arrived at Landi Kotal on 2 January 1907, never having been outside his country.

> He was a man of very strong and determined character, of very superior intellect and surprisingly well-informed on all general subjects.
>
> A few days after his arrival, he astonished [McMahon] by expressing a wish to become a Freemason, but not knowing his motives I gave him no encouragement … it was not until the 22nd of January that I realised how very much he was in earnest … He begged that if it could be done, it should be without the knowledge of any of his staff and people … he had met good men who were Masons; that he knew Freemasonry to be a good thing and he wanted to enter it.

The only place the Amir could become a Mason, if at all, in India would be Lodge Concordia No 3102 which was small and exclusive, being 'restricted to British Civil and Military Officers of high standing.' Given the programme, only one night would be available to take him through all three degrees which meant:

> … all Masonic regulations about stated intervals between proposals, elections and degrees must be waived. Only thirteen days were available in which to accomplish all this!
>
> Lord Kitchener, most fortunately, was at that moment the District Grand Master of the Punjab and I at once communicated to him the facts of the case begging him to telegraph for an all-embracing dispensation to meet the many requirements of the case, to the Grand Master, the Duke of Connaught, who

22   MoFM: NJE 166 (2998) Kit: Centenary Book Kitchener Lodge.
23   Quoted in Jessica L Harland-Jacobs, *Builders of Empire: Freemasonry and British Imperialism 1717-1927* (University of North Carolina Press, 2007) p.255.
24   Harland-Jacobs, *Builders of Empire*, p.266.

happened at the moment to be on a visit to Ceylon. This he did forthwith and at once came the reply, 'I approve of the Amir receiving three degrees and give dispensation. Welcome him into the Craft in my name. Connaught'.

A meeting was called on 2 February at 9.30 p.m., notices being delivered personally. Secrecy was required as the Amir was out of his country 'against the wishes and advice of bigoted advisers who prophesied that nothing but evil could come of his association with foreign infidels ...' Accordingly, a dinner was arranged for the same night with the Commander-in-Chief of India, Lord Kitchener. Usually accompanied by a retinue of staff,

> ... at the last moment, [the Amir] expressed a wish to go unaccompanied by any staff as a special compliment to his friend, Lord Kitchener, and thus he and I went alone.
> Immediately after dinner at which were only Lord Kitchener and his small personal staff, we drove off, unobserved, to the Masonic Hall where Lodge Concordia were waiting to receive us, and the proceedings of the evening began forthwith.[25]

Everything was explained to the Amir in Persian, McMahon acting as translator, a task '... not made lighter by Lord Kitchener who at the conclusion of the 3rd degree delivered a somewhat lengthy but impressive address on the value of Freemasonry which also needed conversion into Persian.' At midnight, when the proceedings ended, the Amir returned with Kitchener to his house and then escorted home by McMahon. The influence Masonry had on the Amir cemented a friendship with Britain which saw him remain loyal to Britain throughout the Great War.[26] Afterwards, '... our loyal friend and ally was struck down by the hand of an assassin; the firm hand that had kept peace on our frontier was removed; Afghanistan turned against us and British troops were sent rushing back in great strength to India. If this had been necessary during the war, the history of that war might have been changed.'[27] Not only had the Amir been lost to Britain, but his initiator and supporter as a Mason, Lord Kitchener had too.

Aged thirty-three, Kitchener had been initiated into the Italian speaking La Concordia Lodge No 1226, Cairo, Egypt in 1883, having been introduced to Masonry by the Duke of Connaught.[28] He remained a Mason for life, belonged to fifteen Lodges and Chapters and served as District Grand Master of Egypt and the

25 McMahon, *The Amir of Afghanistan*, pp.3-7.
26 FJ Moberly, *Operations in Persia 1914-1919, History of the Great War Based on Official Documents* (Government of India, 1928) p.74.
27 McMahon, *The Amir of Afghanistan*, p.11.
28 Royle, p.231; The Duke was Queen Victoria's third son who served in the Indian Army; The Lodge was erased/Closed in 1890.

Sudan and of the Punjab in India. He was involved in setting up new lodges, including being a founder of Drury Lodge (The Actors Lodge) No 2127 on 25 January 1886 yet attended his first meeting there in 1898. At least five Lodges bear his name.[29]

Kitchener's link with Drury dated to the autumn 1885 production *Human Nature* by Augustus Harris.[30] The public areas had been decorated with 'interesting trophies and souvenirs of the Egyptian campaign.' Included was 'a piece of Brussels carpet [...] a relic of considerable interest, for it was brought from Gordon's room in the dismantled Government House at Khartoum by one of Colonel Kitchener's messengers as a proof of his having duly arrived there.'[31] Kitchener attended a rehearsal of the play and having objected to the method of the battle scene was called upon by Harris to 'tell 'em what to do.'[32] He gave his support for the Lodge at the same time. The warrant permitting the Lodge to be constituted was signed by Edward Prince of Wales on 10 November 1885.[33]

On 23 April 1900, when in South Africa, Kitchener visited Bloemfontein's Rising Star Lodge.[34] It is reported that Louis Botha was a Mason, however details of when he became one are not available making it difficult to know whether this influenced the peace discussions between the two men.

Collector and scholar

An avid collector of items, his letters to Marker from India suggest he collected different items as passing fads, although china and porcelain remained constant. A PS from Birdwood to Marker in 1909 illustrates:

> PS: the chief has asked me to add – that he is now collecting swords!!! China my dear Raymond was hardly in it and then absolutely detest the very sight or mention of a sword. Fitz I am sorry to say is stupid about these things and encourages him in the relentless shikan which you will remember well he carries on, when dead keen about such things. I rather gather what he would now like you to do would be to go to the British Museum – stand a complete ground there, sleeping in the building if necessary! Examine all old swords and take with you any you think could be suitably added to his collection! Read all books on the subject of swords and make complete lists of the different kinds of blades and

29   Yasha Beresiner, *Kitchener of Khartoum: Mason Extraordinary*.
30   Augustus Henry Glossop Harris, born 18 March 1852, died 22 June 1896.
31   Marty Gould, *Nineteenth-Century Theatre and the Imperial Encounter* (Routledge, 2011) p.22.
32   Booth, *'Master' and Men*, pp.197-8.
33   MoFM: Souvenir Guide for the opening of Drury Lodge 2127.
34   https://freemasonrymatters.co.uk/latest-news-freemasonry/famous-freemasons-horatio-herbert-kitchener/

waterings, and where others can be obtained. [ask the museum] what are the best books on the subject of swords and armour generally – he thinks there may be old Persian treatises on the subject?[35]

Kitchener was not always able to do his own purchasing and would call on various individuals to assist. In the 1914-18 war, art dealer Frank Partridge[36] would buy for him at the Red Cross Auctions. A few days before he sailed for Russia, Kitchener asked Partridge to, 'buy on his behalf an enamelled bowl decorated with "The Eight Immortals" at a Christie's sale. On 22 June 1916 Partridge attended the auction and bid, 'determined to honour his friend's last request.' The item, Lot 165 was sold for £241 10s and then donated to the London Museum as 'a little tribute to the memory of the great dead.' It was known as the 'Kitchener bowl.'[37]

During his time in Palestine and later Cyprus, Kitchener had developed his interest in collecting porcelain and other items. He learnt the value of archaeological finds.[38] One of his discoveries in Palestine led to a wider discussion and investigation into fake idols. Whilst in Cyprus he was appointed Curator and Honourable Secretary to the proposed Island Museum of Cyprus.[39] His interest in archaeology and artefacts remained, one of his last letters in 1916 being to Archibald Sayce to tell a student to 'remember that some very nice tiles are to be found at Samarra.'[40]

His ability to identify prize pieces and to drive a hard bargain, learnt in the Egyptian markets, apparently led to antique dealers closing their shops when Kitchener was known to be around. It is said he would often buy their best pieces for less than what the dealer had paid; which clearly was not good for business. According to Magnus, friends soon learnt to pack their valuables away so he could not steal them.[41] Grafftey-Smith claims 'local Syrian and Jewish collectors of porcelain and *objets d'art*' in Egypt 'found some comfort in [Kitchener's] passing' as Storrs had driven hard bargains on Kitchener's behalf.[42]

On leaving South Africa, various life-size statues were found to have departed with Kitchener. Magnus claims these were eventually returned in 1909 to South Africa following negotiations between the South African government, Colonial Office and Kitchener.[43] However, four statues had been given to Kitchener by Sammy Marks, a South African mining magnate who had them cast in Rome in 1899 before war broke out. There had been a discussion between Botha and Kitchener about the statues, the

---

35   BL: Add MS 52278, Marker papers, 15 February 1909, Birdie to Conk.
36   Frank Partridge, born 31 January 1875, died 8 August 1953.
37   Trethewey, *Pearls*, pp.512-4.
38   Royle, p.46.
39   Palestine Exploration Fund; Rye, p.69.
40   Sayce, *Reminiscences*, p.417.
41   Magnus, pp.286-7.
42   Laurence Grafftey-Smith, *Bright Levant* (London: Stacey International, 2002) p.23.
43   Magnus, p.232.

desire to have them returned to South Africa being an article in the press. At that stage, Botha saw no value in their return. Two remained at Broome while two were at the Royal Engineer Brompton Barracks in Chatham. In December 1921 Smuts asked that they be returned to South Africa to take their planned place on Church Square and this was done.[44]

Numerous biographers claim Kitchener helped himself to objects he fancied. He clearly had an appreciative eye for collectables, however, claims of helping himself to collections have only been found in accounts of his visit to China and Japan in 1909. The Minister of Railways in China had to mediate Kitchener's interest in the royal China in Manchu. The best pieces had been removed to storage and presence of them denied despite Kitchener having photographs. 'He selected two each of the smaller vases, cups and jars [...] so I stopped him saying that in the decree he was to be allowed only two pieces ... Kitchener then put the jar on top of the vase saying that it was only one piece [...] two cups in his pocket and seized one vase in each hand.'[45] Viscount Lee of Fareham and Lucy Murray comment on his intense interest in items,[46] while Crawford explains '... he kept the handsome gifts which were sent, according to the customs of those countries, on the honourable understanding that they would be returned to their owners! [...] that is the universal system as K must well know: and if he has really committed this grave breach of etiquette he deserved censure.'[47] Kitchener was not well liked on his visit to Japan and did himself no credit at a lunch for Theodore Roosevelt hosted by Lee in April 1910 – 'his instincts and manners – in a less famous man – would be considered overbearing and ill-bred.'[48] There does not appear to be official correspondence on the matter, a letter from the Foreign Office of 13 December 1909 only refers to the King '... express[ing] his special thanks to the Emperor and his people for the more than kind and distinguished manner in which Lord Kitchener has been treated during his stay in Japan.'[49] Kitchener's behaviour to some extent was due to his inherent shyness exacerbated by his tendency to withdraw when upset, which he was on leaving India and having no clear future mapped out. His stern demeanour amongst strangers was open to misinterpretation and given his preference for Chinese collectables over Japanese, his intense interest in specific pieces of furniture may well have been misreading of his humour.[50] But his reputa-

44   Much travelled statues, in *South African Digest*, vol 11, no 2, 5 June 1964, p.16; TNA: PRO 30/57/100, Kitchener to Harrison, 8 October PA13.

45   Christopher Arnander & Frances Wood, *Betrayed Ally: China in the Great War* (Barnsley: Pen & Sword, 2016) p.34.

46   Clark, *Lee of Fareham*, p.109; JC Ker, *'Lest We Forget' Revisited: A Memoir* (Bookbaby, 2017) pp.177-8.

47   Vincent, *Crawford Papers*, p.163.

48   Clark, *Lee of Fareham*, p.109.

49   TNA: FO 262/1474, 13 December 1909, FO to C Komura, no.131 f.279.

50   Kitchener's only female biographer to date, Nandkuverba CI, Maharani of Bhavnagar, *Field Marshal Earl Kitchener of Khartoum, KG* (London: Richmond, 1916) in her chapter

tion for driving a hard bargain when purchasing an item was quite within keeping.[51] According to Horace Rumbold, Kitchener left Japan with twenty-five cases of wares, whether they were of items from Japan or including his Indian possessions is not known.[52] When Kitchener asked in 1915 for 200,000 rifles for the Western Front, Japan refused.[53] His Middle Eastern ways were not Eastern ways.

As with all collectors, Kitchener had disappointments where pieces were 'quite common stuff' and having suffered loss and theft of items in transit.[54] Returning to England in 1910, shortly before he was scheduled to take up the Mediterranean command, the Countess of Jersey recalled a visit to Osterley, where he:

> ... amused himself by sorting our Chinese from our Japanese china, the latter kind being in his eyes 'no good.' Tired of this, he suddenly said, 'Now let us go into the garden and pick strawberries.' 'But,' said I, 'there are no strawberries growing out-of-doors in May.' 'Oh,' he exclaimed, 'I thought when we came to Osterley we *always* picked strawberries.' Fortunately I had some hot-house ones ready at tea.[55]

Having received a jewel-encrusted sword when granted the Freedom of London and other gifts including a cigar case from Queen Victoria, when he was presented with a sword in honour of his achievements by the City of Cardiff, he made it known that a dinner service, furniture or pictures would have been more useful.[56] This did not go down well with the British, but it was indicative of Kitchener's pragmatic approach. He had recently been awarded the KCMG which he only accepted following a parliamentary award of £30,000. The financial award had been made to enable Kitchener to fulfil the social obligations accepting the knighthood would entail.[57] It had been proposed by Queen Victoria on 1 June 1899 and put to the House the following day '... in recognition of such services to confer some signal mark of her favour upon him.'[58] In similar fashion, his request for a dinner service instead of a ceremonial sword would enable him to entertain in a fashion commensurate with his new status, and save him the hassle of having to shop.

Kitchener was 'Incredibly house-proud' as noted by the *Rand Daily Mail* reporter in 1961. An article on Melrose House 59 years earlier described it as, 'something out

---

    Kitchener the Man gives some examples of his humour which could easily have been misinterpreted.

51 Ker, *Lest We Forget*, pp.177-8.
52 Gilbert, *Rumbold*, p.81.
53 Arnander & Wood, *China*, p.45.
54 Vincent, *Crawford Papers*, p.163.
55 Countess of Jersey, p.367.
56 Magnus, p.180.
57 Magnus, p.168; Smithers, p.21.
58 TNA: L/PO/JO/10/9/1665 (no 429), signed Queen Victoria 1 June 1899 Balmoral.

of *Great Expectations*. Miss Haversham undoubtedly lived in just such an example of mid-Victorian "brewers' Gothic".' Although in 1961 it was 'an anachronism', in 1903 it 'was an imposing dwelling by Victorian standards, one of the grandest private residences in Pretoria.' Initially occupied by Lord Roberts during the 1899-1902 war, Kitchener took over the house, owned by George Heys,[59] as his headquarters for the remainder of the war, '... and for nearly two years afterwards.' The reporter continued:

> Kitchener of Khartoum ruled Melrose House with a rod of iron. A staff of hand-picked Indian servants, recruited from Indian Army regiments, ran the great house on military lines. A small army of syces groomed the finest collection of horses ever seen in South Africa in the long-since demolished stables. The mess was the most glittering in the history of the British Army. An invitation to dine at Melrose House was tantamount to a Royal command.

His acquisition of artefacts and statues led to Kitchener's practice of renovating buildings to accommodate his treasures. He developed a taste for this in India when he adapted his Simla residence to be more fitting for the Commander-in-Chief of the Indian Army. Hedin, who spent a week with him in 1906, recorded:

> Lord Kitchener's residence stands at the end of the town of Simla, and is called Snowdon. The visitor enters first a large ante-room, which, with its tasteful arrangement and decoration, makes rather the impression of a reception room or a hall of honour bedecked with trophies. A fine portrait of Gordon Pasha is placed on an easel; opposite stand busts of Alexander and Cæsar. In the wainscot of the staircase is inserted the arm of the presidential chair which Uncle Kruger used in Pretoria, and on the tables, shelves, and friezes are valuable Chinese vases of the Kang-hi (1662-1722) and Kien-lung (1736-1795) periods; for Lord Kitchener is an enthusiastic collector of old Chinese porcelain, but only the very finest finds favour in his eyes. But what strikes the stranger most in this unique hall, and above all attracts his attention, are the trophies and flags from Lord Kitchener's victories in the Sudan and South Africa. They hang down from their staves from an upper gallery, among them the standards of the Mahdi and the dervishes of Omdurman and Om Debraket, besides several Boer flags from the Transvaal and the Orange Free State. In the inner drawing-room we find the same luxurious decoration with Chinese porcelain vases and rare ethnographical objects, among which certain Tibetan temple friezes carved in wood are of great value; they were brought by Younghusband's Lhasa expedition. On the tables lie albums of photographs of Lord Kitchener's numerous tours of inspection in India, and of

59   George Heys, 1852-1939, South African.

his journey through the cold Pamir. At receptions the table is adorned with costly services in solid gold, gifts of the English nation to the victor of Africa.[60]

Unemployed in 1911, Kitchener took the opportunity to purchase Broome Park between Canterbury and Folkestone. This was his first property in Britain, friends and family having accommodated him on his visits. Not having a government posting and given his advancing age, 61, Kitchener felt it time to set down roots. He could no longer justify moving between friends' houses and having sufficient finance, felt justified in making the purchase at £14,000. His time refurbishing official residences had convinced him of the value of having a permanent place where he could display his porcelain, marble and other acquisitions. Although he never got to stay in the main house because of being in Egypt, refurbishing and then needing to be in London, he invited various friends to visit and picnic under the trees.[61] The garden had been his priority, he told Lady Ilchester thanking her for sending 'a lovely lot of trees.' He could now determine where to plant flowers.[62] In 1896 Wolseley described Broome, then owned by the Oxendens:

The house is of red brick, much begabled and said to have been built by Inigo Jones. It is in very bad repair, as is also the old furniture [...] The park is fine and beautifully wooded, and the surrounding country rich in undulating scenery, in no way grand or imposing, but delightfully green and homelike. The house is just 7 miles from Canterbury, along the old Watling Street of the Romans.[63]

Kitchener's favourite niece, Nora, oversaw the refurbishment whilst he was away, the architect Detmar Blow having been involved in the design.[64] During his visits to Broome, Kitchener stayed with his steward, Walter Western, who was reassured by Fitzgerald in June 1915 that '... you cannot do a greater service to the war than to look after the one relaxation which Lord Kitchener allows himself – the building of his house. It gives him such intense pleasure every Saturday when he comes down and

60   Sven Anders Hedin, *Trans-Himalaya: Discoveries and Adventures in Tibet, volume 1 of 2* (Library of Alexandria, 1909) p.3, 18-9, born 19 February 1865, died 26 November 1952.
61   BL: Add MS 51370, The Holland House Papers, to Dear Lady Ilchester, 10 September 1911, f.184.
62   BL: Add MS 51370 The Holland House Papers, to My dear Lady Ilchester, 29 January 1913, f.191; 25 March 1913, f.197.
63   George Arthur (ed.) *The Letters of Lord and Lady Wolseley, 1870*-1911 (London: William Heineman, 1922) p.354.
64   Broome Park Golf Club, *A Brief History of Broome Park and Lord Kitchener*, online: https://www.broomepark.co.uk/wp-content/uploads/2018/05/Broome-Park-A-Brief-History-Leaflet.pdf [accessed 25 March 2019]; Stephen Heathorn, *Haig and Kitchener in Twentieth Century Britain: Remembrance, Representation and Appropriation* (Routledge, 2016) p.56.

sees the good work that has been done.'[65] Kitchener made his first war-time visit to Broome on 28 August 1914. Realising that the war went on 'in spite of his absence,' he would visit again.[66] Later, when he had more time, he would travel down late Saturday afternoons to return on Sunday in time for afternoon tea at the house Lady Wantage lent him in Carlton Gardens before heading to York House which had been placed at his disposal by the King.[67]

Lady Wantage, having met Kitchener in 1897 in Cairo, had made her London house available to him at the start of the war until March 1915. Failing to find another due to the pressures of war, Lord Sandhurst the Lord Chamberlain,[68] suggested York House in the north-west part of St James's Palace. At the time it was being used by the Prince of Wales's National Fund for the Relief of the Poor, which the Lord Chamberlain's Office wanted removed. Fritz Ponsonby, Keeper of the Privy Purse, was concerned that loaning Kitchener the house would set a precedent. However, Douglas Dawson, comptroller of the Lord Chamberlain's Office, countered that '... these were abnormal times and "K is an abnormal Minister of War. At the moment of the greatest crisis the British Empire has ever faced this man steps into the breach, gives up his job in Egypt *and his official residence*, and takes the helm at the WO to see us through the trouble and *to drop it immediately the trouble is over*".' Stamfordham, the King's secretary, agreed it would enable Kitchener to live close to the office and Buckingham Palace and 'would give HM another opportunity of rendering personal help in this time of war and would I expect be generally appreciated as an act of grace and favour to an *individual*.' Kitchener moved in not having seen the property, his staff making the necessary arrangements. Soon after, the King and Queen visited him for tea; the two men were good friends, Kitchener regularly phoning or visiting with news.[69]

His 'own predilection' as announced to Rodd, was 'to retire early from active life and devote the remainder of his years to archaeological investigation.[70] His appreciation of history and the past was reflected in his ready approval of starting the Official History of the Great War whilst the war was being fought. Kitchener argued in August 1915:

> ... that, in view of the length of time such a series would take to complete, work should begin immediately on a single-volume popular history which could be published immediately the war had ended. This was in order to maintain public interest in the larger work and to be able to put the government's case

---

65   Bonham's Auctions, *Kitchener and Broome Park, Kent*, online: https://www.bonhams.com/auctions/17807/lot/85/ [accessed 25 March 2019].
66   Hatfield House: 2 September 1914, Fitzgerald to Lady Salisbury.
67   Hodges, p.15.
68   William Mansfield, 1st Viscount Sandhurst, born 21 August 1855, died 2 November 1921.
69   Pollock, pp.429-30.
70   Rodd, *Memories*, p.37.

contemporaneously with the large number of anticipated accounts by popular authors or participants.[71]

He had a thirst for knowledge and somewhere in his busy schedule found time to master languages before arriving in a given place, discover the history, and undertake scientific studies. He was a vice-president of the Society of East Anglians in London, the family house in Stonham Aspal, near Ipswich being in the area.[72] In Dublin, August 1878, Kitchener gave a talk to the British Association for the Advancement of Science on the survey of Galilee,[73] and during his time in Egypt presented on cotton and other subjects.

Although he made no bones about wanting porcelain and specific gifts from friends and others, Kitchener refused to enter into, or continue, investments where he saw a conflict of interest. When, during the First World War, Lloyd George entered into a contract with a Canadian munitions company in which Kitchener had shares, he sold them.[74] What Kitchener defined as a conflict of interest is not very clear, as he saw none in joining the Chatham and Dover Line to improve the link to Canterbury and Broome Park. In a letter to his financial advisor Arthur Renshaw,[75] 26 April 1911, he thought obtaining a position on the British East Africa Corporation would be no bad thing as he had a farm in that territory. This was before he drew support for his farm from that organisation. His forthrightness extended beyond gifts, as he told Renshaw, 'You might put me on the Texas Board or some such sort'; he was a shareholder in the company TL&M which invested in Texas cattle, land and mortgages.[76]

71   Green, *Writing the Great War*, p.6.
72   *Derby Daily Telegraph*, 7 June 1916, p.2.
73   Magnus, p.40.
74   Royle, p.189; Magnus, pp.286-7.
75   Arthur Renshaw, executor of Kitchener's will. The other executor was Algernon Henry Mills of the bank Glyn, Mills and Currie. Both Kitchener and Mills were directors on Railway companies, and the banking firm was the bank for the Gordon College which Kitchener set up. https://www.rbs.com/heritage/people/algernon-henry-mills.html [accessed 27 April 2019].
76   Magnus, p.310; Peter Lester Payne, *Studies in Scottish Business History* (Taylor & Francis, 1967) p.377.

11

Death and the aftermath

In April 1916, it had been thought Lloyd George should go to Russia. However, as events in Ireland were causing concern it was agreed that Lloyd George should concentrate his efforts there. This was announced on 25 May. On 26 May it was decided Kitchener would go to Russia, despite George Arthur saying Kitchener had received an invitation from the Russian Czar to visit, and on 27 May, Kitchener '... sent the telegram accepting the Czar's invitation as published in Sir George Arthur's book.'[1]

Magnus and others claim Kitchener reacted to his intuition. If so, it was only for appearances. He was a meticulous thinker and mentally organised – he could not have been the Steevens' 'machine' otherwise. This tendency of his to put things in order took on a new significance when he died, many interpreting his actions as 'intuition' or a premonition that he would not return. That he returned the locket containing Hermione's hair to the family and that the Queen Mother was recorded as feeling uneasy about his going, has lent credibility to the intuition claims.[2] As a result, we can reconstruct a fairly accurate and detailed account of Kitchener's last few days, reproduced here to show his breadth of interest and attention to detail amongst the pressures and concerns of the day.

After a trip to France where he saw the 29th Division from Gallipoli,[3] on Friday 2 June he met with the House of Commons in secret session, saw some religious ministers about conscientious objectors, and had his final dinner at Rosa Lewis' hotel where he was well known. Rosa used to put geraniums and sweet peas on the table for him, noting that he saw things differently and was '... too absorbed in interests of the world and [his] country' to get married.[4] Kitchener then went, as usual, to Broome for the weekend. He '... finished arranging the furniture and his collection of

---

1   PA: LG F/25/1/22, Hankey, March 1921.
2   Hodges, pp.18-20.
3   De Lisle, *Sport and War*, p.242.
4   Mary Lawton, *The Queen of Cooks, and Some Kings (The Story of Rosa Lewis)* (New York: Boni & Liveright, 1925) pp.129-31.

porcelain in the great hall,' and had tea with Humphrey Leggett. Together Leggett, Kitchener and Arthur McMurdo had bought adjoining lands in Kenya which they were jointly developing. That weekend, Kitchener signed papers to turn the farm into a limited company, and along the route to Scotland despatched a letter to Leggett from Doncaster suggesting who should take the deceased McMurdo's place.[5]

Keen to get away, but not particularly looking forward to going to Russia, he was resigned to doing what he could. The trip would entail far too much ceremony which he detested and, despite it being summer, travelling through the frozen arctic, for a man accustomed to warmer climes would be challenging. His chauffer, Smith, drove him to London, in a Rolls Royce lent to Fitzgerald by South African mining magnate Abe Bailey.[6] He would arrive in time for tea at 4 p.m. giving him time to change into khaki and get to King's Cross Station in time to leave at 5.45 p.m. Kitchener's life was run to precision and when the car skidded in the rain as it turned into Rochester Road from Vauxhall Bridge, he was said to have passed a comment about 'going a little bit too fast.' Having settled aboard the train, Kitchener uncharacteristically returned to George Arthur on the platform and told him '... to look after things whilst I'm away will you.'[7]

On arrival at Thurso, Kitchener was met by Captain Douglas Faviell of HMS *Oak* and Captain Arthur Gwynne Moreton Meredyth,[8] Thurso's transport officer who escorted the officers to the harbour where HMS *Oak*, a destroyer, would take them to HMS *Hampshire* where Captain Herbert Savill[9] was waiting for them. Luggage and servants followed from Scapa Flow in HMS *Alouette*.[10] With Kitchener and Fitzgerald were Hugh James O'Beirne (Foreign Office), H Frederick Donaldson (Technical Adviser, Ministry of Munitions), Second Lieutenant Robert D McPherson, Leslie S Robertson (Ministry of Munitions), and Brigadier-General Wilfred Ellershaw, together with 723 crew.[11]

The ship hit a mine and sank about eight o'clock on Tuesday night. The *Daily Express* reported on Wednesday, the following day, that Fitzgerald's body had been washed ashore.[12] An unnamed warrant officer survivor, one of twelve, was reported as saying he thought Kitchener '... probably never got on deck (this differs from a report at the time of Lord Kitchener having been seen on deck.) There was not five minutes between the explosions and the disappearance of the ship.'[13]

5   Hodges, p.162.
6   Abraham Bailey, 1st Baronet, born 6 November 1864, died 10 August 1940.
7   Arthur, pp.18-20.
8   Douglas Faviell, born 25 November 1884, died 15 July 1947; Arthur Gwynne Moreton Meredyth, born 21 July 1862, died 14 December 1955.
9   Herbert John Savill, born 20 May 1870, died 5 June 1916.
10   Hodges, p.22.
11   hmshampshire.org
12   *Rand Daily Mail*, 8 June 1916, p.6.
13   'The Mystery of Lord Kitchener', in Littell's *The Living Age*, vol 3 (1919) pp.317-8.

Reactions

People could recall where they were the day the news broke. Kitchener's sister, Frances 'Millie' Parker, was at a charity bazar in Essex when news of Kitchener's death reached her. Margot Asquith rushed into a family baptism at St Paul's Cathedral with the news, Vera Brittan[14] walked with her mother and brother along the Thames at Westminster 'sad and subdued'. Film showings and other gatherings were cancelled while the news sank in.

'It was highly probable that Lord Kitchener's death was brought about by German spies', so on 24 June 1916 a resolution was proposed by Lady Violet Greville[15] at Hampton Court and passed. It stated:

> All persons of enemy origin shall be excluded from all military areas and from Government employment, and that all Germans, naturalised or unnaturalised, be interned forthwith ...[16]

Another, similar in content, was passed by the British Empire Union at Hyde Park led by General Sir Hugh McCalmont on the same day.[17] Condolences and sympathies flooded in, that of the French Government being put to the House of Lords on 8 June 1916.[18] South Africa adjourned parliament once Botha had notified the House of Kitchener's death.[19]

The King wrote to Millie: '... while the whole nation mourns the death of a great soldier, I have personally lost in Lord Kitchener an old and valued friend, upon whose devotion I ever relied with utmost confidence.'[20] Raymond Asquith writing to his wife on the behaviour of Margot, 'As if it mattered these old men being killed ...' A couple of days earlier he had written that of greater 'feeling' for the men on the front than Kitchener's death was having their leave reduced from ten days to six or even five.[21] In contrast to Raymond's view, Henry Smith, a Methodist Chaplain wrote that having struggled to get men to attend services 'the reasons I cannot disclose', for a service in memory of Kitchener he had over 200 men of whom about 150 stood for about an hour.[22] Whilst Roland Mountford wrote from near Berles au Boi:

14   Vera Mary Brittan, born 29 December 1893, died 29 March 1970.
15   Novelist and writer, Lady Beatrice Violet Graham, born 13 February 1842, died 29 February 1932, in 1863 married Algernon William Fulke Greville, 2nd Baron Greville. He died 2 December 1909.
16   'A National Demand', in *The British Journal of Nursing*, p.555, 24 Jun 1916.
17   'A National Demand', p.555, 24 Jun 1916. Hugh McCalmont, Irish soldier and Unionist, born 9 February 1845, died 2 May 1924.
18   PA: HL/PO/JO/10/10/598 (no 343).
19   Derby *Daily Telegraph*, 7 June 1916, p.2.
20   Trethewey, *Pearls*, chapter 12.
21   Raymond Asquith, pp.267-8.
22   *The United Methodist: The Weekly Journal of the United Methodist Church*, p.4.

I suppose Kitchener's death must have caused an awful shock at home. It did not cause such a tremendous stir here. I think the Naval affair, until the truth (or as near it as we shall get) become known, caused much more excitement. The general feeling is that Kitchener has got the war on a business footing, and the rest can now safely be left to his successors. We had a memorial service on the same day as you, but fortunately I didn't have to go. It was our first day out, and the ceremony was held at Brigade Headquarters, half an hour's march away, in the middle of a field, and it rained all the time.[23]

John CC Davidson, private secretary to Bonar Law, wrote to William Lamond Allardyce, Governor of the Bahamas,[24] on 6 June 1916:

It is difficult to put shortly what news there is. In the first place there is the terrible tragedy of the death of Lord Kitchener last night [...] There is some slight consolation in the knowledge that the greater part of his splendid work has been accomplished. He had raised the Army in a way that no one else could have done, and perhaps in this ungrateful world, his reputation in the eyes of posterity might have been less great than it will be had he lived for the recriminations which are sure to take place after the war. Nevertheless, it is a great moral loss, and I think that it will do more than anything else to stiffen the backs of the people.[25]

Later, on 27 June, Davidson confirmed that Kitchener's death had 'stiffened people's backs'. It was '... clearly a mine and the weather was so heavy that it was impossible for the destroyers to continue in company with the *Hampshire*. The great consolation is that Lord Kitchener's work was really, if not actually accomplished, so well established that his annihilation did not mean the disappearance of his organisations and scheme.'[26]

The papers echoed the sentiments. The Derby *Daily Telegraph* reporting the London correspondent of the Birmingham *Daily Post*:

A year ago the death of Lord Kitchener would have been a national disaster. It is not that to-day, thanks to his prevision of the magnitude and duration of the war and the labours by which he has equipped us with men. He had completed the task which he undertook. The passing of the Military Services Act crowns his achievement. What other war plans he had what was in his mind when he took ship for Russia, we may know in due time. Had he lived we might have seen him leading armies in the field and meeting a soldier's death. But death has

23   Letters of Roland Mountfort, p.78, letter dated 16 Jun 1916.
24   John CC Allardyce, born 23 February 1889, died 11 December 1990; William Lamond Allardyce, born 14 November 1861, died 10 June 1930.
25   PA: Dav 31, JCC Davidson to Allardyce, 6 June 1916.
26   PA: Dav 31, JCC Davidson to Allardyce, 27 June 1916.

come to him in the form he desired – so, at least I am informed by a friend to whom Lord Kitchener, not many weeks ago, expressed a personal preference for a sailor's death.[27]

For a man who did not like the cold, Ian Hamilton told a lunch party on 7 June that 'Lord Kitchener had a great dread of cold water, and would die at once if he felt sure in the sea,'[28] this is a rather strange statement. HW Sampson of the South African Labour Party seemed to be more in tune with Kitchener: '… if anyone regretted anything – and it would be a thing that Lord Kitchener himself would have regretted – it was that Lord Kitchener did not meet a soldier's death on the battle-field instead of being driven to the bottom of the sea by what one might call cowardly tactics.'[29]

From the German press reported in the *Berlingske Tidendo*, Copenhagen: 'It is a disaster the horror of which will strike all British hearts. If any single name ever expressed Great Britain's warlike energy and unflinching and manly will, it was that of Lord Kitchener.'[30]

There was an outpouring of grief. Memorial services were held all over the Empire. As early as 11 June at the Canadian Red Cross Hospital at Cliveden, Lord Desborough gave the address on his friend. He described Kitchener's death as 'Nelson's Column falling – something national, almost symbolic gone.'[31] In Cairo, on 13 June 1916, the Kasir-el-Nir Barracks hosted a service. Lodge Corinth No 1122 held a 'Masonic Memorial Service' on 2 September 1916 'in pious memory of Late Field Marshal Earl Kitchener of Khartoum PDGD [adapted from a memorial service to His Majesty the Late King Edward VII, which was used by the combined Lodges of (No 492) St John's and (No 2829) Caribee in the Island of Antigua, British West Indies, in 1910].' The service included the *Processional Ode* by Rudyard Kipling, *Crossing the Bar* by Tennyson, *Now the Labourer's task is o'er; now the battle day is past* … and concluded with Kipling's *God of our Fathers, known of old*.[32] Kitchener's favourite hymn was played at memorial services across the Empire: *Nearer, my God, to Thee*.[33]

Not all were upset by Kitchener's death. The *Rand Daily Mail* reported incidents where there was gloating at Kitchener's death by pro-German supporters.[34] In Russia, Rasputin told the Tsarina it was good Kitchener had died as he could have been very

27   Derby *Daily Telegraph*, 7 June 1916 p.2.
28   Celia Lee, *Jean, Lady Hamilton 1861-1941: A Soldier's Wife (Wife of General Sir Ian Hamilton): A Biography from Her Diaries* (London: Celia Lee, 2001) p.159.
29   *Rand Daily Mail*, 8 June 1916, p.6.
30   Derby *Daily Telegraph*, 7 June 1916, p.2.
31   HA: D/ERv/F132/2, Desborough, *Lord Kitchener As I Knew Him*, (reprinted from the Empire Review).
32   MoFM: Kitchener Biographical file.
33   *Rand Daily Mail*, 10 June 1916, p.7.
34   *Rand Daily Mail*, 9 June 1916, p.6.

harmful to the country, but did not say why.[35] In contrast, the Czar who wrote favourably of Kitchener and was keen that he visit, did not long survive himself. In England, Lord Northcliffe felt 'Providence is on the side of the British Empire after all.'[36]

By the end of the month, 'an entirely new' *Life of Lord Kitchener* was being promoted, that by Ernest Protheroe, a publication of 320 pages, the latest copyright photo of the man and an account of the memorial service at St Paul's on 18 June.[37] A book of poetry consisting of 240 poetical tributes was published by the end of the year.[38]

Friends and family consoled each other and others. Millie wrote to a well-wisher: 'I personally have no hope and the reports are very trying entirely owing to our being given no information as to where the fault lay or the cause of the disaster.' To another she wrote: 'No good life is wasted; the influence remains, but I feel victory without my brother will be much saddened. So many of us will feel this, having lost so many of our loved ones.'[39] Ettie Desborough shared the advice Kitchener gave her on the death of her two sons. She further wrote: '… I have wondered so whether all the small mortifications of the last few months really mattered to him. I think somehow he was above and beyond all that. The last time I saw him was the day he came to Panshanger in April, and I thought him quite curiously happy and at peace.'[40] He had worked through whatever prevented him seeing Byng.

On 31 July, F Kitchener wrote to Ettie from HMS *Raglan*, to thank her for her letter and hoped that a photograph had arrived. He continued: 'I had the good fortune to have spent two weekends at Broome and his last week in London with him. He was very happy at Broome, but was rather dreading the week's work & was so looking forward to his trip to Russia. You have always had my sympathy and it would be a great pleasure to meet you and your husband.'[41]

Fitzgerald was not forgotten either. 'I had a letter from Fitz from the train on Sunday night. Casie will feel that very much. They had a deep and true friendship. I do not think anyone had such a crystal character as Fitz. One's only thankfulness is that he did not survive it. The emptiness of life to him would have been almost too great.'[42] He was buried on 10 June in Eastbourne, the funeral attended by Kitchener's nephew Commander Henry Franklin Chevalier Kitchener, Royal Navy.[43]

35   Apollon Davidson & Irina Filitova, *The Russians and the Anglo-Boer War* (Pretoria: Human & Rosseau, 1998) p.218.

36   Trethewey, *Pearls*, p.437.

37   *The United Methodist*, 29 June 1916, no 448, page 1.

38   Chas E Forshaw (ed.) *Poems in Memory of the Late Field Marshal Lord Kitchener* (Bradford, Institute of British Poetry, 1916).

39   Trethewey, *Pearls*, p.433.

40   Hatfield House: Salisbury papers, Ettie to Allie 8 June 1916.

41   HA: D/ERv/1500/1, F Kitchener to Lady Desborough, 31 July 1916.

42   Hatfield House: Salisbury papers, Ettie to Allie 8 June 1916.

43   Burial of Lt Col OA Fitzgerald, AKA Kitchener's Friend 1916 online: https://www. britishpathe.com/video/burial-of-lt-col-o-a-fitzgerald-aka-kitcheners [accessed 27 April 2019].

Kitchener's estate went to his brother Henry C who died on Muhoroni in 1937. On his death, the title passed to his grandson, Henry Herbert, as his father, Kitchener's nephew Captain Henry Franklin Chevalier, had died in 1928. Henry Herbert was born on 24 February 1919 and inherited the title the year he went to Trinity College, Cambridge. His mother forbade him visiting the estate in Africa and the farm reverted to the state.[44] On Henry's death, 16 December 2011, the title came to an end, the next family member in line being a woman, Emma Joy Kitchener, The Lady Fellowes of West Stafford. Since 2012, Lady Fellowes of West Stafford is also known as The Lady Emma Kitchener following a Warrant signed by the Queen on 9 May 2012 which allows her to 'have, hold and enjoy the same title, rank, place, pre-eminence and precedence as a daughter of an Earl as would have been due to her had her late father Charles Eaton Kitchener (commonly called The Honourable Charles Eaton Kitchener) survived his brother the said Henry Herbert Earl Kitchener of Khartoum and Broome, and thereby succeeded to the title and dignity of Earl Kitchener of Khartoum and Broome.'[45]

Kitchener's legacy continues, not so forcefully as it was when he was alive, but, apart from the famous poster, in ways he would approve. In 1919, a convalescent home for ex-service personnel was opened in Lowestoft, Suffolk, the Kitchener Memorial Hospital. Today, from April to October, it provides half-board seaside holiday and short break accommodation.[46] A Kitchener fund was set up to provide '... scholarships for the sons of officers and men with wide interpretation but with special reference to commerce, industry and science.' In '... the first year over 80 scholarships were awarded.'[47] The first award from the Memorial Fund was announced in December 1916. Mr A Day, late Royal Fusiliers injured at Gallipoli, was presented with a donkey and cart in Poplar.[48] While Maxwell was alive, he interviewed everyone and followed their career. Today, the Kitchener Fund, known as the Lord Kitchener National Memorial Fund, still makes awards and is chaired by The Lady Emma Kitchener, who is also the President.[49]

Less in keeping with Kitchener's ideals of remembrance are a town in Canada bearing his name, numerous streets, a pub in New Zealand, and in post-Second World War Two Britain, a train and a clothing boutique in the 1960s selling pre-First World War military uniforms called *Lord Kitchener's Valet*, which resulted in a recording by

---

44   TNA: CO 533/485/8.
45   *Telegraph* obituary. London Gazette, 23 May 2012, *Warrants Under the Royal Sign Manual*.
46   Kitchener memorial hospital, Lowestoft, online: http://www.kitchenerslowestoft.co.uk/ [accessed 27 April 2019]; Heathorn, *Haig and Kitchener*, pp.52-3.
47   Arthur, *John Maxwell*, p.308.
48   *The Sphere*, 6 December 1916, p.175.
49   LKNMF online: http://www.lknmf.com/index.html and The Kitchener Scholars' Association online: https://www.kitchenerscholars.org/ [accessed 27 April 2019]; Heathorn, *Haig and Kitchener*, pp.52-3.

the New Vaudeville Band, *I Was Lord Kitchener's Valet*.[50] Three years after Kitchener's death, he was still popular, especially among the women according to an article in *The Strand Magazine* on 'Good looks in men: what types do women like best?'[51]

50 Railways, online: https://en.wikipedia.org/wiki/List_of_BR_%27Britannia%27_
    Class_locomotives; *I Was Lord Kitchener's Valet* online: https://www.youtube.com/
    watch?v=nvFb4GxvsCk.
51 *The Strand Magazine*, pp.485-90.

Conclusions

Of his nearly 64 years before the outbreak of the First World War, only twelve, and those inconsecutive, were spent in England. By 1919, having spent 671 days in office as Secretary of State, Kitchener was the only Field Marshal to have died at the hand of the enemy.[1] His last eighteen years were spent in the limelight, the celebrity of the day, but he remained a mystery.

Lloyd George could not figure him out, equating him to 'a lighthouse – a sudden blinding flash of light, followed by utter darkness.'[2] In his memoirs, Lloyd George asked '… was [Kitchener] a great man, or was he a disappointment? […] After having been in close touch with him and having seen him at work every week and almost every day, for nearly two years, I could not even then quite make up my mind about his qualities.'[3] George Booth, a cousin of Millie Parker's husband, thought 'Kitchener was a great man. He was inexplicable at times, but he really knew great things.'[4] Guy Wilson, the financial adviser who worked with Kitchener in South Africa, wrote:

> The more I see of Kitchener the more I am disposed to call him 'the man of contradictions'. I am convinced that he would gladly be burned at the stake rather than save his life at the cost of a lie. Of this I am confident. But to get the best of a deal in the interest of his country, I have known him lie like the proverbial trooper.[5]

---

1   Arthur, p.360. 141 men have held the rank of Field Marshal in the British Army since 1736. The last appointment was made in 1997, although in 2012, Prince Charles was promoted a 5-Star General. Two honorary Field Marshals have since been appointed. William Robert 'Wully' Robertson, born 29 January 1860, died 12 February 1933, CIGS 1915, is the only soldier to have held every rank in the British Army from Private to Field Marshal. Sir Henry Wilson was assassinated while in army uniform on 22 June 1922 in Ireland. TA Heathcote, *The British Field Marshals: 1736-1997: A Biographical Dictionary* (Barnsley: Pen & Sword, 2012).
2   Royle, p.299.
3   Lloyd George, *Memoirs*, vol 1, p.450.
4   Royle, p.299.
5   Wilson, *Letters to Nobody*, p.14.

Contrast this with Biddulph's secretary who noted that whenever Kitchener could, he would put himself before duty, whilst both Cromer and Baring, pointed out that Kitchener had a knack of misinterpreting orders he did not like.

Kitchener's priorities changed over the years. As a young soldier he wanted action. He was ambitious, and action was the way to prove himself. He was confident in his abilities but realised he would have to convince others. Learning early on that one had to take opportunities when one could, accounts for his blatant manipulation of events. Having befriended Pandeli Ralli, he discovered how to work the system for his benefit, in a way more socially acceptable than his days on Cyprus. Reciprocally, he discovered helping others up the ladder, helped him too. Once on the career ladder, his drive to safeguard Britain as centre of the British Empire, and his monarch, came to the fore, giving credence to Wilson's assessment.

What he achieved, he did against the odds. For much of his career, he battled against the War Office, British Army and establishment press where people were jealous of him and what he achieved. They did what they could to undermine him.[6] This led to many occasions where Kitchener could retaliate against accusations levelled at him but he chose to keep quiet, or rather got confidantes to smooth things over. This enabled Kitchener to maintain a visage of aloofness; a means of protecting himself, but it also gave rise to Kitchener being accused of saying things his subordinates said in trying to explain his situation, or conveying their own views, such as the order to 'kill all the wounded Dervishes'.

Rennell Rodd, a friend since 1892, explained:

> Kitchener undoubtedly had vision … His face not less than his manner suggested the contemplative spirit. Those curious very blue eyes of his seemed to look beyond you to the desert horizons where so much of his life had been spent. His intuition rather than his reason saw beyond the actual moment, and then he elaborated far-reaching plans for execution when the time should be ripe. Having once determined on a course he was unreceptive to new ideas, and worked towards his end with machine-line precision. Intellectually the past attracted him.[7]

What Rodd failed to identify in this passage is the work Kitchener did surreptitiously before he determined his course. He asked lots of questions, had experts advise, and where appropriate and when needed applied himself to study, invariably when others were not around – as none have mentioned this other than his language studies on board ship, his study of Turkish law and that he would take copies of *Country Life* away with him. The reports he wrote on Palestine whilst he was still junior with no access to administrative staff, and the scientific papers he delivered, provide clear evidence that he found ways of becoming familiar with the material.

---

6   Spiers, *Sudan reconquest*, p.41.
7   Rodd, *Memories*, p.37.

Fritz Ponsonby gives some insight into how Kitchener mastered talks. On his first visit to Balmoral in 1898, Balfour offered to help Kitchener write his London Guildhall speech. After trying to dictate to Kitchener, who kept interrupting, Balfour took Kitchener's notes when he was seeing the Queen and dictated a speech to Ponsonby. Kitchener seeing the result, 'roared with laughter.' He felt '... the whole place would scream with laughter at such beautiful language coming from me,' so took what Balfour had written and rewrote 'the whole thing in my own language' which 'was a great success.'[8] This suggests that his 1909 'plagiarised' Indian farewell speech was tongue-in-cheek; Kitchener having fun at Curzon's expense. In 1915, Kitchener admitted to Riddell that he '... often stole paragraphs from [journalist] dispatches to use in my own.'[9]

He was not good at dealing with pressured decision making: Atbara, Paardeberg, and Gallipoli being the prime examples.[10] In fact, Arthur sums Kitchener up quite well in the *Times Literary Supplement* of 1920:

> He was, in fact, never a mere soldier in the narrow sense. He was rather a strategist, if we understand by strategy that difficult border land between politics and the conduct of military operations. As a tactician, he was frequently at fault, and both Omdurman and Paardeberg deserved many of the strictures passed upon them.[11]

It was suggested he was more of a mathematician; logical-mathematical according to Howard Gardner's Multiple Intelligence theory:[12]

> For this man nothing was too small, nothing too distant, nothing too large. He was never so engrossed in the task of the moment – when his faculties might seem to be stretched to the task of its accomplishment – that he could not see things on the far horizon. Some men take no thought of the morrow; others, again, while seeing the foreground and middle distance in fair detail, have but a blurred vision of things near the sky line. He saw all, not as in a picture with the illustrations of perspective, but as in a plan where dimensions and distances figure as they are and not as they seem.[13]

Kitchener had an innate ability to see the bigger picture and his mathematically inclined brain enabled him to see patterns. In mapping Palestine he visualised the

---

8   Ponsonby, *Recollections*, pp.43-4; Ridley & Percy, *Arthur Balfour and Lady Elcho*, pp.155-6.
9   Riddell, *War Diary*, p.76.
10   Magnus, p.153.
11   Times Literary Supplement, *The real Lord Kitchener* (1920) vol 305, p.347.
12   Howard E Gardner, *Multiple intelligences: New horizons in theory and practice* (Hatchette, 2008).
13   Times Literary Supplement, *The real Lord Kitchener* (1920) vol 305, p.346.

Biblical battles where they took place, saw the value of the plane for military intelligence and how an army should or could be structured in order to function as an entity. By default, he struggled with personal relationships.

An avid learner, Kitchener learned from his mistakes, and having mastered a skill he added it to his arsenal which allowed him to tackle bigger and bolder obstacles. His dual interest in diplomacy and administration worked in tandem to make him a reformer – from transforming the Egyptian Army, the Indian Army, Egypt, and finally the Empire military infrastructure. Each step saw the timeframe for change reduce, until his worst nightmare came true: having to create, or revamp, an army whilst at war. Innately he knew he would never be able to transform the War Office so avoided it until he could not. By the time he arrived at the War Office in 1914, he knew what needed to be done and how best to do it, as well as the personal sacrifice it would take, personalities aside. Had he succumbed earlier to a stint in the War Office, in whatever capacity, his drive and sense of purpose might well have been diminished.

It is tempting to say Kitchener had it all mapped out; that he aimed for the top. The only evidence there is of a goal is his expressed desire to be the Viceroy of India or Agent of Egypt if the former did not materialise. As to a rank in the army or social status, there is nothing on record – yet found – but the dual nature of his personality was expressed to Rodd: he would get back to archaeology, to the great outdoors, making discoveries and solving puzzles. That was the essence of the man: an explorer who visited multiple countries, observed and studied their manner of war, and solved puzzles. He was a fixer, not a sustainer. Intrigue aside, by the time Kitchener was sent to the Dardanelles, his job at the War Office was ostensibly over. He had overseen the transformation of Britain from a peace-minding nation into a fighting machine. On a personal level, he needed a new challenge.

'He had not a trace of the hypocrite in his composition, nor even that quality which emerges into the hypocrisy of moral decency. If he was going to break the moral law in any way, he said so. He used to shock and surprise the respectable terribly.'[14] He had his own moral code, as Wilson observed. He said what was on his mind, working through problems aloud which often led to misunderstandings, especially if the person acted on what they had heard without knowing the wider context or how Kitchener operated. On occasion he opened himself to misuse by others for their own purposes, his loyalty being the determining factor.

Kitchener was loyal to a fault, including to his monarch: most of whom he served becoming good friends. It was Asquith's mention of the King's desire that he became Secretary of State for War despite his concerns about the War Office, and it was a discussion with the previous King which saw him first accept the Mediterranean command and then turn it down in 1909. Yet, his drive for peace only became known when he made his farewell speeches in India and even then people did not quite believe this true of a soldier – particularly one as ambitious as Kitchener was believed

---

14   Cecil, *Egyptian Official*, p.188.

to be. His pushing for peace in South Africa was interpreted as eagerness to get to India while his letter to the Khalifa was not public knowledge.

Similarly, as much as it was a soldier's job to prepare and be prepared for war, but to avoid it starting at all costs, he was a disciplinarian. For the military machine to function effectively, no part could be allowed to malfunction, hence the accounts of him disciplining men for 'appearances' sake'. However, when he could, and if the situation warranted it, such as farm burning, he turned a blind eye. And no evidence of the fifty-one executions he was said to have sanctioned by the age of fifty-one has been found. Of 140 courts martial which came before him in 1901, fourteen recommended the death sentence of which one was upheld, the others commuted, twelve were 'remitted' which included half receiving a reduced sentence, forty-six sentences upheld, one he 'declined to interfere' and the remainder were commuted.[15]

Kitchener worked behind the scenes, his door reportedly always open, and what conversations took place when he went out on his dressing-gown inspections in the mornings we will never know. It was the local population in Egypt who made use of the open-door opportunity rather than his own people who preferred to complain to the press and superiors that Kitchener was cold and unapproachable. Specialists he trusted were given free reign and had his backing. Those he did not trust or who he felt were incapable, he did their job until someone able could take over. Those who suffered this humiliation objected to him centralising control. He understood the complexity, from an economic and effectiveness perspective, some things such as transport and supplies needed to be centrally coordinated, whilst others needed greater flexibility to meet local conditions. He never mastered coaching, mentoring or showing subordinates what to do, but achieved results by setting challenges for those he felt able, and tolerated their making mistakes.

Kitchener led from the front, the cultures and situations he worked among demanded it. If it was not on his charger, it was showing what needed to be done. He never asked anyone to do something he was not prepared to do himself. The rank and file appreciated it, the senior officers not, as it was not in their nature; they directed from the rear. It was a sign of their status, their having served their time, or bought their position. For Kitchener, status was earned and came with the territory; the roles he assumed, Commander-in-Chief Indian Army and British Agent, required he perform in certain ways – which he did, exceedingly well. He was to some extent an actor.

He fell between cultures – born to English British parents, his habits and values were not quite British. He embraced the cultures amongst whom he lived, especially in Palestine and Egypt. His charm was being different whilst meeting the basic British etiquette requirements. Militarily, he thought out of the box. His training as a Royal Engineer and experiences having been on the front line with non-British forces,

---

15   TNA: WO 92/8 and WO 92/10. Records of courts martial in Sudan and Egypt could not be traced. The death sentence was carried out on 'Native Jonas' for murder.

although part of the British Army, gave him an insight into tactics and strategy which did not sit comfortably with senior officers and diplomats in Britain. Those who knew him and made the effort to understand him, valued his ideas but still at the end of the day judged him according to British values, regarding him as an outsider, not quite one of them.

What is striking about the issues which led to his downfall, is that he did not have a complete picture. This was the challenge of being in an administrative role behind the lines and the bureaucracy of the armed forces where a chain of command had to be followed. Had it been Kitchener and the soldiers, things would probably have worked out as each would do what was required. This had been the case in Sudan and largely South Africa where war was fought against a single enemy. The complexities of the First World War, multiple enemies, meant greater political input and co-ordination from afar with multiple Commanders-in-Chief making demands which could not be discussed as in the past; a situation exacerbated as Kitchener was technically in a non-military role. Political intrigue and the desire to protect one's reputation in case of error meant greater glossing over of situations and less chance of finding viable solutions. The nature of the war made this inevitable, and unless all involved in strategic decision making could put personal feelings aside to make objective decisions, no one person can be held accountable for the chaos and loss of life which ensued.

In many aspects, Kitchener was ahead of his time. His egalitarianism is striking – across culture, gender and religion. Yet, he was a man of his time believing in the superiority of the British Empire as embodied in the white man. Education was, for Kitchener, of vital importance to ensure a solid grounding before field experience honed the ability. Decisions on who he thought would be a better ally were based on his assessment of a country's humanitarianism. He had no qualms about overthrowing the Ottoman Empire for this reason and similarly preferred Japan to China. He had an incredible ability to compartmentalise his thoughts and views. His great love of Chinese porcelain was completely dissociated from his views of the country's management. He discerned between the faith of a people and how the government or rulers misused religion to further their own aims, Turkey being the prime example, as was the Madhi. The future of Palestine, despite his affinity for the territory, its history and life-long membership of the Palestine Exploration Fund,[16] was left to the politicians, so long as the territory was removed from Ottoman control. He favoured British institutions and sense of fair play over the French. There are numerous comments of his trip through the desert suggesting a British influence would be helpful – not British control, but education. Kitchener could see the damage British institutions would potentially cause when they clashed with other established cultures. For this reason, he was against missionaries moving into Islamic areas, but where knowledge could be imparted to enable and empower, he was all in favour. Improving people's well-being

16 Daiches, *Zionist Review* (May 1917) p.25.

and economic position, through education and access to basic necessities, would, in his opinion, reduce exploitation and increase the chances of peace.

The way he expressed his ideas and the mannerisms he developed stemmed from him being an introvert and shy. His early rough living caused him to appear clumsy and brusque and his enthusiasm for something led to him gushing and appearing pushy. As people gave in to his enthusiastic appreciations as well as his learning to drive a hard bargain, his reputation for getting what he wanted increased. Riddell captured him well:

> He has clear conceptions of what he requires and good judgement. His weakness is due to the fact that he does not understand the peculiarities of the English people. He is more or less a foreigner. He says himself that he does not understand the conditions that prevail here. He has made the mistake of trying to do everything himself or through the War Office. He knew what was wanted and should have called in business men to make the arrangements. [...] he has been fumbling around without any proper plans for procuring [what he wants]. [...] Kitchener has the Oriental method of talking. He is not direct [...][17]

Kitchener had many weaknesses. His time in the spotlight highlighted these, but there was something likeable about him as Guy Wilson noted: 'Perfidious K, with all thy faults, I love thee still.'[18] Cecil did not '... like him at that period [Sudan]. He was much more uncouth and uncivilised at that time than he was later. He used to have little consideration for any one, and was *caussant* and rude [...] his "nerves" showed in roughness and harshness.'[19] Kitchener refined his behaviour as he mixed more with the British military, political and social establishment. However, he never lost the essence of who he had been which came to the fore when he found himself in strange, uncomfortable or stressful situations, such as visiting Japan and China. According to Cecil, Kitchener had some health issues which impacted on his behaviour. He suffered from 'a most acute form of headache,' had digestion issues and suffered from extreme heat:[20] being more red-head making him more susceptible.

It is often said that when a person relocates country, home traits become more marked. Similarly, whilst the Empire has little resonance in Britain, for the outlying territories then, and now as part of the Commonwealth, Britain, or rather the idea of Britain, became the aspiration.[21] Kitchener's behaviours remained a mix of European, rural Irish and Swiss, and Middle Eastern, but, from his time as Commander-in-Chief

---

17   Riddell, *War Diary*, p.75.
18   Wilson, *Letters to Nobody*, p.16.
19   Cecil, *Egyptian Official*, p.185.
20   Cecil, *Egyptian Official*, p.189.
21   Difficult to articulate, *The Conversation* provides some insight: http://theconversation.com/the-ties-that-still-bind-the-enduring-tendrils-of-the-british-empire-89308 [accessed 4 May 2019].

in India, he sought to safe-guard the British Empire as well he could. Thus, 'when the present [First World] war broke out, Kitchener became the chief guardian of the Empire,'[22] albeit reluctantly. In contrast, many others willingly travelled to do their bit to protect the 'motherland' rather than remain on guard in their home country.

Following the trajectory of Kitchener's life, it is difficult not to draw the conclusion that he was destined for the role he undertook in August 1914. Few others had similar opportunities, or, if they did, made the most of them. Whether by design or fortune, by the time the Great War broke out in 1914 Kitchener had the necessary experience and insight into Britain's armies and enemies to take the leading military role. He knew what needed to be done, the question was whether those at the centre of the British Empire could trust someone from the colonies to lead them through their time of need. Kitchener had spent his life struggling against the invisible barrier of class and social structure, learning sufficiently along the way to overcome. But at the end of the day, his 'downfall' was the result of others' lack of understanding, and unwillingness to accommodate, a man who ultimately did not fit into the idea of 'British', and whom they had put into an anomalous position as part of a 'great experiment.'

22   Daiches, *Zionist Review*, p.25.

Bibliography

Archives

South Africa
Brenthurst Library: MS 272, Reitz collection
Cory Library: Aubrey diaries

United Kingdom
Bodleian Library: MS Milner Dep 175
British Film Institute [BFI]: ID 501778, http://www.colonialfilm.org.uk/node/1207; ID 612293
British Library Manuscripts: Add MS 51370 The Holland House Papers
Add MS 52276-52278 Correspondence and Papers of Lt.-Col. Raymond John Marker
Map DMO/ADD/12
Hertfordshire Archives and Local Studies [HA]: Desborough papers
Hatfield House
Imperial War Museum [IWM]: Smith-Dorrien papers 87/47/3; 87/47/8
Museum of Freemasonry [MoFM]: Kitchener biographical file: LF 1105 and other files
National Army Museum [NAM]: Maxwell collection 7807-25
Parliamentary Archives [PA]: ALC/1/7 file 7/117b
    Bonar Law: BL 117/1/12
    BLU 1/MAXS/5
    Davidson: Dav 19; Dav 31; Dav 31
    Lloyd George: LG E/3/14/4; F/25/1/22; E/2/19/4
    Stratchey: STR
Swindon Archive: Methuen collection 1742/48/3
The National Archives, Kew [TNA]: CAB 2/3, CAB 37/56/27; CAB 38/28/35
    CO 323/63/10; CO 323/64/7
    FO 262/1474; FO 78/4892;
    HL/PO/JO/10/9/1665 (no 429); HL/PO/JO/10/10/598 (no 343)
    PRO 30/40/2; PRO 30/57
    WO 107/14; WO 142/240; WO 25/3914/304; WO 32/5491; WO 32/5636; WO 32/6380

New Zealand
Museum of New Zealand

Journal articles

Abushouk, Ahmed Ibrahim, 'The Anglo-Egyptian Sudan: From collaboration mechanism to party politics, 1898-1956', in *Journal of Imperial and Commonwealth History*, 38:2, 207-236 (2010)

Adams, RJQ, 'Asquith's choice: The May coalition and the coming of conscription, 1915-1916', in *Journal of British Studies* (July 1986) vol 25 no 3, pp.243-63

Anonymous, 'The seamy side of war: A reply', in *Galliard's Medical Journal* (January 1999) vol 70 no 1

Anonymous, 'The First Field Dressing', in *Journal of the Royal Army Medical Corps* (2001) vol 147 issue 3

Brown, Nathan, 'Brigands and state building: The invention of banditry in modern Egypt', in *Comparative Studies in Society and History*, vol 32, no 2 (Apr 1990)

Brux, Adolph August, 'Arabic-English Transliteration for Library Purposes', in *The American Journal of Semitic Languages and Literatures*, vol 47, no 1, part 2 (Oct, 1930) pp.1-30

Callwell, CE, 'Good old times at the War Office', in Littell's *The Living Age*, vol 300 (1919)

Camp Levkouiko, Cyprus, 'Notes from Cyprus', in *Blackwood's Magazine* (Aug 1879) *Church and State*

Daiches, Samuel, 'Lord Kitchener: In memoriam', in *The Zionist Review*, vol 1, no 2 (June 1917)

Dardanelles Commission Report

Dawson, R McGregor, 'The Cabinet minister and administration: The British War Office 1903-16', in *The Canadian Journal of Economics and Political Science* (November 1939) vol 5, no 4, pp.451-78

HHK, 'A visit to Sophia and the heights of Kamerleh – Christmas 1877', in *Blackwood's Magazine* (Feb 1878)

Jackson, HW, 'Fashoda, 1898', in *Sudan Notes and Records* (1920) vol 3, no 1, pp.1-11.

Katz, David Brock, 'A clash of military doctrine: Brigadier-General Wilfrid Malleson and the South Africans at Salaita Hill, February 1916', in *Historia*, vol 62, no 1 (2017)

Kempthorne, GA, 'Medical Staff Corps and Army Hospital Corps, 1854-1898', in *Royal Army Medical Journal* (December 1928) vol 51 issue 6

King, Philip J, 'Edward Robinson: Biblical scholar', in *The American Schools of Oriental Research*, vol 46, no 4 (Dec 1983)

Leeson, DM, 'Playing at war: The British military manoeuvres of 1898', in *War in History*, vol 15, no 4 (2008)

Mouton, FA, '"The good, the bad and the ugly": Professional historians and polit-ical biography of South African parliamentary politics, 1910-1990', in *Journal of Contemporary History*, vol 36, no 1 (June 2011) pp.57-74

Peter's Finger, 'Lord Kitchener and the bombardment of Alexandria', in *Journal of the Society for Army Historical Research*, vol 18, no 72 (1939)

Samson, Anne, 'Origins of the Legion of Frontiersmen and the formation of MI5/6', in *SOQT: Soldiers of the Queen*, issue 172 (2018)

Skillington, Florence E, 'Post Medieval Cossington', in *Transactions*, Leicestershire Archaeological and Historical Society, vol 20 (1938)

Sloane, Geoff, 'Haldane's Mackindergarten: A radical experiment in British Military History,', in *War in History*, (July 2012) vol 9, no 3, pp.322-352

Smith, Iain R & Stuki, Andreas, 'The colonial development of concentration camps (1868-1902)', in *The Journal of Imperial and Commonwealth History*, vol 39, no 3, Sep 2011, pp.417-37

Tollefson Jr, Harold H, 'The 1894 British takeover of the Egyptian Ministry of Interior', in *Middle Eastern Studies*, vol 2, no 4 (1990)

Verner, Willoughby, 'With Kitchener in the Gordon relief expedition', in *The Nineteenth Century* (August 1916)

Wufford, Letitia, 'Imperialists at work and play: The papers of General Sir John and Lady Maxwell', in *The Princeton University Library Chronicle*, vol 51, no 2 (Winter 1990) pp.141-8

Newspapers

Auckland Star
Derby *Daily Telegraph*
Evening Standard
Glasgow Herald
Hansard, HC Debates
London Gazette
Morning Post
New Zealand Herald
New Zealand, *Dominion*
Palestine Exploration Fund, *Quarterly Statement*
Rand Daily Mail
South African Digest
Telegraph
The Caledonian
The Conversation
The Literary Digest
The Living Age, vol 3 (1919)
The Morning News, Belfast

The People
The Sphere
The Strand Magazine.
The Sydney Herald
The Sydney Morning Herald
The Times
The United Methodist: The weekly journal of the United Methodist Church
Waimate Daily Advertiser, 21 April 1900
West Sussex Gazette

Published primary and secondary sources

An officer, *The Sudan Campaign 1896-1899* (London: Chapman & Hall, 1899)

Arnander, Christopher & Wood, Frances, *Betrayed Ally: China in the Great War* (Barnsley: Pen & Sword, 2016)

Arthur, George (ed.) *The Letters of Lord and Lady Wolseley, 1870*-1911 (London: William Heineman, 1922)

Arthur, George, *General Sir John Maxwell* (London: John Murray, 1932)

Arthur, George, *Life of Lord Kitchener*, 3 volumes (Macmillan, 1920)

Ash, Eric, *Sir Frederick Sykes and the Air Revolution, 1912-1918* (London: Frank Cass, 1999)

Atkinson, Diane, *Rise Up Women! The Remarkable Lives of the Suffragettes* (London: Bloomsbury, 2018)

Atwood, Rodney, *General Lord Rawlinson: From Tragedy to Triumph* (London: Bloomsbury, 2018)

Atwood, Rodney, *The Life of Field Marshal Lord Roberts* (London: Bloomsbury, 2014)

Atwood, Rodney, *Roberts and Kitchener in South Africa 1900-1902* (Barnsley: Pen & Sword, 2011)

Babington, Anthony, *For the Sake of Empire: Capital Courts Martial 1914-18 The Truth* (New York: St Martin's, 1985)

Bagley, JJ, *The Earls of Derby 1485-1985* (London: Sidgwick & Jackson)

Baker-Carr, CD, *From Chauffer to Brigadier* (London: Ernest Benn, 1930)

Ballard, Colin R, *Kitchener* (London: Newnes, nd)

Barker, AJ, *The First Iraq War – 1914-1918: Britain's Mesopotamia Campaign* (Enigma, 2009)

Barrow, George de S, *The Fire of Life* (London: Hutchinson, 1942)

Bastion, Peter, *Andrew Fisher: An Underestimated M*(Sydney: University New South Wales, 2009)

Beckett, Ian FW & Corvi, Steven J, *Haig's Generals* (Casemate, 2006)

Beckett, Ian FW, *A British Profession of |Arms: The Politics of Command in the Late Victorian Army* (Oklahoma: University of Oklahoma, 2018)

Begbie, Harold, *Kitchener: Organizer of Victory* (Boston: Riverside Press Cambridge, 1915)

Bell, GKA, *Randall Davidson Archbishop of Canterbury*, vol 2 (London: Oxford UP, 1935)

Beresiner, Yasha, *Kitchener of Khartoum: Mason extraordinary*

Blyth, Henry, *Skittles: The last Victorian Courtesan, the Life and Times of Catherine Walters* (London: Rupert Hart-Davis, 1970)

Bonham's Auctions, *Kitchener and Broome Park, Kent*

Booth, JB, *'Master' and Men: Pink 'un Yesterdays* (London: T Werner Laurie, 1926)

Boyle, Andrew, *Trenchard* (London: Collins, 1962)

Brice, Christopher, The military career of General Sir Henry Brackenbury 1856-1904 (PhD, DeMontfort University Leicester, 2009)

Brice, Christopher, *The Thinking Man's Soldier: The Life and Career of General Sir Henry Brackenbury, 1837-1914* (Solihull: Helion & Co, 2012)

Brock, Michael & Eleanor, *Margot Asquith's Great War Diary 1914-1916: Views From Downing Street* (Oxford: Oxford University Press, 2014)

Broome Park Golf Club, *A Brief History of Broome Park and Lord Kitchener*, online: https://www.broomepark.co.uk/wp-content/uploads/2018/05/Broome-Park-A-Brief-History-Leaflet.pdf

Brown, Alison M, Army chaplains in the First World War (PhD, University of St Andrews, 1996)

Buchan, John, *Francis and Riversdale Grenfell: A Memoir* (London: Thomas Nelson, 1920)

Buchan, John, *Lord Minto: A Memoir* (London: Thomas Nelson, 1924)

Buchan, John, *The History of the South African Forces in France* (London: Thomson Nelson & Son, 1920)

Bullard, F Lauriston, *Famous War Correspondents* (Boston: Little, Brown & Co, 1914)

Burial of Lt. Col. O.A. Fitzgerald, AKA Kitchener's Friend 1916 online: https://www.britishpathe.com/video/burial-of-lt-col-o-a-fitzgerald-aka-kitcheners

Burleigh, Bennett, *Khartoum Campaign 1898 or the Reconquest of Sudan* (London: Chapman & Hall, 1899)

Callwell, Charles Edward, *Experiences of a Dug-Out 1914-1918* (London: Constable, 1920)

Callwell, Charles Edward, *Small Wars: Their Principles and Practice* (London: HMSO, 1896)

Carden-Coyne, Ana, *The Politics of Wounds: Military Patients and Medical Power in the First World War* (Oxford: Oxford University, 2014)

Carter, Mark Bonham (ed.), *The Autobiography of Margot Asquith* (London: Weidenfeld & Nicolson, 1995)

Cassar, George H, *Kitchener as Proconsul of Egypt, 1911-1914* (London: Palgrave Macmillan, 2016)

Cassar, George, *Kitchener's War: British Strategy from 1914-1916* (Nebraska: Potomac, 2014)

Cecil, Edward, *The Leisure of an Egyptian Official* (London: Hodder & Stoughton, 1921)

Celia Lee, Jean, *Lady Hamilton 1861-1941: A Soldier's Wife (Wife of General Sir Ian Hamilton): A Biography From Her Diaries* (London: Celia Lee, 2001)

Chamberlain, Austen, *Down the Years* (London: Cassell, 1935)

Chapman-Huston, Desmond and Rutter, Owen, *General John Cowans: The Quarter-master General of the Great War*, vol 1 (London: Hutchinson, 1924)

Chatterjee, Partha, *A Princely Imposter? The Strange and Universal History of the Kumar of Bhawal* (Princeton: Princeton University, 2002)

Cheiro, *Palmistry For All: Containing New Information on the study of the Hand Never Published Before* (London: Herbert Jenkins, nd)

Child-Villiers, Margaret Elizabeth Leigh, The Dowager Countess of Jersey, *Fifty-One Years of Victorian Life* (London: John Murray, 1922)

Clark, Alan (ed.) *A Good Innings: The Private Papers of Viscount Lee of Fareham* (London, John Murray, 1974)

Collins, LJ, *Theatre at War, 1914-18* (Basingstoke: Macmillan, 1998)

Corrigan, Gordon, *Mud, Blood and Poppycock: Britain and The Great War* (London: Cassell, 2004)

Corvi, Steven J & Beckett, Ian FW (eds.), *Victoria's Generals* (Barnsley: Pen & Sword, 2009)

Cracoftspeerage, Special Remainders, http://www.cracroftspeerage.co.uk/online/content/index22.htm

Crisp, Frederick Arthur (ed.), *Visitation of England and Wales*, vol 19 (private print, 1919)

Crosby, Travis L, *Joseph Chamberlain: A Most Radical Imperialist* (London: IB Tauris, 2011)

Daiches, Samuel, *Lord Kitchener and His Work in Palestine* (London: Luzac, 1915)

Daisy Princess of Pless, *Daisy Princess of Pless* (New York: EP Dutton, 1920)

Davenport-Hines, Richard, *Ettie: The Intimate Life and Dauntless Spirit of Lady Desborough* (London: Weidenfeld & Nicholson, 2008)

Davidson, Apollon & Filatova, Irina, The *Russians and the Anglo-Boer War* (Pretoria: Human & Rosseau, 1998)

Davray, Henry D, *Lord Kitchener: His Work and Prestige, With a Prefatory Letter by SE Monsieur Paul Cambon* (London: T Fisher Unwin, 1917)

de Gruchy, John W, *The Church Struggle in South Africa* (Fortress, 2005)

de Lisle, Beauvoir, *Reminiscences of Sport and War* (London: Eyre & Spottiswood, 1939)

de Watteville, H, *Lord Kitchener* (London, Blackie & Son, 1939)

de Wet, Christiaan Rudolf, *Three Years' War* (New York: Charles Scribner, 1902)

DNW, *Kitchener's niece: The Suffragette Who Outraged Her Uncle and Was Abused in Prison* (2016)

DNW, Woodliffe medals

DRW, *Shot at Dawn* (3 June 2017)

Earl of Birkenhead, *Points of View* (London: Hodder & Stoughton, 1922)

Edmonds, James, *A Short History of World War 1* (London: Oxford UP, 1951)

Egmont-Hake, A. (ed.) *Soldiers of the Queen: Roberts of Kandahar* (London: London Publishing, 1900)

Esenbel, Selçuk (ed.), *Japan on the Silk Road: Encounters and Perspectives of Politics and Culture in Eurasia* (Leiden: Brill, 2018)

Fanny, Lady Blunt, *My Reminiscences* (London: John Murray, 1918)

Faught, Brad, *Kitchener: Hero and Anti-Hero* (London: IB Tauris, 2016)

Fawcett, Millicent Garrett, *What I Remember* (New York: GP Putnam's, 1925)

Fisher, John, *Curzon and British Imperialism in the Middle East, 1916-1919* (London: Routledge, 2012)

Forshaw, Chas E (ed.) *Poems in Memory of the Late Field Marshal Lord Kitchener* (Bradford, Institute of British Poetry, 1916)

Fosbrooke, TH, 'Rothley', in *The History of Rothley* (Leicester Archaeological Society, 1921)

Fox, Paul, *Severed heads: The Spoils of War in the Egyptian Sudan* (Making War, Mapping Europe, 2015)

French, David, *British Economic and Strategic Planning 1905-1915* (London: George Allen, 1982)

Fromkin, David, *A Peace to End All Peace: The Fall of the Ottoman Empire and the Creation of the Middle East* (New York: Henry Holt, 1989)

Gardner, Howard E, *Multiple Intelligences: New Horizons in Theory and Practice* (Hatchette, 2008).

Gay, Hannah, *The History of Imperial College London, 1907-2007: Higher Education and Research in Science, Technology and Medicine* (London: Imperial College, 2007)

Germains, Victor Wallace, (A Rifleman), *The Truth About Kitchener* (London: John Lane, 1925)

Gilbert, Martin, *Horace Rumbold: Portrait of a Diplomat, 1869-1941* (London: Heinemann, 1973)

Gollin, Alfred M, *Proconsul in Politics: a Study of Lord Milner in Opposition and Power, With An Introductory Section, 1854-1905* (Anthony Blond, 1964)

Gould, Jennifer Margaret, The women's corps: The establishment of women's military services in Britain (PhD, University College London, 1988)

Gould, Marty, *Nineteenth-Century Theatre and the Imperial Encounter* (Routledge, 2011)

Grafftey-Smith, Laurence, *Bright Levant* (London: Stacey International, 2002)

Great War in Africa Association, www.gweaa.com

Greaves, George Richard, *Memoirs of General Sir George Richards Greaves*, written by himself (London: John Murray, 1924)

Green, Andrew, *Writing the Great War: Sir James Edmonds and the Official Histories 1915-1948* (London: Frank Cass, 2003)

Grew, Edwin Sharpe, *Field Marshal Lord Kitchener: His Life and Work for the Empire* (London: Gresham, 1916)

Grob-Fitzgibbon, B, *Turning Points of the Irish Revolution: The British Government, Intelligence and the Cost of Indifference, 1912-1921* (Springer, 2007)

Halperin, Vladimir, *Lord Milner and the Empire* (London: Odhams, 1952)

Hamilton, Ian, *Anti-Commando* (London: Faber & Faber, 1931)

Hamilton, Keith, *Bertie of Thame: Edwardian Ambassador* (London: Royal Historical Society Studies in History, 1989)

Hankey, MP, *Supreme Command*, vol 1 (London: George Allen & Unwin, 1961)

Harland-Jacobs, Jessica L, *Builders of Empire: Freemasonry and British Imperialism 1717-1927* (University of North Carolina Press, 2007)

Heathcote, TA, *The British Field Marshals: 1736-1997: A Biographical Dictionary* (Barnsley: Pen & Sword, 2012)

Heathorn, Stephen, *Haig and Kitchener in Twentieth Century Britain: Remembrance, Representation and Appropriation* (Routledge, 2016)

Hedin, Sven Anders, *Trans-Himalaya: Discoveries and Adventures in Tibet*, volume 1 of 2 (Library of Alexandria)

HMS *Hampshire*: hmshampshire.org/

Hobhouse, Emily, *The Brunt of the War and Where It Fell* (London: Methuen, 1902)

Hobhouse, Margaret Heyworth, *I Appeal Unto Caesar: The Case of the Conscientious Objector* (London: George Allen, 1917)

Hocking, Andrew, *Oppenheimer and Sons* (Maidenhead: McGraw-Hill, 1973)

Hodges, Arthur, *Lord Kitchener* (London: Thornton Butterworth, 1936)

Hodgkinson, Peter Eric, British Infantry Battalion Commanders in the First World War (PhD, University of Birmingham, 2013)

Hook, Gail Dallas, *Protectorate Cyprus: British Imperial Power Before World War I* (IB Tauris, 2015)

Hotto-Lister, Ayako, *The Japan-British Exhibition of 1910: Gateway to the Island Empire of the East* (Richmond, Japan Library, 1999)

Hull, Edward, *Mount Seir, Sinai and Western Palestine: Being a Narrative of a Scientific Expedition* (London: Richard Bentley, 1885)

Hunter, Archie, *Kitchener's Sword-Arm: The Life and Campaigns of General Sir Archibald Hunter* (New York: Sarpedon, 1996)

Hunter, Archie, *Power and Passion in Egypt: A Life of Sir Eldon Gorst, 1861-1911* (London: IB Tauris, 2007)

Hutchinson, George Thomas, *Frank Rhodes: A Memoir* (Private circulation, 1908)

Jabotinsky, Vladimir, *The Story of the Jewish Legion* (New York: Bernard Ackermann, 1945)

Jackson, HC, *Osman Digna* (London: Methuen, 1926)

Jastrzembski, Frank, *Valentine Baker's Heroic Stand at Tashkessen 1877: A Tarnished British Soldier's Glorious Victory* (Barnsley: Pen & Sword, 2017)

Jerrold, Walter, *Earl Kitchener of Khartoum: The Story of his Life* (London: J Johnson, 1916)

Jolliffe, John (ed.), *Raymond Asquith: Life and Letters* (London: Century, 1980)

Jusserand, JJ, *What Me Befell* (London: Constable, 1933)

Kennedy, Christopher M, *Genesis of the Rising 1912-1916: A Transformation of Nationalist Opinion* (Peter Lang, 2010)

Ker, JC, *'Lest we forget' Revisited: A Memoir* (Bookbaby, 2017)

King, Peter, *The Viceroy's Fall: How Kitchener Destroyed Curzon* (London: Sidgwick & Jackson, 1986)

Kitchener memorial hospital, Lowestoft, online: http://www.kitchenerslowestoft.co.uk/

Kitchener, HH, 'Notes on British Lines of Communications with the Indian Ocean' (1886)

Kitchener, HH, Despatch, Dongola 30 September 1898 online: http://www.northeastmedals.co.uk/britishguide/sudan/despatches1_dongola_hafir.htm

Kitchener, HH, *Survey of Galilee, A Paper Read Before the Geographical Section of the British Association*, [in Dublin] August 1878

Lady Briggs, *The Staff Work of the Anglo-Boer War, 1899-1901* (London: Grant Richards, 1901)

Lady Wantage, *Memoir of Lord Wantage VC, KCB* (London: Smith, Elder & Co, 1907)

Lambert, David and Lester, Alan (eds.) *Colonial Lives Across the British Empire: Imperial Careering in the Long Nineteenth Century* (Cambridge: Cambridge University, 2006)

Lamothe, Ronald M, *Slaves of Fortune: Sudanese Soldiers and the River War 1896-1898* (Woolbridge: James Currey, 2011)

Lawrence, Margot, *Shadow of Swords: A Biography of Elsie Inglis* (London: Michael Joseph, 1971)

Lawton, Mary, *The Queen of Cooks, and Some Kings (The story of Rosa Lewis)* (New York: Boni & Liveright, 1925)

Lee, John, 'Sir Ian Hamilton after the war: A Liberal general reflects', in Hugh Cecil & Peter H Liddle (eds), *Facing Armageddon: The First World War Experienced* (Barnsley: Pen & Sword, 2003)

Lees-Milne, James, *Through Wood and Dale: Diaries 1975-1978* (London: John Murray, 1998)

LKNMF online: http://www.lknmf.com/index.html

Long, Walter, *Memories* (London: Hutchinson, 1923)

Longmore, Thomas, *Gunshot Injuries: Their History, Characteristic Features, Complications and General Treatment* (London: Longmans, 1877)

Lord Lloyd, *Egypt Since Cromer*, vol 1 (London: Macmillan, 1933)

Lord Newton, *Lord Lyons: A Record in British Diplomacy*, vol 2 (London: Edward Arnold, 1913)

Lord Riddell, *War Diary 1914-1918* (London: Ivor Nicolson & Watson, 1933)

Lowndes, Marie Belloc, *A Passing World* (London: Macmillan, 1948)

Lowndes, Mrs Belloc, *The Merry Wives of Windsor* (London: Macmillan, 1946)

Mackay, Thomas, *The Life of John Fowler* (London: John Murray, 1900)

MacLaren, Roy, *Canadians on the Nile, 1882-1898* (Vancouver: University of British Columbia, 1978)

Magnus, Philip, *Kitchener: Portrait of an Imperialist* (Penguin, 1958)

Marchioness (Katharine Marjory) of Tullibardine (ed.), *A Military History of Perthshire, 1899-1902* (Perth: RA & J Hay, 1908)

Marquess Curzon of Kedleston, *Leaves From a Viceroy's Note-Book* (London: Macmillan, 1926)

Marquess of Zetland, *Lord Cromer* (London: Hodder & Stoughton, 1932)

Massoud, Mark Fathi, *Law's Fragile State: Colonial, Authoritarian, and Humanitarian Legacies in Sudan* (Cambridge: Cambridge UP, 2013)

Maurice, Frederick Barton, *Life of General Lord Rawlinson of Trent from His Journals and Letters* (London: Cassell, 1928)

Maxe, FI, *Seymour Vandeleur: The Story of a British Officer; Being a Memoir of Brevet-Lieutenant-Colonel Vandeleur, DSO, Scots Guards and Irish Guards, With a General Description of his Campaigns* (London, National Review, 1906)

May, Edward S, *Changes and Chances of a Soldier's Life* (London: Philip Allen, 1925)

McGauran, A, Notice Paper of The Parliament of the Commonwealth of Australia, No 117, 2002-3

McKenna, Neil, *The Secret Life of Oscar Wilde* (Random House, 2011)

Melik Society: www.melik.org.uk

Menzies, Mrs Stuart (Amy Charlotte), *Lord William Beresford VC: Some Memories of a Famous Sportsman, Soldier and Wit* (London: Herbert Jenkins, 1917)

Minto, Mary, *India, Minto and Morley: Compiled from the Correspondence Between the Viceroy and the Secretary of State* (London: Macmillan, 1934)

Mitchinson, KW, *Gentlemen and Officers: The Impact and Experience of War on a Territorial Regiment 1914-1918* (Andrews UK, 2012)

Moberly, FJ, *Operations in Persia 1914-1919, History of the Great War Based on Official Documents* (Government of India)

Morgan, Kenneth O, *Lloyd George Family Letters 1885-1935* (Cardiff: University of Wales, 1973)

Morgenthau, Henry, *Ambassador Morgenthau's Story* (New York: Doubleday, Page & Co, 1919)

Morris, Jan, *Farewell the Trumpets: An Imperial Retreat* (London: Faber & Faber, 2010)

Morton-Jack, George, *The Indian Army on the Western Front: India's Expeditionary Force to France* (Cambridge: Cambridge Military History, 2014)

Moscrop, John James, The Palestine Exploration Fund: 1865-1914 (PhD, University of Leicester, 1996)

Nandkuverba CI, Maharani of Bhavnagar, *Field Marshal Earl Kitchener of Khartoum, KG* (London: Richmond, 1916)

Nash, NS, *Betrayal of an Army: Mesopotamia 1914-1916* (Barnsley: Pen & Sword, 2016)

Nevakivi, Jukka, 'Lord Kitchener and the partition of the Ottoman Empire, 1919-1916,', in K Bourne & DC de Witt (eds.), *Studies in International History* (London: Longmans, 1967)

Nevinson, Henry Woodd, *Fire of Life* (London: James Nisbet, 1935)

O'Brien, Phillips, *The Anglo-Japanese Alliance, 1902-1922* (London: Routledge, 2003)

Okoth, Assa, *A History of Africa: African Societies and the Establishment of Colonial Rule 1800-1915* (Nairobi: East Africa Pub, 2006)

Pattison, RG, *The Cape Seventh Class Locomotives* (Kenilworth: Railway History Group of Southern Africa, 1997) pp.48-50

Pauley, Jennifer Anne, The social and political roles of Edith, Lady Londonderry 1878-1959 (PhD, University of Ulster, 1994)

Payne, Peter Lester, *Studies in Scottish Business History* (Taylor & Francis, 1967)

Pearson, Hugh Drummond, *Letters from Abyssinia, 1916 and 1917: With Supplemental Foreign Office Documents* (Los Angeles: Tsehei, 2004)

Perry Shore, Caroline & Jones, Alan, *An Enchanted Journey: The Letters of the Philadelphian Wife of a British Officer of the Indian Cavalry* (Pentland Press, 1994)

Peters, Arne, *Carl Peters and German imperialism 1856-1918: A Political Biography* (Wotton-under-Edge: Clarendon, 2004)

Pollock, John, *Kitchener Comprising the Road to Omdurman and Saviour of the Nation* (London: Constable, 2001)

Ponsonby, Frederick, *Recollections of Three Reigns* (London: Eyre & Spottiswoode, 1951)

Porter, Andrew, 'The South African war and imperial Britain: a question of significance?', in Gregory Cuthbertson, Grundlingh, Albert & Suttie, Mary-Lynn, *Writing a Wider War: Rethinking Gender, Race and Identity in the South African War, 1899-1902* (Cape Town: David Phillips, 2002)

Pottle, Mark (ed.), *Champion Redoubtable: The Diaries and Letters of Violet Bonham Carter 1914-45* (London: Weidenfeld, 1998)

Presland, John, *Deedes Bey: A Study of Sir Wyndham Deedes 1883-1923* (London: Macmillan, 1942)

Price, Warwick James, 'K', in *The Sewanee* Review, vol 24, no 4 (Oct 1916)

Prime, Adam John, The Indian Army's British Officer Corps, 1861-1921 (PhD, University of Leicester, 2018)

Prior, Robin & Wilson, Trevor, *Command on the Western Front, The Military Career of Sir Henry Rawlinson, 1914-18* (Oxford: John Wiley, 1992)

Pugh, James, *The Royal Flying Corps, the Western Front and Control of the Air, 1914-1918* (London: Routledge, 2017)

Purdy, Martin, *Roman Catholic Army Chaplains During the First World War: Roles, Experiences and Dilemmas* (MA thesis, University of Central Lancashire, 2012)

Queen Victoria, *The Letters of Queen Victoria* (Cambridge University Press, 2014)

Railways, online: https://en.wikipedia.org/wiki/List_of_BR_%27Britannia%27_Class_locomotives

Ridley, Jane & Percy, Clayre, *The Letters of Arthur Balfour and Lady Elcho, 1885-1917* (London: Hamish Hamilton, 1992)

Riedi, Elizabeth, *Imperialist Women in Edwardian Britain: The Victoria League 1899-1914* (PhD, University of St Andrew's, 1998)

Rodd, James Rennell, *Social and Diplomatic Memories, 1902-1919* (London: E Arnold, 1922)

Roper, Michael, *The Records of the War Office and Related Departments, 1660-1964* (London: Public Record Office, 1996)

Rowell, Cora, *Leaders of the Great War* (New York: Macmillan, 1919)

Royal Commission on War Stores in South Africa, vol 1, *Minutes of Evidence* (London, HMSO, 1906)

Royle, Charles, *The Egyptian Campaigns 1882 to 1885* (London: Hurst & Blackett, 1899)

Royle, Trevor, *The Kitchener Enigma* (London: Michael Joseph, 1985)

Rye, JB & Groser, Horace G, *Kitchener in His Own Words* (London: T Fisher Unwin, 1917)

Samson, Anne, *Britain, South Africa and the East Africa Campaign, 1914-1918: The Union Comes of Age* (London: IB Tauris, 2005)

Samson, Anne, *Jan Smuts and the British War Cabinet 1917-1919* (MA Dissertation: University of Westminster, 1998)

Samson, Anne, *World War 1 in Africa: The Forgotten Conflict of the European Powers* (London: IB Tauris, 2013)

Sandes, EWC, *The Royal Engineers in Egypt and the Sudan, the Reconquest Reappraised* (Chatham: The Institution of Royal Engineers, 1937)

Sayce, Archibald Henry, *Reminiscences* (London: Macmillan, 1923)

Schnitzer, Shira D, *Imperial Longings and Promised Lands: Anglo-Jewry, Palestine and the Empire, 1899-1948* (DPhil Modern History, University of Oxford, 2006)

Shalladay, Jim, *Canada's Wheat King: The Life and Times of Seager Wheeler* (University of Regina, 2007)

Sheffy, Yigel, *British Military Intelligence in Palestine* (London: Routledge, 2012)

Sherson, Erroll, *Townsend of Chitral and Kut* (London: William Heinemann, 1928)

Simeon, James Lomote, 'Llewellyn Henry Gwynne', in *Dictionary of African Biography*

Simkins, Peter, *Kitchener's Army* (Barnsley: Pen & Sword, 2007 reprint)

Smithers, AJ, *The Fighting Nation* (London: Leo Cooper, 1994)

Snape, Michael Francis, *The Royal Army Chaplains' Department, 1796-1953: Clergy Under Fire* (Boydell, 2008)

Snape, Michael, *The Redcoat and Religion: The Forgotten History of the British Soldier From the Age of Marlborough to the Eve of the First World War* (London: Routledge, 2005)

Snook, Mike MBE, Wolseley, Wilson and the failure of the Khartoum campaign: An exercise in scapegoating and abrogation of command responsibility (PhD: Cranfield University, 2014)

Spiers, Edward M, *Sudan: The Reconquest Reappraised* (London: Routledge, 1998)

Stapleton, Timothy J, *Military History of South Africa: From the Dutch-Khoi Wars to the End of Apartheid* (Santa Barbara: Praeger ABC-Clio, 2010)

Steevens, GW, *With Kitchener to Khartoum* (Edinburgh: William Blackwood, 1901)

Storrs, Ronald, *The Memoirs of Sir Ronald Storrs* (New York: GP Putnam's, 1937)

Strachan, Hew, *World War 1 in Africa* (Oxford: Oxford University, 2004)

Surridge, Keith, British civil-military relations and the South African War (1899-1902) (PhD, King's College London, 1994)

Swinton, ED, *Eyewitness: Being Personal Reminiscences of Certain Phases of the Great War, Including the Genesis of the Tank* (New York: Doubleday, Doran & Co, 1933)

Sylvester, AJ, *The Real Lloyd George* (London: Cassell, 1947)

Symes, Stewart, *Tour of Duty* (London: Collins, 1946)

Taylor, Elizabeth, *The Old World and the New: The Marriage and Colonial Adventures of Lord and Lady Northcote* (Newcastle Upon Tyne: Cambridge Scholars Publishing, 2013)

Taylor, James, *'Your Country Needs You': The Secret History of the Propaganda Poster* (Glasgow: Saraband, 2013)

The British Journal of Nursing

The Kitchener Scholars' Association online: https://www.kitchenerscholars.org/

Thomas, Nicola, Negotiating the boundaries of gender and empire: Lady Curzon, Vicerine of India 1898-1905 (PhD, University of Oxford, 2001)

Times Literary Supplement, *The real Lord Kitchener* (1920) vol 305, p.548.

Tisdall, EEP, *Unpredictable Queen: The Intimate Life of Queen Alexandra* (London: Stanley Paul, 1953)

Townsend, Charles, *Easter 1916: The Irish Rebellion* (London: Penguin, 2006)

Trethewey, Rachel, *Pearls Before Poppies: The Story of the Red Cross Pearls* (History Press, 2018)

van de Waal, Jérôme, *The Catholic Church in Ireland 1914-1918: War and Politics* (Dublin: Irish Academic, 2003)

van Emden, Richard, *Boy Soldiers of the Great War* (London: Bloomsbury, 2012)

van Heyningen, Elizabeth, *The Concentration Camps of the Anglo-Boer War: A Social History* (Johannesburg: Jacana, 2013)

Vincent, John Russell, *The Crawford Papers the Journals of David Lindsay, Twenty-Seventh Earl of Crawford and Tenth Earl of Balcarres (1871-1940), During the Years 1892 to 1940* (Manchester: Manchester University, 1984)

Viscountess Milner, *My Picture Gallery 1886-1901* (London: John Murray, 1951)

Vizetelly, Edward (Bertie Clere), *Cyprus to Zanzibar by the Egyptian Delta* (London: C Arthur, Pearson, 1901)

von Dumreicher, André, *Trackers and Smugglers in the Deserts of Egypt* (London: Methuen, 1931)

Waller, David, *The Magnificent Mrs Tennant: The Adventurous Life of Gertrude Tennant, Victorian 'Grande Dame'* (New Haven: Yale University, 2009)

Warner, Philip, *The Man Behind the Legend* (New York: Atheneum, 1986)

Watson, Charles Moore, *The Life of Major-General Charles William Wilson, Royal Engineers* (London: John Murray, 1909)

Wheeler, Harold FB, *The Story of Lord Kitchener* (London: George G Harrap, 1916)

Wheeler, Stephen, *History of the Delhi Coronation Durbar* (London: John Murray, 1904)

Whitehead, Ian R, *Doctors in the Great War* (Pen & Sword, 2013)

Wilkinson, Henry Spenser, *Thirty-Five Years: 1874-1909* (London: Constable, 1933)

Williams, Basil, *Cecil Rhodes* (New York: H Holt, 1921)

Williams, Jeffery, *Byng of Vimy: General and Governor General* (Barnsley: Pen & Sword, 1992)

Wilson, Arnie, *Snow Crazy: 115 Years of British Ski History* (Rickmansworth: TSL, 2018)

Wilson, Charles, *From Korti to Khartoum* (Edinburgh: William Blackwood, 1886)

Wilson, Guy Fleetwood, *Letters to Nobody, 1908-1913* (London: John Murray, 1921)

Wilson, John A, *Signs and Wonders Upon Pharaoh: A History of AMERICAN Egyptology* (Chicago: University of Chicago, 1964)

Wingate, Francis Reginald, *Mahdiism and the Egyptian Sudan: Being an Account of the Rise and Progress of Mahdiism, and of Subsequent Events in the Sudan to the Present Time* (London: Macmillan, 1891)

Zewde, Bahru, Relations between Ethiopia and the Sudan on the Western Ethiopian Frontier 1898-1935 (PhD, University of London, 1976)

Ziegler, Philip, *Diana Cooper: The biography of Lady Diana Cooper* (Harmondsworth, Penguin, 1983)

Zulfo, Ismat Hasan (trns Adam Clark), *Karari: The Sudanese Account of the Battle of Omdurman* (London: Frederick Warne, 1980)

Index

The period 1815-1914 is sometimes called the long century of peace. It was in reality very far from that. It was a century of civil wars, popular uprisings, and struggles for Independence. An era of colonial expansion, wars of Empire, and colonial campaigning, much of which was unconventional in nature. It was also an age of major conventional wars, in Europe that would see the Crimea campaign and the wars of German unification. Such conflicts, along with the American Civil War, foreshadowed the total war of the 20th century.

It was also a period of great technological advancement, which in time impacted the military and warfare in general. Steam power, electricity, the telegraph, the radio, the railway, all became tools of war. The century was one of dramatic change. Tactics altered, sometimes slowly, to meet the challenges of the new technology. The dramatic change in the technology of war in this period is reflected in the new title of this series: From Musket to Maxim.

The new title better reflects the fact that the series covers all nations and all conflict of the period between 1815-1914. Already the series has commissioned books that deal with matters outside the British experience. This is something that the series will endeavour to do more of in the future. At the same time there still remains an important place for the study of the British military during this period. It is one of fascination, with campaigns that capture the imagination, in which Britain although the world's predominant power, continues to field a relatively small army.

The aim of the series is to throw the spotlight on the conflicts of that century, which can often get overlooked, sandwiched as they are between two major conflicts, the French/Revolutionary/Napoleonic Wars and the First World War. The series will produced a variety of books and styles. Some will look simply at campaigns or battles. Others will concentrate on particular aspects of a war or campaign. There will also be books that look at wider concepts of warfare during this era. It is the intention that this series will present a platform for historians to present their work on an important but often overlooked century of warfare.

Submissions

The publishers would be pleased to receive submissions for this series. Please contact series editor Dr Christopher Brice via email (chrismbrice@yahoo.com), or in writing to Helion & Company Limited, Unit 8, Amherst Business Centre, Budbrooke Road, Warwick, Warwickshire, CV34 5WE.

Books in this series:

1. *The Battle of Majuba Hill: The Transvaal Campaign 1880–1881* John Laband (ISBN 978-1-911512-38-7)

2. *For Queen and Company: Vignettes of the Irish Soldier in the Indian Mutiny* David Truesdale (ISBN 978-1-911512-79-0)

3. *The Furthest Garrison: Imperial Regiments in New Zealand 1840–1870* Adam Davis (ISBN 978-1-911628-29-3)

4. *Victory Over Disease: Resolving the Medical Crisis in the Crimean War, 1854–1856* Michael Hinton (ISBN 978-1-911628-31-6)

5. *Journey Through the Wilderness: Garnet Wolseley's Canadian Red River Expedition of 1870* Paul McNicholls (ISBN 978-1-911628-30-9)

6. *Kitchener: The Man Not The Myth* Anne Samson (ISBN 978-1-912866-45-8)

7. *The British and the Sikhs: Discovery, Warfare and Friendship c1700–1900* Gurinder Singh Mann (ISBN 978-1-911628-24-8)

8. *Bazaine 1870: Scapegoat for a Nation* Quintin Barry (ISBN 978-1-913336-08-0)